Dave Pelz's Short Game Bible

Dave Pelz's
Short Game
Bible

*Master the Finesse Swing
and Lower Your Score*

DAVE PELZ

with James A. Frank

AURUM PRESS

First published in Great Britain 1999 by Aurum Press Limited, 25 Bedford Avenue, London WC1B 3AT.

This edition published by arrangement with Broadway Books, a division of Random House Inc, New York, New York, USA.

Grateful acknowledgment is made to the photographers whose photos are reproduced in this book. Photo on page vi by Dan Sellers. The following photos in the text were provided by F. Vuich/GOLF Magazine (Figures 4.15.1, 7.20.1–6, 7.22.1–9, and 9.14.3). All other photos in the text were provided by Leonard Kamsler. The photos in the color insert were provided by F. Vuich/GOLF Magazine, Sam Greenwood/GOLF Magazine, and Leonard Kamsler.

A catalogue record for this book is available from the British Library

ISBN 1 85410 648 1

Designed by Tina Thompson

Printed and bound by MPG Books Ltd, Bodmin, Cornwall

9   8   7
2006   2005

Dedication

Eddie . . . Eddie . . . Eddie . . .

You've been with me from the beginning. We started Pelz and Son Golf when you helped me build out a little office and make wax patterns for investment cast putters in our basement. I'm sure you slipped more grips onto Teacher putters and caught more wedge shots from Tour pros than any kid alive. You stayed with it, balanced three-ball putters and helped manufacture frequency matched Featherlite clubs in the struggling years, then managed to get your engineering degree on borrowed money. At early Short Game Schools you set up equipment before the students came, then picked up the balls after everyone left. And, of course, you built the laser measurement devices we used in teaching.

You've given me test ideas, run the tests, then helped me write articles on them for GOLF Magazine. And you've done so much, including production, for my TV shows on the Golf Channel. I think you've held reflectors and positioned cameras on more photo shoots than I've been on myself. As Technical Director of the first two Dave Pelz World Putting Championships, you were incredible.

And you're still there for me: mapping golf courses for our research projects, designing and building equipment for the Pelz Golf Institute, writing your own articles for *Junior Golfer* and the "Pelz Report" newsletter, developing learning aids for U.S. Golf Aids, and picking me up after I've fallen into a ravine building the Cordillera Short Course.

I want to tell you how much I admire you as a person, for the job you do, and for the way you make those around you feel. And there is still nothing more fun than hopping into our FlexJet (times change, don't they?) and flying off to run another test, then playing a round of golf together. I couldn't have done these things, especially this book, without you.

I dedicate all the joy this book is going to bring to so many golfers around the world to you. I am so proud of you, son, and I hope we can go on forever.

Eddie . . . Eddie . . . Eddie . . . I love ya, man!

Contents

Acknowledgments

First I would like to mention and thank all of the PGA and LPGA Tour professionals who have contributed enormously to my understanding of the scoring game and have been of such help in my quest to learn about it. They have given me honest feedback, never letting me get away with any unwarranted assumptions, and so many have grown to be good friends over the years. I truly appreciate you all.

In addition, I want to thank Jim Simons, Tom Jenkins, D. A. Weibring, Tom Sieckmann, Peter Jacobsen, Payne Stewart, Vijay Singh, Steve Elkington, Lee Janzen, and Tom Kite. These special people are more to me than great players; they are great human beings, and friends.

Jim Simons was the first Tour player I met while taking data, and he became a good friend. Jim has given me many honest, thoughtful answers as to what he was feeling, what he believed, and what he experienced during competition. In the years we worked together, Jim developed one of the best short games on Tour (and I'm not just saying that; the data bears it out): He won all three of his PGA Tour titles shortly (within 7 to 10 days) after grinding with me on his short game, and Jim . . . I thank you for those thrills, too.

Tom Jenkins has been another friend, and an invaluable source of inspiration. We worked together while he was on Tour, and his focus and dedication quickly proved what our concepts could do if you worked with them. Then he served as lead instructor at my Short Game Schools for a few years before going back out on Tour. T.J. has what is possibly the most repeatable, beautiful wedge swing of them all, is an absolute magician from sand, and I rate him among the finest wedge players in the world today. T.J., you are the greatest.

D. A. Weibring is another longtime friend, who brought his knowledge, skill, and feedback to my work. D.A. is one of the more naturally talented players I've worked with. A man with great natural touch, his feedback comes from an entirely different area from that of some other players. I have benefited tremendously from having worked with him over the years. I feel lucky just to know you and your family, D.A., and to know you are my friends.

There is only one Tom Sieckmann. After winning tournaments around the world, he brought his game to the PGA Tour, and won there, too. I can assure you, I learned more from Sieck than he learned from me. It is a pleasure to continue working with Sieck. Now that he is playing the Tour only part time, he has become the Publisher and Editor of the "Pelz Report," the newsletter of The Pelz Golf Institute. Sieck, your sincerity and credibility are like a beacon of light to my day when I see you, and I look forward to continuing our study of the game together.

Peter Jacobsen is one of the most talented and gifted players I have ever seen. A few years ago when he was healthy and his short game was sharp, I believed no one could consistently beat him. During that time, he won two PGA Tour events, led the Vardon Scoring Average statistics for most of the year, and played on the Ryder Cup team. He proved to the world just how good he really is. Peter, remember, when they can't beat you from inside 60 yards, they can't beat you. And I thank you for your honesty, your feedback, and your friendship.

Payne Stewart is nothing but class. His swing is smooth, his rhythm is great, his talent is enormous. And working with Payne is a real treat. There is never a moment when you are in doubt about what opinion he has, about whatever I've said or asked him to do. I love that. P.S., I get more done with you in less time than working with anyone else. Just being there when you hit shots better than most people in the world, with your *eyes shut,* is an experience I will always treasure.

Vijay Singh first came to my school at Cordillera, in Vail Valley (Colorado), at an altitude of 8,000 feet. You cannot believe how far he can hit the golf ball in that rarified air. It was a real treat to work with you then, Vijay, and since, to see how beautifully you adapted our concepts to your game. When I work with a powerful player such as you, it is so rewarding to see the finesse touch you developed and use so deftly. Vijay, it was an additional thrill to watch you win your first major championship at the PGA, and I hope to see you win many, many more.

Steve Elkington has the best swing in the world. If he can stay healthy for a while, he will probably be the best player in the world, too. When Elk is on, no one can beat him, because he is so good in all the games of golf (you'll see what those five games are later in this book). Elk, you've made great strides in your short game and your putting, and I hope you will make what I've just said come true in the coming years. You have given me tremendous insight into your inner game, with how you integrated my advice into your on-course strategy and performance. Thanks for the pleasure of being your friend, and I'm looking forward to more in the future.

And Lee Janzen, what can I say? Like all our students, he paid to come to school. But sometimes I feel that it was stealing, because I enjoy grinding with him so much. Lee has to be the most fun person in the world to work with. His personality is incredible, his sense of humor never stops, and his work ethic is unparalleled. All of this in a person with the heart of an assassin (on the golf course only). If you can be beaten, Lee Janzen will beat you. Lee, after you won your second U.S. Open you showed the world what class really is, and we all love you for that. It is with great pride that I call you my friend.

I thank you all, Simmie, T.J., D.A., Sieck, Jake, Payner, Vijay, Elk, and Lee, from the bottom of my heart, for your attention, focus, caring, feedback, and honesty. I love you guys.

A Special Tribute to Tom Kite

Last, but certainly not least, comes Tom Kite. This one-of-a-kind Texan deserves special recognition, not because he has been a better friend or a closer companion, but because he became, quite simply, the *best* short-game player in the world. He proved to me and to the world—although the world didn't seem to notice—that a great short game is a key that fits all courses and leads to golf success.

Tom Kite is not a superior athlete, not a particularly long hitter, not the world's greatest ball-striker. In fact, according to the data, he was not among the top 60 on Tour in ball-striking. However, he is golf's fourth-leading all-time money winner, is among the all-time leaders in scoring average, has one of the best records in Ryder Cup play in history, and has been the best short game player for the last 20 years.

In 1980, after a meeting with Tom and five other PGA Tour players in which I showed him his short-game data, he was the only one to immediately add a third, higher-lofted wedge to his bag. He began practicing his distance wedges, applying his intelligence, determination, stubbornness, practice habits, and undying desire to win, to the task. As we worked throughout that year, he became, according to my data, the Tour's best wedge player by the end of the season. As far as I can tell, Tom has remained so ever since.

His accomplishments are impressive. For 15 years, his birdie percentage on par 5s has been near the top on the PGA Tour. While pretty impressive on its own, that statistic becomes more so when you realize that the number of par 5s he hits in two is relatively low compared with many other Tour players. He didn't do this with distance, but with his short game.

Kite holds numerous course records, but the most impressive to me was the 62 he shot at Pebble Beach when he won the 1988 AT&T National Pro-Am. In that round he hit only 10 greens in regulation, and besides some great putting, holed two wedge shots from off the green. During his U.S. Open victory in 1992, he finessed the ball better than anyone believed possible in treacherously windy conditions, hitting to the greens with 14 wedges in 18 holes, and shooting even par 72 to win. In early 1993, he completed the five-round Bob Hope Chrysler Classic at 35 under par. That score beat the existing tournament record by 6 shots, beat the second-place player by 7 shots, and third place by 10.

I also love the fact that he won an 18-hole Ryder Cup match 6 up with 5 to play. His stunned opponent was 5 under par when he was closed-out. And in 1997, he holed out from off the green 5 times in one round, to win a tournament in France.

And best of all, in 1981, his first year of short-game dominance, he recorded some numbers I find the most remarkable. My data showed Tom getting up and down an astounding 85% of the time for shots inside 60 yards, while getting up and down over 70% of the time from the sand. As a result, he finished in the top 10 in 21 of 25 tournaments; a record I feel will be more difficult to break than any other he has set.

All this from a man who could barely see (until he had his eyes fixed with Lasik surgery), and has, in my opinion, mediocre God-given athletic talent. Tom, I thank you for working with me and being my friend. I know you are a great family man, and as a fellow Austinite with a king-sized heart, a great work ethic, and a large dose of smarts, you are smart enough to be the best in the short game. While others may hit it longer and straighter, you take home the money, and I salute you for that!

My Staff, My Wife, and My Cameraman

I also want to acknowledge the contribution of my staff of instructors from my Scoring Game Schools in Boca Raton, PGA West, and Cordillera. These are the world's best short-game teachers, and they have helped me in so many ways, it is difficult to do them justice. What I can say is thanks, you are the best, and let's keep trying to get better.

Of course, this book would have been clearly impossible to write without the support of my wife JoAnn, who as COO of The Pelz Golf Institute, runs not only the company, but my life. My dear, you know I love you for that, too. Anyone who knows us, knows this is not an exaggeration.

I also want to thank my staff at the home office of The Pelz Golf Institute in Austin, Texas, who helped prepare the photo and video sequences, photographs, and illustrations that make the concepts of this book come to life. A special thanks go to David Watford and Joel Mendelman for their tireless artistic and graphic contributions, and to Eddie Pelz for not only keeping it all together, but for doing it mainly after midnight.

And finally, my thanks to Fred Vuich and the good people at GOLF Magazine, who provided me with many photographs from our photo shoots, to Jim Frank— my favorite editor on earth, and especially to the best golf photographer in the world, and I'm proud to say my friend, Leonard Kamsler. Leonard, you ARE THE BEST!

Foreword
by Lee Janzen

Everyone wants to shoot better scores. The best players in the world all agree that the key to lower scores is improving your short game. We all spend time pounding range balls and trying to find that perfect groove so we can hit pure shots, but our most valuable time is spent working on shots from 100 yards into the greens.

Practicing your short game will help your scores, but practicing techniques that narrow your chance of error will dramatically improve your scores. Dave Pelz has spent many years compiling data on every shot imaginable—from distance wedges, pitching, and chipping to sand play and trouble shots. From his research, Dave has developed the basic fundamentals that ensure better scoring.

Read this book and then practice the shots you learn. You will enjoy new skills that impress your playing partners and lower your scores.

I have experienced an improved short game every time I have worked with Dave. I think everyone who works with the information in this book will improve his or her ability to score, too.

I could not have won my second U.S. Open without Dave Pelz. He has improved my scoring game, and I know he can help you, too.

Introduction

I didn't call this book "THE" short game bible. It's "MY" short game bible, *Dave Pelz's Short Game Bible.* I make that distinction because it is the work-in-progress record of my research, what I understand about the game, and how I teach the short game of golf.

This book is not intended to say "everything" about the short game and all of its shots or to convert golfers to any particular theory or method of play. My short game bible contains my research on how the game *is* being played and my thoughts on how it *can be played better,* i.e., how golfers can shoot lower scores.

My intent is to help golfers improve; to help them develop their scoring ability; to help them become better players and to enjoy the game more.

I believe scoring and self-improvement are what the game is all about. The challenge to each golfer's ability to post a score is the very essence of the game. In this regard, I have been doing research for years on how and why golfers shoot the scores they do. Some time ago I established The Pelz Golf Institute, creating a medium for all my testing, results, thoughts, and questions regarding the playing of the game. The Institute was founded to conduct research "for the good of the game." Its purpose is not to discover clubs to drive the ball farther or to make equipment better in any way. Rather, the goal of the Institute is to discover, understand, and develop better ways to teach golfers to play and enjoy the game.

This book comes straight from the Institute. It relates the short game as it is taught in my Scoring Game Schools, so it may seem different from other golf instruction books. That's because it *is* different. This book focuses as much on understanding as it does on technique, because our research has shown that golfers learn faster, and better, if they learn both why and how at the same time. While the traditional instruction you expect is all here, it may be in a different place than you expect or couched in slightly different terms. I encourage you to read the book as you find it, and see if you don't quickly internalize the concepts and improve your short game shortly thereafter.

Please take a few seconds to consider the following.

Has it ever occurred to you that:

- Golf balls are better balanced today, flying farther and straighter and spinning better than ever before, by measurable amounts.
- Drivers are lighter and stronger, irons are better balanced, and shafts are lighter and more flexible in the right places than ever before, by measurable amounts.
- Greens are smoother, faster, better maintained, and they roll more smoothly than ever before, by measurable amounts.
- Tour professionals hit longer, straighter, and better shots, hole more putts, and shoot lower scores than ever before, by measurable amounts. They are so much better that most tournament courses have to be "toughened-up" to keep the pros from shooting regularly in the 50s.
- And yet, the average score of the average American golfer has not gone down in the last 30 years!

It's true. Even though average golfers *are* hitting their longest-ever drives on their local courses (yes, the Big Bertha/titanium phenomenon is real), they still aren't shooting lower scores. One of my goals in publishing this book is to change that.

My short game bible will show you why and how shooting lower scores is completely reasonable, as well as why "where you putt from is more important than how well you putt," and why "if you can wedge it, putt it, and drive it, you can play this game."

There is help in this book for all golfers, from Tour players to beginners, in learning to score better. I sincerely hope it is easy for you to use, that you'll refer to it over and over again and get full benefit from it. After you read, feel free to call us or communicate with us (see Resources in the back of this book) with your questions or comments.

I seriously invite you to write, e-mail, or call because I love feedback. I'm going to be teaching lots of people, and the next book in my scoring game series (*Dave Pelz's Putting Bible*) is well on its way. Your results, comments, or experiences may help me get my points across better in the years to come and allow us all to enjoy this great game more. So get after it and enjoy.

CHAPTER 1

Score Counts in Golf

Who Cares About Score?

1.1 Defining the Scoring Game

In golf, how you play inside of 100 yards is the prime determinant of how you score. I don't say this play *completely* determines your golf score, just that it is the most significant factor when it comes to writing numbers on your scorecard. I base this statement on more than 23 years of studying golfers and compiling data, which show that 60% to 65% of all golf shots occur inside 100 yards of the hole. More important, about 80% of the shots golfers lose to par occur inside 100 yards. These results led me to focus on what happens inside 100 yards, what I call the "scoring game," to concentrate my teaching there, and to found the Dave Pelz Scoring Game Schools.

Every golfer's scoring game is a combination of many shots and many deci-sions. In teaching players how to score, I simplify things this way: I define the game played from 100 yards in to the edge of the greens as the "short game"; the game played on the greens is obviously the "putting game"; and the judgments and decisions made on game management and shot selection constitute the "management game." As you can see in Figure 1.1.1, I've broken the game of golf into five categories, what I call "the five games of golf," which also include the "mental game" (fear, anxiety, confidence) and the "power game" from outside 100 yards.

Learn to play all five of these games well and you will become a good golfer. And the more you improve your performance in these games, the more you will enjoy your golf.

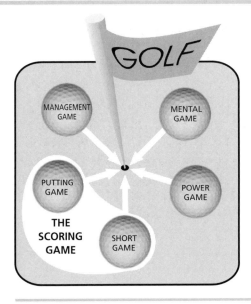

Figure 1.1.1: The five games of golf

1.2 Why Is This Book Necessary?

My *Short Game Bible* focuses completely on play from 100 yards in to the edge of the green. To a true golfer, scoring is what the game is all about, and your short game plays a vital role in determining scoring ability. We don't all have the same natural talent, we can't all hit 350-yard drives like Tiger Woods, and we will never all look the same when we swing a golf club. But if you are in reasonably good health, if you can walk the meadows and see the clouds, smell the grass and hear the birds, if you can feel the breezes and make contact with the little white ball, you can learn to score better. And this book will help you do it.

This is not a book about generating more clubhead speed with your driver or hitting the golf ball farther. Rather, my *Short Game Bible* details what I have learned and how I teach the short game, including the distance wedges, pitches, chips, sand shots, lobs, and bump-and-run shots. I hope it will help you learn something about them.

Now, the first point I want to make is about putting. Sound a little strange? Stick with me.

1.3 The "Golden Eight"

What do you think is the most important distance in golf? The 250 yards of the tee shot? The 150 yards of the perfect approach? The 20 yards of most chips? Or putts from inside three feet? Actually, it's none of these. Golf's most important distance is the "Golden Eight," the eight feet that separate a two-foot putt from a 10-foot putt.

More simply put, the Golden Eight is the distance difference between making and missing most of your putts.

I've studied thousands of golfers, at all skill levels, and found that nearly everybody makes almost every putt from inside two feet. Go a little farther away, to three feet, and golfers begin to miss (even Tour pros make only 85% to 95% of their three-footers). Step back to five feet and pros hole about 65%, while amateurs, if they're lucky, are making about 50%. And at six feet, the best in the world, the PGA Tour professionals, sink about 50%, plus or minus 5%. From 10 feet, no one consistently holes better than 25%. And from over 15 feet? One in 10, best case, even for the pros.

So your best chance of making a putt is if it's inside 10 feet. And how do you get it there? Answer: the wedges, pitches, chips, and bunker shots of your short game.

Why the Short Game?

1.4 Giving Your Short Game Its Due

There are more than 15,000 golf professionals in this country, most of whom teach the game. There are another 7,000-plus assistant pros who teach (and another 5,000-plus who want to teach), and 25 or so successful golf schools. What most of these teachers and schools have in common is that they emphasize the full swing, what I call the power swing. That is what golfers expect to be taught, and that's what they get. As a result—and I'm not being critical, but it's a fact—the short game takes a backseat in the teaching of golf.

I am publishing this book because your short game deserves more attention than that. Your short game is not like any of golf's other games; it should not be played as if it's a throttled-down version of the power game, as some pros teach. Golfers who use muscle control and deceleration to turn their power swings into short shots are doomed to frustration. The short game needs to be taught separately because—and here comes the good part—it is the most important skill you can improve to lower your scores.

As mentioned above, the short game controls the "Golden Eight" feet. If statistics prove that you'll probably miss a 10-footer but you're almost 100% from two feet away, then you'd rather be putting from two feet than 10, right? How do you get there? For most of us, most of the time, the length of our first putt is a function of our short game.

My research also shows that the short game is the single greatest influence on the success or failure of players on the PGA Tour. I'll explain the data in detail later, but right now, suffice it to say, I believe—and can prove—that it is the short game that wins the big money, wins the big tournaments, and keeps the pros on Tour year after year.

(Don't get too hung up on the pros. My data, which I'll refer to over and over in this book, has been collected from players of all skill levels, not just Tour players but also middle- and high-handicappers, even beginners.)

And here's another piece of information that may surprise you, especially if you're an average or new golfer: The higher your scores, the *more* you need a good short game. Beginners and high-handicappers hit fewer greens than better players, which means they face more short-game shots per round. The more you need your short game, the better it has to be if you're going to become a good player (i.e., a low scorer). So while the short game is the bread-and-butter skill to the Tour players, it's of even greater consequence to "normal" golfers.

1.5 Learn How to Learn

The purpose of my *Short Game Bible* is not simply to tell you how great short-game players look or swing. It's to help you learn how to be a better wedge player, a better sand player, and a better chipper and pitcher of the golf ball when you get close to the greens. But before you can achieve a better short game for yourself, you must first learn both what you need to know and how to learn it.

In one after another of my schools around the country, I see golfers struggling to master their short games when they have no real understanding of what it is they're trying to accomplish. In these cases, it doesn't matter how hard they try, how much they practice, how diligent they are, or how much they care. When they don't know the skills and techniques required to execute good shots, or how to practice to learn them, they will not be successful in learning them. The truth is, very few golfers, even at the Tour-player level, understand the details and realities of their short games.

Therefore, what I want you to learn from this book is:

1. What you need to learn
2. How to learn it
3. Methods for ingraining your learning so your results will serve you on the golf course

By reading this book you will not only learn *how* to become a better short-game player, but you will actually *become* one. If that happens, I've done my job and you will enjoy the game all the more. We'll both be satisfied, because not only will you shoot lower scores but also you'll know how you developed that ability. You'll be able to fine-tune and touch up your short game later, perhaps many years later, after some bad habits may have snuck into your game.

My ultimate goal is to help you to become your own best teacher, and to help you use that skill to improve your short game for as long as you continue to play.

1.6 The Pelz Overview of Scoring

My *Short Game Bible* can best help your short game if you both understand what's being said and follow the recommended drills. It also will help if you understand where this information fits into the overall development of your ability to score. Figure 1.6.1 shows how I view your learning process, and how this book can fit in to help you improve your scoring game.

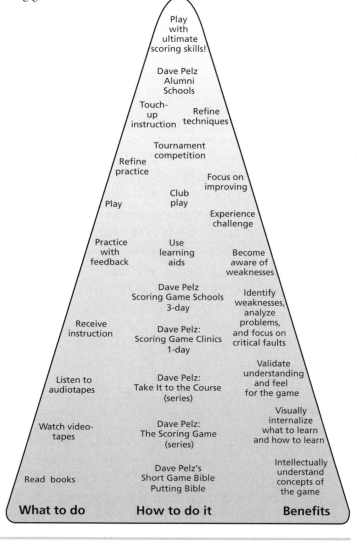

Figure 1.6.1: Pyramid of Learning: where Pelz teaching fits into your learning program

Play with ultimate scoring skills!

Dave Pelz Alumni Schools

Touch-up instruction   Refine techniques

Tournament competition

Refine practice

Focus on improving

Play   Club play

Experience challenge

Practice with feedback   Use learning aids   Become aware of weaknesses

Dave Pelz Scoring Game Schools 3-day   Identify weaknesses, analyze problems, and focus on critical faults

Receive instruction   Dave Pelz: Scoring Game Clinics 1-day

Validate understanding and feel for the game

Listen to audiotapes   Dave Pelz: Take It to the Course (series)

Visually internalize what to learn and how to learn

Watch video-tapes   Dave Pelz: The Scoring Game (series)

Intellectually understand concepts of the game

Read books   Dave Pelz's Short Game Bible Putting Bible

What to do   **How to do it**   **Benefits**

Don't be intimidated or discouraged by the number of different shots and areas of practice that are comprised by the scoring game. At every skill level, the putting and short-game skills are easier to learn and groove than the skills of the power game. (The management game is the easiest to learn, but only once you have repeatable skills in the power, short, and putting games.) None of the concepts or motions in the short game are difficult if you take the time to understand them and then properly practice them. It's all a matter of knowing what to do, how to do it, then doing it often enough.

All of the learning aids, books, and video- and audiotapes referenced in Figure 1.6.1 may not be available when you are first reading this book, but they are all works in progress. If you are interested, contact the numbers or addresses listed in the Resources (page 427).

Where I Come From

1.7 How I Got Here

I've been playing golf almost my entire life. I played in my first tournament when I was seven. I remember because I got my picture in the newspaper for playing a match against a man aged 77. We had a heck of a match, both shooting about 150. I don't remember who won, but I do remember that picture. As a now-famous seven-year-old, I was hooked on golf for life.

At 12, I lost in the finals of the Youngstown, Ohio, Pee-Wee tournament, and I was convinced that the lucky bounce Tony Joy got to beat me was just the experience I needed to survive, to be a winner from then on. Later, at Boardman and Willoughby High Schools in Ohio, I played first positions on the golf teams. I played just well enough to get a few college coaches interested, although my sister could beat me until I was 16. They didn't allow her to play on our team, however, because it embarrassed the boys when she beat them.

I attended Indiana University on a four-year golf scholarship. Even though my main reason for going to college had been to get prepared to play the PGA Tour, I majored in physics, a grounding that has served me very well. By the end of my Indiana years, I finally realized I was more likely to succeed in a laboratory than on the PGA Tour. Although I thought I could play pretty well, I kept being beaten by other Big Ten golfers, like John Konsic of Purdue, Jack Rule of Iowa, and especially a big kid from Ohio State named Nicklaus. I could read the writing on the wall.

I registered and briefly attended graduate school at the University of Maryland, but dropped out when I got a job in space research at NASA's Goddard Space Flight Center outside Washington, D.C. I gave up golf for a few years, as I couldn't afford to belong to a private club. Instead, I took up auto racing. I put aside my clubs in favor of a Jaguar, a Sports Car Club of America competition license, and a helmet. After two years of racing and my third crash, I realized that if you have a bad day on the golf course you get disgusted and angry, but at least you live to compete another day. Have a bad day on the race course and they bury you.

I loved my job at NASA, but once a golf nut . . . So I started playing again. When I wasn't working, I played in tournaments; at night I put my research skills to work on my game. I was just good enough to compete on a national level, qualifying for the 1974 U.S. Amateur at Ridgewood Country Club in New Jersey. I lost in the second round, not only because I ran into a better player, but also because the putter I was using, a club of my own design, was disallowed by the United States Golf Association.

1.8 A Businessman? No!

Shortly thereafter, I was approached by a group of local businessmen who knew I'd designed a putter that had had a dramatic effect on my game. They agreed to set me up in business if I would leave NASA. They said we'd all make a fortune, but it didn't quite work out that way.

While my wife and three children were somewhat apprehensive about my new career, and my parents were aghast, I assured them everything would be fine. Then I promptly lost everything I had ever made. In the first year, I lost the $75,000 the investors put up. In year two, I mortgaged my home, both cars, and emptied my NASA retirement fund, a total of $40,000, and lost that. By the third year, I'd been befriended by a number of PGA Tour players, six of whom invested in me because they thought my research was helping their games. I lost their $25,000. In the fourth year, I thought I was a success because I was losing less than the year before, but my accountant told me I'd been bankrupt for two years. I thought I was doing fine and reasoned that if I kept at it, I'd get there soon.

Soon came very slowly, as shown in Figure 1.8.1. I didn't make a significant profit until almost 18 years later. But I'm still in golf, and still loving it. I eat it, sleep it, dream it. Just ask my wife, my family, and my friends among the club and Tour pros. The reason golf still excites me is that as a student of the game, I continue to learn new things on a regular basis.

Let me admit right now that this isn't the first time I thought I was a "student of the game." I thought the same thing in college. Back then, I kept statistics on the

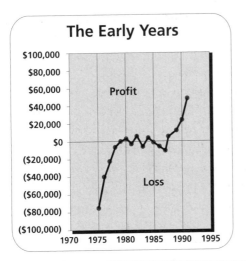

Figure 1.8.1: Pelz profit history

number of fairways I hit, my greens in regulation, three-putts—you name it, I quantified it. I thought I understood golf.

I was wrong. Dead wrong.

How All This Happened

1.9 The Day That Changed My Life

Since starting in the golf business, I've totally changed my view of golf. That change began one day during the Kemper Open, which used to be played at Congressional Country Club outside Washington, D.C. I was trying to decide if I wanted to stay in the golf business or not. I'd been losing quite a bit of money (it was only the beginning of my losses, but I didn't know that then) and wasn't feeling very secure, when I found myself watching a Tour professional named Gay Brewer warming up on the practice tee.

Let me tell you a little about Gay Brewer. He won the 1967 Masters. He had another dozen or so victories on the Tour. He is still playing on the Senior PGA Tour today. He has always been a consistent money winner. He is a player.

But a swinger? No sir. He had perhaps the worst-looking golf swing I'd seen on someone who can really play. Instead of a one-piece takeaway, his first move was to put the clubhead low to the ground and behind him. Then he brought the club straight up in the air so at the top of his backswing it pointed out in front toward his caddie. Then he waggled it three or four times to make sure anybody who might be watching was unsure just what was happening. From there, he made a reasonably solid move down and through the ball, hitting powerful, low hook shots. It was not an impressive sight. (It still isn't, but it's still the swing he uses today.)

I stood there watching Brewer hit hook after hook, and I thought, "This man won the Masters. This man is a player. He's among the top 10 money winners on the PGA Tour. In many events he beats Jack Nicklaus and Tom Weiskopf, both of whom own reasonably good-looking golf swings. How does he do it with that swing?"

As if that weren't enough, standing next to Brewer on the range was a young fellow who had the most beautiful swing I'd ever seen. His backswing, downswing, and follow-through were all as Ben Hogan had prescribed: on the proverbial plane of glass. His shots traveled on long, high, penetrating trajectories; his drives consistently flew 20, 40, sometimes 50 yards past Brewer's; and he looked better with every club in the bag. He looked like an awesome player, but I didn't recognize him. I checked the name on his bag and still didn't recognize him, so I looked him up in the press guide. There I found out that this fellow had been on Tour for four years and had never finished in the top 100 on the money list. He was not a great player.

Watching Brewer and this young fellow, a question formed in my mind: "How can this beautiful golf swing not outperform Gay Brewer's incredible move?" At that time, I assumed the reason had to be putting.

Just then, they left the driving range together, walked to the practice green, and started to putt. I followed and watched in amazement as the young man executed one of the best-looking, most rhythmic putting strokes I'd ever seen. He made putt after putt, pouring them into the cup. Then I turned to watch Brewer, who had, in fact, a worse-looking putting stroke than he had a golf swing. He brought the putter inside on the takeaway, lifted it up, and shoved it straight out away from his body to a position three to four inches outside the target line. Then he turned the putterface down and made a forward stroke that looked as if he were trying to kill a bug sitting on the outside-back quadrant of the ball, which squirted off his putter as the club smashed into the green. There was no follow-through, nothing that even resembled a stroke as we know it today. It was amazing.

Again I thought, "Masters champ? Top 10 money winner? Great player?" It was at that moment, as I watched Gay Brewer practice missing four-foot putts, that it occurred to me that maybe I didn't understand this game.

1.10 I Followed, Watched, and Wondered

It so happened that Brewer and the young man were paired together that day. I knew I had to watch them for a full round and find out if Brewer truly was a better player. (To this day, I don't reveal the young man's name because he never made it on the Tour. He tried for another year or two, lost his Tour card, and I don't think he ever tried again.)

So out I went, walking and watching every shot the two of them hit for 18 holes. Then came the moment that changed my life.

They finished the round and left the 18th green. I'd been very impressed with the young man's play. He had hit the ball well, struck a number of good-looking shots, and putted well. "The kid played well today," I said to myself. "He may not have made much money so far, but he must be improving. He'll be a real fine player someday."

As for Brewer, I didn't remember one good thing about his round. I didn't notice his game, because nothing he did was impressive.

I was preparing to go out and watch some more players and see if I could learn anything important about the game, when my life changed. While I was standing next to the scoreboard, the scores from the morning rounds were posted: Brewer had shot a 69, the young man a 73.

Gay Brewer, whom I hadn't noticed or been impressed with at all, had taken four fewer strokes than the young man who had hit the ball so beautifully. At that instant, I concluded that I truly did not understand the game of golf. I said, "Pelz, you're going to get killed in this business, because you don't get it. You must not understand how the game is played if you think that kid is a better player than Gay Brewer."

1.11 The Scoring Game Taught Here

Forget going out to watch any more players that day. I went home and sat by myself in my study. I tried to think and think and think. Why, after all the tournament golf I'd played, after all the practice rounds and balls I had hit in my life, why did I not know enough to tell a great player from someone who couldn't make it on the Tour?

The answers didn't come overnight. But they have come. They have come to me over the years. The more I study the game, the more I study people, the more I measure the ways golfers play and swing, the better I understand how they can improve their ability to score. My goal has become to understand the game well enough to make it simple for golfers to score better and enjoy the game more.

If you are ready to find out what I've learned about the short game, read on. I'll explain the realities of golf in Chapter 2, and why a good short game is vital to your ability to score in Chapter 3. Then, in Chapters 4 to 13, I'll teach you how to develop and own a good short game for yourself.

Understanding the Game and Its Realities

What Is Important in Golf?

2.1 What Is a Good Swing?

Once upon a time—before I watched Gay Brewer that fateful day—I thought I knew something about the game of golf. I had been able to look at a golf swing and evaluate how well the clubhead stayed on one plane. I judged the quality of every golfer I looked at or played with by the "in-plane-ness" of his swing.

I also gave credit in my judgments of a swing to its smoothness and rhythm. For example, when I'd look at a Tom Weiskopf, Gene Littler, Al Geiberger, or Tom Purtzer, I thought they had great swings (and, indeed, they did). They were beautiful, smooth, in balance, and conformed to my notions of perfection. And when a swing looked great to me, I assumed it was great, and that the player who made it was great. I had spent my practice and game-development time trying to make my swing look like those, assuming that by doing so I would myself become a great player.

When I'd run into great players whose swings were herky-jerky, out of plane, or unorthodox in some way—players like Arnold Palmer, Lee Trevino, Chi Chi Rodriguez, Moe Norman, and Gay Brewer—I would think, "Ugh." I don't know how they do it, but I'm very glad I don't swing like that.

Until the day I followed Gay Brewer, I had always let my "Ugh" evaluation lie there. I'd never tried to understand why or how those "Ugh" swings could win major tournaments, how "Ugh" swings could belong to truly great players. But I hadn't studied physics for four years without learning a little about the scientific method of understanding and solving problems. I knew the results—these play-ers' records—weren't matching my theories of good swings and greatness. I knew something was wrong with my understanding of the game. I had to be missing something.

After four hours of watching Gay Brewer, I wondered if his success could be chalked up to the size of his heart. I realized there had to be some other way to evaluate a golf game, because it obviously wasn't just the beauty, plane, or rhythm of his swing that determined his results.

It took me several months, and a great deal more observation, before a new evaluation system began taking shape in my mind. It occurred to me that a valid way to scientifically judge the quality of a golf swing was by measuring its effec-tiveness, its success, the accuracy of its performance. A player could make the worst-looking swing in the world, I decided, but if the ball went into the hole, then the shot was perfect, assuming he had been aiming at the hole. And if this "Ugh" player could hole 1,000 shots in a row, then he would be the best at that swing, no matter how bad he looked doing it. I realized that we can judge the quality of golf swings by their results, just as we judge the quality of golfers not by how they play a hole but rather by how many strokes they take. After all, it's not how, it's how many. It's the score that counts.

With this realization, my concept of game analysis changed from looking at swing mechanics, rhythm, and anything else physical to measuring the error in its result. In the simplest terms, how close the swing put the ball to the target became the measure of its quality. How close was all that mattered. This evaluation carried no bias or qualitative assumptions. It was not an impression or opinion, but a measurable fact. And if this measurement of swing quality proved more closely related to the quality of a golfer's performance, scoring, or number of career wins, then perhaps I had found a new and better way to evaluate both the game and the golfer.

2.2 A Little Slack, Please

Before moving on, please realize that I'm not saying bad-looking swings are al-ways better than good-looking swings. It's only true when the bad-looking swing produces better results, consistently knocking the ball closer to the pin. And the emphasis is on *consistently.*

I am not saying that swing mechanics are not important. Of course they are. The world's best teachers do a great job of improving swings by teaching simpler, more efficient techniques. David Leadbetter, Peter Kostis, Hank Haney, Gary

Smith, Jim McLean, Jim Flick, Rick Smith, Robert Baker, Gary Wiren, Butch and Dick Harmon, Michael Hebron, Gary McCord, Dean Reinmuth, and the other top teachers all do a great job. I count them among my friends and among golf's "improvement specialists." But I *am* saying that swing mechanics are not everything in golf, as some golfers believe. What matters is performance, and there is a cold, hard, analytical way to measure any golfer's performance, with whatever club is in his hand: Measure where the ball goes.

2.3 Shot Performance Evaluation

The best measure of the quality of a swing is the golfer's accuracy in moving a ball from point A to point B.

For example, say a golfer is 100 yards from the hole, as illustrated in Figure 2.3.1: From point A (where the ball is) to point B (where the hole is) is 100 yards. This is the original distance of the desired shot, assuming the hole is the desired target. If he hits a pitching wedge and the ball finishes 21 feet from the hole (point C), his miss distance or error is the distance from B to C—from the target to the ball's final resting spot. If you divide the shot-error distance (B – C), by the original shot distance (A – B), your result is the percentage error in this shot. In this case it is 7 yards/100 yards = 7% error.

So how good a swing was it? It got the ball 93% of the way to the hole, so I called it a 7%-error swing, because it produced an error of 7%. In my analysis, if he had made a perfect swing, with 0% error, the ball would have gone into the hole. When a golfer holes a bunch of shots, no matter how bad or good his swing looks, I say he is making a bunch of "perfect" (0% error) swings. A simple evaluation system: The smaller the error, the better the swing.

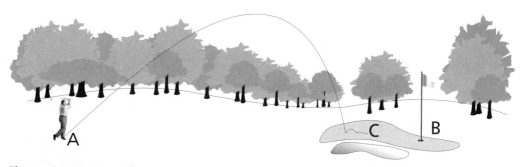

Figure 2.3.1: A shot from 100 yards aimed at B comes to rest at C

Once I gather enough percentage-error measurements with a particular club in a players' bag, at least 100 shots, I call the average of this data the percentage error index, or PEI, for that player with that club. The PEI is an assessment of his ability to perform with that club. When I compute an average from more than 1,000 shots, I consider the PEI an absolute indication of the player's skill with that club.

Performance is now one of the key ways I evaluate a golf swing. Back then, when it was new, I tried it out by following Tour players to see how they performed with every club in their bag. Maybe Gay Brewer of the amazing swing was beating other players because he was making better-performing (i.e., better PEI) swings. I'd know if he was doing something right because that something would be based on performance. Would he be a 15%-error wedge player, a 25%-error putter, or a 5%-error driver? I could find out. I had a way to learn how players play the game.

An Analytical Look at the Game

2.4 Data, Data, and More Data

The first thing I learned after recording enough data was that the average PGA Tour player has an average PEI for all his full swings (drives, 4-irons, 9-irons, etc.) of 7, meaning an average of 7% error. I also learned that if he had a PEI of 7 for his shots from 100 yards to the green, sticking the ball about 20 feet from the pin, he would think that wasn't too bad. From a full wedge swing, a 20-foot putt for birdie was okay. Most pros seemed satisfied with that.

What he wasn't happy with was having a 200-yard shot, hitting his 3-iron, and plugging the ball into the bunker. From the plugged lie he couldn't blast out close to the pin, meaning he had to get real aggressive to save his par. So he rolled his first par-saving putt four feet past, missed the putt coming back, and took a double bogey.

After his round he said, "My 3-iron killed me! I'm a terrible long-iron player. I hit my 3-iron 40 feet left of the hole and it cost me a double bogey. It ruined my round. My long-iron play was my downfall again." He trudged off to the practice range and beat on that 3-iron for the rest of the day.

The funny thing is, I measured the error on the 200-yard 3-iron shot and it was 14 yards—42 feet. That's a 7% error. He hit the same "quality" shot with a 3-iron that he hit with a full wedge. He was tickled pink with the wedge; he was red with rage over the 3-iron. But he was convinced he didn't know how to swing a 3-iron.

I say his swing with the 3-iron had the same quality of motion as his swing with the wedge. The numbers prove it.

When you're talking about the performance quality of a swing, the determining factor is the position of the clubface through the precise moments of impact. That motion determines where the ball is going. By measuring the result of the shot, you are measuring athletic performance—how well the player positioned the club through impact. So how good was he?

In the example cited earlier, he was just as good from both places. But the farther you get from the green, any given percentage error through impact will produce greater miss distances, and sometimes more serious repercussions. That's an important concept that most golfers don't understand.

2.5 The Man in the Raincoat

The concept of measuring swing performance (PEI) drives the concepts in this book and much of my subsequent research. Over the past 23-plus years, I've taken data on players from the PGA and LPGA Tours to measure their PEIs, their strengths and weaknesses. I have walked and measured the courses, learning and charting the yardage between virtually every tee and every pin, bunker, and tree. I have taken all my data during tournament rounds, because when I first came upon the concept I tried it during practice rounds, which were less costly to get into (this was when I had no money and I needed to conserve dollars). However, I found that the pros don't perform during practice rounds: They don't complete their rounds, they don't hit all their shots, they don't putt out, and they don't care about performance. They just hit balls, sometimes trying bizarre shots to determine distances or the effects of the wind. Often they pick up and walk, worrying more about distances than firing at the flag.

(This is an interesting sidelight to the Tour players. They really don't work on their games during practice rounds. They study the golf course. They hit shots to see what kinds of reactions they'll get from the greens, the fairways, and the bunkers, and they learn how to fit their games to the different courses they play. It's fascinating. Watch the pros during a practice round; unless there's some money on the line—which there sometimes is—they aren't playing. They're learning.)

So to compile PEI data, I had to measure shot results during tournament rounds. There I was, Thursday morning at 7:30, with the first group on the first tee. Who were they? A bunch of no-name rookies—Jim Simons, Andy North, and Tom Kite—made up the first group I ever followed. And, as you might expect, it was pouring rain.

I started walking with them, and I was a sight. I was carrying a great big lab notebook (Fig. 2.5.1), and I was wearing a raincoat and holding an umbrella (not easy with a notebook in one hand while trying to write in it with the other). I was 6 feet 5, weighed 285 pounds, and I *was* the gallery. No one else was out there. Not many had yet heard of these three guys, but I was with them for every shot. All the way, in the rain.

They teed off. I'd watch each one hit the ball, scanning the sky for it, then run down outside the ropes to measure where the shot finished. I tried to determine where they were aimed—at the center or the side of the fairway—so I could later figure the percentage error for the drive. I did this for all three guys. Then they hit their second shots, and I ran to the green, went to one side to see a ball in the bunker, scribbled in my notebook, moved around to see where the second ball was on the green, wrote something else, ran around again to see the third ball, and opened my notebook again. Man, I was moving around.

Later I learned that by the third hole they were saying to each other, "Watch this big fat guy. What in the world do you think he's doing?"

On the sixth hole of the very first round I ever charted, the group decided to send Jim Simons over. He introduced himself and said, "Sir, what are you doing?" This was my introduction to Jim, who has since become a good friend; a three-time winner of the PGA Tour, he is now a stockbroker. He has always been a fine gentleman.

Figure 2.5.1: DP with notebook, in the data-acquisition mode

However, on this day, he surprised me. I was caught off guard in the rain, didn't quite know what to say, so I stammered out that I was studying his game, trying to determine where his strengths and weaknesses were. He was taken aback and said, "Oh, you're evaluating my game? How?"

I said, "I'm measuring the percentage error of your shots, measuring the distance you miss your target on each shot . . ." and I quickly drew a sketch (similar to Fig. 2.3.1) to explain the concept of PEIs to him.

He got into it. "That's interesting," he said, and then he asked me what I'd learned.

"Well, in six holes you haven't hit seven of the clubs in your bag yet, so I really don't know. But when I get some solid statistics, I'm sure I'll find out something."

"That impresses me," he said, and he pulled out his business card—"Jim Simons, PGA Tour Professional"—and he added, "Mr. Pelz, when you find out the weaknesses in my game, call me at home anytime. You just let me know."

Jim then introduced me to Andy and Tom, and after that, I followed those three every chance I could.

I met a number of players that way. After I'd been out on Tour almost every weekend for a month, I met Lanny Wadkins. I was following the group he was in, watching them hit, running down the fairway, taking data in my notebook. The group watched me lumbering along the outskirts of the course, doing my thing. Then Lanny came over to see me: "Hey, what are you doing?"

This time, I was ready. I'd spoken to a lot of players in a few weeks, become friendly with a few, and by now I knew how to explain my ideas to them. So I started telling Lanny about measuring his shots, how far they finished from his intended target, percentage errors . . . and I look up and he's running away from me like I just lit a match under his tail. He didn't want to hear any facts, no scientific data, thank you very much; he didn't want to hear anything about it.

Jim Simons and Lanny Wadkins are very different individuals. Simons is analytical, fact-oriented, a numbers sort of guy. Lanny is a total "instinct" player. Don't confuse him with facts. Analysis? Forget it. Lanny does his thing (very well, I should add) and isn't interested in what anybody else thinks about it.

This was how I initially formed relationships with the Tour players. Guys like Kite, North, Simons, Tom Jenkins, Joe Inman—players who could look at my notes and figures and say, "You know, that means something. I can learn something from that." Those were the players who would come work with me.

I'm not saying that you have to be a scientific type to get something out of this book. Not at all. You don't have to study the numbers or think about percentages to improve your short game. What you do need, however, is to understand what these numbers have taught me about the short game and how I can help you. Because I can now accurately detect your problems and tell you what to work on. Stay with me and you'll learn what your weaknesses are and how to fix them, and you never have to think about any numbers, I promise.

2.6 The Reason to Caddie

It makes sense now, and the players believe me now, but back then even the interested ones needed to be convinced. As soon as I had enough data to talk to the guys, they didn't believe the results. I was showing them cold, hard facts, honest data, no opinion on my part, and they didn't believe it. I learned then that people see their lives through a filter, they see what they *want* to see. They don't like to face their weaknesses, while they love to talk about their strengths. (They also don't like to *practice* their weaknesses, while they overpractice their strengths, but more on that later.)

They'd say to me, "Look, Pelz, I know I hit a couple of bad shots with that club, but I'm not that bad. I had a couple of bad lies, and you were outside the ropes so you don't know."

To get through to some of these guys, I had to caddie for them. Then I could walk inside the ropes, I could see the lie, and they couldn't give me a hard time afterward about it being in a divot or the crosswind up at the green. They also could tell me before hitting the shot exactly where they were aiming, and so on.

About this time I switched from my big logbook to a handheld tape recorder. I'd whisper into it where the player was aiming, how far the shot was, where the target was, how far he missed it by, and at the end of the round I entered the data into a computer and did the calculations. It was a lot of work, but I got it done, and it was accurate.

Who Does What, How Well?

2.7 How Good Are the Tour Players?

This was my life for a couple of years. First walking outside the ropes watching players, then caddying for those I got to know well. I got to know, by game if not personally, many players with every club, driver to putter.

In one round walking with one group I'd get three complete rounds of golf—

about 210 shots from three guys. If I caddied for someone in the morning, I'd follow three more guys in the afternoon, and I'd measure and record the performance error from every club in their bags on every shot they hit in every round I followed.

As I compiled more data and looked at the percentages, I began seeing patterns. At the start, I learned that for the first 10 rounds I didn't know a player at all. After 10 rounds, I had begun to learn something. By 20, I had him down pretty well, and by 40 rounds there were no more secrets. I knew his strengths and weaknesses, the quality of his game in every area.

At first I expected every club or shot category to be unique. Then the greater similarities took hold. For example, the woods really weren't that different from one another: If a guy was pretty good with his driver, he usually was pretty good with his 3-wood, too. (This is true of Tour players; later, when I began working more extensively with amateurs, it proved to not always be the case.) Likewise, all his long irons—1-, 2-, and 3-irons—were similar. The medium irons—4, 5, and 6—had much the same PEIs. Same for the short irons.

I started seeing consistent patterns within categories, and as I gathered more numbers and improved my computer analysis, I realized something that was startling at the time: The drivers and fairway woods weren't all that different from the long, medium, and short irons. There was a PEI for each player, and all those clubs were within about 1% (plus or minus) of it.

Here's an example of what I mean. After 40 rounds, I had Jim Simons's numbers for all his clubs. They were something like 8.1, 7.9, 7.6, 7.7, 8.0, 7.4, 7.8, 7.5, and so on from driver through 9-iron. It was essentially the same number for every club. What it told me was that the full swing didn't change very much. Yes, even the pros hit their drives a little farther off-line than their shots with other clubs; but in terms of percentage error, their drivers weren't much worse (or better) than their 9-irons.

Simons was a just-under-8% player for his full shots, on average, after hundreds and hundreds of shots. Andy North was a little better, about 7.3. Tom Kite was 7.5. Nothing too different about any one of them. I looked at player after player, and over a period of three years I gathered a lot of numbers, more than enough data on more than 100 of the 150 or so who were out there winning money.

On average, the Tour players had—and still have—about 7% error in their full swings: 5% was the very best, 10% shots were poor. A 1%- or 2%-error shot was truly rare, while a 15% to 20% error was awful, and also very rare.

2.8 No Two Were the Same

So here I was, with about three years' worth of research and a lot of good friends on the Tour. I told them what my numbers told me, where they were good and not so good, what the data were saying they should work on. It was about this time, too, that a few of them gave me some money to continue working, to continue showing up on the Tour and helping them with their games. I still hadn't made my breakthrough, but I was getting close.

What was missing? The full swing is only one part of the game. As I mentioned in Chapter 1, golf is five games, and the full-swing power game is only one of them. Remember, the others are the putting game, the short game, the management game, and the mental game. The numbers couldn't tell me anything about the mental game, but they were saying all kinds of things about the short game and putting.

Every player—every one, bar none—had a very different PEI for his full swing than for his wedges, which was usually at least twice and, for some players, three times as high. Simons was 8% with his full swing but about 17% with his wedges, which is more than twice as bad. North was 7.3% with his full swing and 16% with his wedges, while Kite was 7.5% and 13%, respectively. And these three were among the *better* wedge results.

Every player's numbers changed for his wedges, and that surprised me. A list of five PGA Tour players' PEI data is shown in Figure 2.8.1, with the same data in graph form in Figure 2.8.2.

CLUB	D	3W	1i	2i	3i	4i	5i	6i	7i	8i	9i	PW	SW	P
PGA TOUR PRO														
A	9.2	8.6	7.2	7.8	6.9	7.7	7.9	7.6	7.0	7.7	7.4	16.1	18.1	23.0
B	7.9	7.9	7.4	7.7	7.1	7.0	7.6	8.1	7.4	7.3	7.8	13.8	17.2	25.5
C	8.3	6.8	6.7	7.2	7.0	7.4	6.8	6.8	6.9	7.7	7.1	15.5	19.0	27.6
D	9.5	8.2	8.6	8.0	8.1	8.5	8.0	7.7	8.5	7.2	8.0	14.9	14.6	31.1
E	5.4	5.7	5.3	6.0	5.2	5.1	5.7	5.5	5.2	5.3	5.6	13.9	21.0	24.4

Figure 2.8.1: Percent Error Index (PEI) for five PGA Tour pros

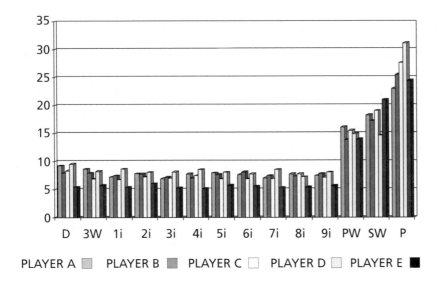

Figure 2.8.2: Percent Error Index (PEI) for five PGA Tour pros

There was something there I didn't understand. If a player's PEI for a 6-iron was the same as that for a 3-iron, which was the same as the player's driver and 9-iron PEI (all within about 1%), that meant that the distance from the pin or target was not a factor in determining PEI value. But why were the wedge PEIs so different? And so much worse for every player? Especially since wedge swings look simpler to execute than a full-bore driver swing, why can't the pros seem to execute them as well?

As if that wasn't bad enough, my initial putting PEIs were even worse. The three guys had putting PEIs of 40, 31, and 26. Forty percent error! Why were they so inept with their putters? It took me a while to work out that one, but there was a very simple answer: I was measuring putting error incorrectly.

This was when I realized that PEIs fell into three ranges, and followed the same basic patterns for all the players. The range for full-swing PEIs went from 5% to 9% from the best to the worst ball-strikers on the PGA Tour. The wedge data varied more from player to player, from 13% to just above 26%. Putting PEIs varied from just above 5% up to 10%. Nobody had low PEIs in all three categories, and the good ball-strikers (low full-swing PEIs) tended to have poor (high) putting PEIs. That's when I first realized I wasn't dealing with one game of golf. I was dealing with at least three, and three different skill sets, in what I had always assumed was the single game of golf.

Putting PEIs Must Be Measured Differently

When I first calculated putting percentage errors, I used the same formula I was using for full swings. If you face a three-foot putt and you miss just over the lip, the ball runs maybe two feet by, and that's a 67% error. By taking the error left after the shot and dividing it by the distance before the shot, you come up with some very big errors in putting. This was before I learned that the optimum roll speed for a putt (to optimize its chance of both hitting and staying in the hole) was one that would roll the ball 17 inches past the hole if it missed. When I refigured the putting PEIs based on that fact, they came down into the range of 5% to 10%.

2.9 Are PEIs Important?

The next step was to see which game mattered the most. I listed the players in order, starting with the player who had the lowest full-swing PEI at the top, down to the highest. Who had the best full-swing PEI? Lee Trevino, with a 5.02% error for all his swings. Also very good was Tom Weiskopf, but he wasn't second best. That was Miller.

No, not Johnny Miller. Allen Miller. He was the second-purest ball-striker I ever charted, but you probably never heard of him because he didn't stay out on Tour. A wonderful amateur player, Allen is now a teaching pro in Buffalo, New York. His full-swing PEI back then was 5.06%, and to this day that is the second-best male PEI I've ever measured. (Not only can he teach the full swing but he can demonstrate it, too.)

Then I listed the players by official money-winnings and correlated the two lists. The number-one ball-striker I measured was 15th in money over a three-year period. The number-two ball-striker was 200th. Number three was 85th; four was 35th; five was 129th. And the 65th-best ball-striker was number one on the money list. There was no significant correlation between how well the pros struck the ball and how much money they made. The analysis said that how well you hit the golf ball didn't matter in determining the scores you shot or how much you won on the PGA Tour. I couldn't believe it!

To use a phrase that was popular when I was doing this analysis, it blew my mind. I'd just spent almost 20 years of my life trying to improve my swing so I could hit the ball better and be good enough to play the Tour, plus another three years chasing the pros across the country and taking data, and I felt exactly the way I had when Gay Brewer's score went up at the Kemper—that I knew nothing about golf. But because I'm stubborn, I didn't quit. I hung around and thought about it until I figured out what was wrong. I knew the PEI data was accurate, as was the PGA Tour money list, so it had to be something in my interpretation of the data.

It was. My data wasn't saying that scores don't depend on how well you strike the ball. It was telling me that if you hit the ball with between 5% and 9% accuracy (which all Tour players do), the exact number within that range does not influence money won. It said that a drive that finishes in the center of the fairway is not measurably better for your score than a drive at the left or right edge of the fairway. It also said that players who hit iron shots to within 5% to 6% of the pin don't make much more money than those who hit them to within 7% to 8% of the pin.

After getting over that shock, I felt it was time to look for another correlation. At the time, I was trying to make a living by designing putters, so I decided to check the correlation of putting PEIs to money winning. I ran the same statistical correlation: best putting PEI at the top, down to the worst at the bottom. Next to that I put money winnings. And? I saw a weak correlation in the data, so weak it wasn't obvious at first glance. Again, the best putters were not the highest money winners. In fact, the best putters were not even bunched near the top of the money list. What the putting PEI data showed was that the better a player putts, the more money he wins—*all other things being equal*. In other words, while putting doesn't determine the money rankings, it helps to putt better.

All that was left was the short game, the shots hit with partial-effort swings (most often wedges) from within 100 yards of the green. I plotted the short-game PEIs the same way as before, alongside the money-winnings, and bingo! There was the strong correlation. I learned that the best short-game PEI belonged to Hale Irwin, who was right at the top in money won over the three-year data period. Tom Kite was 15th on the short-game PEI list and 18th on the money list. And Allen Miller? He was at almost the same spot well down the short-game PEI list as he was on the money list. Up and down, all along the money list, there was a strong and meaningful correlation between how well players hit their short-game shots and how much money they won on Tour. Any player who was good with his wedges was also good at cashing checks.

Understanding Helps

2.10 Why Is the Short Game So Important?

I had made a very important discovery: that short-game performance is more important than either putting or the power game in determining the score a player shoots and how much money he makes on the PGA Tour. Later, I would learn that the same is true for amateurs (with respect to scoring ability, of course, without the money earnings). But I had yet to figure out why. It was time to go back to my original data, to the thousands of shots I'd charted, to understand the importance of the short game. For each of those shots I had measured with each player, I knew not only the percentage error, but also the distance the ball flew and where it finished. I began making new charts.

In the center of a piece of paper I drew an X. That was the target. Then I plotted how close to the target, and exactly where, each shot finished. I did it for all clubs, grouping long, medium, and short irons, and then plotted frequency contours like those you see on a topographic map, which indicated where the shots missed their targets most often.

When I plotted all the players' 1-, 2-, and 3-irons, I saw that, as a group, Tour players tended to miss the target primarily either left or right with these irons, not long or short. Their distances were surprisingly accurate: The average distance error was only a couple of yards, just 1% or 2%. The directional error, however—the error left or right—was almost 7% on average, which for a long iron of 180 to 200 yards meant they were missing left or right of the target by 12 to 14 yards (about 35 to 40 feet). There was no question: The problem with the long irons was direction, not distance, as seen in Figure 2.10.1.

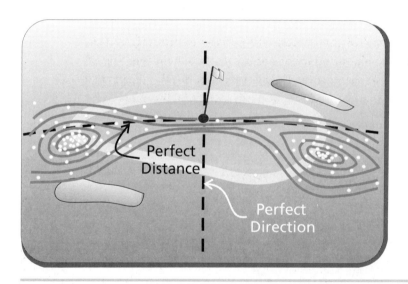

Figure 2.10.1: Shot scatter for long irons (1-, 2-, and 3-irons)

I wondered why a player could hit the ball within three yards of the correct distance but only within 13 yards of the right direction. I didn't get it.

I did the same thing for the medium irons, the 4-, 5-, and 6-irons, and found virtually the same pattern, as shown in Figure 2.10.2. The distance error was still very small, plus or minus two yards, while the directional error was plus or minus 11 yards. Although these shots were a little closer to the pin than the long irons

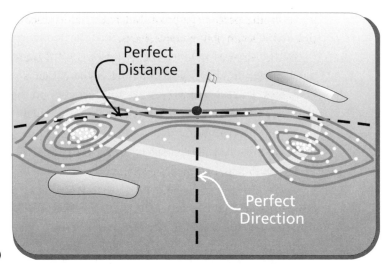

Figure 2.10.2: Shot scatter for medium irons (4-, 5-, and 6-irons)

(and still the same percentage error), the misses again were primarily in direction, from side to side.

With the short irons, the 7-, 8-, and 9-irons, the pattern held true (Fig. 2.10.3). Distance error was down to plus or minus one or two yards, but direction was off by eight yards left or right. Again, the overall error was about 7%, the same as that for the long and medium irons, and still significantly greater in directional error than distance error.

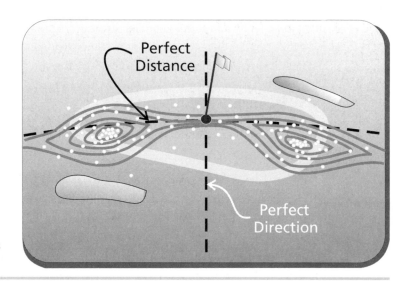

Figure 2.10.3: Shot scatter for short irons (7-, 8-, and 9-irons)

As I said, the shots within each category of irons fell primarily into two groups, one on each side of the target. As I plotted the frequency contours, a picture began to emerge. (Now remember, I was spending hours poring over the data and computer printouts, all by myself.) Suddenly the patterns looked to me like women's brassieres. The left side was always a little higher on the chart than the right, because shots to the left (draws and hooks) go a little farther than shots to the right (fades and slices), but they all looked like brassieres.

Because of the consistent shape of the shot patterns, I call this phenomenon of shots grouping left and right of the target the "bra effect." Until I saw this data, I had always assumed most players miss their shots in a random (circular) pattern around their target. Not so. While some players miss predominantly left, others tend to miss right. But very few power-swing shots miss absolutely on-line.

2.11 The Data Speaks

On all the full-swing shots, I saw the same pattern: Players were very good at controlling distance but very poor at controlling direction in terms of total error. While shots often would be within a few feet of the hole in distance, they would usually still be far off in direction. Why was that? How could someone not hit the ball straight while hitting it the right distance? How could they be so accurate, 1% to 2% error in distance with their full swings, when they couldn't hit it to better than a 7% or 8% error in direction?

After thinking about it, the answer became obvious. It's not that golfers don't practice direction—they practice it all the time; they're almost always hitting at a directional target and seeing the miss direction as the shot falls left or right of target. However, the direction of a shot is controlled by the rotation of the clubface through impact, and the timing of the swing. It is a result of the player's athleticism, coordination, swing mechanics, rhythm, timing, and the quality of his physical performance through impact.

If the best players in the world, who practice for hours almost every day of their lives for 10, 15, 20 years or more, only manage to hit the ball straight to within 5% to 9%, then direction must be very difficult to control. And you know what? It is. The clubface travels along a fairly flat swing plane, rotating 180 degrees (from 90 degrees right to 90 degrees left of target) through the region of impact, on all full-swing power shots. To get the face of the club at the perfect angle at the moment of impact is one of the greatest challenges in all of sport.

But why were they so good at distance? Again, it's obvious: Distance is not as much a function of a golfer's swing as of his club selection.

Tour players don't normally select 7-irons for 200-yard shots; they take a 3-

iron. They don't use 3-irons for 150-yard shots, they use 7- or 8-irons. So while direction is critically controlled by a player's face angle at impact, distance is primarily controlled by his club selection, caddie, and the yardage book—each of which is very accurate. All the player has to do is make reasonably solid contact.

The same is true for amateurs. If you know you're 150 yards away, you don't try to hit a sand wedge. You take your 150-yard club, your 6- or 7-iron. And when you use the right club, as long as you make a reasonably good swing, the ball flies about the right distance. But it doesn't go dead straight unless you put a *very* good swing on it—that is, a well-timed swing with exactly the correct face angle at impact.

What all this means is that when you're making a full swing, golf is primarily a game of direction. Most golfers don't realize that. They worry more about which club they choose than how straight they're going to hit it. But having the right club doesn't matter nearly as much as your directional accuracy with it.

2.12 Now We're Getting Somewhere

If you understand the data above, and everything I just said, now consider its exact opposite. Because that's what happens in the short game.

After I plotted the Tour pros' contour lines for the full swing, I did it for shots between 40 and 60 yards. These are partial swings (I call them "finesse swings") with the wedges, shots that don't go the normal distance you associate with the club's full-swing potential. Their plotting showed exactly the same pattern of shot dispersion as the power-swing shot patterns—the bra effect—except the bra was rotated 90 degrees (see Fig. 2.12.1).

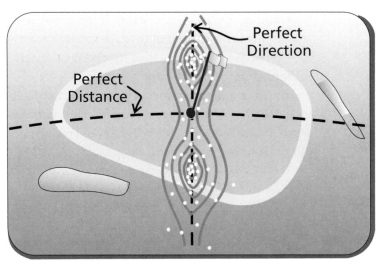

Figure 2.12.1: Short-game shot scatter (from 40 to 60 yards)

In the short game, the nature of the pattern is reversed. All of a sudden pros hit their short-game shots straight to better than 2% error, which is plus or minus two yards left or right. However, they didn't hit these shots the right distance within six to 12 yards (13%–26%). They were well long or short by a significant amount a high percentage of the time. Suddenly the problem in golf changed from direction to distance.

While this initially astounded me, again, the more I thought about it, the more it made sense.

Think again about how a player determines the distance for a full-swing shot. He grabs the correct club for that distance and makes a normal swing. But how does he determine the distance for a short-game shot? In his head. For a 50-yard shot, he doesn't have a 50-yard club in his bag. He can't take out a 50-yard club and make a full swing. So he does the best he can, grabbing a 90-yard club and throttling down.

The shortest club in the bag of every Tour player I was working with at the time was a sand wedge, which, with a full swing, hit the ball about 90 yards. Stand any one of the players at 40 yards and tell him to hit his 90-yard club and what does he do? He misses it by an average of at least six to eight yards, because he doesn't have what is required in his head to make his 90-yard club go 40 yards.

You Make It or You Don't

2.13 The Conversion Curve

Is distance control really important in the short game? Go back to putting: Can you make as many putts from 10 feet as you can from two feet? Look at the putting conversion curve in Figure 2.13.1.

Your ability to score is significantly influenced by your ability to minimize your number of putts per round. If you leave yourself lots of one-foot putts, you'll make them 100% of the time. Lots of 10-foot putts? You're down to a 20% conversion rate. Putts longer than 20 feet? You're looking at two- (and three-) putts most of the time.

The key distance for leaving short-game shots from the hole is about six feet; that's where the pros' conversion rate is 50%. My data shows that the pros were hitting wedge shots to within six feet of the hole in direction, but not distance. Their full-swing shots were pretty close to six feet away in distance, but they were far more than six feet away in direction. So whether they were hitting long

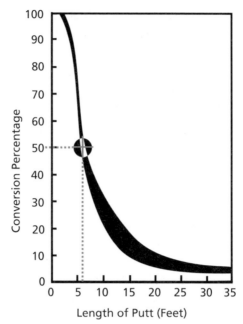

Figure 2.13.1: Putting conversion curve

irons, short irons, or wedges into the green, they weren't one-putting very often.

How to deal with all this? The answer is simple. To score better, hit your long irons straighter and your short-game wedges closer to the right distance.

How do you hit your long shots straighter? I don't know. But the golf world has convinced most golfers to spend most of their practice time trying to learn. I think that's a bad decision. To make significant improvement in the power game takes good instruction, athletic ability, timing, rhythm, talent, and a lot of practice. But once you've improved your ball-striking, it doesn't improve your scoring ability much, because you're still not going to one-putt greens from where even good long-iron shots leave you.

Based on my research, I made the decision years ago to forget the power swing. Rather, I decided to teach people to hit their short-game shots the right distance, because it isn't that difficult to do. And once you learn how, you will shoot lower scores.

(Many golfers have a poor short game because they've never had a way or place to practice it. Most practice areas don't have a target green for hitting these shots, letting you see whether your ball lands long or short of where you were aiming. Even when there is a target green, golfers don't know how far away they are; they make a swing but don't receive the proper feedback. I'm also sorry to say that most golfers don't understand how to practice or what to work on in their short-game swings, so any practice they do get in doesn't accomplish much. I'll cover all that later on in this book.)

2.14 If It's Straight, It's Good

For most golfers, in practice and in play, as long as their shots go straight, they think they've hit a good wedge. While I was caddying on Tour, I witnessed something that put this problem into perspective.

I was carrying for Tom Jenkins (T.J.). He was 51 yards to the pin, lying two on a par 5. His playing companion was right in front of him, same lie, same everything, but 50½ yards away.

T.J. hit first. He got over the ball, made a nice little waggle and a beautiful swing, and hit the ball right at the pin. As it was coming down, T.J. was holding his finish and saying, "Oh baby, be the right distance. Be perfect." The ball flew right over the pin (it almost hit the top of the flagstick), landed, and stopped immediately, six yards past the pin. It covered the flagstick all the way, finishing just a little long. T.J. walked to the bag, handed me his wedge, and said, "I hit it perfect. I thought it was in the hole. It's a little long, but it felt so good. That was a perfect swing." He was pleased.

As we stood there, our playing companion got over his shot, made a nice little waggle, and executed his 50-yard wedge swing. Immediately after the moment of impact, he turned his back on the shot, twisted his face and body in anguish, slammed his club into the ground, and said a few things not to be repeated here.

He was sick: I thought he was going to slit his wrists or throw up in his golf bag. He had pulled his 50-yard wedge shot six yards to the left of the hole, which to a Tour player looks and feels like a terrible shot. To hit it that far off-line was disgusting. He had contempt for his own ability, he was mad, he was upset, he hated himself, and although he had hit the ball solidly—exactly 50 yards—he had missed six yards left.

I listened to the two players talking as they walked to the green. T.J., facing an 18-foot birdie putt, was happy because he had just made a good swing. His companion was ready to quit the game forever because he had pulled his wedge shot, made a terrible swing, and was facing an 18-foot birdie putt from a different direction.

As the physicist caddie, with equal PEIs running around in my head, I just chuckled. The balls didn't know the difference, the putters didn't know the difference, the golf course didn't know the difference, and, of course, both players scored the same—a par 5—both missing their 18-foot putts. Yet one player thought he hit a great wedge approach shot, whereas the other thought he hit a terrible shot. So go the perceptions of golfers.

2.15 The Scoring Game

In Chapter 1, I mentioned that the scoring game was made up of the short game and the putting game. Early in this chapter, I showed you how to evaluate the true performance of golf swings and how the game falls into different categories of skills and results. A few pages back, I tried to convince you that in the full-swing game, direction is what you should worry about since your choice of club is what primarily controls your distance. (Please be aware of your directional control. It is really important. Most sand traps sit left and right of target areas because course architects are no dummies.)

Then I showed you how just the opposite is true for the short game. Because the club is more lofted, the swing plane more vertical (causing less clubface rotation through impact), and the shots shorter, direction takes care of itself. When you're holding a wedge, it's distance that should concern you, because if you don't hit the ball the right distance, you can forget about having a high probability of holing those birdie putts.

Finally, let me repeat the main point of this chapter: If you want to score, the most important "game" to improve is your short game. Second most important is your putting game. And the least important game is your power-swing, ball-striking game, the game you've been practicing all these years.

CHAPTER 3

The Five Games of Golf

Something's Wrong Here

3.1 "The Golf Swing" Is a Myth

Do you believe golf's "Golden Rule," that "he who rules the short game collects the gold"? And do you believe me when I say golf is really five different games? And I mean *really* different, as distinct from each other as tennis is from bowling. If you don't believe me yet, you should by the end of this chapter.

The next few pages are vital to your long-term capability to become a better golfer. Why? Because most people have trouble learning something when they don't understand or believe the underlying foundations of those lessons. So read carefully until you truly understand and believe what the words are saying.

When I was learning the game, every lesson featured the professional explaining that there was really only one swing in golf. No matter who it was, the pro would say something like this: "The 5-iron swing is a miniature version of a drive swing, the chip shot is a miniature 5-iron swing, and the putt is a miniature chipping swing. Since there is only one move and one grip in golf," he would continue, "if you get your swing started properly and groove it, you can use that swing for almost every shot in golf." The pros referred to this as the "unified swing theory," which many professionals have been teaching for the last 50 years.

It sounds good, it certainly sounds reasonable, and it makes the game sound simple. But there's one problem: It's wrong.

Nobody ever measured or proved it. Like so many other accepted truths in golf, it has no basis in fact. A good player probably said it during a press conference, it was quoted in the newspapers, and it became a law of the game. Nobody said anything different.

But I will, because I don't believe it anymore. And if you want to learn to score better, start by not believing it either.

3.2 The Great Ones

To get this incorrect notion out of your head, let's look back at some of the great players the game has produced. There are many players who have been exceptional at one part of the game while being relatively ordinary at another part. Look first at the great power-swingers. My personal list of the best full-swingers to play the game includes Ben Hogan, Lee Trevino, Mac O'Grady, Tom Purtzer, Tom Weiskopf, and two Canadians, Moe Norman and the late George Knudson. They all struck the ball extremely well from tee to green, they all had consistent shot patterns and repeating results, and their shots consistently landed close to where they planned.

And they were all relatively poor putters. When I say "relatively poor" I realize that they were good enough to play on Tour, so they weren't what you could call "bad" putters. But compared with their full-swing ability, their putting was at best *unremarkable.*

At the other end of the talent spectrum are the world's great putters. That group includes George Archer, Bob Charles, Ben Crenshaw, Dave Stockton, Don Pooley, Loren Roberts, and Brad Faxon. All are terrifically talented at rolling the ball into the cup, but are relatively poor ball-strikers. This isn't to say they don't hit excellent golf shots; however, their tee-to-green shots often are poor, their ball-striking is inconsistent, and they don't make solid contact on a regular basis.

All of which proves my point that if golf were only one swing and you were really good at it, it would seem logical that you would (or at least could) be good at all aspects of the game. However, *this has never happened!* All the great ball-strikers and all the great putters—who have such obvious talent in one part of the game—have a just as obvious lack of superior performance in another part. They validate my belief that the different games are different fundamentally, and that there is no one swing for all of golf.

Three Physical Games

3.3 There Are Three Swings and Five Games

By studying the PEI data discussed in the previous chapter, you will see strong variations in performance among the power, short, and putting games of every player. I have yet to see a player who performed at the same accuracy level (same PEI value) in any two games, let alone all three. There is no question that something different is going on in the way golfers learn and play these games. These three swings even look different if you know what to look for, and by categorizing them individually they become easier to teach and learn.

If you accept the possibility that each game is unique—and, therefore, that different swings must be learned—I can detail those differences. But this is what I meant at the beginning of this chapter when I said you have to understand before you can learn. Think about this again: There isn't one swing, there are three. And there isn't one "game," there are five. That's a big leap, I know. It might be easier if I wait to explain the unique features of the short game relative to power and putting, and I first touch on the two "mind" games.

The fourth and fifth games—the mental and management games—are as different from each other as they are from the power game. I won't go into great detail here, but you will understand what they involve when I mention what they relate to:

- Mental game: fear, confidence, anxiety, aggression, determination, focus, concentration, emotional control, etc.
- Management game: shot selection, skill evaluation, strategy, statistical analysis, risk-vs.-reward balance, competitive situation, etc.

Very different, yet very similar. Both games involve what goes on inside your brain while it controls your body. Both are related to your physical motions by your mind's control over them. And like those muscle-controlled actions, both games can be learned, taught, practiced, and improved or degraded.

Okay, back to the three physical games. If golf derived from a single swing and you were a coordinated, gifted athlete who was good at that swing, then it would seem that you would be good at all parts of the game. But I challenge you to name one golfer who has been great at all three.

Certain players are better in one game than another because, while the fundamentals of the three physical games are different, the teaching of all three (and more important, the learning) has been the same. For way too long, the same principles have been used in the instruction of all three games. But I'm contending—and proving—that what's good for the full-swing ball-striker is bad for his putting, if he learns and uses the same theories. The principles of the three games are so different that even the words and concepts used to describe them are dissimilar. Let me show you.

Jack Nicklaus

Even the greatest player in history, Jack Nicklaus, had relative weaknesses in his game. Where Nicklaus was truly remarkable was not in his full swing, although it wasn't bad (I measured his power PEI at 42nd, which means 41 players who played at the same time hit shots more accurately from point A to point B). Jack was in the top 25 PEIs in putting, and his short game was mid-30s—except for his sand play, the only true weakness in his game (128th by my data). His excellent lag putting covered for his poor sand play ability, because it allowed him to play away from bunkers, which he "managed" to do. So he wasn't the greatest in any of the three physical games, but he was very good in them all. Without question, his greatest strength was a mastery of the mental and management games. There has never been anyone to compare with his course management, composure, and use of strategy to make the most of his physical attributes. In perhaps the greatest use anyone has ever made of the management game, Jack "managed" to let more players lose to him than anyone I ever studied.

3.4 The Power Swing

I am not too interested in, nor do I ever teach, the full swing. But I'll mention some of its mechanics here so you can notice and feel the differences between it and the other two swings.

The modern power swing starts with a one-piece takeaway: The clubhead, shaft, hands, arms, elbows, shoulders, chest, and hips all start turning (rotating) away from the ball together. They move at the same angular rate, and continue to move until the lower body and hips become restricted and can no longer turn. When the hips stop moving, the upper body—the arms, shoulders, and chest, plus the shaft and clubhead—continue to move, coiling against the lower body. This coil creates tension and stores energy to be released later, on the down-and-through swing.

During most of the backswing, the hands and arms remain in front of the chest, and another event occurs: the cocking of the wrists. As the backswing continues, the upper body meets so much resistance from the lower body that it can coil no further. In the final backswing motion, the arms, elbows, and hands then actually stretch or turn against the chest as the clubhead reaches the absolute top.

The swing down and through should be initiated by the re-turning of the lower body. This lower-body turn leads everything else toward and through the impact zone: The lower body pulls the upper, the upper body pulls the arms, the arms pull the hands, the hands pull the shaft, and the shaft pulls the clubhead. This chain of events means you create centrifugal force and maximum energy for release, as each component of the swing adds its own energy through impact.

In Figure 3.4.1 you see vocabulary I use to describe some concepts and fundamentals of the power-game swing. These fundamentals are so different from those of the scoring game that I won't coach any of my players on their full swings. I recommend that they find a good full-swing teacher, and also important, change their mind-set when switching from one game to the other.

POWER GAME
Athletic Ability - Talent - Full - Strength
Connection - RHYTHM - Quickness
Coordination - Speed
Release - Coil

HIT

Figure 3.4.1: Power-game vocabulary

3.5 The Putting Game

The fundamental mechanics of the putting stroke are the opposite of those of the power swing. The putting stroke has no lower-body turn, no coil of the upper body against the lower, and no cocking of the wrists. The head and trunk remain still while the arms swing with a slight rotation of the shoulders. There should be no forearm rotation, a key element of every other swing: Forearm rotation is a killer of good putting, making it difficult to achieve consistent directional results. But because the forearms rotate in every other swing, most golfers let them rotate through their putting strokes without realizing it, to their great detriment. Figure 3.5.1 shows some typical putting-game vocabulary, which, as you can see, differs drastically from that of the power game.

PUTTING GAME
Solid - RHYTHM - Feel
Pure - Acceleration
Smooth - Simple
STROKE

Figure 3.5.1: Putting-game vocabulary

The great ball-strikers tend to be poor putters, because their power-swing funda-mentals sneak into their putting-stroke motions. If Moe Norman or Mac O'Grady had been anywhere among the top half of putters and short-game players, they might have dominated the game for years. The same is true for George Knudson, even Ben Hogan. (Some will argue that Hogan did dominate, in the late 1940s and early 1950s, but he probably could have done better, and was well known for putting problems. I never took data on Knudson and Hogan, but I have observed their putting strokes in person and on video, and both contained seriously flawed fundamentals.)

What about Lee Trevino? Like Hogan, Lee has a wonderful record filled with major championships and many other victories. And as mentioned earlier, his full-swing PEI was the best I ever measured, consistently around 5% all the years I watched him. But despite holing some important putts in his career, Trevino was not a good putter: His putting PEI is only average, and I classify his putting as merely adequate. He won as much as he did despite his putting, not because of it. If you get a chance, ask him; I'm sure he knows this about himself. By my book, if Lee had putted like Ben Crenshaw, you might never have heard of the man named Nicklaus.

3.6 The Short Game

Now to the swing of the short game, the finesse swing, which is neither fish nor fowl. It differs from the full swing, because the upper body should not be "con-nected" to the lower (though they should be turning at the same rate and through the same angles, so they look as if they could be connected). The takeaway of the finesse swing looks identical to the takeaway in the power swing, but when the hips stop turning, the upper body—shoulders, arms, hands, and club—stop turning, too (no coil), so there is no energy stored between the upper and lower body as there is in the power swing. On the downswing, then, everything comes through impact together: The lower body doesn't drive or lead, so it produces very little power. Everything goes back together, then comes down and through together, producing what I call a "synchronized" turn. As a result, every finesse swing, regardless of length, appears to have the same effort and rhythm.

The finesse swing differs from the putting stroke because the forearms rotate, the weight transfers, the knees move, and the hips rotate both back and through the shot. You see none of this when putting (that is, you *should* see none of this when putting). Figure 3.6.1 lists some descriptive words we use on the finesse swing, a list almost completely different from the power- and putting-games' vocabularies.

SHORT GAME
Effortless - Positive - Beautiful
Crisp - RHYTHM - Touch
Soft - Music
SWING

Figure 3.6.1: Short-game vocabulary

3.7 The Differences

Analysis of PEI data was the first thing that ever suggested to me the idea that there might be different games and different swings in golf. Then, when I examined the swings of the three games, I found measurable differences and knew I was onto something. After making a comparison of the games' swing fundamentals, and the vocabularies of the games, I was sure it was an absolute lock that the games were independent of one another. I finally figured out that even the basic intents, purposes, and goals of the three games are different, too. But it took me time to understand all that, just as it may be taking you some time right now.

Look again at the three "vocabularies" shown in the last few pages, the lists of words we commonly use to describe each of the three games. Notice that the only true similarity is in the area of rhythm: All three games need to be played with good rhythm to be accomplished successfully.

Can you imagine a great putter making a big coil in his backstroke? Or releasing his forearms through impact? Or staying connected and turning his body through his putting stroke? There is no way! The three games are, by their very natures, different. Which means that if you want to be good in them all, you must learn the different fundamentals that allow you to be good in each of them. For more proof of these differences, look at the last word of each list: The great ball-strikers "hit" their drives; the great finesse players "swing" through their pitches and chips; and the world's best putters "stroke" their putts.

It also helps to realize that the goal of each game is different. Think about your intent when you play shots in each of the games:

1. The goal of your *power swing* is to hit the ball as far as you can, within the constraints of reasonable accuracy. From 9-irons to drives, which you want to hit as far as you can, you allow yourself to be somewhat inaccurate in direction so you can get the distance you need. You want maximum power with reasonable accuracy.

2. The goal of your *putting stroke* is to give up all sources of power, achieve the simplest motion you can master, and provide maximum precision to strike the ball down a given line at an appropriate speed. This is almost the complete opposite of your full-swing intent. Accuracy is at a premium; maximum power is useless.

3. The goal of your finesse swing in the *short game* is a compromise between the above two. You want to hit the ball as accurately as possible, but you still need adequate power in your swing. You want the accuracy of the shot's trajectory, behavior, and landing zone to be maximized. You must give up some accuracy control because you need some power, but you try to do so with a rhythmic swing, not a hit, for the best compromise.

Three games, with three swings and three sets of fundamentals to learn. Each is simple, easy, and learnable. But nobody has conquered all three yet, because they have not realized that they should be separated to be learned best.

The Short Game Dominates

3.8 The Golden Rule

In Chapter 2, I explained how I compared ball-striking ability with money earnings and learned that how well a Tour pro strikes the ball with a full swing does not correlate in any statistically significant way with how much money he earns. When I first saw this result, I was quite surprised.

Why? Because for many years I planned and tried to play the game professionally. I figured to do that I would have to hit the ball better, which would lead to better scoring, which would lead to my being able to play for a living. By the time I was conducting my correlation studies, I'd given up any dreams of a pro career. But I was still amazed that my data contradicted my long-held assumptions about ball-striking. I didn't understand how hitting the ball better could do anything except win more money. After examining this data in detail, I realized that what it showed wasn't that ball-striking is unimportant, but rather that if your full-swing PEI is between 5% and 9% (the extremes of all players on the PGA Tour), then how well you strike the ball within that range doesn't affect how much money you will make.

The reason for this is the "conversion curve." The conversion curve, shown on page 29, is the most important illustration in this book, and may be one of the most important concepts in the game of golf. Very simply, it tells you the chances of converting a putt, on average, from any given distance.

Needless to say, from all the rounds I've charted and all the data I've obtained, I have recorded thousands upon thousands of putts. I know exactly how well PGA Tour pros putt from every distance. If you examine this curve carefully, you'll find that no one makes a high percentage of putts from outside of 10 feet, and almost everyone playing at the professional level makes most of their putts inside two feet (if not, they won't be playing on the Tour for long). So the most drastic differences in putting conversion rates occur between two and 10 feet—as mentioned earlier, the "Golden Eight" feet.

Let's bring this back to the real world. When Lee Trevino (a 5% ball-striker) hits a 5-iron from 180 yards to 5% accuracy, he still faces a 27-foot (nine-yard) putt. That's a fine 5-iron, better than the average Tour player by several feet. But most Tour players will two-putt from 40 feet, 30 feet, 20 feet, even 10 feet; so the fact that Trevino generally hits it closer to the pin doesn't give him a very meaningful advantage for one-putting more often. It does give him this small advantage every time he hits a power-swing shot onto a green in regulation, which occurs around 10 times a round. So statistically, on average, for being the best ball-striker Lee receives a small advantage in putting conversion probability over the entire rest of the field about 10 times a round, if his putting skill is equal to theirs.

On the other hand, when Tom Kite (who improved from a 13% to a 5% short-game PEI) hits a wedge from 40 yards to six feet, and Trevino, who is a 15% wedge player from 40 yards, puts the ball three times as far from the hole, 18 feet, then Kite statistically gains almost half a shot (again assuming equal putting skills). It is an absolute cinch that Kite will hole more putts from six feet than Trevino will hole from 18 feet.

The advantages gained from hitting good short-game shots occur seven to 10 times a round (Tour players miss, on average, about five greens in regulation, and hit short-game shots to a high percentage of the four par-5 holes each round); that can add up to a difference of several shots. You can see why the short-game performance of all Tour players has a strong correlation with their money earnings. It is entirely reasonable—and proper—that the people who execute the finesse game the best tend to win the most money, have the lowest scoring averages, and are the most consistent winners on the Tour.

I also have taken data on the LPGA Tour, and the results are identical for the ladies.

So now you understand my "Golden Rule" of golf. Because of the conversion curve, and the fact that 60% to 65% of all shots in golf occur within 100 yards of the green, it is clear that "he who rules the short game collects the gold."

3.9 Pros I've Worked With

Over the years, I've been fortunate to work with many pros, both men and women, from the U.S., European, Canadian, and Asian tours, as well as amateurs from around the world. I've instructed the national teams from Germany and Italy, and made presentations for the PGA of America to club pros throughout the United States. Thirteen years ago, I began opening my Scoring Game School facilities, where I've taught Tour pros—from the PGA and LPGA Tours (Fig. 3.9.1 lists them)—plus some 15,000 amateurs, all of whom have paid to attend. Most of these amateurs are not low-handicappers, but they are serious golfers, and all of them, including the professionals, want to score better.

Every one of these golfers has the same problem. While some are poor chippers, others can't get out of the sand, and many can't pitch accurately in the 15- to 30-yard range, they *all* have the problem of the conversion curve. No one has ever complained to me about getting the ball consistently too close to the pin with

PGA/Senior Tours

Michael Allen
Billy Andrade
Paul Azinger
Hugh Baiocchi
Chip Beck
Bill Britton
John Brodie
Mark Brooks
Olin Browne
Jim Carter
Brandel Chamblee
Michael Christie
Keith Clearwater
Lennie Clements
Jay Delsing
Bob Dickson
Bob Duval
Danny Edwards
Steve Elkington
Robin Freeman
Lan Gooch
Gary Hallberg
Mark Hayes
Ryan Howison
Joe Inman
Peter Jacobsen
Lee Janzen
Tom Jenkins
Steve Jurgensen
Tom Kite
Steve Lowery
David Lundstrom
Rocco Mediate
Allen Miller
Walter Morgan
Bob Murphy
Andy North
David Ogrin

Joe Ozaki
Tom Pernice
Mark Pfeil
Dan Pohl
Don Reese
Tom Sieckmann
Jim Simons
Tim Simpson
Vijay Singh
Mike Standly
Payne Stewart
Mike Sullivan
Peter Townsend
Howard Twitty
Grant Waite
Dewitt Weaver
D. A. Weibring
Bob Wolcott

International Tours

Ralph Berhorst
T. C. Chen
Scott Dunlap
Peter Fowler
Torsten Giedeon
Thomas Gogele
Paul Hoad
Robert Karlsson
Colin Montgomerie
Bryan Norton
Jesper Parnevik
Cliff Potts
Terry Price
Costantino Rocca
Luigi Scarfiotti
Peter Smith
Heinz-Peter Thul
Ian Woosnam

LPGA Tour

Kristy Albers
Missie Bertiotti
Jill Briles-Hinton
Kim Catherein
Noelle Daghe
Beth Daniel
Heather Drew
Michelle Estill
Allison Finney
Marlene Floyd
Jane Geddes
Suzy Greene
Caroline Hill
Becky Iverson
Cathy Johnston-Forbes
Caroline Keggi
Emilee Klein
Hiromi Kobayashi
DeeDee Lasker
Sally Little
Melissa McNamara
Barbra Mizrahi
Liselotte Neumann
Sandra Palmer
Cindy Rarick
Susie Redman
Patti Rizzo
Annika Sorenstam
Muffin Spencer-Devlin
Sherri Steinhauer
Jan Stephenson
Kris Tschetter
Deborah Vidal
Colleen Walker
Karen Weiss
Maggie Will

Figure 3.9.1: Professionals who have worked with Dave Pelz/Dave Pelz Scoring Game Schools

their short-game shots, and most golfers are certainly two-putting, or worse, most of the time. And their scores aren't as low as they want them to be.

Every one of my schools starts with testing to identify players' weaknesses so we can maximize their improvement. Through my research, I've learned that 80% of a player's handicap is determined by his play within 100 yards of the green. But when I ask students how they spend their practice time, almost all say they spend 80% of their time practicing the full swing. Most students report spending less than 10% to 15% of their time on their putting, and almost no time practicing their short game.

In this light, it's interesting to note that the students with the greatest improvement are the ones who come back to work with us the most often over a long time period—like Tom Kite, who, after 18 years, still occasionally comes back to school. The returning alumni also are the ones who practice the most and improve the most. Please take this as proof of the importance of the short game to lowering scores, because you just can't get too good at the short game.

The better you play it, the lower you will score.

CHAPTER 4

Mechanics of the Short Game

Before Your Swing

Before I begin teaching you how to make the best possible short-game swing, I must explain a number of concepts. It's likely that some of these will be totally new to you, at least in relation to your golf game—things like the effects of adrenaline, the need for stability, and the importance of feedback. But just to be sure you know you're still reading a golf book, I'll also deal with a number of "golf-friendly" concepts such as grip, ball position, alignment, and swing plane. As you read this chapter, remember what I said earlier: You can't learn to play golf optimally without first understanding what it is you are trying to learn. All of these notions must be understood if you are going to learn to make a consistently reliable finesse swing. They are vital to its execution and success, and once you internalize their meaning and importance, you can begin to improve with dramatic efficiency.

4.1 Muscles and Adrenaline

I wish I had a nickel for every time I heard a golfer, pro or amateur, say, "I'm hitting it great on the practice tee, but I can't take it to the course." He blames himself for not being a good pressure player, or thinks he hasn't practiced enough, or simply feels incompetent. The irony is that a player who can do it all on the range probably is practicing a swing that cannot possibly be taken to the course by *anyone* with *any kind* of talent. He is grooving a move that wouldn't stand up for the greatest Tour professional with the greatest nerves in the world. But he doesn't realize that, so he keeps practicing, hoping a little more sweat will make the difference.

It won't, owing to the way adrenaline affects his body and his muscles. Adrenaline is released into the body when a person gets excited or scared; there's nothing we can do about it. Adrenaline makes our muscles get stronger, sometimes very much so. This extra power can be helpful if we need to escape from heavy rough or bad lies. It can be managed in the power swing if you know it's coming: Simply change your club selection. However, if you rely on muscle control for your short game, adrenaline effects can be deadly.

Adrenaline will flow whenever the golfer feels pressure. If you face a hard or important shot and you rely on muscle control to "hit" your short-game shots, chances are good that any "touch" you may have had—even just a few minutes before on the practice range—will be gone. There's no flow of adrenaline when you're practicing, so any touch learned on the range vanishes when pressure appears, even when you make what feels like a really good swing.

4.2 Dead Hands

The way to tame adrenaline, then, is obvious: Don't use your muscles to power your short game. Instead, let the power come from the energy provided by your finesse-swing motion.

The muscles that kill touch in your short game are the incredibly strong yet small muscles of your fingers, hands, wrists, and forearms. You must make a conscious decision to keep those muscles out of your short shots and use what we call in our schools "dead hands." If you're swinging with dead hands, those small muscles have only two jobs: (1) to cock the wrists during the backswing; and (2) to hold on to the club so it doesn't fly out of your hands during the rest of the swing. If you can do that, you can beat the adrenaline effect.

If you want to produce the same shots on the course that you practiced on the range, especially under pressure, you must stop using your muscles during practice and begin using the length and rhythm of the finesse swing to power those shots. Through practice, you learn how long your swings have to be to produce the shots you want. (In later chapters you'll learn about different swing lengths and how to create them.) You feel the centrifugal force and natural motion of the swing powering the shots, rather than "hitting" shots with your hand and arm muscles. And you hold your finish, retaining the feel of your swing until each shot lands and you can see how far it flew.

While practice swinging, you should focus on finding a smooth, repeatable rhythm that you can imagine producing the results you want. Once you can see, feel, and judge the proper motion with a practice swing, you'll be able to repeat it in a real swing; from there it's a small step to doing the same thing during a match when your heart is pounding and your muscles are pumped full of adrenaline. Take several practice swings until you make one that looks and feels really good, that will produce the shot you want, the way it did on the practice tee earlier that day, last week, and last month. This is called "making a preview swing." Once you see and feel that rhythm and make a perfect dead-hands preview swing, it's easy to step up to the ball, repeat it, and produce the result you expect on the course.

4.3 Alignment Is Critical

In my golf vocabulary, the terms setup, alignment, aim, body alignment, and address position are all related to the same thing. They relate to the target direction of your upcoming golf swing and how your body is postured and oriented to that straight line from ball to target (because of ground slope or wind, your swing-line target may not always be the same as the pin direction). And one more thing: No matter what you call it, the setup and alignment of your body is one of the most important fundamentals of your short game.

In every game of golf, if you align your body improperly your instincts will subconsciously make swing compensations intended to hit the shot in the desired direction. Because your instincts are to control and execute these compensations with your hands, and are totally target-oriented, correct alignment is critical if your body is going to learn to make fundamentally correct swings with dead hands. Aim correctly and it's easier to make good swings, because from a good position, good swings cause good results; aim poorly and a good swing will hit a bad shot, so you'll have to make compensations to produce the desired results. And in the short game, a compensating swing is a bad swing.

4.4 Parallel Left

For most short-game shots, I recommend you use what is called "parallel-left" alignment. (You won't use parallel left for the cut-lob and uneven lies, but that leaves more than 95% of the shots inside 100 yards.) Here's how you get your body in the proper parallel-left setup.

Every time you practice, take the club you are going to hit and carefully lay it down in line with your intended target (Fig. 4.4.1). Squat down behind your ball to see this line precisely. Next lay your 2-iron parallel to and one foot inside your hitting club, leaving room to hit many shots between them. Your 2-iron is now your "aim club," as shown in Figure 4.4.2.

Walk behind both clubs and look down the aim-club line. Your aim club should be aimed slightly left (maybe a foot) of your exact target. This is true "parallel-left" alignment, the perfect alignment for your body and swing to swing along.

Pick up your hitting club and address your ball with your feet, knees, hips, and shoulders parallel to your aim club (Fig. 4.4.3). The toes of both shoes should be the same distance from the aim club, when your feet are perpendicular to the shaft. If you are aimed properly parallel left and use a dead-hands motion, your club will naturally swing parallel to your shoulders, traveling down your target line through impact.

Without moving your body, and keeping your left heel in place, lift and swing your left toe 30 to 45 degrees toward the target (Fig. 4.4.4). This creates a slightly

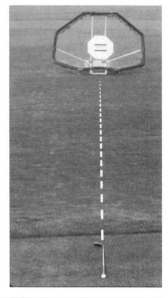

Figure 4.4.1:
Hitting club aimed directly at your target

Figure 4.4.2:
Aim club parallel-left of perfectly aligned hitting club

Figure 4.4.3:
Feet, knees, hips and shoulders setup square to parallel-left aim club

Figure 4.4.4:
Perfect parallel-left alignment: lead toe flared 45 degrees toward target

open stance, which will encourage your hips to turn through impact without resistance from your lower body.

Using an aim club on the course is a violation of the rules (the USGA thinks it makes the game too easy, which should prove to you it's a good idea). However, practicing this way will help you groove better short-game swings and teach you to recognize and feel when your setup is correct on the course.

Major Concepts for the Short Game

4.5 Every Swing Has a Bottom

Picture a 30-yard wedge shot that you hit fat. Got it? Now stick that sick, fat feeling in the back of your mind. I'll come back to it later.

Near the bottom of every swing, at the point where centrifugal force extends the hands, wrists, and clubhead away from the shoulders, the clubhead travels on an almost perfectly circular path. And because the swing is inclined to the ground, it has a low point. Every golfer has a unique, precise bottom to every swing.

Theoretically, if the club consistently swings with a rhythmic, coordinated turn of the golfer's body, then the low point will consistently occur at the same point in the swing, and therefore the same point in the stance, every time.

You don't have to be a genius to find the low point: Take a swing and see where the divot begins and ends. Between those two points, at the bottom of the divot, is the low point. If you make consistently good swings, like those of PGA or LPGA Tour players, with no body slide and no significant collapsing of your hands and wrists, the bottom of your swing will occur in the same place every time, at a spot about two inches forward of the center of your stance (Fig. 4.5.1).

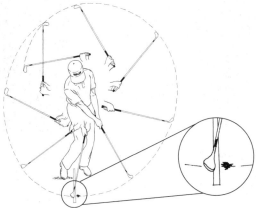

Figure 4.5.1: Low point (bottom) of swing is where divot occurs

The fact that the perfect swing does not bottom out at the center of the stance surprises many golfers. But if you think about it, the low point is forward of center because the body transfers weight forward during the downswing, moving your center of mass slightly forward through impact. So your divots should *not* be dead center in your stance, but two to three inches ahead.

Why do I think the positions of your divots are important? Because I see so many of my Scoring Game School students hit fat wedge shots. They position the ball forward of where their natural swing divots start, and they hit that dreaded fat shot I mentioned earlier.

While you may think you can control your divot location, you really shouldn't alter the physics of the rotation, centrifugal force, and weight transfer in your swing. These are the forces that determine where the bottom of your swing occurs, and they will—unless you use the small muscles in your hands and wrists to alter their natural occurrence.

Of course, you *can* change the physics of your swing. Swing with only your right arm and your divot will move back in your stance, almost back to your right shoulder (Fig. 4.5.2). Swing with your left arm only, as shown in Figure 4.5.3, and your divot will move forward in your stance. But use a conventional two-hand, two-armed swing and normal body rotation back and through, and your divots will be two to three inches forward of your stance center (Fig. 4.5.4). Your divots

RIGHT ARM ONLY

LEFT ARM ONLY

NORMAL SWING—2 HANDS

Figure 4.5.2: Right-arm-only swing creates divot inside back foot, behind stance center

Figure 4.5.3: Left-arm-only swing creates divot inside front foot, well forward of stance center

Figure 4.5.4: Perfect swing creates divot two to three inches forward of stance center

Finding the Center of Your Stance

It's important to understand where the center of your stance really is. It's not halfway between your toes, because your feet are almost always angled in or out to some extent, and golfers tend to balance their weight on the ground through their ankles. I define the midpoint of your stance as the centerline between your ankles. You can see and measure that spot, which is important when you're trying to place the ball correctly, as explained below. Here's how to find your stance center.

Stand as shown on the left in Figure 4.5.5, with both feet pointing exactly perpendicular to your target line and your aim club, and your pants raised to reveal your ankles. (Wearing shorts makes this easy.) Imagine two lines extended out from the middle of your ankles, perpendicular to the target line. Position your wedge shaft exactly between these lines, where the ball is in the photo. That's the middle of your stance. Now turn your left toe toward your target by 30–45 degrees without moving your left heel (on the right in Figure 4.5.5). The ball is still in the center of your stance.

Why is this important? Look at the left sequence of Figure 4.5.6, which shows a typical golf stance. My left foot is turned out about 40 degrees toward the target, which is good, while my right foot is essentially square to the target line. Judging by my toes, the ball looks centered in my stance. However, when accurate ankle lines are added in the right sequence, you can see that the ball actually is well forward of my stance center.

If you establish a procedure of first placing your ball at your stance center when both feet are square to the line, *then* rotating your lead-foot toe toward the target, you can attain a perfectly centered ball position every time.

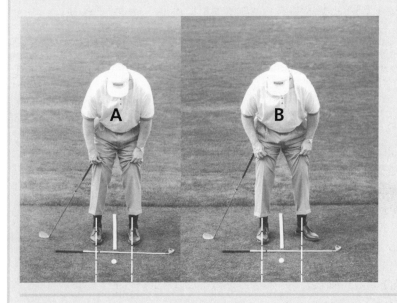

Figure 4.5.5:
Ball positioned
at stance center
(between ankles)
in both photos

Figure 4.5.6: Golfer attempts to place ball at stance center (left), leaves ball forward of center (right)

will occur there every swing, more consistently and more accurately than ever, as long as you don't move them with your hand and arm muscles (in which case you won't play well under pressure).

Once you learn the dead-hands swing and where your divots occur relative to the center of your stance, you can learn the exact ball position that will let you swing your wedges without fear of hitting behind the ball, even on tight or hard-pan lies. This will allow the complete elimination of the fat shot from your short-game repertoire.

4.6 Ball Position Is Fundamental

How important is ball position? Try this experiment in your backyard or at the practice range. Address a ball as you normally would for a 20-yard pitch shot, in the middle of your stance. Without moving, have a friend pick up the ball and move it 12 inches toward your target so it's out in front of you. Still without moving your feet, try to hit the ball to your target. Now set up normally again (ball centered in the stance) and have your friend move the ball a foot back in your stance. Again, try to hit it to your target. Can you make contact with both balls? Can you feel how you have to use your hands and wrists? Can you feel how different this is compared to your normal, dead-hands swing?

Of course, 12 inches is an exaggeration. But golfers often move the ball forward and back a few inches in their stance, up and down along the target line, without thinking. Nothing much looks different (Fig. 4.6.1) and they assume they can hit the ball solidly and cleanly—controlling the bottom of the swing arc—no matter where the ball is in their stance. In fact, this is virtually impossible to do without using the muscles of the hands and wrists. My point is that if the ball is anywhere in your stance except in the exact position to be hit with your dead-hands swing, you'll have to use your hand muscles, exposing yourself to the effects of adrenaline.

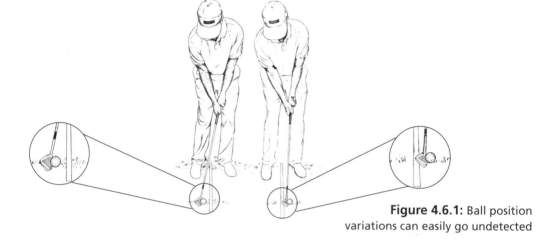

Figure 4.6.1: Ball position variations can easily go undetected

Yet many golfers have been taught to hit higher, softer shots by moving the ball forward in their stance. For lower shots, they're taught to move it back. You can get away with moving it back a bit, because by making a good dead-hands swing, you still hit the shot solidly—just a little lower than normal. But I can't tell you how wrong it is to move a ball forward in your stance for short shots. You're asking for fat shots. If you want to hit the ball higher, use a more lofted wedge and make solid contact from the center of your stance.

In my schools, I've measured thousands of mishits. I've learned that most fat shots—when the club hits the ground behind the ball before hitting the ball itself—are caused not by swing problems but by ball-position problems, often as little as an eighth of an inch too far forward. Yes, ball position is that important. And there is no margin for error in the forward direction.

Although I know you know that the little (golf) ball should be hit before the big (earth) ball, I want you to look at Payne Stewart making perfect contact on a wedge shot. Figure 4.6.2 shows this sequence, courtesy of a high-speed camera.

Figure 4.6.2: Perfect swings produce perfect shots when club-ball contact is perfect

4.7 Don't Go to Fat City

After hitting a fat shot, most golfers say they got too anxious and "looked up" to see where the ball was going. Not only do they say that, they believe it. But when I measure their swings and ball positions, I usually find that the ball is too far forward and that they are making swing compensations with their hands in an attempt to hit the ball cleanly from that incorrect spot.

Quite honestly, these same golfers perform okay after a few shots on the practice tee, after they have a chance to get their compensations and timing correct and produce good shots. However, look at the post-impact positions of a few of these bad-ball-position swings (Fig. 4.7.1). Can you see the knee dips and wrist flips required to hit the ball before hitting the ground? Can you see the bad swing habits developing in the subconscious? Every one of these golfers placed the ball two to three inches forward of where it should have been; they also all had the same problem—poor wedge-shot results under pressure.

Be sure you understand the physics of ball position:

1. A good finesse swing will produce good shots only if the ball is positioned correctly in your stance.
2. Play the ball too far forward and you'll either hit it fat or be forced to learn "hand-powered" swing compensations that will make you generally less consistent and specifically worse under pressure.

Figure 4.7.1: Bad ball position forces golfers to make compensating swings

3. Play the ball too far back and you have about a two-inch margin of error, from which you can still hit playable shots with dead-hands swings, although they will fly a little lower than you desire.

You can never learn a dead-hands finesse swing without first learning the proper ball position, because only the correct position allows a dead-hands swing to produce solid contact and good shots.

I'll come back to ball position in later chapters when discussing specific shots. Until then, these are my rules for where the ball should be (Fig. 4.7.2):

1. For *chip shots,* position the ball back in your stance, off the back ankle. You want to hit the ball with a descending blow, trapping a minimal amount of grass between the clubhead and the ball, and creating a low, running trajectory.

2. For all *distance wedge and pitch shot* swings from normal lies, when you expect a normal trajectory, position the ball in the exact center of your stance (between your ankles, not your toes). Your front foot should be turned toward the target by about 30 to 45 degrees.

3. In a *bunker,* you want to contact the sand behind the ball, scoot the club under and past the ball, and use the sand to blow the ball out. To hit behind a ball from a good bunker lie, first aim to the left, then position the ball inside the heel line of your left foot (details in Chapter 9). Placing the ball in the center or behind the center of your stance forces you to move your natural swing bottom (divot) backward, which can be accomplished only by collapsing your wrists or leaning backward and creating a reverse weight shift (neither of which will work consistently).

Figure 4.7.2: Perfect ball position moves from back ankle (chip), to stance center (pitch), to inside left heel (sand)

Most golfers start with the ball too far forward on their finesse shots, particularly chips and pitches, and too far back in the sand. Nearly 80% of our students, even some Tour pros, begin our schools with the ball ahead of the swing's natural low point on 30-yard pitches and chip shots. That's why so many of these shots are hit fat. The results worsen when the shot is important: Under pressure, hand and wrist muscles get stronger and tighter, inhibiting the player's ability to control where his divot occurs.

Remember, ball position is crucial. Physics proves it.

How to "See" Ball Position Accurately

When ball position is incorrect, the body subconsciously tries to make compensating corrections to achieve solid contact with the little ball (the golf ball) before contacting the big ball (the earth). This leads to a variety of inconsistencies and mistakes in the short game.

When the ball is *too far forward* in the stance (Fig. 4.7.3), the golfer will slide his hips forward, toward the target, at the start of the downswing, in an effort to reach the ball and not hit behind it. The more the hips slide, the harder it is for them to rotate. This can be especially problematic for tall golfers, who tend to bend their knees and then find it virtually impossible to make a proper hip turn through the shot.

Balls positioned *too far back* create a different problem (Fig. 4.7.4). The golfer instinctively feels the need to reverse weight shift to get the ball higher into the air, because

Figure 4.7.3: Only a forward slide (note golfer's left knee line) can prevent this shot from being hit fat

Figure 4.7.4: For ball too far back in stance, golfer moves weight back on through swing to compensate

"good-contact" shots come out too low. This type of swing leans back, frequently producing sculled low-liners.

The best way to get your ball positioned correctly, centered between your ankles, is to address the ball with your feet together and perpendicular to the target line as shown in Figure 4.7.5, then carefully spread them an equal distance from your stance center (Fig. 4.7.6). Then, without moving your heel, turn your lead toe out to achieve the perfect stance with perfect ball position (Fig. 4.7.7).

Figures 4.7.5–7: Perfect ball position step #1: feet together, ball in exact center of stance. Perfect ball position step #2: spread feet equally on both sides of ball, keep feet square to swing-line. Perfect ball position step #3: turn left toe 45 degrees toward target

4.8 A Concept of Stability

Why is stability being discussed in a book on how to score in golf? Three reasons: Because good short-game players swing their short-game clubs in a stable motion; most golfers don't understand what that means or why it's good to do it; and it's a key reason most golfers don't get away with mistakes while good players do.

You *need* to understand stability, so read on.

Look at a swing sequence of a new student in one of my Scoring Game Schools hitting a 30-yard wedge shot (Fig. 4.8.1); we videotape all our students making this swing so we can learn about them and learn from them. Look at this phenomenon, which we call "long-to-short" swinging (long backswing, short follow-through); it is very common in the short game and very wrong. Use this image only to learn what *not* to do. Unfortunately, not everything bad about long-to-short swinging can be seen in still photographs, so I'll explain how it causes deceleration and unstable club positions through the impact zone. Even if you couldn't keep awake during your high-school physics class, I'm sure you can follow this.

When many golfers start their swings for a 30-yard shot, they take the club back the same way they do on full-swing shots. But as they swing down from the top of the backswing, the clubhead (because the backswing was too long) begins moving too quickly for the required length of shot. About two feet before impact, each golfer subconsciously senses he is generating too much speed, so his brain fires the message "Ohmygod" to slow the hands, slow the clubhead, and keep his 30-yard shot from traveling 50, 60, or even more yards.

Figure 4.8.1: Long backswings and short follow-throughs create unstable wedges through impact

Once the Ohmygod has struck, the hands stop pulling the club and, instead, the club begins pushing the hands and shaft. What was once an accelerating swing becomes an unstable, decelerating motion.

The Ohmygod itself isn't so bad, for without it the ball would sail past the target. The problem is the physical reaction of the club to the slowing of the hands and shaft. Once the clubhead begins pushing, the motion becomes unstable, and unstable clubheads produce bad shots.

We see Ohmygods in many of our students' wedge shots. So we remove the clubs from their hands, take them inside, and give them a little lesson in physics.

4.9 Pull Carts and Clubs Are Stable

I have a simple example to demonstrate stability. Think about the pull cart (called a "trolley" in Britain), which used to be very popular on public courses but has lost favor to the electric cart. Figure 4.9.1 shows a pull cart loaded with clubs, ready to be pulled around a course. Figure 4.9.2 illustrates an overhead view of the same pull cart, but it's being pushed. The direction that the golfer is pushing is shown by the arrow; the cart's anticipated reaction to that push is indicated by the dashed arrow.

If the pushing force were directed exactly through the cart's center of mass (where the weight of the clubs is centered), the cart would roll exactly in the direction of the force. However, when the pushing force is directed to one side of the center of mass, the cart will rotate around its center of mass, as shown.

The explanation is physics: If a force pushes from behind a mass and is not directed exactly through the center of mass, then the mass must rotate. Figure 4.9.3 illustrates this at an extreme, with the force trying to push the cart straight down

Figure 4.9.1: The pull cart (trolley) can be stable if pulled, unstable if pushed

Top View

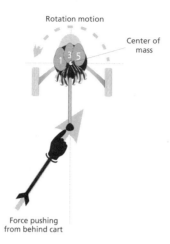

Rotation motion

Center of mass

Force pushing from behind cart

Figure 4.9.2: Pushing from behind usually causes a "pull cart" to rotate

the fairway, making one pushing correction after another, first left, back to the right, to the left, and so on.

Now look at Figure 4.9.4, which shows the same cart and same force but different physics. Now the force is pulling the cart: The force is being applied from in front of the mass, pulling it, and the laws of physics are simple but completely opposite. When a mass is pulled from in front, the mass must align with and follow

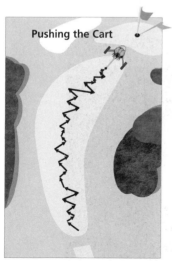

Pushing the Cart

Figure 4.9.3: Pushing the cart causes unstable motion down the fairway

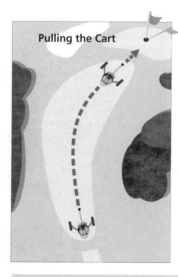

Pulling the Cart

Figure 4.9.4: Pulling the cart creates a stable motion

the force. The mass cannot rotate, but must follow the direction of the force. When pulled, the cart is stable, will follow you wherever you go, and needs no directional guidance.

How is a pull cart like a wedge swing? The mass of the clubhead is very heavy like the mass of a pull cart, the shaft is like the cart's handle, and a force can be applied from either ahead or behind (pulling or pushing).

From the top of the backswing, the golfer pulls the mass down toward the ball, creating an initially stable swing. The heavy clubhead follows the lightweight shaft in the direction of the golfer's hands, as the laws of physics dictate. If the golfer continues to accelerate and consistently pulls the clubhead through impact, the club will continue to travel on a stable, repeatable path. Of course, at some point every clubhead and every swing must slow to a stop, so at some point every swing becomes unstable. But you must not let your clubhead become unstable until *after* it has hit the ball. An Ohmygod will immediately make your motion unstable by slowing your hands and changing the physics so the clubhead begins to push the shaft.

A very important part of your job in the short game is to swing your wedges with motions that are stable through impact. A stable swing provides better, more consistent results than an unstable one.

Let's talk about results. If the ball is hit squarely on the sweet spot, both stable and unstable clubheads traveling at the same speed react essentially the same way: the clubhead slows down, the ball speeds up, and the clubhead does not twist at impact. However, golfers don't always make perfect contact on the sweet spot of a wedge, as shown by our sweet-spot detector tape (Fig. 4.9.5). Most short-game

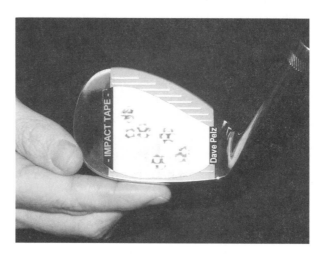

Figure 4.9.5: Sweet-spot tape measures impact location on wedge face

shots (like most drives, 5-irons, even putts) are mishit to some degree, missing the sweet spot sometimes by as much as a half or three-fourths of an inch. Even on the new oversized clubs, that's a significant miss.

The swing's stability through impact has a dramatic effect on the result of a mishit. If it's unstable, the clubhead is free to rotate as the force dictates, turning with a severity directly related to contact distance from the sweet spot. For example, say contact is toward the toe: The heel will kick forward—more the farther contact is from the sweet spot—robbing energy that should be transferred to impact.

But with a stable swing, when the clubhead is being pulled through impact, its motion will be better. The accelerating clubhead won't rotate as much from a mishit, because it's trying to follow the pulling shaft, and less energy is lost. The resulting shot will be better, sometimes dramatically so.

I have measured mishits off both stable and unstable swings and found significant differences. For example, on two 30-yard wedge swings, when both clubheads missed the sweet spot by three-fourths of an inch, the unstable swing flew the ball 22 yards while the stable swing shot carried 28 yards. Even though it was mechanically the same mistake—missing the sweet spot by the same amount—the shot hit with a stable swing would leave a reasonable putt to save par, while the unstable swing would drop the ball into a bunker, water, or other trouble well short of the desired landing spot.

Finesse Swing Strategy

4.10 "Short-to-Long" Has It

By now I hope you understand why it's better to make a stable (pulling) wedge swing than an unstable (pushing) swing through impact. In short, you want the clubhead to be accelerating when it meets the ball. But even with physics squarely on my side, I don't teach acceleration through impact. I've tried that and it doesn't work. Rather than making a good pulling swing, men equate acceleration with hand and muscle power, so when consciously trying to accelerate, they use their hand muscles, which puts us back where this chapter began, suffering from the effects of adrenaline and likely to fail under pressure.

There's a better way to be sure to make an accelerating swing: Make a short backswing and a longer follow-through. This assures acceleration without muscles, and stability in the dead-hands finesse swing.

Look carefully at the two swing sequences (Figs. 4.10.1 and 4.10.2) and try to imagine them in action. Imagine them smooth, rhythmic, and effortless, because

Figure 4.10.1: Payne Stewart demonstrates a stable 15-yard wedge shot

that is the way both Payne Stewart and Lee Janzen swing. With absolutely no effort from their hand and wrist muscles, they make stable wedge swings every time. Their hands don't begin to slow (causing instability) until their shots are in the air. Their swings minimize whatever impact errors they make, so they rarely hit bad finesse shots.

Figure 4.10.2: Lee Janzen makes a 30-yard swing (looking downline)

4.11 Intellectualizing Comes Up Short

Every golfer understands that if you make a long backswing, you cannot accelerate the club faster and faster as you approach impact and still hit a short shot. Rapidly moving clubheads tend to hit long shots, not short ones. It is also easy to grasp that if you take a short backswing and accelerate to a point approximately two to three feet past impact (as shown in Fig. 4.11.1), you will be rewarded with minimal adverse effects from swing errors and mishits because the swing is stable when it meets the ball. But golf balls don't care how smart you are or how much you understand. My research has shown that golfers get the idea of "short backswing, long follow-through," yet they still find it incredibly difficult to do on the course.

There is something about most golfers' mental outlooks that causes them to be insecure at the top of a short backswing. My experience leads me to think that the golfer gets to the end of a short backswing and thinks, "I can't get it there from this position; I'm going to leave it short." This thought pattern occurs even when I have measured and pointed out to this golfer that he has hit his last 20 shots too far past the target. He still wants to hit those shots with his muscles; it's instinct, and it is very difficult to overcome.

Don't be discouraged if you don't attain stability right away. It's perfectly normal to have an insecurity about the short backswing. It takes time to convince yourself that short backswings and long follow-throughs are the components of a superior wedge swing. (We teach this concept at my Scoring Game Schools, and it often takes many swings to create this new habit.)

But if you learn nothing else, learn this: A sure killer of a good finesse game is the overlong backswing. The moment you take the club back too far, your chances of making contact with an accelerating, stable motion are ruined.

Figure 4.11.1: Maximum velocity two feet past impact assures a stable clubhead through impact

Finesse-Swing Mechanics

4.12 The Synchronized Turn

As I mentioned in Chapter 2, the short game has its own swing, which is distinctly different from the power game's hit (in which the hand muscles are active) and the putting game's stroke (where there is no body rotation and no wrist cock). I call it the finesse swing.

But I don't want you to begin learning the swing until you are comfortable with everything I've said up to this point. Do you understand how dead hands eliminate adrenaline problems? How setting up parallel left prevents hand-compensation? Where ball position should be relative to the bottom of your swing arc and divot? And how to make a short-to-long stable swing? If so, you are ready to learn the synchronized turn and true finesse swing.

Simply turn your upper body at the same speed that you turn your lower body from start to finish. Synchronize your upper and lower bodies to turn and rotate together on the swing back and forward. This doesn't mean they are connected. Rather, they are turning together in a synchronized motion.

The easiest way to feel this synchronization is to assume your address position for a 30-yard wedge shot, drop your club, and put both hands on your hips, thumbs toward the front. Squeeze your elbows together behind your back. This will lock your upper and lower body together. Now turn back, as in your backswing, and through to a full finish, as if you were hitting that 30-yard shot (Fig. 4.12.1). Do this as many times as it takes you to "feel" the synchronized motion.

Figure 4.12.1: Perfectly synchronized, the upper body (shoulders and chest) and lower body (hips) turn together in the finesse swing

Do not allow one part of your body to coil against another part, as you do in a power swing. Your shoulders never coil against your hips (Fig. 4.12.2), your arms don't coil against your chest. By eliminating all coiling, you stop power from being produced by your lower body. You don't want the legs driving, leading, or accelerating the rest of your body into impact.

If there's no coil, no lower-body drive, and you don't add any hand, wrist, or arm muscles (keep dead hands), you should be able to produce a low-power swing. And low power is what the finesse swing and the short game are all about.

Figure 4.12.2: To avoid a coil, the shoulders and hips must turn together (never separately)

4.13 Rhythm and Timing: The Power Source

I worked for NASA for 15 years before I turned my mind totally to golf. While there, I learned something that has helped many Tour professionals improve their short games. The lesson I learned and passed on is: "Big Muscles for Power, Small Muscles for Touch and Refinement."

At NASA, when we were beginning to launch payloads to the moon, we found we couldn't simply aim, fire the main rocket engines, and expect a bull's-eye. We learned we could never harness or control the incredible power of those monstrous rockets accurately enough to be successful. What we did find those big engines could do, however, was lift the spacecraft up from earth and throw it into some reasonable earth orbit. Then, after we measured what orbit it was in, with very small engines controlled and timed very precisely, we could kick the capsule out of earth orbit toward the moon. After it left earth orbit, we'd determine exactly how long and in what direction we would have to fire the even smaller "fine-tune" thrusters to adjust the final trajectory into a perfect lunar orbit to allow the lunar lander to descend to the surface.

The thrusters that refined the motion to perfection were approximately the size of a human hand. They were small and had very little power, but they were sufficient to finesse the final orbit so the astronauts could set up a perfect landing.

This space-age example translates directly to your short game. Imagine your synchronized body turn as the main rocket engines, supplying the main power to get the ball in the general vicinity of your target, while your dead hands are the small thrusters that fine-tune your shots to the hole.

But haven't I been saying don't use your hands? Yes, and I meant it. You cannot consciously use your hands to add power to finesse shots and have them supply fine-tuning as well. If the muscles of your hands and wrists kick in to help power a shot, they are no longer available for subconscious fine-tuning. To get power from a muscle it has to be firm and strong, contracting and tight. Muscles in that condition can't supply small increments of touch refinement at the same time.

For the power to hit 10-, 30-, and 50-yard finesse shots, use the rhythm of a synchronized body turn. Let your subconscious deal with your dead hands, using them to fine-tune and *feel* your touch.

One way to make all this work is to keep the hands relaxed, the arms relaxed and extended. This way they can move naturally as a result of the forces generated by the swing. Don't make them work, but let the momentum of your finesse swing get them moving.

Here's the recipe: Combine a dead-hands swing with the synchronized turn. You'll cook up a minimum-power finesse swing that provides the opportunity to develop maximum touch.

4.14 The World-Class Finish

I divide all finesse swings into two types, those for shots that carry over 30 yards and those for shots that carry less than 30 yards. The distinction is based on how each swing should finish.

For the longer finesse shots—those between 30 yards and just short of your power-swing distance with the same club—make a full, complete finish, transferring all your weight onto your forward foot (Fig. 4.14.1). Having kept your hands

Figure 4.14.1: A world-class finish for shots longer than 30 yards: weight on left foot, right toe touching for balance only

from supplying power to the swing, there is no reason to bring them back to stop the finish short. Stability demands that the clubhead is accelerating at impact; by continuing to a full finish, you increase the likelihood that you'll be accelerating when club meets ball.

I've also found that asking a student to concentrate on making a full finish removes his instinct to "hit" shots. I always show each student a video of what he looks like making a perfect finesse swing, finishing in a perfectly balanced position. We call this position the world-class finish, because it looks as good as the best players in the world.

One final note about the world-class finish. Do not allow your body to slide forward or your left knee to flex laterally toward the target during the down- and through-swing (Fig. 4.14.2). As you make a synchronized turn through impact your left knee should be almost straight—but not rigid. This encourages turning completely onto your left foot in the follow-through and finishing with most of your weight there. A straight left knee also allows your back foot to be pulled around and forward so only the toe is touching the ground (someone standing behind you should see every cleat on the bottom of your right shoe).

For shots under 30 yards, you can't use a full finish because you'll carry the shot too far. So between 10 and 30 yards, shorten both your back- and through-swing lengths, using shorter swings for shorter shots. For stability's sake, make

Figure 4.14.2: Allowing the left knee to slide forward prevents a good turn (or full weight transfer onto the left foot)

sure your follow-through is always at least 50% longer than your backswing.

A good reference is the 15-yard pitch swing, which usually requires a back-swing length that takes the shaft to horizontal and a follow-through finish with the shaft about vertical, as shown in Figure 4.14.3.

On these shorter swings, make sure you keep your hands out of the action of the shot. I see too many students whipping their hands and club behind them in what I call a "styler finish" (Fig. 4.14.4). I'll tell you again: If you use your hands to

Figure 4.14.3: A smooth swing from shaft horizontal to vertical produces a 15-yard carry

Figure 4.14.4: The "styler" finish (hands low and behind body at finish) demands hand and arm muscle control

"style," or supply power, or determine where your divot occurs, or for *anything,* you won't be very good under pressure.

4.15 Cocking the Wrists

Probably the most misunderstood element of the golf swing is the wrist cock. Hold your right hand straight out in front of you, your thumb pointing toward the sky. In this position, the hand can move two ways: side to side (left to right), and up and down. Many golfers think wrist cock is the side-to-side motion— absolutely not. That is wrist hinge or collapse, a motion usually unwanted in a golf swing and used only rarely in the short game, when extraordinary circumstances demand it (more on this later).

To get a feel for the proper wrist cock, set up in your wedge address position with a club gripped properly in your hands. Without moving anything other than your wrists, lift the club straight up as if you want to hit yourself in the nose with the clubhead (don't cheat and lift your forearms). This up movement is the cocking of the wrists; they are fully cocked when you can't move them any farther (Fig. 4.15.1).

The cocking of the wrists should occur gradually throughout the backswing, starting just after the initiation of the one-piece takeaway (again, exceptions later). It should be completed just before reaching the top of the backswing, no matter how short or long the backswing is for the shot.

Figure 4.15.1: Wrists should cock up, not hinge back or through

Many golfers ask: Doesn't cocking my wrists make my swing wristy? My pro told me to simplify my swing by keeping my wrists stiff. Do you agree?

An absolute no to both questions.

Wristy swings are the result of hinging, or collapsing, wrists (no difference; golfers use both these terms for the same thing), bad moves if you do them in either direction. A proper wrist cock aids the finesse swing by providing a reliable source of consistent power that doesn't involve the muscles. The centrifugal force generated by the body's rotation will always uncock the wrists for you through impact. And nothing could be more repeatable than that.

Although there are a few instances in the short game when you don't want a wrist cock, the "no wrist cock" swing is a special condition used in chipping and to produce the ultimate soft shot with the slowest possible head speed. I'll cover these in Chapter 7.

4.16 The Finesse Grip

Most teaching professionals feel the grip is the most important fundamental in golf. I disagree, at least in regard to the short game. There the grip falls somewhere down the line behind alignment, ball position, and stability. My evidence for this priority ranking includes a number of good short-game players with strange grips

(Paul Azinger comes to mind). Having said that, I think there is a preferred short-game grip, and using it will make this game easier.

One way to take the hands and arms out of a power-producing mode is with a new grip, different from what you use to swing your woods and irons, the full-swing clubs. Setting up for a full swing, most golfers take a strong grip—the hands turned slightly away from the target, and the Vs formed by each thumb and fore-finger pointing between the chin and right shoulder for right-handers (Fig. 4.16.1). From this starting position, the hands and forearms should release through impact, returning to the square position (defined as the back of the left hand perpendicular to the target line) through the impact zone and turning the clubface over to produce a draw, a little extra power, and extra yardage.

But that is exactly what we don't want in a good finesse game. We don't want the power, we don't want the draw spin, and we don't want the small muscles of the hands and forearms providing power. We want them just for touch and accuracy.

The grip I recommend for all finesse shots—chips, pitches, distance wedges, and sand—starts with the hands in the square position (Fig. 4.16.2) and keeps them there through impact. The quieter they are, the better, so the clubface reaches impact in the same position every time. Most people call this a fairly weak grip: The Vs formed by thumbs and forefingers should point to the center or left (nearer the target) side of your chin (Fig. 4.16.3), with the palms parallel to each other and perpendicular to the target line.

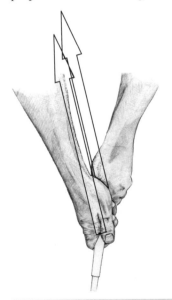

Figure 4.16.1: The power-swing grip

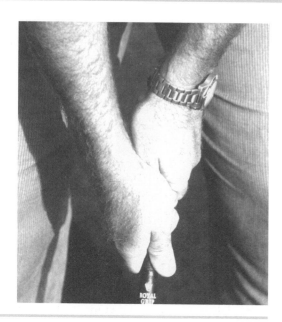

Figure 4.16.2: The finesse-swing grip

(A technical note: Many golfers and golf professionals talk about the Vs formed between the thumb and forefinger. What they really are referring to is the position of the hand, indicated by the forefinger line as shown in Figure 4.16.3. Don't be fooled by a player who has the same hand position as that shown in this photo but places his thumb alongside the shaft rather than on top of the shaft, producing what looks like a V point to his right shoulder [Fig. 4.16.4]. Remember, you care about the hand position in the grip and where the forefinger line points, not where the thumb or V points.)

To optimize your performance, I believe you actually could use three grips—one each for the power game, finesse game, and putting game. As explained in Chapter 2, each game is unique and could use its own grip. If you've been playing for a long time, you might have trouble getting comfortable with three distinct grips; if you don't have a lot of time to practice and get comfortable with a new finesse grip, don't change. But if you do decide to make a change, be prepared to put in many long hours of practice and play many shots under pressure before you feel confident with it.

Strong Is Wrong
I think the too-strong grip is a major reason many great full-swing ball-strikers have trouble with the finesse game. They tend to have strong full-swing grips that provide extra power in the long game but unwanted power in the short game.

Figure 4.16.3: Finesse grip,
thumb on top of shaft

Figure 4.16.4: Finesse grip,
thumb on side of shaft

4.17 The Finesse Swing Plane

Another fundamental of the finesse swing is posture, the position of your body before and during your swing motion. If you don't think posture is important, lie flat on your back and try to hit a golf ball. The angle between your upper body and lower body has a strong influence on your body's ability to rotate and swing a club. The angle between your spine and the ground determines what level, or swing-plane angle, you must swing on. Thus, your swing plane and body angles can change with the length of each club and with the slope of the ground beneath your feet on each successive shot.

But this is golf, and we love the challenge. The question is how can you determine how much you should angle your spine (bend over at the waist) for your best finesse-swing posture? Before you try to work out the answer, you must understand the conflicting influences that make every golfer's posture a compromise. The conflicting factors are:

1. Standing more vertical makes it easier to turn your body around your spine. Try it. Stand tall and you'll have no problem turning everything together, back and through (Fig. 4.17.1), perfectly synchronized. But you can't hit a golf ball from that position.

Figure 4.17.1: Standing vertically, baseball swings keep shoulders and hips synchronized together instinctively

2. The more you bend over, increasing the angle between your spine and hips, the more difficult it is to rotate your hips. Try this: Bend completely over, as in Figure 4.17.2, and try to rotate your hips. It's almost impossible to make a full lower-body turn in synchronization with your shoulders from this position.

3. The closer you get your spine angle to perpendicular to the line from shoulders to ball, the easier it is to use centrifugal force to make a swing repeatable.

Figure 4.17.2: Bending over too far prevents hips from rotating, makes synchronization almost impossible

So we compromise, trying to find the "just right" bent-over position that also allows for a smooth, synchronized turn back and through your finesse shots. Bend over too much (creating too flat a spine angle) and you can feel your body rotation being inhibited. Stand too tall (making the spine angle too vertical) and you'll have trouble hitting solid shots, because your natural swing plane won't pass through the ball.

If you've never heard the term "finesse-swing plane," it's the imaginary surface—often represented by a thick pane of glass—that passes through your shoulders and the ball when you are at address (Fig. 4.17.3). The clubhead should stay in that plane throughout the swing (Fig. 4.17.4). While the concept of swing plane

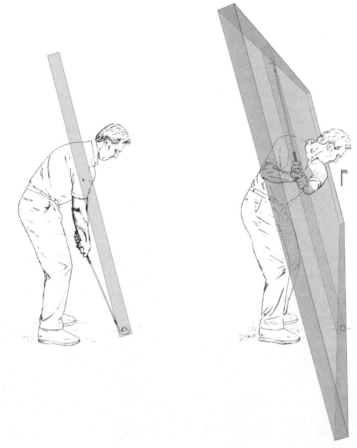

Figure 4.17.3: The finesse-swing plane as it appears if your eyes (camera lens) are "in" the plane

Figure 4.17.4: The finesse-swing plane as it appears when you stand on (with your eyes above) the "ball-target" line

is complex in the power game, in the short game it is very simple. After you have determined your posture and committed to a dead-hands, synchronized finesse swing, the finesse-swing plane is the very steep angle that includes the ball and both of your shoulders. And you definitely want to keep your clubhead in the plane throughout your finesse swing.

Only Certain Camera Positions Can Measure Swing Plane

If you're thinking of using video or photographs to check your clubhead and swing plane, be sure the video camcorder or still camera lens is placed precisely somewhere *in* the plane. A camera cannot "see" if a clubhead is in, or just above or below, the plane unless its lens is itself in the plane. This means the camera cannot be along the ball-target line unless its lens is on the ground at ball level.

Viewed from an off-axis position behind (Fig. 4.17.5), the swing plane passes from the ball through the center of the player's shoulder sockets.

My favorite camera position is about 24 inches inside the target-ball line and about 36 inches above the ground. From this position you can see the target and the ball flight on camera most of the time, while still measuring the swing plane. The drawback is having to bend over or squat down to see through the camera during setup and action viewing.

Figure 4.17.5: To record with camcorder lens in swing plane (to see if club is in-plane), tripod must be positioned inside ball-target line

A good finesse swing is similar to swinging a rock on the end of a string. As you rotate your shoulders around your spine, the rock (clubhead) swings out and straightens the string through impact. If you use a dead-hands swing, get your clubhead in the correct position at the top of your backswing (no matter how short the backswing may be), and begin with perfect posture, a synchronized turn through impact will make perfect contact every time. Nothing, and certainly no human muscles, will ever be more repeatable than centrifugal force through impact.

Good alignment and posture, an in-plane swing, and a good turn through impact are all you need.

Fundamentals of Learning

4.18 Hold, Watch, and Feel: Learning from Feedback

Another benefit of a full finish to your finesse swings (when the shot is long enough to allow it), is ending the swing with your head up, following the shot in the air to its completion. It's very important to hold your body finish position until the ball lands and you can see the results. The correlation between how you swung and how the ball flew will never be fresher in your mind. That is just the feedback you need to prepare your subconscious to play your best in the future.

As you hold your finish, feel the swing you just made and watch how the ball flies and where it stops. To become a great player, you've got to notice flight trajectories, carry distances, and how your shots react on the greens, and file those impressions away with your kinesthetic sensations of the swing—length, rhythm, and so on—so your brain can correlate the information for future benefit. You don't have to think about all of this, but you do have to see these results: Feel your swings, watch your shots, and let your subconscious do the rest.

That is what learning is all about: assembling and assimilating information in your brain so it learns what your swing needs to look and feel like and how the ball will react when you do it that way. And the best part is that you don't have to think about it: It happens automatically if you pay attention. As you see more and more shots and store them with your kinesthetic awareness, your brain refines and builds better memories to draw on in the future.

However, none of this happens if you don't watch and receive the required information in your brain. You must do it in real time, as it happens. Biofeedback studies have shown that a human's short-term-feel memory is very short: Every eight seconds, you lose about 30% of the sensations or feelings you have generated—if no new ones have come along. If you do add new sensations, they immediately cover up the old.

If you can make a habit of holding your finish and retaining the feelings of each shot while watching its flight, then what you see and feel within that first eight seconds will be correlated in your mind and you will have optimized your process of learning touch for distance.

Golfers who hit shots and turn away in disgust, or drop their shoulders, hunch over, or move in any way, lose the feelings of their swings. Then they can't correlate what they did with the results. You can practice that way forever and never improve. But if you get to the end of your follow-through, hold it, and watch your shot land (usually four to six seconds after you strike it), you'll probably hold on to 80% of the feeling generated during the swing. It's still in your mind and body, and your brain will deal with it.

You can't remember the feeling of a swing made a few minutes ago if you've made several new ones since. But if within eight seconds you see the ball land five yards past your target, which was at 43 yards, your mind will file away an input of that vision correlated with a strong set of feelings and sensations in a memory of what produced that 48-yard shot.

Watch the great players. Both when they practice and when they play they hold their finish on shots until they see the results of their swing motion. In putting you should hold and feel your arm swing at the finish. In the short game it's your finesse turn, your body's motion, that determines where your shot is going, and therefore that is what you must hold in your finish position. You can lower your arms after wedge shots, because they didn't control the shot, but you must hold and feel your final body position, letting your brain correlate the sensations with the result.

4.19 Good and Bad Finesse Swings

Before going on to Chapter 5 and the details of controlling distance, let's review the finesse swing as you should now perceive it.

Your perfect finesse swing begins from a perfectly postured setup, aligned parallel left of your target, the ball centered between your ankles. Your weak finesse grip has the back of your left hand facing the target, the forefinger lines pointing at your nose. Beginning with a one-piece takeaway, everything moves away together and stops together at a short backswing position. There is no upper-body coil, no excess storing of energy, and your fully cocked wrists have the clubhead in the perfect swing plane, which extends high above and slightly behind your shoulders.

On the downswing, everything moves together, perfectly "synchronized" and accelerating with dead hands through and past impact. The clubhead is stable, achieving its maximum velocity two to three feet after contact with the ball. The through-swing continues to a full, high finish, your right hand almost touching your left ear. At the finish, nearly all your weight is on your left (front) foot, with the right toe touching the ground for balance. You made a smooth body turn, with no hint of a forward slide and no lateral motion of your left knee toward the target. Your left leg was almost straight as you held your finish, standing on your left side, feeling the swing and watching the shot's result.

You became an *ever-so-slightly-better* player as a result of that swing. You are ready to move on—slowly, incrementally, inexorably continuing to improve your short game.

CHAPTER 5

How to Score

Distance Control Is the Problem

5.1 Research on What Works

One of the things I am most proud of is that since the beginning, I have kept all of my teaching techniques, my Scoring Game School programs, and the training of my staff based in fact, research, and experimental data, all of which relate to the realities of the game. We don't teach old wives' tales, or pass along good-sounding homilies expressed by great players. We teach what our research shows us works for real golfers who practice and improve. The same is true for my *Short Game Bible*.

I mention this so you know how my "3 x 4 System" for controlling wedge distances was discovered, and how it will help you learn to score better. I also want you to realize that this is not something I created by myself, sitting in a darkened room theorizing how golf might be played better. I discovered this system while working with PGA and LPGA Tour players who helped me to see as much as I helped them improve. I didn't create it, I just recognized it and named it, and have been teaching it to golfers ever since, helping them learn to score better. When you understand how 3 x 4 works, you will have more fun mastering the system—and watching your scores start to fall. You don't have to worry "Will it work?" or "Should I try another system?" This system works, every time, for those who learn it. But first you need to understand it.

5.2 Do You Think Distance?

At the end of the last chapter, where I listed the ingredients of the perfect finesse swing, I gave an example that included wanting to hit a wedge shot 43 yards. Have you ever thought that precisely, or, rather than think yardage at all, do you simply say to yourself, "It's a sand wedge," and fire away? It makes a big difference. The ability to hit your short-game shots specific distances—say, 21 yards when the pin is 24 yards away, or 12 yards when you need to land the ball at that spot so it can roll to the pin—is what my scoring-game system is all about. Scoring is not about hitting every shot perfectly. Scoring is about getting away with your misses, avoiding penalties, taking advantage (by saving a stroke) of the good shots you hit, and getting up and down when you miss the green. Scoring is about optimizing your talents by playing to your strengths and away from your weaknesses, and lowering the numbers you write on the scorecard.

Once you begin mastering the finesse grip, perfect ball position, clubhead stability through impact, short-to-long swings, and the synchronization of your finesse swings, this development and honing of your skills allows you to bring more precision into your short-game shot distances. How exact do you need to be? You need to stick the ball in the "Golden Eight" range, consistently leaving yourself putts inside 10 feet. As the putt conversion curve shows, once outside of 10 feet, it doesn't much matter where you are: The odds of making putts decrease so rapidly, your score doesn't change much whether you're putting from 20, 30, or 40 feet. You'll probably two-putt all of them.

I find it ironic that many modern courses indicate yardages to the center of greens from about 300 to 100 yards. But they don't mark any sprinklers inside 100 yards, where knowing yardage is most important. I don't mind knowing that the yardage is 165 yards, but whether it's accurate to a yard or two one way or the other doesn't matter. None of us can hit the ball straight enough from that far away to make the next putt anyway. It's from 30 yards—or 60, or 47—where we can control the shot's accuracy to within one or two yards, that we need to know the exact distance, because we can almost always leave our shots in the "Golden Eight" from there.

5.3 In the Early Years

My method of learning the feel for hitting short-game shots definitive distances began to evolve from my work with the Tour pros, whose shots I had measured and charted. After several years of racing around to record their shots, I was able to call back Jim Simons, Tom Kite, Tom Jenkins, Jan Stephenson, and several other interested players, and tell them what I'd learned about where their games were strong and where they were weak. I sat down with them and my mountain of data, and talked about the thousands of their shots I'd recorded, and how I had assigned each of their clubs a Performance Error Index. I also explained how the strongest correlation to scoring averages and money winning was found with the short-game PEI, and how I thought they could score better and win more by improving in this area. So that was where we concentrated our efforts.

About the same time, as I was trying to convince some of the world's best golfers that they should listen to me, I read a book on learning theory. It said that the secret of efficient learning is feedback—immediate, accurate, reliable feedback that correlates the feelings of actions with the subsequent results: accurate and reliable to provide consistent learning patterns without confusion; immediate to allow the actions to be associated with feelings, which fade from memory by 30% every eight seconds.

Humans can't learn much about their actions without receiving feedback on the results of those actions. For example, it takes only one experience to learn not to place your hand on a hot stove: We feel the heat, the burn, the pain. The pain is feedback, immediate, reliable, and very accurate. We know that if we put our hand on a hot burner again, we will get burned again.

That's not what happens at the driving range. If we go to a range and hit wedges, often we're hitting at a distant target or the nearest flag, usually 100 or 150 yards away. Hit the wedge straight and we assume it's a good shot, but we've learned nothing about how far it flew or how quickly it would have stopped on a green. That is what most golfers think of as practicing their wedges.

I told these pros that we had to improve their short games, but not simply by spending more time on the range. The PEI data had proven how important it was for players to improve the precision of their wedge play if they wanted to win more money; more specifically, my plotting of their shots proved that they had to work on distance, not direction. I explained that they had to learn to feel the swings for exact distances, so they would be able to produce these distances when needed. They had to practice their wedge games by receiving feedback on how far they hit every practice shot. So when they had time off the Tour, they came to work with me and we would practice their pitching- and sand-wedge games for distance control inside 100 yards.

Learning from Feedback

5.4 Fast Eddie

The only way I could think to teach Tour pros precision distance control was to take them out to a practice area, give them visible targets at known distances, and reward them with immediate, accurate, reliable feedback on each swing until they learned to do it right.

In those days we alternated among three ranges: Columbia Country Club in Chevy Chase, Maryland; the Naval Academy in Annapolis, Maryland; and the Old Gunpowder Golf Club in Laurel, Maryland. We would place eight plastic laundry baskets 10 yards apart from 20 to 90 yards; between every pair of baskets we placed nine golf balls, one at every yard. I drafted my son Eddie, at the time an avid 10-year-old baseball player, and had him be the precise target, standing at the desired target distance somewhere along the line of baskets.

During each practice session, the Tour pros would hit their shots from a designated starting line so measurements were accurate to within one yard. I would sit close to them, face on, holding a walkie-talkie so they could hear distance results coming back from Eddie, who would be standing downrange at a specified distance, with his baseball glove on one hand and the other walkie-talkie in the other. I had trained Eddie to catch each shot not straight overhead, but by turning sideways and grabbing it close to the ground, so that if he didn't move, the glove would point almost to the exact spot that the ball would have landed. Eddie became extremely proficient at catching the ball, pointing to the spot where it would have landed, looking to determine the exact yardage of that spot, then calling it in on the walkie-talkie. A crude but immediate, accurate, and reliable feedback system.

Using this system, the player could hit a shot, watch it fly, and almost immediately upon its landing hear Eddie call in the yardage. This is how we began. This is how they learned, standing with bodies motionless to retain maximum feel until the yardage feedback for each swing was received.

5.5 Learning Through Repetition

Aiming at the 50-yard basket, Jim Simons would swing his wedge; a few seconds later, he would hear the yardage—"58." He'd hit another one—"57." And another —"60." Another—"59." After a few of these, Jim would get disgusted, give himself a pep talk on doing better, make an adjustment in his swing, and hit again. The yardages would then come back—"42," "41," "56," "44," "55," "45," "53," "48." After a while, usually 10 to 20 balls later, we'd hear the magic number—"50."

After staying at that yardage for a few shots—giving Simons a chance to become accustomed to carrying it exactly 50 yards (which he would do surprisingly well once he had the feel for the proper swing)—I'd ask Eddie to go to a new yardage—say, 70—and we'd repeat the process. After another 20 to 30 shots, we'd move Eddie again—say, to 30 yards, then 90, then 60, 25, 40, and all around. Simons, Kite, Stephenson, and Jenkins each hit thousands of wedge shots and received immediate, accurate feedback at the conclusion of each shot and, very important, while still holding their follow-throughs.

We believed at the time that if the player did this long enough, sooner or later he or she would learn how to produce a shot of approximately the right yardage on the first try. It worked, although not immediately. We found that no matter how good a player became during a practice session, he (or she) would have regressed by the time we started a new session the next day. However, with almost every session, he would get better more quickly than in previous sessions. So we kept on practicing with feedback, and the improvement began to be measurable on the course and in tournament play. More finesse shots began to finish close to the holes, more up-and-downs were being converted, and their bank-account balances began to grow.

5.6 Here Comes Rhythm

The players and I continued these distance-wedge practice sessions whenever they could take a few days off from the Tour. As time passed, I noticed that several characteristics of their wedge swings were changing.

The first thing I noticed was that after a few wedge sessions, the swings of the players began to look different: They had become more rhythmic. Each player seemed to be swinging with less effort, and somehow the wedge swings were smoother than they had been in the beginning. What I later realized was happening was that their subconscious minds were learning to correlate the "feel" of their swings with the distance their shots would fly. The smoother the swing, the easier it can be felt, recognized, and repeated. Herky-jerky swings are hard to "feel" and remember; smooth swings are easy. They were subconsciously developing synchronized finesse swings long before I knew what a synchronized finesse swing was.

As I studied these swing changes, I realized (1) they were no longer coiling in their backswings, and (2) the rhythm of their moves was becoming consistent with their personalities. Tom Jenkins was swinging with a consistently faster rhythm than was Kite, and Kite was swinging faster than Simons. I realized that the sequence of speed was similar to the way they walked and their personalities. Jenkins is a quick-moving, fast-talking, fast-walking person; Kite is more average speed in every way; and Simons is slower than both in all the above ways. Their wedge rhythms were becoming reflections of their beings. It sounded reasonable, so I didn't think much more about those observations until I saw the next change.

After watching thousands of shots, I saw that the "hit" was being removed from their swings. As I watched their upper and lower bodies moving together back and through, creating a smooth, rhythmic, effortless motion, I could see they were removing their hand and forearm muscles from supplying the power for the shots. After grinding, sweating, concentrating, and competing against one another, always with almost instantaneous feedback, the players stopped hitting shots with their muscles and converted to using purely rhythmic swings. I should point out that this happened instinctively, through their subconscious control systems, not as a result of following my theories. They found that their shots were more accurate, more reliable, and more easily reproduced when they took their hands and the "hit" out of their swings.

5.7 The Players Knew at Impact

Then something else happened. About six months after starting these distance-wedge feedback sessions, I got a late-night phone call from Simons, who was out on Tour. He said, "Pelzy, guess what I did today? I had my caddie on the range, I was hitting shots to him, he was calling back my distances, and I found that I knew what my shot distance was going to be before he called it back. I could make my swing, hold my finish, say the yardage, and it would be within one yard of being right. Every time.

"I've learned the right and wrong feels of the distances I want to hit," Jim said. "Even if I'm trying to hit it 60 yards and I hit it 64, I know as soon as I've done it."

I was tremendously excited. So I called Jenkins and told him what Simons had done.

T.J. said, "Big deal. I've been doing that for weeks. Whenever I make my swing, as soon as I've reached my finish I know exactly how far it's going to go."

Time passed, our distance-wedge sessions continued, the players were feeling good about our work, and their scores were continuing to improve. Then another phenomenon. One day I was sitting in my chair, watching Jenkins swing, listening to Eddie call in the yardages. By this time, T.J. seemed to enjoy quietly calling out his estimate of the distance numbers before Eddie could radio them in. Suddenly I realized that I knew the yardages even before Tom verbalized them. Simply by watching T.J. swing, from a position facing him, I could tell how far he was going to hit the ball almost before he hit it. I didn't understand how this was possible—I wasn't even sure I believed what had happened. I didn't say anything, but just continued to watch, look, and listen, thinking the precise distances to myself.

5.8 I Knew at Impact

Finally, I could no longer resist, and as Jenkins was hitting balls, I called out a number just after impact. Lo and behold, it was right on the money, which amazed him as much as it did me. He stopped and asked how I did that. I said I didn't know for sure, but that I was convinced I could tell how far he was going to hit the ball before he made contact.

I told him I didn't have to see the follow-through because it was always the same, extending to a full finish whether he was hitting the ball 40 yards or 80. I simply needed to see his backswing and know what club he was swinging. I would bet him that by watching his swing, without ever looking at the ball flight, I could tell him how far he had hit it.

I remember we stopped and discussed this for quite a while, because neither of us understood how I could know how far he was hitting his shots, especially since I never looked away from him, never watched the trajectory of the ball. I was doing it simply by watching his swing.

It's important to remember that by this time his swings had become very rhythmic and very repeatable, and I had seen thousands of them. But we still didn't know how I was judging his distance so accurately.

Over time, the same thing happened with the other players, and before long I figured it out. I was subconsciously watching and gauging the length of their backswings. Something very positive had happened to all these players: First, they removed muscle control and the "hit" from their wedge swings, then each fell into the rhythm of his own swing. Then, after they'd made that rhythm a constant from day to day, week to week, even month to month, they found they could control the distance of their finesse shots by varying the length of their backswings.

It's vital for you to realize that this system of controlling the length of your shots with the length of your backswing works only if you always swing at the same rhythm (*your* rhythm) and always follow through to a full, complete finish. If you do, the velocity of the clubhead at impact is simply a function of the length of the backswing: The farther back you take it, the faster the clubhead is traveling when it reaches the ball. And the faster the clubhead is moving, the longer the shot. It is a simple, physical relationship that I learned by watching my friends hit thousands and thousands of shots. Short backswings for short shots, long backswings for long shots. It's such a simple concept, and it works so well.

As I developed my ability to predict shot yardages from swing visions, I began to name the different swings I saw. There was the full swing. Then there was the ¾ swing, when the ball flew three-quarters (75%) of the full-swing distance. And there was the ½ swing, when it flew half (50%) of the distance of the full swing.

How Timing Provides Answers

5.9 Timing the Wedge Swings

As I got to know more and more players, and watched more and more swings, I realized not only that there was a characteristic shot three-quarters of the length of their full-swing distance for each player, but that it was always the result of the same-length backswing—just about when the left arm was parallel to the ground and the left hand was as high as the left shoulder (they were all right-handed players). You can see Tom Jenkins's ¾ backswing position, which created a shot of three-quarters of his full-swing distance with that club, in Figure 5.9.1.

There was also a ½-shot distance swing, with another repeatable backswing position that proved surprisingly consistent for the players: the left hand stopped at a position just below the hips (as shown in Fig. 5.9.2).

As I continued working with various Tour players, we needed to refer to swings between the ½ and ¾ positions, but we had nothing to call them until one day it dawned on me that from a frontal view (as seen in Fig. 5.9.3), the length of every player's backswing could be precisely correlated to the hour hand of a clock.

Imagine that his left shoulder is the center of the clock, and his left arm is the hour hand (forget the club). In these terms, the full swing, for the full-length wedge shot, is the result of making a synchronized turn to the maximum "zero-coil" posi-

Figure 5.9.1: Tom Jenkins, at his ¾ backswing position

Figure 5.9.2: Tom Jenkins at his ½ backswing position

Figure 5.9.3: Tom Jenkins at his full (10:30) finesse backswing position. The player's left arm can be imagined to be the hour hand of a clock

tion, where the left arm is at 10:30 on a clock face. So we called that his 10:30 swing. The same system described the previous ¾-length shot as a 9:00 o'clock swing, because the left arm is horizontal at the top of that backswing (as shown in Fig. 5.9.1). The third repeatable and often recurring swing, the ½-length swing, also could be accurately described as a 7:30 swing (again, as in Fig. 5.9.2).

By using time descriptions of the three different backswing lengths, we created and named the three most commonly used finesse swings (and shots) as 7:30, 9:00 o'clock, and 10:30. These three are the basic finesse swings, which every good player should "own" because they are easy to execute and they produce three known, repeatable, and controllable distances. It is the same as having three different clubs in the bag that produce those same distances. By "timing" the wedge swings, we also created an infinite array of swings and shot distances in between the three reference swings.

By practicing and grooving these three swing lengths, my players multiplied their easily reproducible distance shots with each wedge in their bag. They had the full-finesse-swing yardage (about 90 to 95 yards for their sand wedges), which they achieved by making a synchronized backswing that went back to the 10:30 position. (Note: The 10:30 finesse swing usually flies the ball about 10 yards shorter than a full coil-and-hit power swing for the same club.) They also had a shot at around 68 to 73 yards, the result of swinging back to the 9:00 o'clock position (75% of 90 yards); and a 45-yard shot (50% of 90 yards), which came from swinging back to 7:30.

While the exact yardages differed from player to player, the 50%, 75%, and 100% ratios remained almost constant. Having named the backswing lengths by the hour hand of a clock, the players now possessed the ability to produce a complete range of distances simply by thinking about the "time" of their backswing. If they wanted to hit the ball slightly farther than their 9:00 o'clock distance, they took their backswing to 9:15 or 9:30. A slightly shorter shot became an 8:30 swing. To set this concept in your mind, look carefully at Figure 5.9.4, and imagine these three swings all in the same rhythm. It's that simple. With constant-rhythm finesse swings, distance is controlled by backswing length or time.

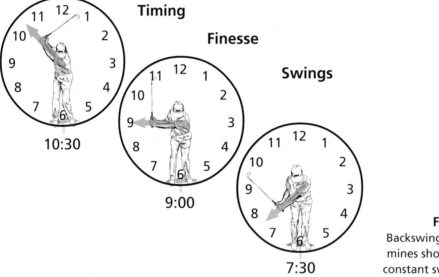

Figure 5.9.4: Backswing time determines shot distance at constant swing rhythm

5.10 9:00 O'clock Is Best

About this time in the discovery and development of our distance-wedge control system, my players were very excited. They were feeling better about being able to produce known, repeatable carry distances on the course, hitting shots closer to the pins on par 5s, making more birdies, and saving more "up-and-down" strokes around the greens. They also were making more cuts, shooting lower scores, and, as a result, making more money. Tom Jenkins quadrupled his official money winnings in his next year on the Tour. Jim Simons won his first PGA Tour event. Tom Kite not only more than doubled his official money, he won both the number-one spot on the PGA Tour money list and the Vardon Trophy for lowest scoring average the next year.

The system didn't work only for men. After working on their distance-wedge control, both Jan Stephenson and Kite won their Tours' "Most Improved Player" titles the next year. And Jan was voted "best short game" on the LPGA Tour by her peers. And she deserved it. She was driving them crazy with her precision inside 100 yards.

As more players adopted and adapted to the system, we made more and more discoveries about its usefulness. It turned out that most of the players were experiencing a similar phenomenon: While their overall wedge games were improving, they realized they were developing both "favorite" and "unfavorite" yardages. There were distances they came to love, as well as those they'd try to avoid (although less comfortable with some distances, they were still much better hitting those shots than ever before).

Jim Simons became so good at 45 and 71 yards that whenever he had shots of those lengths, he felt he might hole them out. Tom Kite felt the same way at 75 yards, as did Tom Jenkins. What I found interesting was that every player reported that their favorite distances were shots produced with their 9:00 o'clock swings. Since working with this initial group of players, a fair number of Tour professionals have come to my Scoring Game Schools and learned the system. Almost every one has come to the same conclusion: The 9:00 o'clock swing is the most reliable, most easily reproduced, and most consistent distance producer in the game.

I mention this as a positive event to look forward to in your finesse-game development, when one distance swing becomes your favorite. When you can make a smooth, rhythmic, 9:00 o'clock finesse swing (or whatever swing you prefer), you'll have the most reliable, repeatable swing you've ever had, particularly under pressure. When these feelings happen, you'll find yourself truly enjoying standing over the ball and knowing, before you swing, exactly how far the next shot is going to go.

One more little bonus I should mention. Once you begin to get the feel for your three principal distances, you will find that those distances just short of and just beyond each of them are also not difficult to produce: They are just a little more or less time on your finesse swing clock. It becomes as easy to swing to 9:15 as it is to visualize 9:15, and that really is pretty easy.

5.11 Working with a System

There are a few practical recommendations I can make for learning to time your distance wedges.

You should realize by now that the finesse swing will work with all the wedges in your bag, regardless of brand name, loft angle, or shaft length (assuming you have an acceptable lie in the grass). For most people, however, all your wedges means just a pitching wedge and a sand wedge.

Don't be afraid to hit your sand wedge from the fairway. It should have about four to five degrees more loft, and be about one-half inch shorter, than your pitching wedge (if not, you need to get one that is; see Chapter 10). Because of these differences, the same 10:30 finesse swing with both clubs will produce shots about 15 yards different. For example, if your pitching-wedge distances are 90 yards (10:30 swing), 67 yards (9:00), and 45 yards (7:30), then your sand wedge with the same three swings should fly roughly 75 (10:30), 56 (9:00), and 37 (7:30) yards. These won't be your exact yardages, but you get the idea.

Before worrying about having to run out and buy more clubs, first groove your 9:00 o'clock and 7:30 swings. You already can make a full swing with your wedge, so you know how to make a 10:30 finesse swing. Just take the coil and "hit" out of your old wedge power swing, and keep your upper and lower bodies synchronized. Remember, your 10:30 finesse swing is as full as it gets (no coil allowed), and in this swing your shaft should never get back to horizontal. Because of the shorter shaft, more upright swing plane, and the requirements of dead hands and synchronization, you should never take any club back past 10:30 in a short-game shot.

It's also vital, as you work on your three reference finesse swings, which will all have the same rhythm, that you get immediate and reliable feedback after every shot. From shot to shot, day to day, week to week, even from year to year, you will constantly be correlating swing lengths with shot carry distances. Your swing rhythms should always be constant and look like you, just the way your walking stride looks like you. If you maintain your rhythm and use dead hands, your finesse swings will perform under pressure like you've never seen before.

Begin each swing with a "slow-ish" one-piece takeaway to the top of the backswing (slow by your standards, not in comparison to anyone else). Come down and through the impact zone aggressively (not hard, but positive: Imagine "saaawish-swish" is your backswing-to-through-swing rhythm), and make a full, high, well-balanced finish. You should be able to hold your pose with your weight fully on your left side and only the right toe touching the ground. You can own these three swings if you include all the principles for the finesse swing outlined in Chapter 4 and spend enough time to train your subconscious mind to repeat them.

One more time: *The rhythm of all the swings must be the same, and the backswing lengths for each of the three reference swings must be repeatable.* If they're not, they won't produce repeatable distances in practice or on the course. You can practice your 9:00 o'clock backswing at home in front of a full-length mirror (you won't believe what 10 or 20 swings every night for a few months will do for your ability to repeat these moves). Or get a learning aid to help you learn the look and feel of the 7:30 and 9:00 o'clock backswings (see "SwingStop" in Chapter 12).

One last piece of advice. Cock your wrists continuously, gradually as you make your backswing (exceptions are discussed in Chapter 6), and have them fully cocked before you get to the right backswing "time." If you wait to cock your wrists until you've reached the right time, the swing will carry on as you cock and get too long for the distance you want. Also, keep your left arm extended throughout the swing, until it folds at the finish. Not only will this keep your swing radius constant, but it's the easy way to judge backswing time and length.

Shorter Swings Are More Difficult

Like the pros, you'll probably find the 9:00 o'clock swings the easiest to make and the 7:30 much more difficult. I've seen this over and over again, with thousands of students. Though I'm not exactly sure why, I'm absolutely sure it's true.

I've also noticed that men seem to have a more difficult time with short backswings than do women. Men seem very insecure when trying to make short backswings such as in the 7:30 swing, when their hands barely get above their thighs. This insecurity seems to come because men fear not being able to hit the ball far enough with a short backswing, even though they consistently hit their shots too far with their normal swings. Maybe it's a male ego thing. When men first take up the game, they control their clubs and "hit" with their hands, trying to avoid whiffing. This seems to become a habit that is difficult to break.

Another problem with the 7:30 swing is that there is not much time to get your body parts synchronized. It's the same feeling you may have over very short putts: You jab with the hands because you feel there's not enough time to get into the flow and rhythm of the stroke. With a wedge, it may seem easier to "hit" the ball than to wait for the smooth, 7:30 finesse swing to come through it. But I never promised to teach this game the most instinctive way. Just the best, simplest, and most effective way.

So it is important when making the 7:30 swing to think rhythm back and through with both your hips and upper body synchronized. In our schools we often mention thinking about the swing as going "saaawish-swish": That's "saaawish" on the backswing, "swish" on the downswing (the backswing takes a little longer because it starts from a standstill).

5.12 Turn Away and Turn Through

To understand and learn to achieve the different swings, it helps to have a simple way to identify them. Lay your club on the ground in an "aim-club" position pointing at the target (see Chapter 4 for more on using an aim club), and assume your parallel-left address position for a 30-yard wedge shot. Then place both hands on your hips—thumbs forward—and tuck your elbows as far behind your body as you can, so your shoulders and hips are locked together (as shown in Fig. 5.12.1).

Figure 5.12.1: Setup with both lower and upper body positioned parallel left of aim club

From the address position, imagine you are going to make a finesse backswing, and turn your hips and shoulders together as far back as you can, keeping your head still and your shoulders in synch with your hips. When you reach your limit with no stretch or pressure (as far as you can turn comfortably), you have turned to what we call your #4 backswing-turn position (Fig. 5.12.2). We divided the finesse turn for each golfer into four positions: The maximum turn without coil is #4. Position #1 is one-quarter of that turn, #2 is half, and #3 is three-quarters of the full turn, as shown. Every golfer will have his own unique four backswing-turn positions based on his flexibility.

Now look at Figure 5.12.3, where the same four backswing body-turn positions are combined with the upper-body and arm positions of the 10:30, 9:00 o'clock, and 7:30 reference distance-wedge backswings, and the 15-yard pitch backswing. I like to show these separate "body-only" photographs so you can make a mental note: Although I'm talking a lot about arm positions when I discuss timing wedge swings, I'm *always* referring to synchronized wedge swings. Don't forget, your body must turn, too! This finesse-swing system doesn't work if you use only your hands and arms to hit wedge shots.

Now return to your address position, and with your hands still on your hips and shoulders pinched behind you, make sure your left toe is flared toward your target direction at least 30 degrees. Turn forward to a full-finish position—99% of your weight on your left foot, and your right foot up resting on its big toe. This is your "turn through" to your #5 finesse-turn position (Fig. 5.12.4). Stand in front of a mirror and turn back and forth slowly through this full range of motion,

Figure 5.12.2: Body positions for finesse- (synchronized-) backswing turns #1, #2, #3, and #4

Figure 5.12.3: Arm positions for 15-yard pitch, 7:30, 9:00 o'clock, and 10:30 backswing turn positions

keeping your shoulders and hips synchronized: You can feel and see five finesse-turn positions on your follow-through, which in later chapters will be correlated with finish positions in other finesse swings and shots. I emphasize the body positions (not arm positions) here again because so many golfers don't turn their lower body properly, or completely through, during their wedge swings.

Figure 5.12.4: Finesse through-swing positions #1 through #5

I said before that the 7:30 swing is difficult for many students to master. Identifying and being aware of your turn positions can help. Now that you know them, start at address, hands on hips and shoulders pinched behind, and make a slow turn away to your #2 back-turn position. Then turn through to your #5 through position, and you have completed the heart of a 7:30 finesse swing. You didn't use a club, didn't use your natural rhythm, and didn't see a ball fly, but the finesse turn is the heart of your finesse swing. If you can't turn your body properly, you have no chance of involving a club and ball, and making a good finesse shot. However, if you stand in front of a full-length mirror, making these moves and occasionally stopping to see what they look and feel like, you'll get it in no time.

Make the 7:30 finesse turn a few times until it is mechanically perfect (no coil, no pressure, in balance). Then begin to work it into a "saaawish-swish" rhythm that feels natural. In fewer than 10 or 20 swings, and less than five minutes, you will be feeling good about this turn motion and be ready to try it with a golf club. But no ball! Not yet. Stay in front of your mirror for some good feedback.

Imagine holding a wedge in your finesse grip and make the same #2 turn back with your body, swinging your arms to the 7:30 backswing position with wrists

Figure 5.12.5: The 7:30 backswing position, wrists cocked

cocked, as shown in Figure 5.12.5. Hold them there for a few seconds: Look at them, feel them, internalize them. Then turn through to your #5 full-finish position, your wrists recocking, your weight moving forward onto your left (lead) foot, everything still synchronized as in Figure 5.12.6. Again, see and feel this position, trying to internalize all the sensations. Once you're comfortable, add the motion, slowly at first, then a little faster with a little more rhythm, until you reach your natural speed and natural "saaawish-swish" rhythm. That's a perfect 7:30 finesse-swing motion. Practice it enough in front of your mirror, without a ball, until

Figure 5.12.6: The 7:30 finesse-swing motion

Figure 5.12.7 (top): My 7:30 finesse swing **Figure 5.12.8** (middle): My 9:00 o'clock finesse swing **Figure 5.12.9** (bottom): My 10:30 finesse swing

Back Swing Length	Back Swing Turn Number	Through Swing Turn Number to Finish
7:30	2	5
9:00	3	5
10:30	4	5

Table 5.12.1: Distance-wedge swing and body-turn positions

it looks really good to you, and it will be a lot easier later on the course.

Now that you know the backswing body-turn positions (listed in Table 5.12.1), understand the timing of backswing lengths, and are aware that upper- and lower-body synchronization are essential in a finesse swing, let me show you how it works for me. In the following swing sequences, you can see that my 7:30, 9:00 o'clock, and 10:30 distance-wedge swings are simple backswing-length adjustments to the same basic finesse swing, which I always try to make at the same rhythm, finishing in the same position (Figs. 5.12.7 to 5.12.9).

How "3 × 4" Works

5.13 My "3 × 4 System"

With the 7:30, 9:00 o'clock, and 10:30 finesse swings grooved into your game, you can add three more distances inside 100 yards to your repertoire simply by adding another wedge, different from your other two, to your bag. Many manufacturers make more lofted "L" or third wedges, with about five degrees more loft than the standard sand wedge. Some even make the extra lofted "X wedges," with about 64 degrees of loft (four or five degrees more than an L wedge).

A little reminder: No matter how many wedges you carry or what their lofts, they are not as important at this point in your development as working on your ability to make quality finesse swings. This means how well you control the distances your short-game shots fly, and how well you deal with getting those shots into the "Golden Eight" feet around the hole. No matter how many wedges you have to choose from, if you can't make the proper finesse motions to the correct backswing times, then nothing else matters. So learn to make your finesse swings first, and then you are ready for my 3 × 4 wedge system.

Actually, you already know the basics of the system. It consists of learning to play three distinct shots with the three finesse swings of 7:30, 9:00 o'clock, and 10:30 backswings, with each of four different wedges to produce 12 known and reproducible carry distances inside 100 yards (see Fig. 5.13.1).

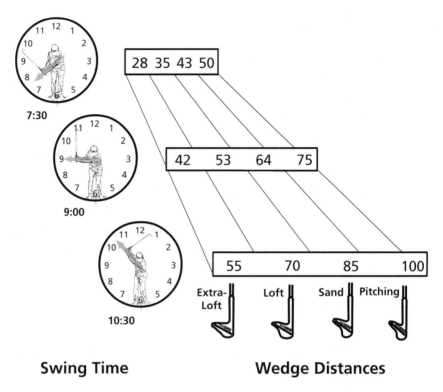

Swing Time   **Wedge Distances**

Figure 5.13.1: My 3 x 4 wedge system: 3 swing times with each of
4 wedges produce 12 known, repeatable distances

The math is simple: 3 swings times 4 wedges equals 12 distances. But the philosophy calls for something more: You want to *own* these 12 shots.

> TO CONTROL YOUR SHOT DISTANCE ACCURATELY ENOUGH TO MAKE
> YOUR NEXT SHOT (PUTT) IMMINENTLY HOLEABLE.

Consider that the "mission statement" of your short game. And consider the implications. It would be like having 11 extra clubs in your bag when you're competing with someone of similar skill who has only one club and no idea how to control the distance for any shot inside 100 yards. Who do you think will win?

And remember: You can be as talented with all 12 finesse shots as you are with one, because the same swing works for them all. The only difference is the length (time) of your backswing, which you vary to match the length of your shot.

5.14 Good News–Bad News

First the good news. My 3 x 4 System is simple, easy to understand, easy to practice, and easy to execute. Every golfer I've ever seen use it has improved his short game and ability to score.

Now the two pieces of bad news: (1) You have to give up one or two of the eight irons (2 through 9) you're used to playing with; and (2) You have to keep track of 12 new shot options inside 100 yards, shots you've never had before.

In the next few pages, I will explain why the good news of switching to the 3 x 4 System outweighs the bad. Read these pages carefully. Don't think that you're now suddenly able to master every up-and-down situation. No matter how many wedges you carry or how many finesse-swing lengths you learn, your scores won't go down until you get good enough with your short-game shots to stop them within the "Golden Eight" and make the next putt.

5.15 Is This Mission Impossible?

If you saw a set of golf clubs for the first time and were told how far each club carried the ball, it might be difficult to remember all those numbers. But having played for a while, you have no trouble remembering that your 7-iron carries the ball 140 yards. That knowledge is part of your game. I'll now show you how you can avoid having to remember any numbers while improving your game from 100 yards in.

Go to a practice range and hit between 10 and 20 solid shots (which may require 25 to 30 swings) with your pitching wedge using your 9:00 o'clock finesse swing. Walk off (or, even better, "shoot" with a laser range finder) the carry distances of the solid shots, write down the yardages, then average the numbers to determine your 9:00 o'clock pitching-wedge distance for that day. Do this for a few days to find your best estimate for the average distance you can expect when you hit a shot with that club and swing.

Do the same with your 10:30 and 7:30 swings while you're there. This will give you three numbers: the average yardages for your 7:30, 9:00 o'clock, and 10:30 swings with your pitching wedge. Write them on a little piece of paper or adhesive dot (Fig. 5.15.1) and stick it to the shaft of the pitching wedge. Put them upside down on the back of the shaft so you can read them when you are ready to hit without taking too much time. Cover the dot with a piece of clear tape, long enough to wrap around your shaft and stick on itself. This will protect the numbers from wear, tear, and weather. (If you're worried, it's perfectly legal by USGA rules to do this.)

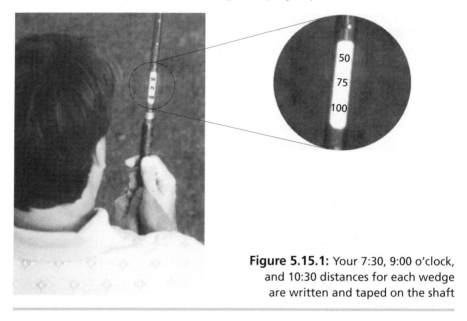

Figure 5.15.1: Your 7:30, 9:00 o'clock, and 10:30 distances for each wedge are written and taped on the shaft

Do the same thing—hit 10 to 20 shots, average the distances, repeat over a few days, arrive at three averages—for your other wedges. Tape those numbers to the shafts. Now it will take you just a second or two to be confident of your yardage and club for the swing you want to make. You don't have to remember distances on the course: They'll be right at hand when you need them.

Whenever you have a shot inside 100 yards, guess which club has a shot distance closest to the distance you need and pick it out of the bag. Quickly check that you chose the right club, make a good, realistic practice swing to the right time on the backswing, and—if you feel good—fire at the pin.

Your Subconscious Always Wins

5.16 Don't Think

When you have the yardages and the swing images in your mind's eye, short shots become a joy to hit. There is no thinking required. You've already practiced the distance swing after you measured your yardage and chose your club, so just swing. You'll soon think of the three distances for each wedge the way you think of the yardages for the other clubs in your bag. By the time the tape wears off, you probably won't need to replace the numbers (until you get new clubs and need to measure new distances for them).

Every golfer has an average distance he expects to hit his 7-iron. Say yours is 140 yards. You don't stand with your 7-iron in your hands and think, "140, 140, I have to make an exact 140-yard swing." No. You think, "140 yards, that's a perfect 7-iron," so that's the swing you try to make, a perfect swing with the 7-iron in your hands.

The same thing will happen with your wedge game after you commit to the 3 x 4 System and practice enough. You'll be looking at a shot of 72 yards and think, "What will hit this 72 yards? Okay, that's a 9:00 o'clock swing with my sand wedge. Just make a smooth, rhythmic, perfect 9:00 o'clock swing." And that's exactly what you'll do . . . and 72 yards is how far the ball will fly!

After a few practice sessions and playing a few rounds with wedges that fit you and your 3 x 4 System, with your yardages taped to the shafts, you'll find that you remember the distances without looking at them. But it's comforting—and perfectly legal—to leave them there. You can check before every shot without taking any extra time. Just make sure your distance numbers are clear and easily legible on your shafts. And if you're suddenly unsure standing over the shot, flip the club over, check that number, and be confident that you've chosen the right club. It's a very satisfying feeling to know you have the right club and the right swing for the shot at hand. It makes the swing easier to execute.

Your Wedges May Not Be Acceptable

As you become more proficient with the finesse system, you'll want your 12 shots to provide the most even coverage over 100 yards. You might not find your standard pitching and sand wedges up to the task. A big reason for this could be the length of their shafts. The sand wedge should be half an inch shorter than the pitching wedge; the L (lofted) wedge should be half an inch shorter than the sand wedge. If you add a fourth (X) wedge, as I strongly recommend, that should be half an inch shorter still. Furthermore, the heads of each wedge should get progressively heavier as the clubs get shorter and more lofted, and the lie should be slightly more upright as you move closer and closer to the ball.

5.17 Preshot Routine

In my lifetime of studying the game of golf, I have made many observations that I cannot prove, and I usually don't talk much about them. I can prove most of what I teach in this book, but I want to tell you two ideas for which I have no data, test results, or research. That doesn't mean they aren't true. In fact, I strongly believe they are true, or I wouldn't pass them on. But the scientist in me demands I begin with that warning.

While watching the great players, I've noticed two things you must come to understand if you hope to come close to maximizing your true potential in playing golf:

1. How you prepare, and what you do before swinging a club, affects the way you swing it.
2. The more consistent, repeatable, and boring your preshot ritual becomes during practice, the more efficiently your subconscious can take control of your swing mechanics on the golf course.

Here is where I must define what I mean by "preshot routine," while sharing some thoughts on how to best prepare yourself to both practice and play.

A preshot routine is a repeatable sequence of things a golfer does prior to hitting a shot. If he doesn't do anything repeatably, he doesn't have a routine. It doesn't have to be a single repeatable routine for all shots in golf: He can have one preshot routine for his power swing, one for his finesse game, and a different one for putting. However, the preshot routine must always stay the same for any given shot, all the time.

Every good preshot routine has two distinct parts: preshot preparation and preshot ritual. The preparation comes first, followed by the ritual; then the golfer can hit his shot.

This does not mean a player always prepares to hit a shot by taking the same number of practice swings. It does mean he always covers the same preparation, in the same sequence, before hitting each shot. Even from here I can see you're confused, so let me offer a few examples.

5.18 Preshot Preparation

Before you decide what shot to hit and how, you must weigh several, and sometimes many, variables. What follows are the common ones; on some shots, you may have to consider others.

When you arrive at your ball, first look at your lie. Is it okay? If not, what compensations will you have to make to hit the ball solidly? Grip down on the club a little? Move the ball back in your stance a bit? Swing across the line to cut the ball from left to right? Or for clean contact, how sharply descending must the swing be?

What about the distance to the pin (or if you aren't shooting at the green, to your predetermined target)? How far do you want the shot to fly? How much wind and which way is it blowing? What trajectory will work best? What club do you need? What swing key do you want to be thinking about?

As you handle these considerations, your mind factors, calculates, and evaluates how they influence club selection. Sometimes it's easy, other times not so easy.

Every shot requires a different line of thinking. But it's as you mull over these questions that you must make all your shot and swing decisions and—this is most important—commit to them. You can't have any doubts when you're standing over the ball ready to make your swing.

After making your first set of decisions—what shot to hit and with what club—the next step is to focus on visualizing the shot in your mind until you can see it clearly. Then imagine the swing that will make that shot happen. Make several practice swings to internalize the look and feel of the perfect swing, standing as close to the actual grass and slope as possible (but be careful not to move the ball; that's a penalty).

The goal of the preparation process is to see and feel the exact swing you are going to make before you try to make it happen for real. One or two practice swings may or may not be enough. Your last practice swing must feel exactly right for the shot you want to hit. If it feels right, you're ready to go; if not, make another or two, or three, or four more, if necessary, until you are completely comfortable. (This doesn't have to drag out your pace of play: Start your preparation before it's your turn to hit.)

When your mind's eye says, "Yes, that's the swing I want, that's my 'preview swing,'" lock onto that image. With the look and feel of the perfect swing fresh in your mind and muscles, you are ready to move into your preshot ritual and hit the shot.

5.19 Preshot Ritual

Think back to when I was working with my original three Tour players and they were beginning to develop rhythmic, repeatable swings. I noticed that as they refined and improved their finesse games they all had developed consistent preshot rituals.

I define the preshot ritual as the "always-exactly-repeatable set of rhythmic motions a player executes in the last five seconds before the start of the swing." Not only did my original players develop consistent preshot rituals, but every great player I have ever watched since then has one, too.

The reason for a preshot ritual is simple: The rhythm you have immediately before a swing affects the rhythm of that swing. A good preshot ritual tells you when to start the swing. It prepares you both mentally and physically to repeat the swing motion and rhythm you have practiced so often, preparing you to succeed in executing the shot you want to hit. It also gives your subconscious a count-down, which lets every part of your body know exactly when things are going to begin.

The preshot ritual is nothing more than a simple, rhythmic, repeatable set of motions that you *always* use to get your swing going. These movements should take the same amount of time, and move at the same rhythm, for every shot with-in a game. (The power game has its own ritual, the putting game its own, and so on. Their rhythms are different, but within each game the rhythm remains consis-tent.) This repetition tells your subconscious when the real swing is going to begin, and that it is going to be just like it was on the practice tee and just like the preview swing. There should be no thought in executing the ritual, only a clear focus on repeating the perfect preview swing. The preshot ritual is doing nothing more than telling your subconscious control system, which you have trained in practice, "One, two, three . . . go!"

My finesse-swing preshot ritual goes like this: It starts with two slight knee flexes, during which I say to myself, "Okay," which means I just saw and felt a per-fect preview swing and I'm starting my ritual to go. I waggle once as I look at the target for the last time, waggle once again as I look down at the ball, then forward press and start my backswing. The sequence and timing of my finesse preshot rit-ual motions are always the same, and the same rhythm applies to the finesse swing that follows.

My ritual is nothing special. It's just the habit I've grooved after hitting thou-sands of wedge shots. Tom Kite has a very different and much more rhythmic rit-ual—which includes bouncing the clubhead—that helps set up his rhythm and tempo. Then he tenses, relaxes, flexes, and goes. Every golfer is different because every person's body, metabolism, and tempo are different. Don't copy a ritual from a great player; instead, develop the ritual that is right for you.

You must have a good preshot ritual, but don't think it's the answer to your problems. It won't hit the shots for you. You'll still have to practice to develop your

Checklists

Preshot Preparation

(time can be variable from shot to shot, but shouldn't take more than 25–30 seconds; Fig. 5.19.1)

1. Check lie, distance, wind, landing area
2. Consider risk of mishit, gambling percentages
3. Choose club, visualize the shot, commit to the shot
4. Imagine the swing, swing key, and commit to the swing
5. Internalize look and feel with practice swing(s)
6. See and feel the perfect preview swing; when it feels perfect, go to your ritual

Figure 5.19.1: Your preshot routine is preparation. Timing can vary, number of practice swings can vary

Figure 5.19.2: Your preshot ritual, the last 5 seconds. Timing is always the same

Preshot Ritual

(time must always be repeatable, consistent; Fig. 5.19.2)

1. Always move at the same rhythm, *your* rhythm, just like in practice
2. Don't think about the future, shot results, or consequences; focus on doing your ritual
3. Let your ritual lead you into repeating your preview swing
4. Watch and feel how good the swing and shot that follow are

finesse-swing mechanics as well as your feel for distances and shot behaviors. But it's foolish to devote all that practice time without developing a consistent preshot ritual. Nothing will do more to optimize your ability to internalize and habitualize from your practice sessions, and help you transfer those habits to the course when you need them.

5.20 Religion Helps

And still that's not the end of it. Simply deciding on a preshot ritual is not enough: You must perform it on every shot, including on the practice tee. You don't have to repeat the entire preparation process on the range, since the situation won't change too much (unless you're working on special shots, in which case it is a good idea to get used to analyzing every shot). But *always,* before every full swing, wedge shot, or putt, religiously execute your preshot ritual. That's the only way to train your subconscious to accept it and make it a habit.

By always practicing properly, always using your ritual, and never doing it any other way, your subconscious will gain maximum trust in it. And this will give you the best chance of performing under pressure. Never lie to yourself, never do it quickly to get it over with, never drag out the time to make sure you do it properly. Perform your preshot ritual on the course with the same rhythm and tempo you had in practice. This allows your subconscious to take control of your swing. After a few thousand times, you won't even realize you used a ritual or made a swing. And that's when you know you're succeeding.

The pros I work with have told me many times that they can't remember making a swing, especially an important one, under pressure. They remember their thoughts during the preshot preparations, how good their preview swing felt, and how they knew they would perform successfully. This feeling is something referred to as being "in the zone." I think it is simply you and your subconscious being in perfect communication. You have trained your subconscious properly, and it is trusting you completely to perform the ritual and get out of the way: You do the preparation and the ritual, your subconscious will execute the shot.

It's not magic, it's not mystical, it's not something only the pros can do. It does take time, repetition, commitment, and consistency. It's a habit you can develop if you use it religiously on every shot, every time, on the practice tee and on the course. And it does work.

CHAPTER 6

Distance Wedges

Short-Game Shots

6.1 Which Shot?

One of the reasons I love the game of golf is that it never takes prisoners. It is out there, the same for all of us, never claiming to be fair, or easy, or difficult. It simply says, "Here I am. Let's see what score you can shoot today."

And every today is different. The tees are set differently, as are the pins. The greens are always different, because of the weather and the height of the mowers. Also changing daily are the length of the rough, the effects of wind and rain, and the firmness of the turf.

All of which means you're continually asking yourself, "Which shot should I hit here?" For example, the pin is 53 yards from your ball, which is sitting perfectly in the fairway. You decide to carry the ball 50 yards in the air, just a little less than your 9:00 o'clock "L-wedge." Say, 8:30. No problem.

"Saaawish-swish"—the preview swing feels perfect, so you are ready to go. The air is clear and crisp, the breeze is light, your rhythm is good. You step into perfect alignment, execute your ritual, and "saaawish-swish," make the perfect 8:30 finesse swing. Contact was perfect, ball flight looks perfect, it may go in the hole. How perfect!

Then the ball lands six inches to the right of the pin, takes a big bounce to the back of the green, dribbles over the back, scampers down the hill, and tumbles into the creek. You're in the water. Double-bogey city.

Isn't this a great game?

6.2 There's More to Scoring Than Hitting Shots

The short game is more than choosing the right shot: You also have to plan for its reaction on the green. Sometimes it's wise to allow a margin for human error, as well as for nonhuman error.

Re-examine that shot in detail. You thought the pin was 53 yards away, but really it was 51, a minor miscalculation. You hit the ball almost perfectly, except it carried 51 yards instead of 50, not bad. The green was slightly firmer than you expected, so your first bounce was harder, and went farther, than planned, four yards to the back of the green instead of three. And it rolled forward instead of biting like you wanted. And you didn't know the hill behind the green had just been cut, allowing the ball to find the water.

Nothing more than a combination of small mistakes and misjudgments, resulting in a double bogey instead of a birdie after a well-hit shot. It happens all the time. That's golf.

In the short game, unlike the power game, what happens after the ball hits the ground is often as important to the final result as the way it was struck. Put another way, selecting the right shot often is as important as how you hit it.

Your performance on every short-game shot will always be a result of not only how well you choose which shot to hit, but also how well you execute your physical swing and the ball's behavior after it leaves your club. (By performance I mean how close you come to achieving the desired result, the same as the PEIs back in the second chapter.) It isn't enough to make a good swing and clean contact: You also must have judged (or "read") the behavior requirements of the shot.

Magnifying the importance of shot behavior on the ground is the fact that there is very little chance for forgiveness in the short game. If you hit a poor drive or a bad long-iron shot, your short game usually can save you. Play badly around the greens and your score almost always rises. The research proves it.

6.3 Four Basic Shots

From my years of studying this game, watching where Tour professionals and amateurs save and lose strokes, I've divided short-game shots into four basic categories. Of course, within those categories are an infinite number of variations and modifications, depending on the conditions of play. Here are the categories (and the chapters in which I will discuss them):

1. Distance wedges (from 30 to 100 yards off the green)—Chapter 6
2. Pitches around the green (from inside 30 yards)—Chapter 7
3. Chipping (from within a few steps of the green) and the bump-and-run (from inside 100 yards)—Chapter 8
4. Sand shots (from inside 100 yards)—Chapter 9

Every one of these shots is important because they are the ones we all, amateurs and pros, face nearly every time we play. How often can be determined in Chart 6.3.1. Look along the horizontal axis and find your total-game handicap. Then move vertically up to the curve, and from where this intersects move across to the vertical axis to see the average number of short-game shots hit to the greens per round (which is slightly more than the number of greens you *miss* in regulation). How you perform on these shots largely determines the final score you post after every round you play.

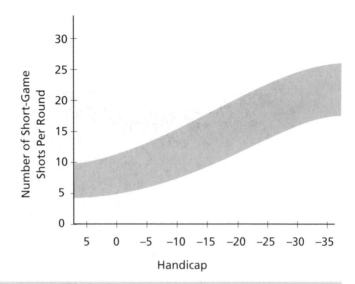

Chart 6.3.1: Short-game shots per round vs. handicap

Luckily, the "generic" shots (good lie, no special difficulty) in all four categories can be handled with the same swing motion, the finesse swing I've been describing in the last few chapters. In case you've forgotten, it's a smooth, synchronized, rhythmic turn with all parts of the body moving together. (If that last sentence doesn't make sense, go back and reread Chapters 3, 4, and 5, because you can't master the short-game shots without first mastering the finesse swing.)

The Distance Wedge

6.4 From 30 Yards or More

When your ball is between 30 and 100 yards off the green (roughly 20 to 75 yards for women), in a reasonably good fairway or rough lie, a distance wedge is usually the best choice, because it optimizes your chances of precise distance control. The swing must go back to at least 7:30 length and through to a full finish. It must have a synchronized turn (moving at your body's natural rhythm) and a full finish, or the 3 x 4 distance-control system won't work. The distance is controlled by club selection and the length of your backswing.

What about 10- or 15-yard shots? They fall into the pitch shot category (discussed in Chapter 7), because they require a less-than-full finish.

What follows are the directions for hitting a distance-wedge shot.

6.5 Distance-Wedge Execution

Your stance should be 14 to 18 inches wide, just about shoulder-width. For a longer shot (which calls for a longer backswing), you might stand a little wider for balance; for a shorter shot, slightly narrower. Your entire body, including both feet, knees, hips, and shoulders, should be aligned parallel left.

Stand tall, with your body in an athletic position—knees slightly flexed, upper body bending forward slightly from the hips, weight centered on the balls of your feet. Don't crouch too much or spread your feet too far apart, as these moves restrict lower-body motion and put control of the swing into your hands and arms. Because you're standing tall and holding a short club, you should be fairly close to the ball. Your arms should hang loosely, almost straight down from your shoulders, leaving four to six inches between your hands and legs (Fig. 6.5.1). Don't crouch, as this pushes your arms away from your body and flattens your swing plane, or get your back too vertical, which inhibits the synchronization of your swing motion,

Figure 6.5.1: Good distance-wedge posture

since your arms must be lifted and dropped more from that position (Fig. 6.5.2).

The ball should be centered exactly in the middle of your stance, which places it two to three inches behind the bottom of your arc. Check this with both feet square to the target line (Fig. 6.5.3). Once the ball is centered between your ankles, keep your left heel in place and turn your left toe about 30 to 45 degrees toward the target; while the ball will appear to be back-of-center relative to your toes (Fig. 6.5.4), it remains perfectly centered.

Use your finesse (neutral to weak) grip and reasonably light grip pressure (Fig.

Figure 6.5.2: Too bent-over and too vertical distance-wedge posture

Figure 6.5.3 (left): Perfectly centered distance-wedge ball position (feet square to swing line)
Figure 6.5.4 (right): Perfectly centered distance-wedge ball position (left foot flared toward target, ready to swing)

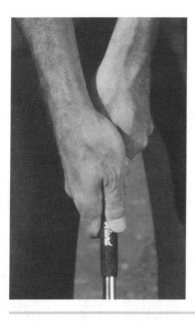

Figure 6.5.5: A perfect finesse grip holds and controls the club in the last three fingers (not the palm) of each hand

6.5.5). Your upper hand should be about a quarter-inch from the butt end of the club. You should be able to feel the clubhead as you waggle and swing. If you can't feel the weight of the head going back and through, close your eyes and concentrate on this feeling. If you still can't feel the club, you're probably gripping too tightly and have too much muscle tension and control in your hands. Lighten up!

Your swing plane is determined by your size and posture. Envision this plane as a line from the ball through your shoulders, as shown in Figure 6.5.6. With short clubs such as your wedges, which position your body fairly close to the ball, your swing plane should be quite steep. You will feel that your swing is as much vertical (above your body) as horizontal (around your body), with the shaft well above and behind your shoulders at the top of your backswing (Fig. 6.5.7).

The club should feel light when it is above your body. Coming down it should remain in the swing plane, naturally controlled by centrifugal force through impact. This will allow you to make a dead-hands swing and keep your hands, arms, chest, and hips synchronized: all together . . . back and through. Look at the sequences in Figures 6.5.8 and 6.5.9, where two-time U.S. Open champion Lee Janzen is flying his sand- and lob-wedge shots 40 and 50 yards in the air, each ending up next to the pin. For reference, this swing should have a very different feeling than your driver swing, which is much more horizontal, swings more around your body, is more behind you at the top of your backswing, feels much heavier, and involves your hand and arm muscles to a greater degree.

Figure 6.5.6: The finesse-swing plane includes both the ball and your shoulders
Figure 6.5.7: The clubhead should stay in the swing plane until you stand up in your finish

Figure 6.5.8: Lee Janzen's 7:30 swing (looking downline)

Figure 6.5.9: Lee Janzen's 9:00 o'clock swing (looking downline)

6.6 Distance-Wedge Recap

1. Start the swing by moving everything—legs, hips, upper body (shoulders, arms, hands, and club)—together and in rhythm away from the target.

2. The arms move with the rest of the body: They do not initiate the motion or add any power. The fingers and hands are dead, doing nothing besides holding the club and cocking your wrists.

3. Don't set your wrist cock prematurely; it should be accomplished gradually during the backswing, and be completed before you reach the top or end of your backswing.

4. During the through-swing, keep everything synchronized as you swing down and through the ball. Body rotation and the club should still be speeding up until a few feet past impact. This natural, muscle-free stability is produced by a follow-through longer than the backswing.

5. Swing through to a high, full finish regardless of the length of the back-swing, and hold your finish position while you watch the results, with 99% of your weight on your front foot (use your back toe for balance only).

If you want to see what I consider a perfectly synchronized distance-wedge swing, examine the sequence of Tom Jenkins in Figure 6.6.1. If you can learn to keep your finesse swings synchronized this well, your short-game shots will improve for sure.

Figure 6.6.1: T.J.'s perfectly synchronized finesse swing

Shot Behavior

6.7 What Happens After Impact

The other half of a distance-wedge shot is the behavior of the ball after it lands on, or just short of, the green. While exact shot behavior is impossible to predict or describe in these pages, I can give a general outline of what to expect from your distance-wedge efforts, and a few numbers that may help guide you when practicing this part of your game.

As a general rule, I would describe the distance-wedge shots with the four wedges like this:

The *pitching wedge* (PW) provides a somewhat low, penetrating trajectory, with medium backspin, resulting in a shot that bounces forward from a shallow pitch mark in the green surface, then rolls a fair amount. This shot is perfect for playing short of elevation changes on a green, so the ball bounces and then rolls up to the next level by the pin. This shot also is great in windy conditions, especially against the wind. The PW is a good choice off tight lies, but expect a lower trajectory and more spin.

The *sand wedge* (SW) creates a high, crisp trajectory with lots of backspin, and a shot that lands and makes a medium-deep pitch mark in the green. From this pitch mark, the ball usually bounces only modestly forward, then spins back almost to where it first hit the green. Don't use this shot with too much wind, because of its high spin; into the wind, it will up-shoot and go nowhere. The SW has too much bounce on its sole (bottom) to be effective from tight lies. However, the bounce makes the SW an excellent choice from deep grass (rough) and soft sand.

The *lofted wedge* (LW) provides a high, soft trajectory with modest backspin (unless hit hard from a longer distance), and a shot that lands softly and makes a medium-deep pitch mark in the green. Because the LW comes down almost vertically, the first bounce is more up and down than forward, and the ball tends to stop fairly quickly. If the shot is hit crisply from a tight lie, the increased backspin can pull it back short of where it first landed, sometimes even off the green. The LW is an excellent choice from greenside bunkers and for many soft lob shots around the green from the fairway or short rough. It is *not* a good choice from deep rough or very tall grass.

The *extra-loft wedge* (XW) provides the ultimate high, soft shot, one that controls its behavior on the greens with an almost vertical landing trajectory. While it does have some backspin, it's usually not too much, because this shot is rarely hit hard. (Hit the X-wedge hard and it will fly too high, becoming almost useless.) The XW works best when hitting high, soft shots to difficult pin positions on hard, fast greens, without having to play cut shots (which are somewhat more difficult to control). These shots usually make shallow pitch marks on the green as they come in softly and from short distances. The XW is the best club from the sand for short shots (under 10 yards' carry), and for getting the ball up quickly over high bunker lips.

In the four video sequences in Figure 6.7.1, you can see the measurably different launch angles of these four shots. I'll detail what to expect on the greens as a result.

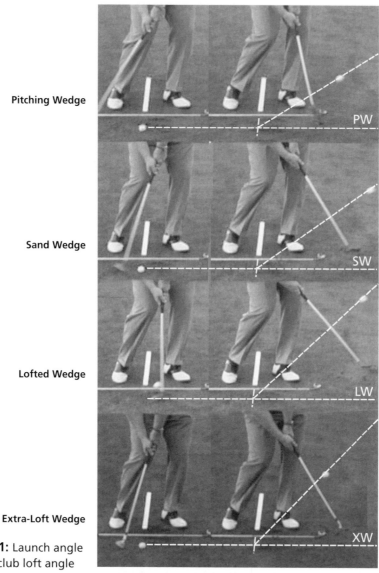

Pitching Wedge

Sand Wedge

Lofted Wedge

Extra-Loft Wedge

Figure 6.7.1: Launch angle varies with club loft angle

6.8 Average Expectations

Table 6.8.1 lists the average general characteristics one can expect from distance-wedge shots from the four clubs described earlier, when hit from level lies into flat greens of normal firmness. Do not take these descriptions as gospel: Shot behavior will always vary based on type of grass, green speed, firmness and moisture content, wind, the ball's lie, and the player's finesse-swing action.

CLUB	PW	SW	LW	XW
Trajectory Height	Low	Medium	High	Extra-High
Spin	Medium	Maximum	Medium-High	Medium
Roll-to-Carry Ratio	20% to 50%	0% to 30%	−15% to 15%	−20% to 10%
Desirable Lies	Fairway, Rough	Plush Fairways, Deep Rough	Fairways, Light Rough	Tight Fairways, Light Rough
Undesirable Lies	Deep Rough	Tight	Fluffy	Fluffy
Performance	Good in General	Good (under 85 yds.) Poor (over 95 yds.)	Good (under 60 yds.) Medium (over 60 yds.)	Good (under 40 yds.) Poor (over 45 yds.)

Table 6.8.1: General characteristics of distance wedges from grass

6.9 The Ball's Pitch Mark Controls Roll

Before your shot, do you assume that how fast your ball will stop on the green depends on how much backspin you put on it? Most golfers do.

Before your shot, do you think about how deep a crater, or pitch mark, your ball is going to make in the green? Most golfers don't.

In fact, the depth of your shot's pitch mark in the green can have a greater effect on the shot's subsequent behavior than backspin. As illustrated in Figure

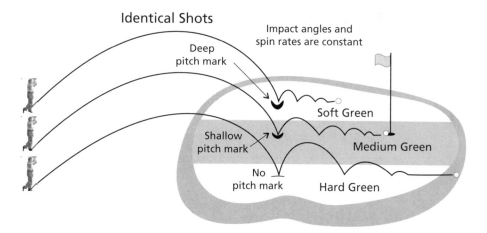

Figure 6.9.1: The depth of your pitch mark affects the behavior of your shot

6.9.1, the depth of the impact craters made by identical incoming shots can vary with the firmness of the green surface, influencing how far the ball bounces. The forward momentum of every short-game shot is affected by either the depth of the pitch mark it has made, or was not allowed to make, due to green firmness.

Most golfers subconsciously understand this, especially in the context of wet, soft greens. Every golfer who follows the pro Tours knows that when greens are soft, the pros get up and down more often and shoot lower scores. Why? Because they hit high, soft shots that stop almost exactly where they land on the soft greens (their shots make deep pitch marks in the soft, wet greens, so the ball can't bounce forward). The pros call this "throwing darts," because each shot sticks where it first hits the green, and shot behavior on the greens becomes very predictable at "zero movement."

Figure 6.9.2 shows how pitch-mark depth is also affected by a shot's angle of impact. It shows that on surfaces of the same firmness, three different approach angles can have a dramatic effect on pitch-mark depth (as long as the surface is not concrete-hard). Again, pitch-mark depth affects the first bounce forward. Note that neither example is concerned with how much spin is on the ball: Spin is a separate factor and has its own effect, which is often significantly influenced by the pitch-mark-crater depth.

I emphasize pitch-mark depth because it especially controls how quickly your shots will stop when you are hitting distance wedges and pitch shots to elevated and lowered greens. Examine the examples in the sidebar (next page) and make sure you understand the effect of green elevation on how balls will behave, even

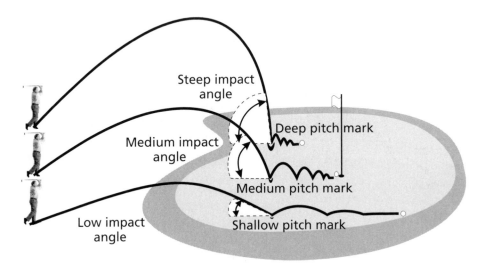

Figure 6.9.2: Angle of impact affects pitch-mark depth

when the greens are perfectly flat and of constant firmness. What you'll learn is that hitting a 31-foot-high distance-wedge shot to a soft green elevated 30 feet above you is like hitting onto a cement-hard green. Your shot will make no pitch-mark crater and will roll like you can't believe.

Pitch-Mark-Depth Effects

It's easy to understand that the depth of a ball's crater is affected by the incoming angle of impact. Less obvious is that the angle of impact can be affected by the elevation of the green relative to the golfer and the slope of the ground from which the golfer hits the shot. Look how the three angles of impact in Figure 6.9.3, for the same wedge shot, are totally dependent on the elevation of the greens. Since angle of impact affects the depth of the pitch mark and the first bounce, it significantly controls the behavior of the shot on the green.

Examine an example of this effect, shown in Figure 6.9.4, when two golfers hit the same-distance shot, with the same height and spin, to the same flat green. The only difference is that one hits his shot from below the green surface while the other one hits from above. Owing to the different angles of impact, the two shots make different-depth pitch marks and behave completely differently upon landing.

Now look at Figure 6.9.5, where the same thing happens to two different golfers, again hitting the same shots to the green but this time off lies of different slopes. These effects occur all the time on the course, with golfers blaming themselves for not putting enough (or too much) spin on their shots. If anything, they should be blaming themselves for not understanding the effect of angle of impact and pitch-mark-crater depths.

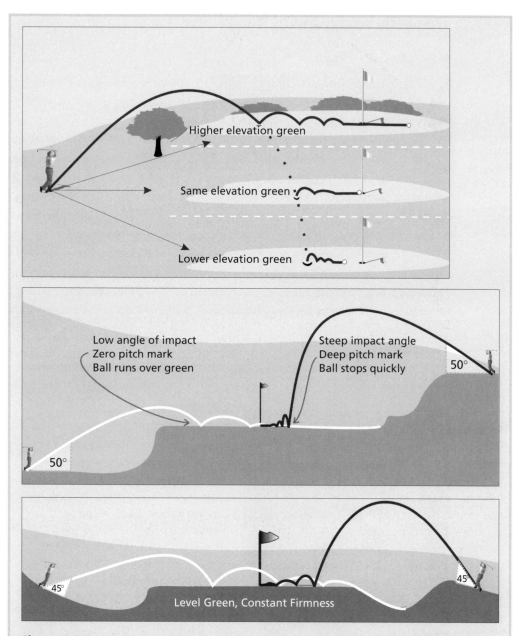

Figure 6.9.3 (top): Green elevation affects pitch-mark depth and shot behavior
Figure 6.9.4 (middle): Identical shots (produced by identical swings) behave differently, depending on green elevation **Figure 6.9.5** (bottom): The slope of your hitting ground affects your results on the green

Distance-Wedge Swing Variations

6.10 The Grip-Down

While the primary distance controls in the 3 x 4 System are length of backswing and club selection, there is one other way to adjust shot distance without violating or interfering with the rest of the system.

You don't want to "hit" the shot a little harder or "take a little off" your swing, since those have adverse effects on a rhythmic dead-hands finesse swing. And you certainly never want to decelerate into impact or shorten your follow-through to reduce carry distance. The other way to adjust distance is to change the length of your club: To take four or five yards off a shot, grip down on the shaft about four or five inches, move a little closer to the ball, and make the same swing.

Maybe, for your swing, four or five inches won't equal exactly four or five yards; the test on page 125 will clarify the relationship with your finesse-swing shots between gripping down and shorter carry distances. When you run this test, don't try to reduce distance by a set number of yards. Rather, find a grip-down position that feels comfortable (Fig. 6.10.1) and see how many yards that grip takes off your shots.

The ultimate performance would be to learn a precise grip-down distance for each of your original 12 distances, giving you a total of 24 accurate shots inside

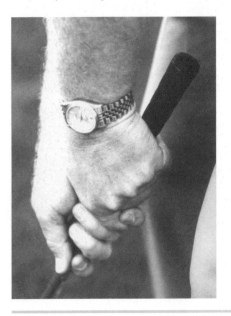

Figure 6.10.1: Grip down the shaft to decrease shot distance

Calibrate Your Grip-Down Distance Loss

The 3 x 4 System creates 12 known and repeatable distances. Run this calibration test on each of those "swing x club" distances.

At your practice range, find a target area that will give you accurate feedback on ball-flight distance. A good place would be an easily viewed slight uphill slope at the approximate calibration distances needed for that day's test—for example, at your 9:00 o'clock L-wedge distance of 42 yards. Spread two towels on the ground, one at your precise distance for that swing (in this example, 42 yards), the other towel five yards closer (37 yards).

Warm up your swing to a different target, then get 10 balls for the test. Try to make 10 identical, perfect 9:00 o'clock swings, hitting all 10 balls to your target towels, gripping down about four inches on your L-wedge shaft on every other shot. Figure 6.10.2 shows identical swings with alternating shaft lengths. Note how much shorter your grip-down shots fly, on average, and you have a first estimate of your grip-down distance effect. If you repeat this test several times, you will begin to get an accurate and repeatable idea of the actual distance effect. By repeating the test over several different days, you can measure this effect quite accurately, and start using it effectively on the course.

Figure 6.10.2: Identical swings with different-length clubs produce different distances

100 yards. Sound unbelievable? Jan Stephenson did exactly this on the LPGA Tour. She taped all six numbers onto each of her wedge shafts, and no one on the ladies' Tour could touch her near the greens.

6.11 Low Trajectories

The easiest way to vary shot trajectory from a normal lie is to change the loft of the club you use. If you need a higher, softer shot, use a wedge with more loft. It is a lot easier than creating a different swing or changing your mechanics.

Still, you'll face situations when you want to change the character of a shot, which is done by making slight changes in technique. To lower wedge-shot trajectories—when hitting directly into a crosswind—either move the ball back two to three inches in your stance or lower your follow-through and finish with your hands low, shoulder-high at most. Either change will slightly reduce the wind effects on your shots, which can be significant on distance wedges.

If you want a more pronounced effect, make both changes, which creates a "knock-down" wedge shot (Fig. 6.11.1). The trajectory is even lower, while main-

Figure 6.11.1: The knock-down wedge swing

taining a fair ability to stop shots on the green with lots of backspin. (Note: You must not use your hands in the knock-down shot. Be sure to swing through impact keeping your synchronized body turn, but let your hands keep going out toward the target on the follow-through rather than folding up and finishing high, as in a normal distance-wedge shot, Fig. 6.11.2.)

To lower your shots even more, position the ball about four inches back in your stance and again use a low-hands follow-through. This will minimize any wind effect on your shot.

As you practice different-length finishes, you'll see that even though the ball stays on the clubface only a very short time, your follow-through has a real effect on ball flight. The higher your hands finish, the higher the trajectory; the lower the follow-through, the lower the shot flies. If you watch Paul Azinger on the PGA Tour, you'll see his follow-through is usually low, his hands barely rising above his chest, which is why he strikes low, boring shots (as I'm demonstrating in Fig. 6.11.3).

Figure 6.11.2: The 9:00 o'clock distance-wedge swing

Figure 6.11.3: A slightly knocked-down 9:10 distance-wedge swing

Paul's low shots are very repeatable, very reliable, and he is a great player. However, it takes a lot of practice and skill to execute this shot without "hitting" at the ball at impact. As skilled as "Zinger" is, when the greens get hard and fast, it becomes more difficult for him to hit to some tight pin positions and keep the ball on the greens. Most golfers who try to play a short follow-through get very "handsy" and "muscley" in the impact zone, resulting in poor control, especially under pressure. So go with the low finish only when a low shot is absolutely necessary and a lower lofted club won't get the job done.

6.12 The Cut Lob

While it's okay to occasionally play the ball back in your stance to produce lower shots, it is *not* okay to play the ball forward in your stance as a means of getting a higher trajectory. Playing the ball forward leads to one of three results, and two of them are bad: From a forward ball position, golfers either hit shots solidly (but with distance results that aren't great), hit a thin skull (terrible result), or hit it fat (terrible result).

Playing the ball significantly forward of your stance center moves it ahead of the bottom of your natural swing arc. If nothing else in the swing changes, the shot has to be hit fat; more likely, the golfer uses his hands or a body slide to alter the swing (producing some solid shots and some thin skulls).

As you learned before, the bottom of a good finesse-swing arc and the divot are where they are. That's physics. The only way you alter that is by giving up your true finesse swing. And if you don't change your swing, you will hit behind the ball. Then what happens is that after a few fat shots "fat fear" sets in, and the subconscious creates a new swing motion that includes a forward knee slide during the downswing (Fig. 6.12.1), a "handsy-through-impact" action (Fig. 6.12.2), or both.

Figure 6.12.1: Forward ball position promotes forward knee slide

Figure 6.12.2: Forward ball position promotes handsy wrist action and fat fear

Both compensations are attempts to hit the ball before the ground. Both create bad contact, bad shot trajectories, and bad distance control, especially under pressure when the hands don't work as well as they did on the practice tee.

To hit a higher shot, the first choice should always be to take a more lofted club and make your standard dead-hands finesse swing. The second choice is to open the clubface, aim your swing line to the left of the target, and keep your ball exactly in the center of your stance, relative to your new swing line (Fig. 6.12.3). Keeping the ball in the middle of your stance ensures crisp contact, and you can hit the ball as high as you want simply by opening the clubface enough and aiming far enough left. Remember, higher shots usually fly shorter distances, so be sure to make a longer backswing (and, as always, a full finish) to get these shots all the way to your target.

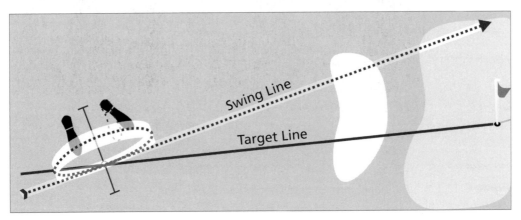

Figure 6.12.3: Ball position should be centered between ankles for the cut-lob shot

6.13 Calibrate Your Cut-Lob Technique

For any cut shot, you must open the face of your wedge, which can be done many different ways. I suggest simplifying your options by adopting one standard open-faced position, the "45-degree-open" look, as shown in the sequence of photographs in Figure 6.13.1. Start with a normal finesse grip and square club-address position shown on the left (aligned parallel left), then loosen your grip without moving the left-hand position and rotate the shaft to open the clubface until the face lines are at a 45-degree angle to the aim club (center figure). Retighten your left-hand grip, still without moving the left hand, reestablish your original finesse-

Figure 6.13.1: The proper way: Rotate your clubface open while maintaining your finesse grip

grip position relative to your body, and flare your left toe toward the target (shown on right). This is the normal address position, with a normal finesse grip relative to your "aim club," except the face of the wedge has been rotated open to the 45-degree-open position.

Now that you know how to establish a consistent open-faced wedge setup, take a towel and a laundry basket to your practice range, where you can calibrate how that clubface performs. Walk 30 steps from the pile of balls you'll be hitting and set down your basket as your target. Walk seven steps to the right and lay down the towel, which becomes your calibration towel. Return to the pile of balls. Pick a nice area of grass from which to hit and set up your aim club parallel left of the target basket (for help setting an aim club, see section 4.4).

With a normal square clubface, hit five shots with your normal distance-wedge swing to your target basket. Next, without changing anything else, rotate your clubface open to the 45-degree-open position, keep your grip square to the target, and hit five more shots. If you truly swing just the way you did before, with your swing still going down your aim-club line through impact toward the basket, these five shots should go off to the right and fall short of the calibration towel (due to the open clubface).

Continue using the same setup (aiming parallel left of the basket, the clubface 45 degrees open) and hit five more shots. Again, the balls should fly off to the right and short of the basket. The amount they fly to the right and short is your cut-lob calibration angle and distance.

Walk out and measure your calibration distance by first moving the towel to the middle of your 10-ball scatter pattern (Fig. 6.13.2). Measure visually how far short and to the right the towel is compared to your target basket. Pick up the towel and move it the same angle to the left and the same distance past your basket as your open-faced shots finished right and short. Now the calibration towel is your new swing line and swing-distance-calibration target, to help you set up to hit shots dead to the real flagstick on the course (Fig. 6.13.3).

Practice hitting cut-lob shots to the target basket by setting up and swinging to your new calibration towel, using your 45-degree-open-faced wedge. The more you practice this way, with an aim club aligned left and an identifiable calibration towel on the range, the better you will learn to set up and swing properly to the left, so you can hit cut-lob shots accurately to a flagstick on the course.

Figure 6.13.2: Measure your cut-lob calibration angle and distance right and short of your target

Figure 6.13.3: Set up and aim long and left to hit perfect cut-lob shots to the target basket

Distance Wedges from Difficult Lies

When faced with a bad lie, you should change your setup. Here's a simple rule: The worse the lie, the more sacrifices you should be willing to make (in carry distance, height, stopping distance, and general shot control or accuracy) to better accomplish the single most important factor in achieving acceptable results— clean, crisp contact of your clubface on the ball. Always remember, it is all too easy to jump out of the frying pan (the bad lie) into the fire (a worse lie, penalty strokes, double bogeys, and worse). The number-one result you want to achieve from a bad lie is a safe recovery to a safe position.

6.14 From Deep Grass

Two comments when playing from grass: (1) The taller the grass, the shorter the shaft and the longer the swing you should use; and (2) Never try to curve a shot when you can't get clean contact between clubface and ball.

When there's a lot of grass around the ball, you won't get good results, or maintain control, if you sweep the club through and trap grass between clubface and ball. The grass and consequent moisture on the clubface produce "flyer" shots, which have slightly more carry and significantly less backspin than normal, solid-contact shots. They usually don't stop rolling until finding trouble behind the green.

The setup changes to make from deep grass are to grip down on the shaft, effectively shortening the club, and to play the ball farther back in your stance. These adjustments create a steeper angle of attack and minimize the grass compressed between the clubface and the ball. Although these shots are never easy, they become more predictable as you learn to make better contact.

6.15 Against the Grain

Always consider the grain of the grass from which you are hitting. If it's growing away from the target, you must swing as if your shot distance is 25% to 50% farther than what it measures (Fig. 6.15.1). The grass is going to grab your wedge and try to stop your follow-through, so always take a little longer backswing and try to continue all the way to a full finish: If your club doesn't get out of the grass, your ball might not, either.

When grass grows toward your target, it may make your shot fly and roll a lot farther. This happens because so much grass gets trapped between the clubface and the ball that all backspin is removed from the shot. It also doesn't help that

Figure 6.15.1: Vijay Singh blasts from greenside rough, against the grain

the ball squirts out on a lower trajectory, further increasing shot distance.

Once you have a practice green to hit to, try to find some long-grass rough 30 to 100 yards away. Don't worry about the grain of the grass, but do notice which way it's growing and then go ahead and hit your shots; either direction is good practice. The more shots you hit out of unusual situations, the more you'll learn how to plan your shots accordingly.

6.16 On Hardpan

Most golfers fear hardpan lies. I love them. Rather than thinking of them as being big trouble, you can count on good results and have extraordinary control from hardpan once you learn how to handle it.

From a bare, hardpan lie on hard dirt, move the ball three inches back from normal position (that is, three inches behind the center of your stance), open the clubface slightly, and aim a little left (for right-handed players), as shown in Figure 6.16.1. Make your normal dead-hands finesse swing. These adjustments will prevent you from hitting the ground behind the ball, bouncing the clubhead into it, and skulling the shot. You'll produce a slightly lower trajectory with more backspin than you normally get from a good lie, two differences you can learn to live with.

Sometimes a low, spinning shot is not what you need from hardpan. To hit the ball higher, open the face of your wedge more. You can even do it with a 64-degree X-wedge as long as it doesn't have too much bounce on the sole.

Before I explain how to hit hardpan shots high, understand what you're trying to do and how the club can help. Take all your wedges and prop them up on your kitchen countertop (lean them against a support, as shown in Fig. 6.16.2, so they stand up). Place a golf ball at the leading edge of each club and squat down so your eyes are at countertop level. Push the ball against each club tightly, so you can see exactly how much margin for error you have to mishit the shot and still make contact on the face rather than the leading edge. Each wedge probably has a different margin for error due to its different sole configurations (called bounce; see pages 279–83 for details) in the square-face position. Realize that if you hit a hardpan shot either thin or fat, the result will be the same because on fat shots the club will bounce up and skull the ball.

Now you want to maximize the margin for error in hitting a shot high. So take each wedge in turn and open the face slowly, back and forth (as shown in Fig. 6.16.3 for the second club from right), while looking at the height of the ball in comparison. Some wedges give fairly good margins for error in the open position,

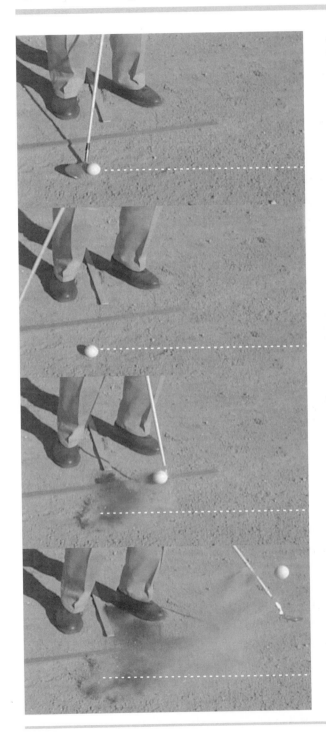

Figure 6.16.1: The hardpan lie

Figure 6.16.2: The bounce on each wedge determines how high its leading edge is above hardpan (relative to a golf ball)

Figure 6.16.3: Rotating the face open raises some wedges' leading edge intolerably high

and some are awful (if none of yours can be opened and still get the face under the center of the ball, you *must* get some new wedges). You should have at least one wedge in your bag that you can rotate open and still use successfully off hardpan surfaces.

Once you know which wedge gives you the most margin for error in the open position, see how high you can hit it. Take some balls, your wedge, and a piece of lumber (a 2" x 12" board, about 2 feet long, as shown in Fig. 6.16.4, is perfect), and head to your backyard. Aim the board to the left of your target, put a ball on the board (Fig. 6.16.5), take your address position parallel to the board, and make sure the ball is centered in your stance, between your ankles. Grip down on your wedge shaft two inches (the thickness of the board), and you're ready. The more you open the face, the higher your shots will fly.

Figure 6.16.4: A solid board (2" x 12") is good for hardpan lie practice

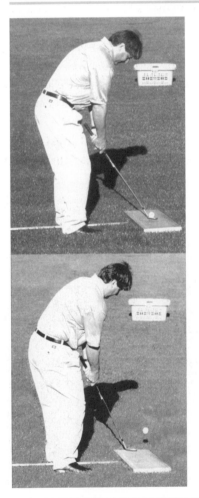

Figure 6.16.5: When practicing hardpan lies, don't set your target basket in line with any windows

Be sure you can't break anything with the occasional skulled shot, because you're going to hit some skulls (the margin for error is *so* small). But once you get reasonably good from wood, you'll be fine off dirt. When you feel real confident, try hitting from cement; you'll be amazed at how you can hit these shots high, reasonably soft, and with lots of backspin. But don't spend too much time hitting off cement or the sole of your club will suffer.

6.17 Ball Above or Below Your Feet

When the ball is above their feet, most golfers have been told to beware of the shot flying left because their swing plane will be flatter (more around their body). This is true. However, there is a more important reason the ball flies left from these lies on short-game shots: The greater the loft of a club, the more it aims to the left when the ball is above your feet. Since the wedges have the most loft, this phenomenon is most effective close to the green. Seen in a down-line view (Fig. 6.17.1), even when the player aims the leading edge of his L-wedge straight (wide band), the loft angle of the face is actually still aiming to the left (narrow rod). Then when his shot goes left, he thinks he made a bad swing.

This effect is not so bad on a 3-iron shot because the loft of a 3-iron is not as great as that of a wedge. Remember: The greater the loft, the greater the aim-left effect.

Figure 6.17.1: Ball above feet: When the leading edge aims straight, the face of a lofted wedge still aims left

When the lie is above your feet, minimize the aim-left effect by gripping down on the shaft, then make up for the distance loss by taking either a longer back-swing or less lofted wedge. This keeps the lie angle of your shaft closer to normal. But you still have to aim to the right to finish close to the pin.

When the ball lies below your feet, the alignment problem is not nearly so bad. Because golfers tend to keep their bodies vertical, crouch down, and use a club with a longer shaft, the only change in lie angle (and thus where they aim) comes if they stand slightly closer to the ball than normal. With the ball below your feet, try not to catch the heel of your club on the ground before impact (play the ball slightly back in your stance), and don't aim as far left on any slope as you would aim right if the slope ran the opposite way (putting the ball above your feet). For more details on this effect, see pages 176–80.

My point here is that you should always be aware of the ground level from which you hit your short-game shots and its effect on where you must set up and aim.

6.18 Downhill and Uphill

Downhill wedge shots are difficult, and it doesn't take much of a downhill slope to create the problem. To understand what's happening, look at Figure 6.18.1, where normal ground level is indicated by the horizontal line and the normal clubhead arc is the curve on the downswing. Both lines are dashed to show where they would extend belowground. Obviously, there is no possible way to make a centri-fically powered swing from this position that will let you hit the small (golf) ball before hitting the big (earth) ball.

This "wrong-ball-first" problem occurs because golfers like to stand vertically in the gravitational field of the earth. They feel out of balance when they're tilted, and make poor swings from such positions. But changing your orientation to the ground is the best solution to hitting downhill shots, as long as the slope isn't too severe.

In Figure 6.18.2, Jon is standing perpendicular to the downhill surface on which the ball lies. If he could swing this way (and keep his balance), hitting this shot would not be a problem. The ball would come out lower owing to the slope of the hill, but he could plan for that by using a more lofted club or allowing for more roll after impact. Most important, he can easily hit the ball solidly before hitting the ground.

This is my first solution to a downhill lie. Set your shoulders parallel to the ground, keep your balance as well as you can on your backswing, then make a good through-swing. Allow yourself to walk forward on your follow-through to

Figure 6.18.1: Downhill lies promote hitting the ground behind the ball

Figure 6.18.2: Tilt shoulders with downhill slope to avoid hitting fat shots

Figure 6.18.3: Tilt with the slope, hit a good shot (stay down through impact), then walk down the slope if you can't maintain balance through your finish

keep from falling over (Fig. 6.18.3). Play the ball in the middle (or slightly back in your stance if you want to provide a little "fudge margin," to avoid hitting the shot fat), and plan on the ball coming out low and running longer than normal once on the ground.

When the downslope gets too steep to stand with your shoulders parallel to the ground and make a walk-through finish, go to plan B. For this, instead of standing down the hill, go back to standing vertically but set up aiming way left, open your clubface (Fig. 6.18.4), and hit a cut shot from the sidehill lie you created. Aiming far left changes the downhill lie to a sidehill lie, with the ball below your feet (left-handers aim the other way). This is still not an easy shot, but if you don't catch the heel of your wedge on the ground before impact, you can hit a cut slice around to your target, and things usually will turn out fine.

Figure 6.18.4: Sidehill cut shots (right) are easier to hit than severe downhill shots (left)

My last-resort shot, plan P (for Prayer) from even steeper downhill slopes (leftmost image in Fig. 6.18.5), is the "muscle chop," swinging down on the ball hard from the left-aim setup (sequence Fig. 6.18.5) and hoping for the best. This should be the last option, because no matter how much you practice, this is a very difficult shot under pressure.

Figure 6.18.5: The downhill chop-cut shot (no lower body turn) is the last resort

6.19 From Sand

When facing a distance-wedge shot that happens to be in the sand, anywhere between about 30 and 100 yards, use your normal distance-wedge swing and move the ball back one or two inches from your stance center (Fig. 6.19.1). Set the face of the club square to your target and make a normal finesse-wedge synchronized turn.

Figure 6.19.1: A normal distance-wedge swing with ball slightly back ensures solid ball contact on long sand shots

The setup adjustment guarantees clean contact—ball before sand—actually pinching the ball against the sand at impact. But this slightly more descending blow adds backspin and takes some yardage off the shot (about 10 yards) compared to the same shot from a good lie in grass. To compensate for this loss of distance, use a slightly longer backswing or the next-longer club.

Many golfers don't understand what happens in the sand, so even when they make a beautiful swing, with beautiful contact, the shot finishes short. If they're lucky, the ball stops on the front of the green; less lucky and they're in another bunker just short of the green.

CHAPTER 7
The Pitch Shot

From Inside 30 Yards

7.1 You Could Toss It On from Here

Now let's move a little closer to the green.

The pitch shot probably got its name because it flies as if someone has made an underhanded toss, or pitch, of the ball into the air and onto the green (Fig. 7.1.1). Not as long as a distance wedge, but longer and higher-flying than the chip, the pitch is lofted onto the green from about three to 30 yards off its edge. After landing, it normally rolls about the same, or a slightly shorter, distance than it flew in the air. You can and will use all of your wedges for pitch shots, and, as you'll soon learn, the conditions of the shot dictate which wedge is best.

Figure 7.1.1: My non–USGA approved "pitch" shot

As you get closer to the green, the second half of each shot increases in importance. What I mean is, with a 5-iron, which flies 170 yards then stops in three or four, what happens on the green is not such a big concern. The premium is on striking the ball—making a good swing—to get the ball on the green. It's almost taken for granted that if you make a good swing and hit a good shot, the ball will stop on the green. (Once you know the softness of the greens that day, you don't think much about them on each shot.)

But as you get closer to the green and start using your distance wedges, you have to worry how and where the ball will stop: Will it kick left or right? Is the landing area uphill? By the time you're close enough to hit a pitch shot, the ball's reaction on the green is critical to your success. So while the physical motion of the pitch swing is easier to execute than the full-power swing, the result of the pitch is judged on a much harsher scale: You either make the next shot, your first putt, or you don't. As a result, these are pressure-packed shots.

There are other factors contributing to the golfer's fear of pitch shots: (1) pitch shots are not well understood mechanically; (2) they are rarely taught by club pros; (3) they look simple; and (4) golfers fear looking foolish, especially on such a simple shot. Magnify these factors by some of the situations when you'll be hitting a pitch: lofting the ball over a bunker, water, or an expanse of long grass around the green. Short shots with severe penalties for nonperformance!

However, as I'll show you, the pitch is pretty simple. You play it much the way you do a distance wedge, except with a shorter backswing and shorter follow-through. The follow-through is still longer than the backswing (to ensure stability), but a pitch never has a full finish: If it did, it would be a distance-wedge shot—and carry the ball too far.

7.2 Execution of the Pitch Shot

The mechanics of the pitch closely resemble those of the distance wedge in many respects. Your feet should be fairly close together, no more than 14 to 15 inches apart (but at least 10 inches apart, even for small women). Don't get them too close together, since your stance needs to provide balance and you need to be able to rotate your lower body in rhythm with the shot.

Start your setup with both feet perpendicular to an aim club (real or imagined) aligned parallel left. Position the ball exactly at the midpoint between your ankles and turn your forward foot toward the target 30 to 45 degrees without moving your heel. This routine assures you will achieve a true centered-in-your-

Figure 7.2.1: The pitch shot setup position

stance ball position (Fig. 7.2.1). The ball should be centered between your ankles for all good lies (just like for distance-wedge shots), to allow contact with the ball before the club reaches its low point or divot. The bottom of your pitching arc, just like your distance-wedge arc, will locate the center of your divot about two to three inches forward of the center of your stance.

Your stance should be athletic, with knees slightly flexed. Hold the wedge lightly in your finesse grip. Stand fairly tall and let your arms relax, hanging straight down under your shoulders.

Many golf pros teach that the lower body should remain totally still during the pitch shot. They reason that you don't need power from the lower body, so they try to simplify the swing by eliminating moving parts. I don't agree.

It's true that you don't want to be driving your legs on pitch shots, but you do need enough lower-body motion to keep your body parts synchronized during the swing. The upper and lower body must move at the same rate, so you don't create power but you *do* create rhythm. And it's difficult to have good rhythm if you don't move your lower body. Golfers who freeze from the hips down become arms-and-hands players. Rather than swinging, they swipe or hit at the ball, producing inconsistent results, especially under pressure.

For example, on a 15-yard L-wedge pitch shot, you should take about a #2 turn away from the ball, and then a #3 turn through (see section 5.12 if you have forgotten the turn calibrations), and your wedge shaft should come from about horizontal on the backswing to vertical on the follow-through (Fig. 7.2.2).

Again, like the distance-wedge shot, the swing plane includes the lines from the ball through your shoulders (Fig. 7.2.3). Keep the club on this plane (until your head comes up as you finish) with a synchronized finesse turn, and you won't have to make any compensations with your dead hands and wrists. Start

Figure 7.2.2: A horizontal-to-vertical shaft swing will deliver a 15-yard (approximately) pitch shot

Figure 7.2.3: The clubhead stays in the swing plane on pitch shots until you stand up in your finish

every shot, on the practice tee and on the course, with your preshot ritual: It won't work for you later, under pressure, unless you ingrain it into your preshot routine along the way.

7.3 Standard Pitch Recap

1. At the perfect time in your preshot ritual, start the swing by moving everything together—legs, hips, upper body (shoulders, arms, hands, and club)—synchronized and in rhythm, away from the target.

2. The arms move with the rest of the body; they neither initiate the motion, nor add any power. The fingers and hands are dead, being used only to hold on to the club, and cock the wrists.

3. Begin your wrist cock as soon as you start your takeaway; it should be accomplished gradually, and be completed by the end of your backswing.

4. During the through-swing, keep everything synchronized as you swing through the ball. Your body rotation and short-to-long swing will produce the natural, muscle-free stability necessary for efficient and repeatable pitching.

If you want to see a great 15-yard pitch, examine the sequence in Figure 7.3.1 carefully. Payne Stewart is so good at these shots, I think he's trying to make it almost every time.

Figure 7.3.1: The 15-yard pitch, Payne Stewart style

Other Pitch Shots

7.4 S-Wedge, L-Wedge, and X-Wedge Shots

Many golfers think pitch shots are hit only with pitching wedges. Not in my book!

All four wedges can and should be used in your pitching game (and in your sand, distance-wedge, and chipping games, as well), because every shot calls for different shot characteristics. If different clubs can help you shape your pitch shots for better and more consistent results, and make them easier to hit, then use them.

Because I firmly believe you should use all your wedges in all these ways, I have renamed my own four wedges *Perfect*, *Sensational*, *Lovely*, and *eXcellent* (PW, SW, LW, and XW), as you'll see in Chapter 10. This removes any tendency to stereotype them by name. So a sand wedge isn't only for the sand, and so on.

However, if you are going to be successful using four wedges inside 100 yards, you have to learn about them, learn what you can do with them, and just as important, learn what you should *not* do with them. In Figures 7.4.1 to 7.4.4, you can see that each of the four wedges creates a different launch angle for its pitch shot, which, of course, produces different reactions on the green. Furthermore, the clubs differ in shaft length, head weight, sole configuration, and lie angle (see

Figure 7.4.1: Pitching wedge launch angle

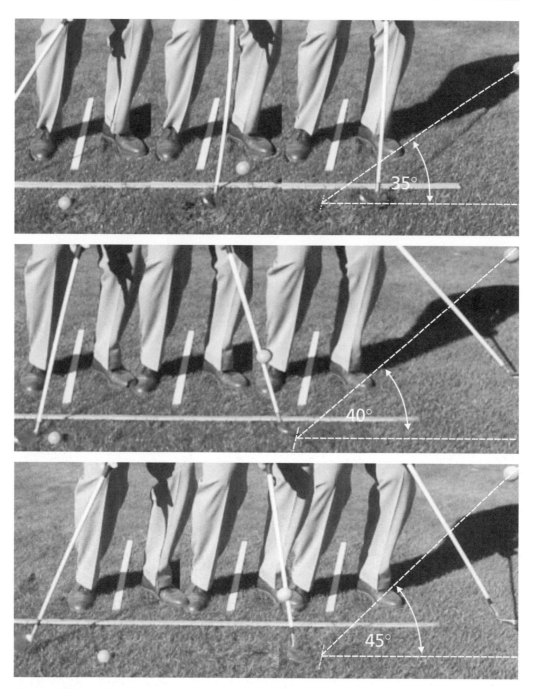

Figure 7.4.2 (top): Sand wedge launch angle **Figure 7.4.3** (middle): Lofted wedge launch angle **Figure 7.4.4** (bottom): Extra-lofted wedge launch angle

Chapter 10 for more about equipment specifications). These differences combine to produce the specific performance of each club.

Most of these clubs also can be used for cut lobs from grass, as well as off hard-pan lies. Likewise, each has an application from the rough and tight fairway lies. It's all a matter of what the golf course gives you. The more options you can handle, the better your chance of hitting the shot you need when you need it.

7.5 Cut Shots

As mentioned in the last chapter, if you need a high, soft shot, the most accurate way to hit it is with a high-lofted wedge with the face square. Similarly, when you want to hit a cut shot, lofting it even higher than the standard wedge shot, don't position the ball forward in your stance. Moving the ball ahead of the center of your stance requires you to move the bottom of your swing arc forward to hit the shot solidly. From this position, golfers either hit fat shots or slide their knees and "chase" the ball with their hand muscles to alter their swings, as shown in Figure 7.5.1. Here, subconscious compensations must be made. Compare this with the beautiful cut-pitch swing of Payne Stewart in Figure 7.5.2.

To hit the high cut-lob pitch shot, follow the directions for a cut-lob distance-wedge shot (section 6.12), modifying it for your finesse-pitch swing. Narrow your stance, open the clubface, aim left of the target, and keep the ball exactly in the center of your stance (between your ankles) relative to your new swing line (Fig. 7.5.3). Spend some time beforehand learning how far left you need to aim to

Figure 7.5.1: Forward ball position requires hands and knees to overwork to avoid fat shots

Figure 7.5.2: Payne Stewart executes a 12-yard cut shot

fly your shots at your target (using the same general procedures as detailed in section 6.13).

Test your cut-lob technique off tight and hardpan lies. This may sound sadistic, but if you're comfortable hitting a cut lob off hardpan, you'll have no problem from a good lie. Remember to keep your hands and arms soft, and let your finesse swing and club do the work. One thing that is very different from your normal pitch is the size of the swing necessary with a cut lob: When the clubface is wide open, it's not unusual to need a 9:00 o'clock backswing to fly the ball just 15 yards.

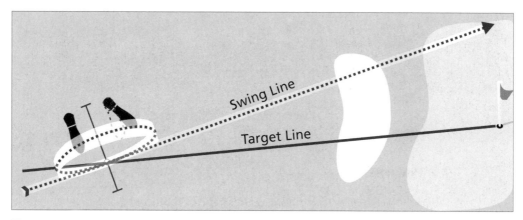

Figure 7.5.3: Setup for a cut-lob pitch shot

Are You Making Compensations?

Once you're comfortable hitting the short cut lob, do me a favor. Go to a private spot—the far end of the driving range or an empty field (so you won't be embarrassed if you hit a few bad shots)—and hit cut lobs with your eyes closed. Set up with your eyes open, place the ball in the center of your stance, and go through your normal preshot routine and ritual. But as you start your takeaway, close your eyes (as I demonstrate in Fig. 7.5.4). Don't open them until the swing is finished, then look and see how you did.

Closing your eyes will reveal if you've been compensating for poor ball position: If the ball is too far forward, you'll have trouble hitting good eyes-shut shots, because you won't be able to compensate with your hands or body. If you hit good shots with your eyes closed, your ball position is fine. If, however, you tend to hit behind the ball, move it back a little in your stance.

I ask my pros to hit practice shots with their eyes closed all the time. They usually perform just as well with them shut as open. What does that tell you?

Figure 7.5.4: The eyes-closed, 15-yard cut-lob pitch shot

7.6 Pinch Shots

Do you understand what produces spin? To impart backspin (spin that would bring the ball back toward the golfer), the face and force of the club must contact the ball below the ball's center of mass. Figure 7.6.1 is a simple sketch of that happening.

Therefore, it follows that overspin (or topspin) is produced by making contact with the club *above* the ball's center of mass (Fig. 7.6.2). However, it's hard to do this without skulling the shot: That's why thin and skulled shots fly so low and so far—no backspin. In reality, most golfers who talk about applying overspin actually are referring to the condition of "less than normal" backspin. It's minimal because although they may have made contact below the ball's center of mass, it isn't much below and the other conditions necessary for backspin are not present.

What are those conditions? Primarily the loft and angle of attack of the clubhead, and the surface below the ball. When the surface is firm, offering good resistance, the ball actually can get "pinched" against it (Fig. 7.6.3). When the ball is pushed down and dragged along a firm surface, the "pinched" cover of the ball is stretched, then snaps back, producing some extra backspin. (It often damages the cover, which you see after the shot.)

The clubhead's angle of attack to the ball is the exact direction of the clubhead's movement (can be horizontal, upward, or descending), through impact. Even when no pinching is involved, the downward swing strikes a more glancing blow, and results in more backspin than when the clubhead moves horizontally, as in Figure 7.6.1, below. These spin differences can significantly affect whether or not the ball stops near the hole.

Figure 7.6.1: Lofted wedge face contacts ball below center, producing backspin

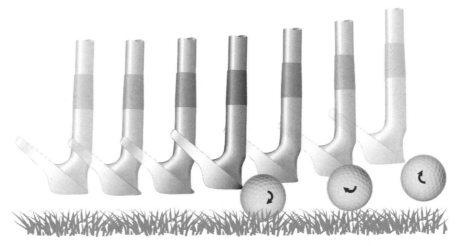

Figure 7.6.2: Skulled wedge shot contacts ball above center, produces overspin

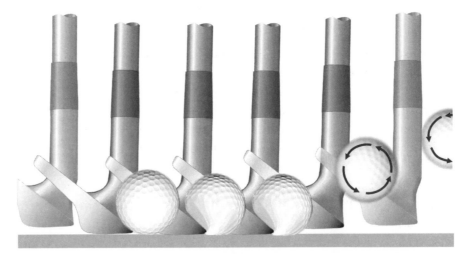

Figure 7.6.3: Descending blow pinches ball against hardpan,
producing maximum backspin

7.7 Minimum vs. Maximum Spin

To consistently pitch your shots and stop them within the "Golden Eight" feet surrounding the flagstick, you should be aware of how much or how little backspin can be imparted on shots from different lie conditions (as shown in Fig. 7.7.1) when:

| ½-inch grass | ¼-inch grass | hardpan dirt/sand |

Figure 7.7.1: A ball's proximity to a firm surface affects how much spin can be applied

1. There's nothing beneath the ball to pinch it against; typically when the ball sits up high in the grass.

2. The surface beneath and close to the ball is fairly firm, so the ball can be pinched against it; e.g., a normal lie on fairway grass.

3. The ball is in direct contact with something hard like hardpan dirt or sand. It's very easy to pinch the ball against the dirt or drag it through the sand with any downward swing. (A horizontal swing will pick it cleanly off the surface with no pinching, or else produce a skulled shot.)

On the golf course, one can use this knowledge of backspin and whatever is below the ball to determine what kind of shot to play, how much backspin it will have, and where you want it to land.

I recommend using one of two swings to control the backspin on your pitch shots—one for maximum backspin, and one for minimum backspin. Both are reliable and consistent. Once you decide which to use, you must read the green for that shot. If you then execute reasonably well, you will end up near the hole.

To achieve the minimum-backspin-shot swing, you must always execute the same way, from all the lies—by making your clubhead travel horizontally through the impact zone. This can be achieved with a stiff-wristed (no wrist cock) swing, in which the angle of approach to the ball is low and stays low after impact, as seen in Figure 7.7.2. It also helps to use as little loft as possible, by taking a lower lofted club, and contacting the ball as near its center as you can.

To produce maximum backspin, create the most descending blow you can and pinch the ball as firmly as possible against the surface beneath it (Fig. 7.7.3). If there's nothing beneath the ball, a more descending motion will produce a low-trajectory shot but only moderately more backspin. Increasing your clubhead loft at impact by opening the face will also increase spin a little, as impact occurs farther below the ball's center of mass. This will produce some backspin, but not as much as in the pinching action discussed above.

Figure 7.7.2: The zero-wrist pitch shot produces minimal backspin

Figure 7.7.3: Pinching with a descending blow maximizes backspin

Shot Behavior

7.8 Don't Hit into Slopes

Here is an example of how golf, especially pitching, is more than simply hitting the shots.

Every year at the U.S. Open, I hear a few players complain about how the officials who set up the course are evil, unfair, and trying to keep them from shooting too far below par. Players think this because every Open course seems to have a few greens that behave oddly. When players hit to these greens, the surface is so hard and fast that the shots don't hold but roll into trouble behind. Unless the shot is absolutely perfect—landing on the right spot near the front, with maximum backspin—it has no chance of staying on the putting surface. But if they try to land the shot short and bounce it onto the green, the ball stops short. The front of these greens appear to be much softer than the surfaces themselves, so the (expletive deleted) officials are blamed for watering the front of the greens but not the greens themselves.

One year, after talking to the course superintendent and learning that the fronts of the greens had not been watered, yet still hearing the players' complaints, I decided to investigate to find out what was really happening. I learned that it was a simple matter of golfers not understanding the physics of slopes and bouncing balls.

Begin by understanding that a golf ball bounces off a firm surface (when it makes no significant pitch mark) like a beam of light bouncing off a reflective surface (Fig. 7.8.1). The physical law describing this says the incoming angle equals the outgoing angle. That's how most drives bounce off a hard fairway (Fig. 7.8.2): The lower the ball comes in, the lower and farther it bounces forward; the higher it comes in, the higher and shorter it bounces out and forward. We see it, and expect it, on drives and fairway wood shots that we perceive as having little spin.

But golfers don't carry that understanding to iron shots flying into greens. There, we make two mistakes: (1) we expect backspin to stop an iron shot close to where it lands; and (2) we have no idea how changing the slope of the landing area changes the angle of the bounce.

Mistake 1 is explained in section 6.9. It's the ball's pitch mark depth that pri-

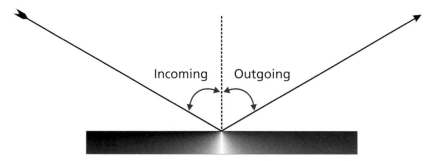

Figure 7.8.1: Light beam bounces off reflective surface; angle of incidence (incoming) equals angle of reflection (outgoing)

marily controls the first bounce, not the spin. When a ball lands on firm fairway grass short of a green and there's no pitch mark, the bounce should follow the laws of physics (the outgoing angle should equal the incoming angle).

It's mistake 2 that gets us. Figure 7.8.3 shows what happens when the slope of

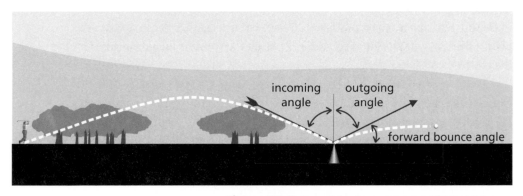

Figure 7.8.2: Low drive bounces low off hard fairway

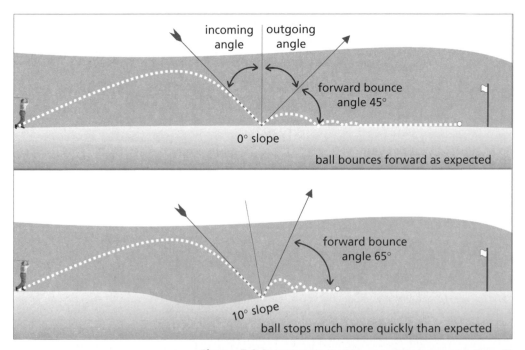

Figure 7.8.3: PW pitch shot bounces 20 degrees higher off 10-degree slope (bottom) compared to flat surface (top)

the landing area is changed by 10 degrees. This changes the bounce angle by *twice* that—20 degrees. (It's a change of 10 degrees on the approach plus 10 degrees on the bounce—20 degrees total.) That's the explanation of U.S. Open greens. A small change in the slope of the landing area makes twice as big a change in the bounce angles of shots landing there.

Here's a more extreme example of this effect (Fig. 7.8.4). Imagine you are hitting a pitching-wedge shot into a hard green with lots of trouble behind it. The area in front of the green has a modest 22-degree slope. Your shot is perfect, so you expect it to land just short of the green, coming in on a normal 45-degree approach angle, and bounce 45 degrees forward onto the green. But when it hits the 22-degree-sloped landing area, the bounce angle is changed by almost 45 (22 times 2) degrees. Instead of bouncing 45 degrees forward, the ball bounces 90 degrees—straight up into the air! It doesn't bounce one inch forward, and wouldn't bounce forward if the landing area were concrete. All because of the physics of bounce angles, not water or U.S. Open officials.

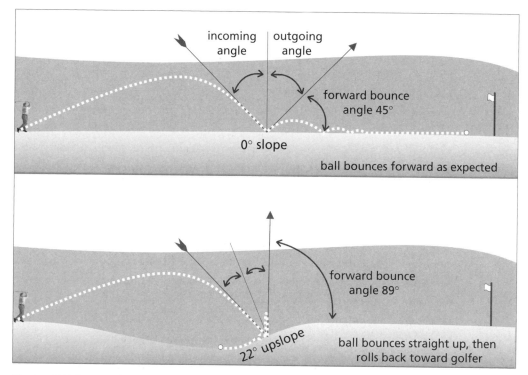

Figure 7.8.4: PW pitch shot bounces straight up, not forward, off 22-degree surface

The lesson is this: Don't land your pitches on slopes. If you try pitching into upslopes, you will probably finish short of the pin. Conversely, when you pitch onto downslopes, the effect is reversed and the ball will bounce forward lower by *twice* the downslope angle, sometimes so far forward it won't even stay on the green. So if possible, always pick the shot that will land the ball on flat ground, where you can judge the first bounce and roll more accurately.

It's worth making the point here that this effect is exaggerated, or much more noticeable, with wedges because their approach angles are so steep. People don't think about it as much with a 6-iron because the shot isn't coming in on such a steep angle and at least still bounces forward (although less than expected), even off upslopes of 20 to 25 degrees.

7.9 After It's on the Green

As I've mentioned previously, every short-game shot has two parts. The first part, the physical execution, is the swing, which produces the different characteristics of trajectory, velocity, and spin that you learn so you can land the shot on a particular spot. The second part is the reaction of your ball to the green after it lands. You must be able to anticipate this reaction, to "read the shot." It's the same if you want to be a good putter: You must be able to perform the mechanics of putting plus read the green to know how the ball will react. To be a good short-game player, you must be able to hit the shot and know what's going to happen to it. Messing up either part ruins the end result, unless you are lucky. And good players don't depend on luck.

You'll never have an accomplished pitching game if you can't land your shots consistently on the spot you want. You must be able to do this with every wedge in your bag. That's the first part, execution, which I've talked about a little bit already and will discuss more in Chapter 12. Right now, it's time to detail the different responses you can expect from pitch shots with each club on the greens.

A key to pitching success is practicing with each of your wedges. Each club will produce a different trajectory, different height, different backspin characteristics, and different bounce and roll behavior on the greens. While this may seem overwhelming, it doesn't have to be. I'm not suggesting you practice, master, and memorize every possible pitch-shot situation. But you do need to practice enough to learn which combinations work best for you and are easiest for you to visualize and produce. You must practice enough to develop a favorite shot, while knowing which shots to avoid. The favorites will become the shots you go to when the pressure is on because you can execute them with confidence and reliability.

The next few sections cover generic behavioral characteristics of the pitch shot. As you read them, some facts will stick out and stay with you; others may not mean a thing. The only way you'll ingrain any of them in your game is to see for yourself what works and what doesn't. My observations are based on research, and I believe in them 100 percent. But, as the old saying goes, you have to "see it to believe it." In the end, you'll have to practice for yourself.

I recommend landing all pitch shots at least three feet onto the green surface and not in the fringe. I would rather hit a higher, softer shot with a 64-degree X-wedge and land it safely on the green, than take a lower lofted wedge and try to bounce the ball through the fringe. The fringe will produce more bad bounces than will the putting surface. Fringes are not designed to be pure, smooth surfaces; greens are. Most fringe areas are not top-dressed, aerified, rolled, verticut, and smoothed to produce the consistent results that great up-and-down play requires. Fringes are for flying over, greens are for flying onto. (Unless you're playing Augusta National, in which case the fringes *are* smooth, and may be safer than those lightning-fast greens.)

How do you control shots after they land on the putting surface? Some players hit the ball low and spinning, while others bring shots in high and soft. Both techniques will work if properly executed and the greens behave predictably (unless pin locations require an unavailable stopping distance). However, I've noticed that the best finesse players use shot trajectory more often than spin to control the bounce and roll on greens. If you watch the likes of Tom Kite, Tom Watson, and Seve Ballesteros, you see a lot of high, soft shots that float up to and stop near the hole. Of course, they can, and do, hit low, spinning shots when necessary. But a soft shot dropping almost vertically will not bounce or roll too far no matter how soft, hard, or moist the green. Soft, high shots are very predictable when well executed. A well-struck, low, spinning shot is still completely dependent on the amount of spin and the condition of the exact spot on the green where it makes contact (for example, spinning balls don't stop well on wet or moist greens). And perhaps most important, the player has to create just the spin he wants with execution and ball contact; it's easier to hit the ball soft and high, with less spin, time after time.

Which shot and club you select should be determined by your skill at executing that shot, plus the shot's margin for error and probability for success. And don't forget your subconscious. If you're not sure about a shot, give your subconscious a chance to help you decide. Imagine the shot, try to make a preview swing and feel it, and see how your subconscious feels. Give it the chance to join in the preparation process for the shot. That's why my short-game mantra is "see it, then feel it, and when you like it, do it."

Very simply, if you feel you can get your ball closer with a flop shot than with a bump-and-run, you should use your flop shot, and vice versa. Remember, the goal is to leave yourself with the shortest possible putt.

7.10 P-Wedge Flight vs. Roll

A look at some pitching-wedge data will give you an idea how these shots react for PGA Tour players. If you get the general flavor of what to expect from these shots when they are well executed, it will help when you begin to practice your own shots.

I ran this test with five different players, each hitting 50 shots at each distance, with a variety of conditions: across, with, and against the grain; on dry and wet green surfaces; on bent and Bermuda grass greens. All shots were hit with the players' normal finesse pitching swings, with no attempt to create extra spin or height. These were simple pitch shots to flat areas of greens rolling at average speed (between 7.5 and 9.0 as measured by a Stimpmeter). I tabulated the results so you can see an average performance, something you could look for when you're facing similar situations.

In Chart 7.10.1, you can see that pitching-wedge shots (49–50 degrees loft) hit

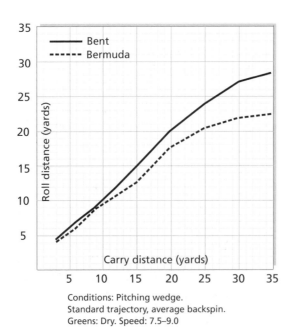

Conditions: Pitching wedge.
Standard trajectory, average backspin.
Greens: Dry. Speed: 7.5–9.0

Chart 7.10.1:
Carry vs. roll distance
for PW shots

across grain rolled approximately the same distance on the bent grass green that they carried in the air. These shots rolled a little less on Bermuda grass. The result gives you a good baseline, and is easy to remember: When you pitch the ball with your P-wedge, expect a 50-50 split of carry distance to roll distance under these kinds of average conditions.

But not all shots are across grain to flat pin positions. In Charts 7.10.2 and 7.10.3, you can see that when the pros pitched with and against the grain, there were large differences on the Bermuda green—hitting into the grain killed the roll, while hitting with the grain increased the roll—but only small effects on the bent grass green. So when hitting a pitch to a Bermuda green, check whether your shot will be coming in with or against the grain of the grass before you decide how far to fly it. On bent, however, it doesn't matter much.

What about wet greens? Shots were first hit to dry greens, across grain, and measured. Then the greens were thoroughly watered, and the same shots hit again. It is clear that pitch shots are more affected by rain when playing to bent greens than Bermuda greens (Chart 7.10.4).

Don't take these data and charts too seriously, because your shots will behave a little differently, based on your swing mechanics. Use this information as a guideline to begin learning about the second half of your pitch shots when you practice.

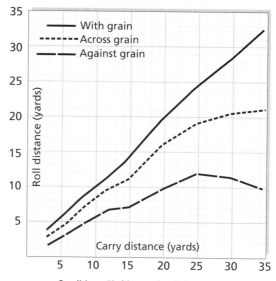

Chart 7.10.2: Grain effects on Bermuda greens

Conditions: Pitching wedge (loft: 49° or 50°). Standard trajectory, average backspin. Greens: Dry. Speed: 7.59.0

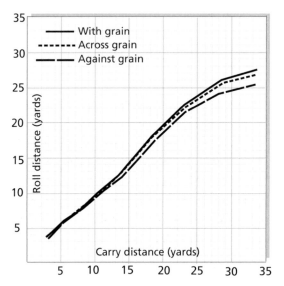

Conditions: Pitching wedge (loft: 49° or
50°). Standard trajectory, average backspin.
Greens: Dry. Speed: 8.0–9.0

Chart 7.10.3:
Grain effects on
bent greens

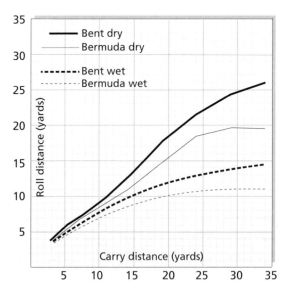

Conditions: Pitching wedge.
Standard trajectory, average backspin.
Greens: Dry. Speed: 7.5–9.0

Chart 7.10.4:
Dampness effects on
bent and Bermuda greens

7.11 Loft Affects Roll

When I was taking the data of the Tour pros, I had them hit shots to the same greens with other wedges besides the P-wedge. This information will further help you learn the details of your game. Again, don't take it as gospel; use it as a general guideline.

When looking at a shot, begin by thinking that if you hit it with a pitching wedge, the ball will roll about as far as it flies. Then modify this estimate by the conditions of the green, as discussed above. Also remember that if you bring your shot in higher, the ball will make a deeper pitch mark in the green and will stop faster.

Look at the pros' average results—on flat, dry, bent, and Bermuda grass greens—comparing shots with a sand wedge and lofted wedge to the pitching wedge (Figs. 7.11.1 and 7.11.2). While the pitching-wedge roll roughly equaled the carry in the air, sand-wedge shots rolled less, about two-thirds as far. L-wedge shots rolled only

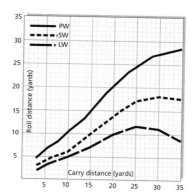

Conditions: PW (loft: 49°–50°);
SW (loft: 54°–55°); LW (loft: 59°–60°).
Standard trajectory, average spin.
Greens: bent. Speed: 8.0–9.0

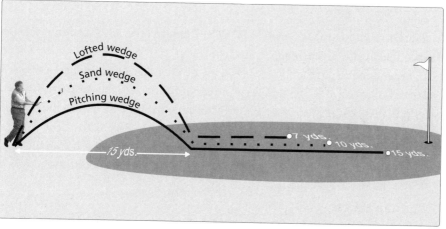

Figure 7.11.1: Carry vs. roll for different loft wedges (bent grass)

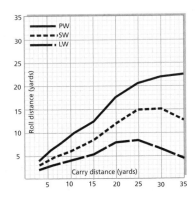

Conditions: PW (loft: 49°–50°);
SW (loft: 54°–55°); LW (loft: 59°–60°).
Standard trajectory, average spin.
Greens: Bermuda. Speed: 7.5–9.0

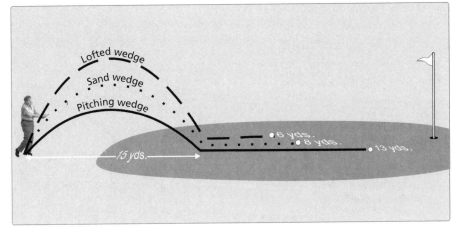

Figure 7.11.2: Carry vs. roll for different loft wedges (Bermuda grass)

one-half as far as they flew (when I say "rolled," I mean how far the balls moved after first contacting the green, bounce plus roll).

These numbers, while not exact for any given golfer or particular shot, are a good indication of what you can expect on your shots. On flat, firm greens, land your pitching-wedge pitch shots about halfway to the hole. If you decide to pitch with your sand wedge, perhaps to carry farther over the fringe, fly the ball about 60% of the way to the hole. If you use your L-wedge, land it about two-thirds of the way to the hole, plus or minus a little based on the green conditions.

7.12 Spin Effects

I also can give you an idea of how the spin put on wedge shots will influence a shot's behavior on the greens. In general, you can increase the spin on any shot by cocking your wrists and making a more descending blow than normal. Playing the ball slightly back in your stance and pinching it against a firm surface will maximize spin. To minimize spin, keep your wrists straight (zero wrist cock), and sweep through impact with as little loft as possible (relative to what the shot will allow). If you don't need either maximum or minimum spin, you probably can get more consistent results by playing your normal pitch swing and producing what I call the "normal" (mid) amount of spin.

I had the Tour pros try the same shots with each of these three spin techniques (maximum, minimum, mid). Chart 7.12.1 shows the results of their pitching-wedge shots. You can see that by pinching these shots, they stopped them in about half the distance of their minimum-spin shots.

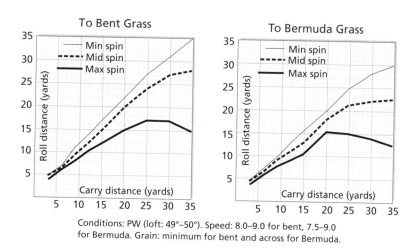

Conditions: PW (loft: 49°–50°). Speed: 8.0–9.0 for bent, 7.5–9.0 for Bermuda. Grain: minimum for bent and across for Bermuda.

Chart 7.12.1: Carry vs. roll effects for different spin rates (PW shots)

Hitting shots with their sand wedges produced the results shown in Chart 7.12.2. This time maximum spin stopped the shots even faster (shorter roll). And when they used their lofted wedges (Chart 7.12.3), their shots stopped shorter, and shortest of all when they were pinched.

There are a few other interesting results in this data:

1. Balls can be stopped faster on Bermuda grass greens than on bent grass greens of similar speed and firmness. Remember this if you play different courses around the country or the world.

2. The higher the pros hit their shots, the less effect spin had on where the balls

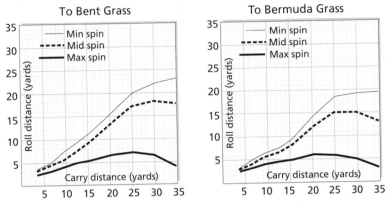

Conditions: SW (loft: 54°–55°). Speed: 8.0–9.0 for bent, 7.5–9.0 for Bermuda. Grain: minimum for bent and across for Bermuda.

Chart 7.12.2: Carry vs. roll effects for different spin rates (SW shots)

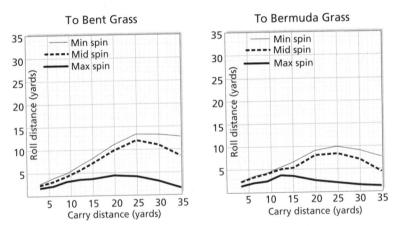

Conditions: LW (loft: 59°–60°). Speed: 8.0–9.0 for bent, 7.5–9.0 for Bermuda. Grain: minimum for bent and across for Bermuda.

Chart 7.12.3: Carry vs. roll effects for different spin rates (LW shots)

stopped. This should prove to you that the higher your shots come into greens, the less important spin is.

Relate this information to the advice everyone hears for short shots: "Get the ball on the ground and running as soon as you can." This axiom is true for those amateurs who cannot control how far they fly their wedge shots. But the pros often get their best results by bringing shots in high, landing them close to the pin—rather than the edge of the green—and not worrying about how far they will roll. As your pitching improves, you'll be able to hit shots this way, too.

7.13 The Grass Menagerie

To be a complete player, you must be knowledgeable about the different results produced by the types of grass you're likely to encounter. In this country, that usually means bent, rye-, blue-, Bermuda, and Kikuya grasses.

Characteristics of shots hit from bent, rye-, and bluegrass are relatively easy to predict, because the grass (unless extremely long) doesn't grab your clubhead as it heads into and through impact. They are finer, weaker blades, so the club slides through them without much effect, and the moisture content and firmness of the dirt below your ball are the main outside influences you need to worry about.

Bermuda grass is much more difficult to pitch from, especially in southern and coastal climates where the grain (the direction the grass grows) runs strongly in one direction or another. Chipping from Bermuda fringe is easy, perhaps easier than from bent, because the ball tends to sit on top of the short, thick, snarly blades. Pitching is a different story, particularly against the grain. Take several serious practice swings when pitching from Bermuda to judge the effect of the grain on your clubhead through the impact zone. Get as close as you can to an exact replica of the grass where your ball lies without moving it. Take several practice swings, watch and feel your clubhead pass through, and visualize what will happen in your real swing. When pitching against Bermuda grain, always move the ball back slightly in your stance to assure solid contact from a more descending blow. You want to get the ball up and out as quickly as possible so that when the club gets caught in the grass and slows down, the shot is already away.

Kikuya grass is the rarest of the grasses mentioned, which is fortunate because it presents the most difficult problems when hitting distance wedges, pitches, and chips. It is the dominant grass in Japan, but I have played on it in California, at Riviera Country Club in Los Angeles. Kikuya plays like triple-strength Bermuda, with similar grain effects. It is tough even when pitching and chipping *with* the grain. To handle Kikuya, use very short clubs and practice making clean, crisp contact with the ball. If you're tall, grip down so your lower hand is completely on the shaft, below the grip; shorter players can get away with a few fingers of the bottom hand actually on the shaft.

What about the different grass on the greens? You will find Bermuda, bent, and ryegrasses on most greens in the United States, and they have seriously different effects on the ball after it lands on the putting surface, as shown in the previous section. But there are many new types or strains of bent and Bermuda grasses, as well as several new grasses, so here are a few general rules:

1. For greens cut to the same grass height, expect more roll on bent greens, a little less on the thicker, stronger-bladed Bermuda.

2. Expect almost no effect from the grain on bent grass, unless it is long enough for you to see it lying in one direction or the other.

3. Bermuda grain will have a strong influence on the roll of your chip and pitch shots. Hitting into the grain, the ball will stop much more quickly; when the grain is with you, the ball will roll farther than normal.

Since you'll be only a few yards off the green on a pitch shot, take a few extra seconds to walk and look from your landing area to the hole to see how the grain runs. Ask someone in your foursome or the pro shop before the round what kinds of grasses are on the fairways, roughs, and greens; it can make a difference.

Pitch-Shot Variations

7.14 Avoid Humps, Look for Valleys

I always recommend pitching to a flat area of a green, not to an upslope or down-slope (see section 7.8 for details), because it's easier to judge how your shot will bounce and roll off a flat surface. However, flat spots are not always available. If you must pitch onto uneven terrain, try to land the ball in a depression, not an elevation. Here's why:

In the center of Figure 7.14.1, I have diagrammed the perfect sand-wedge shot to a perfectly flat green: It lands and then rolls the perfect distance to the hole. However, since no one is always perfect, I've also shown how a shot hit slightly short of or past the perfect landing spot will behave. As logic would suggest, a shot hit three feet short of the perfect landing spot ends up about three feet short of the hole. A shot that lands three feet past the desired mark rolls only about three feet past the hole.

At the top of Figure 7.14.1, there's a hump at what otherwise would be the perfect spot to land the same sand-wedge pitch. But again, since nobody is always perfect, I also have shown how slightly long and short shots will behave. As you can see, these are not so good. The shot that lands three feet short of perfect will hit on the upslope of the hump, bounce up in the air (it's those incoming/outgo-

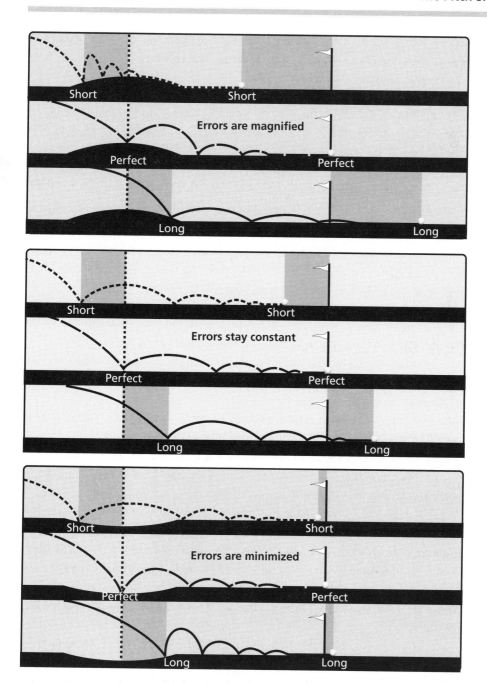

Figure 7.14.1: Pitch-shot execution errors can be magnified, unchanged, or minimized, depending on where they land

ing angles again), and finish nine feet short of the pin; the shot that lands three feet long hits on the downslope, kicks forward, and scoots nine feet past the hole. The hump magnifies any error you make.

Compare the hump to the bottom of Figure 7.14.1, in which a depression or valley is at the perfect landing spot. All three shots—the one hit short, the one hit perfectly, and the one hit too long—finish in the same place right by the hole. The short shot hits the downslope and kicks forward; the long shot hits the upslope and doesn't bounce as far. The one in the middle bounces "normally." And that's why you would like to aim all your shots at valleys rather than humps.

Here's a test. You are faced with a shot that is 30 yards to the pin, as shown in Figure 7.14.2. The first eight yards is sand, so a bump-and-run is out. You can choose a pitching wedge, carry it halfway to the pin, land it on the flat spot on the green, and if you hit it perfectly, it should roll close to the hole. Or you can choose your sand wedge and fly it about 60% of the way to the pin, to land in the bottom of the valley, so no matter how well you hit it, the ball should roll close to the hole. Or you can fly your L-wedge two-thirds of the way to the pin, to the top of the mound, and maximize any error you commit in your swing. It's your choice.

The smarter you play, the luckier you'll get. And the better you understand the game, the easier it is to make the smart decisions. (The answer, by the way, is the sand wedge. But you knew that.)

Figure 7.14.2:
Should you use your
P-, S-, or L-wedge
for this pitch shot?

7.15 Gripping Down

In section 6.10, I discussed how gripping down on your distance-wedge shaft will reduce the distance of those shots. The same principle applies to pitching and all short-game shots. If you are worried about hitting a soft enough shot—say, the landing area is downhill—grip down on the shaft. By effectively shortening the club, you take power out of your shots.

Internalize the feel for a shorter club at your practice green. Drop a few balls about 30 steps from a target pin. Pitch three or four shots to the pin with any club, using your normal swing and execution. Then grip all the way down to the end of the grip, putting your right index finger (for right-handed golfers) just onto the bare shaft, as shown in Figure 7.15.1. Pitch 10 more shots to the same pin. You will have to stand closer to the ball, crouch down a little, and make a much bigger swing to get the balls to the hole. The longer swing indicates that the shorter club has cut the power on the shot.

Figure 7.15.1: Gripping down on the shaft reduces power delivered to the shot

If you really want to get comfortable with the gripped-down pitch shot, find a difficult downhill shot and run the test again. First, pitch with a full-length shaft, followed by several shots to the same pin with a gripped-down grip and shortened club. You'll quickly learn the truth about many delicate shots around the green: It's easier to control the ball with a short club and a long swing than with a long club and a short swing. This truth stands strong for all the wedges.

7.16 Uneven Lies

I've been credited with saying that golfers hit their short-game shots much straighter on the practice tee than on the golf course. Of course, I didn't just say this: I saw it happen and I measured it. Then it took me several years to figure out why.

The reason is the ground beneath the golfer's feet. Many players don't understand that even on short shots around the greens, ground level influences aim.

The importance of aim, and how to aim properly, is discussed at length in sections 4.3 and 4.4. However, those sections assumed you were standing on level (horizontal) ground and hitting shots off level ground. However, many short-game shots start with the ball above or below the player's feet, creating all manner of directional problems.

First, let me define what I mean by the aim, or alignment, of your wedge. Figure 7.16.1 shows the golfer's perspective of a wedge on level ground: The wide bar is aimed from the leading edge of the clubhead toward the target. The smaller, round rod is aimed in the same direction, but points up along the approximate launch angle the ball would leave on if it were hit off the face five lines up from the bottom of the club (which is where most clubs feel the most solid). For clubs soled properly on level ground, both bar and rod point in the same direction. So whether you skull a wedge shot off the club's leading edge or hit it perfectly on the fifth face line, it will fly the same direction (although not the same distance or on the same trajectory). The true launch direction of the well-struck shot is what I call the "face aim" of the wedge, because wherever the wedge face is aimed, that is where the shot will fly (unless the wedge is moving sideways on a cut shot).

Figure 7.16.1: Leading-edge aim
(wide bar) and face aim
(narrow rod) of a wedge

As I said, this doesn't create a problem on level ground. However, many right-handed golfers have been told that when the ball is above their feet, they should aim a little to the right to compensate for the flatter, more around-the-body swing that results in a right-to-left hook.

But that's only part of the truth. Aiming a little to the right works well for full-swing long-iron shots. It does not work as well for short-game shots.

Look at the directional rod coming off the face of a 60-degree L-wedge (Fig. 7.16.2). When you place the ball above your feet and stand in a normal posture, the clubhead is higher than your feet. This not only flattens the swing plane, it also points the wedge's face aim dramatically to the left due to the severe loft of the clubface. The direction of the "leading-edge aim" doesn't change (so if you skull the shot off the leading edge, it will fly straight and not to the left). The problem I discovered follows from the fact that golfers aim with the leading edge of their wedges without realizing that this positions the face aim well left of their intended target.

Conversely, when the ball is below the feet, it probably will go to the right, right? Wrong. When the ball is below the golfer's feet, he does not have to change his posture or his swing plane so much. Instead, he crouches down a little more than usual and uses a longer-shafted club to reach the ball (Fig. 7.16.3). If he makes a good swing, hitting the ball solidly without catching the heel of the club on the ground, the ball usually flies dead straight to where he aimed. So while most

Figure 7.16.2: When the L-wedge leading-edge aim is slightly right of the pin, the face aim is still to the left

Figure 7.16.3: L-wedge leading-edge aim and face aim point in nearly the same direction when ball is below feet

golfers aim a little left to allow for a fade when the ball lies below their feet, I've measured that they miss this shot to the left more often than not.

Once you understand the phenomenon of uneven-lie alignment, it's easy to see why golfers perform poorly around the greens, especially on modern golf courses lined with moguls. (Look at Pete Dye's notorious Stadium Course at PGA West, in LaQuinta, California, in Fig. 7.16.4.) Learn to aim your pitches accurately and you'll have a leg up on your competition before you swing.

Figure 7.16.4: The humps, bumps, and moguls of PGA West are a golfer's "uneven-lie-heaven," courtesy of Pete Dye

Uneven Lies Cause Alignment Problems

Here are three face-aim directions—when the ball is above, below, and level with the feet—for an L-wedge when its leading edge is aimed straight at the target (Figs. 7.16.5, 7.16.6, and 7.16.7).

Compare these to the face aims taken by the same golfer, who now is aiming the

Figure 7.16.5 (top left): L-wedge, ball above feet: when leading-edge aim is at target, face aim is left **Figure 7.16.6** (top right): L-wedge, ball below feet: when leading-edge aim is at target, face aim is almost straight **Figure 7.16.7** (bottom): L-wedge from level ground: when leading-edge aim is straight, face aim is straight

leading edge of his L-wedge slightly right and left to compensate for the effects of the same two uneven lies on his swing plane (Figs. 7.16.8 and 7.16.9). This is how most golfers actually align their wedges, and causes their poor directional results from sidehill lies.

Figures 7.16.10 and 7.16.11, is the proper "leading-edge aim" the golfer should use to accomplish the proper face aim of his L-wedge for these lies.

Figure 7.16.8 (top left): L-wedge, ball above feet: when leading-edge aim is slightly right, face aim is still left

Figure 7.16.9 (top right): L-wedge, ball below feet: when leading-edge aim is slightly left, face aim is also left

Figure 7.16.10 (bottom left): Proper alignment for L-wedge, ball above feet: leading-edge aim substantially right so face aim is at target

Figure 7.16.11 (bottom right): Proper alignment for L-wedge, ball below feet: leading-edge aim only slightly left so face aim is at target

7.17 Tight Lies, Then Hardpan

Pitching from a tight lie, even hardpan, isn't particularly difficult unless you try it while using the wrong club. Wrong in the sense that many wedges have different sole configurations (the bounce on the bottom of the clubhead), which dramatically affect their performance. A sand wedge with lots of bounce, for example, is particularly ill-suited for tight lies.

The sole designs of the four wedges I recommend are detailed in section 10.10, but since we're discussing pitch shots off hardpan, look at Figure 7.17.1. Shown are the sole designs of a typical sand and L-wedge. The large amount of bounce on the sand wedge prevents the leading edge of the club from getting close to the ground; that can be helpful for sand play, but off a hard surface it would cause the club to hit behind the ball, bounce, and send the leading edge into the center of the ball. This is the classic cause of the skulled wedge off hardpan.

The L-wedge, however, has a small flange with not too much bounce, giving the golfer a reasonable margin for error in hitting shots a little thin or heavy without the dreaded skull. The margin for error can be increased by opening the clubface, aiming left, and playing the ball a little back in your stance. This technique is discussed in section 6.15 (distance wedge off a tight lie); the same applies to the pitch shot when using X-, L-, or P-wedges.

From tight lies, you also must not let your muscles get tight or your swing get handsy. Use your dead-hands approach to the finesse swing. Again, you can gain confidence in this shot by practicing with your eyes closed, but only after you learn precisely where to position the ball in your stance, and can hit great shots with your eyes open.

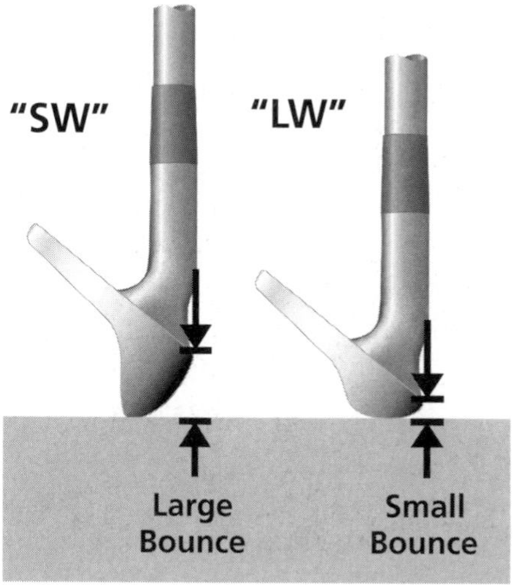

Figure 7.17.1: Different wedges are designed with different amounts of bounce

Special Pitches from Difficult Lies

7.18 From Serious Greenside Rough

You will occasionally encounter serious—what I call "U.S. Open–style"—rough around a green. The grass can be so long and deep that it's difficult to find your ball, even when you know it's only a few feet off the putting surface. When golfers encounter one of these deep-grass lies, they often step up and swing hard, simply hoping for the best. Sorry, but normal techniques won't work, no matter how hard you swing. To extricate your ball and get it close to the hole requires a well-executed plan, a specific method of delivering the clubface to the ball, and a little luck.

I don't want to mislead you: These are difficult shots. There is no surefire way to free your ball and get it near the hole every time. However, there are four shots you can play, one of which should get the ball up and out and onto the putting surface. Each technique is fundamentally different, and requires a fundamentally different mind-set and swing.

The four shots are the "Drop," the "Chop," the "Rip," and the "Blast."

The Drop

The idea here is to drop the club cleanly on the ball, but this shot requires two circumstances to make it possible. First, the ball can be no more than six to 12 inches into tall grass: The shot comes out so softly, the ball cannot travel through much more grass than that. Second, the grass has to be growing straight up so you can drop the club down through the blades and cleanly onto the ball. That won't happen if the grass is folded over.

The drop swing is fairly simple. Position the ball off your right (back) ankle, take a narrow stance, and lean as far forward as you can without losing your balance (Fig. 7.18.1). Take a finesse backswing, fully cocking your wrists (Fig. 7.18.2), and drop the club onto the back of the ball (Fig. 7.18.3). The downswing should drop as straight down as possible.

You're trying to slide the clubhead between the blades of grass, not cut through them. If you lean forward far enough, play the ball back far enough, and choke down on the shaft far enough, you should be able to put the clubface flush on the ball. If you can't make clean contact, don't try this shot.

There is no follow-through (Fig. 7.18.4). Again, the ball will come out of the rough low and soft, so don't try to hit it through too much grass or very far.

Figure 7.18.1 (top left): Setup for the drop shot from deep grass **Figure 7.18.2** (top right): Drop-shot backswing **Figure 7.18.3** (bottom left): The drop shot pops the ball out softly **Figure 7.18.4** (bottom right): The drop shot has no follow-through

The Chop

The chop works from a lie similar to the drop shot described on page 182, except the ball can be more than 12 inches into the deep stuff. Again, you want to get the clubface cleanly through the grass and down onto the ball. But the chop has more power and a follow-through, and you'll probably have to cut a little grass since you're going to drive the ball out of the rough rather than pop it as you do in the drop shot.

Play the ball well back, take a slightly wider stance (but still less than shoulder-width), and lean forward slightly (Fig. 7.18.5). Then make a longer backswing than on the drop shot and make certain your wrists are fully cocked (Fig. 7.18.6). Chop through the grass, delivering a descending blow through the ball trying to take a divot (Fig. 7.18.7), then follow through at least two feet past impact (Fig. 7.18.8). You probably won't make a divot, but trying to swing through will let you feel the power. You should see the ball fly out well ahead of the clubhead with plenty of speed.

The heavy grass will take all the backspin off the ball, so it's going to come out hot. Don't choose the chop to tight pin positions; you need room for the ball to roll after it lands.

Figure 7.18.5: Setup for the chop shot from deep grass **Figure 7.18.6:** Chop-shot backswing

Figure 7.18.7: When chopping, try to take a divot after impact **Figure 7.18.8:** The chop shot and follow-through

The Rip

When your ball is lying so badly, so far down in the grass that neither the drop nor the chop will work, try a rip swing.

I really don't consider the rip part of the short game. It's more a power swing than a finesse swing, but I include it here because it can be effective from a few yards off the green. The plan is to take a short club and rip through impact, ignoring the fact that there's a lot of grass in front of, around, and behind your ball. Rip through impact and move everything, ball and grass included, forward and onto the putting surface. Obviously, this is not a delicate shot that can be controlled with precision: That's okay, its purpose isn't control, just making sure you get the ball out and forward so you don't face a similar shot again.

Play the ball from the center of your stance (ankles), with a wide stance (shoulder-width), and choke down on the shaft as far as you can while still making a reasonable swing (Fig. 7.18.9). Make a big backswing, slightly past 9:00 o'clock (Fig. 7.18.10), and then rip through impact (Fig. 7.18.11), and don't worry where the ball is going to land or stop. The key to getting out is accelerating through impact and a full follow-through (Fig. 7.18.12).

Figure 7.18.9 (top left): Setup for the rip shot **Figure 7.18.10** (top right): Rip-shot backswing **Figure 7.18.11** (bottom left): Ripping through impact moves grass and ball forward **Figure 7.18.12** (bottom right): With such a short club, the rip follow-through is difficult, but important

This is one shot in your short game where I advise using all the muscles in your hands, arms, and wrists. Go ahead and release your power, finish your swing, and make sure you get the ball out in front of you somewhere.

The Blast

Use the blast when the ball is deep and the grass is lying over or clumping around the ball. The pin should be no more than about 30 feet from your lie.

The blast from grass is virtually identical to the blast from sand (detailed in Chapter 9), where you take a long swing with a long club and "scoot" the clubhead under and past the ball. The clubface never actually touches the ball; like sand, the grass blasts the ball softly onto the green. But there is one difference between the blast from grass and that from sand: Coming out of grass, don't expect much backspin, so these shots won't bite when they land. They'll be soft, and they won't roll too far, but there is no way they will bite or spin back on the green.

Holding your club at full-shaft length from a shoulder-wide stance, play the ball forward, off the heel of your front foot (Fig. 7.18.13), and make a pure 9:00 o'clock backswing (Fig. 7.18.14). Then swing through and past the ball (Fig. 7.18.15). The

Figure 7.18.13: Setup for the blast from tall grass **Figure 7.18.14:** Swing back to 9:00 o'clock

Figure 7.18.15: The blast from grass is similar to the scoot-and-spin shot from sand

Figure 7.18.16: The ball always comes out if you finish the swing

ball should come out high and soft. After a little practice, you'll develop good control as long as you complete the swing with a full, high finish (Fig. 7.18.16).

If you commit to finishing the swing, you'll never leave the ball in the rough.

7.19　From Nesty Lies

The nesty lie should be called the "nasty lie," because it is one of the trickiest in golf. As you can see in Figure 7.19.1, the ball actually looks as if it is sitting in a bird's nest. Because the top of the ball is visible, golfers think they can hit it out. However, it is almost impossible to make crisp, clean contact with a normal pitching swing motion.

If you swing hard and the ball comes out hot, it will fly way too far. If you swing too easy and you don't make clean contact, you'll fluff the shot and may have to try it again from just a few feet ahead.

I know of only two ways to get out of the nesty lie. If there's a lot of room for the ball to roll to the pin, use the chop shot, very similar to the chop used from deep grass (section 7.18). It should allow you to make "almost-clean" contact between the club and the back of the ball.

Position the ball well back in your stance; the nestier the lie, the farther back you play it. I've often played this ball behind my back ankle, as in Figure 7.19.2. Grip down on the shaft to shorten the club, lean forward so your natural downswing motion becomes more vertical, make a full-wrist cock on the backswing,

Figure 7.19.1: A nesty lie looks like an egg in a bird's nest

Figure 7.19.2: The chop shot from a nesty lie: Clean club-to-ball contact is the goal

and chop straight down on the back of the ball, expecting a very short follow-through. If you make good contact, the ball will come out low and with no spin, so it rolls a long way on the green.

When the hole is closer to you, try the blast. Just like the blast from tall grass (see page 187), this shot is similar to a blast out of sand except the grass is throwing the ball out with almost no backspin.

Play the ball well forward in your stance (Fig. 7.19.3), open the clubface, and aim left—like a normal sand shot. Make a 9:00 o'clock finesse swing and finish with a high, full follow-through. The ball will come out high and soft, and look like a sand shot until it hits the green. There, rather than biting and checking after the first hop, it will gently release and roll a significant distance.

Figure 7.19.3: Blasting from a nesty lie produces a soft shot without much backspin

7.20 From Tight Quarters

When something such as a tree (Fig. 7.20.1) behind the ball keeps you from making a normal backswing, try the "cock-it-first" swing, which is fun to play. I say it's fun because whenever I'm going to use it during a round, I make normal, full-length preview backswings. Then, as my companions watch, I step up to the ball and use my "cock-it-first" swing. Without fail, they say, "What did you do—why did you practice one way and make a different swing?"

Actually, I didn't change swings. The swing of the cock-it-first is identical to that of the normal pitch shot. The only difference is, the wrists were cocked before the backswing began. Cocking the wrists first reduces the size of the swing arc, so it requires less room than a normal backswing (Fig. 7.20.2), and the club is no longer restricted going back.

I start in a normal pitch address position, then fully cock my wrists without moving any other part of my body (Fig. 7.20.3). From there, I move my arms and body in a normal backswing: If everything turns away together, the top of the backswing looks normal (Fig. 7.20.4). Then, swinging down into the ball, the radius is smaller (Fig. 7.20.5). At impact, my body and club positions are that of a normal pitching swing (Fig. 7.20.6).

This works only if you do everything just like a pitch swing *except* for the early timing of the wrist cock.

Practice on the range by setting your bag or a chair behind you. Alternate shots, first your normal pitching motion with nothing behind you, then the cock-it-first pitch in front of the restriction. With a little practice, you'll find this an easy shot to master, and fun to pull off.

Figure 7.20.1: Someone put a tree behind my ball **Figure 7.20.2:** My normal backswing won't work

Figure 7.20.3: Cock your wrists up first in the "cock-it-first" swing
Figure 7.20.4: The "cock-it-first" backswing looks like a normal backswing at the top

Figure 7.20.5: Your normal finesse downswing will fit inside the tree

Figure 7.20.6: The "cock-it-first" swing arrives at impact looking the same as every other finesse swing

7.21 From Impossible Stances

Here is another fun finesse swing, which will come in handy when you can't make a reasonable golf swing from a normal stance. You'll use it when the ball is sitting well higher than normal—sometimes waist high or higher (which can happen when you're in the bunker but the ball is outside it, as in Fig. 7.21.1)—on the wrong side of a tree, or too close to a fence or hedge. In these predicaments, most golfers would try to swing left-handed. If the pin is inside 30 yards away, I prefer to use the same club as if my lie were perfect, but swing backward.

The backward swing is a simple, wrist-free motion (Fig. 7.21.2). Stand as close to the ball as you comfortably can without worrying about hitting yourself in the foot. The ball should be slightly in front of your toes (Fig. 7.21.3). Place your left hand on your right shoulder: The shoulder is your pivot point, and holding it with the left hand will remind you to keep it in place throughout the swing, ensuring solid contact and a reasonably good shot.

The backswing is about twice the length of the normal swing you'd make for a shot of the same distance. (You need a larger swing motion since there is no wrist cock providing power.) Keep the right shoulder still and focus intently

Figure 7.21.1: When the ball is well above your feet, shots become difficult

Figure 7.21.2: The backward swing

Figure 7.21.3: Ball position for the backward swing should be forward of your feet

on the ball throughout the swing. Practice and you'll get pretty good at it.

If you need to fly the ball more than about 30 yards, the left-handed swing using the back side of your 3-iron or putter probably will be required to give you the necessary distance.

7.22 From Shallow Water

Most golfers never consider hitting a ball out of the water. They're perfectly happy to take the penalty, utter a few deletables, and play on. However, if you can hit a ball out of sand, you can hit it out of water—as long as it's not more than a few inches below the surface and you don't try to hit it too far (Fig. 7.22.1).

To hit the water shot, you must have either a solid stance on the bank or be willing to take your shoes off (or get them wet). The pros hit this shot all the time because saving a stroke means more money to them than the cost of shoes. (They don't pay for shoes anyway.)

The key is to remember that water is like sand. Just like in sand, your wedge can either bounce off the water or dig into it. And again, just like when you are in sand, the ball should be positioned in your stance well forward for good lies (near the top of the water), and back in the middle of your stance for the buried (underwater) lies.

Figure 7.22.2 shows what to do when no more than one-third of the ball is underwater. Open your X-wedge all the way—90 degrees, so the face points to the sky—which positions the maximum surface area of the clubhead on the water at the bottom of the swing arc. Also play the ball forward in your stance, to ensure that the club will not cut into the water; rather, it will splash, bounce off the surface, and scoot under the ball.

Figure 7.22.1: The shot from water is just like a shot from sand

Figure 7.22.2: The one-third underwater shot

Figure 7.22.3 shows a ball about two-thirds in the water. Open the face about 45 degrees and move it back in your stance a little so it cuts into the water to the depth of a ball. The deeper the club cuts into the water, the harder you have to swing to maintain clubhead speed through impact.

When the entire ball is just under the surface (Fig. 7.22.4), play it back in the middle of your stance, square the clubface, and prepare to swing through firmly enough to move all the water and the ball.

Figure 7.22.3: The two-thirds underwater shot

Figure 7.22.4: The completely underwater shot

If your ball is two or more inches below the water's surface, play the ball slightly back of your stance center, and turn the club so it enters the water, toe first. It will then dig as deep as the power of the swing will take it. Don't try this shot if your ball is more than four inches below the surface, as few golfers have the necessary swing power.

By examining the splashes in Figures 7.22.2, 7.22.3, and 7.22.4, you can better understand how the clubhead is interacting with, and powering through, the water:

Staying Dry

If you are worried about getting wet from any water shot, wrap a towel around the right (back) side of your body. That way, when the water comes down, the towel will be there to protect you during the finish of the swing. Remember, your face and clothes may get wet, but they will dry later. If you don't save your water strokes, they stay on your score forever.

1. Ball one-third below the surface, clubface wide open: The club bounces off the water so almost no water moves forward. The ball comes out cleanly, much like a bunker shot but with less backspin.

2. Ball two-thirds below the surface, clubface open 45 degrees: As intended, the club gets deep enough into the water to get to the bottom of the ball. A significant amount of water is carried forward by the club. The ball will come out low and with no spin.

3. Ball totally underwater, clubface square: The club digs the ball out. A lot of water moves forward, and even more moves up. This shot requires a significant amount of power, so don't swing easy.

CHAPTER 8

Chipping and the Bump-and-Run

The Mechanics of Chipping

8.1 So Simple—Yet Difficult

Chipping is the second-easiest motion in golf. Only the putting stroke is mechanically and physically simpler to perform. And yet, for many golfers, chipping is their worst shot. Their level of inaccuracy when chipping is so high (as measured by my PEI data), that it was initially very hard for me to understand why. But I've got it now.

After studying the chipping swings and shots of a number of both Tour professionals and golfers in my schools, I have come to this conclusion: The chipping swing is *too* easy. What I mean is, because it is easy to do, you can learn to chip with bad technique and, at least in the early stages of your game development, your chips look good compared to your other shots. Later on, however, this poor technique will severely limit your effectiveness. Compounding the problem, when you finally decide it's important to improve—when you finally realize how many strokes you're losing—you don't know how or what to do to improve.

New golfers have no idea how costly poor chipping can be to their games. They don't know that they'll chip at least two to five times in every round for the rest of their golf careers. And they don't realize how unforgiving each chip really is. If you stub or chili-dip a chip (hitting the ground behind the ball), it adds a stroke to your score and you have to try again. When you run the ball way past the hole and have to chip coming back, it's the same thing—a wasted shot. Even when you think you chipped pretty well, if the ball doesn't stop inside the "Golden Eight" feet, you'll probably miss the first putt—another wasted stroke!

In an earlier chapter I mentioned one of the cardinal rules of the short game: "Hit the little ball (the golf ball), before you hit the big ball (the earth)." This is es-

Beginners, Take a Chipping Lesson

Have you ever heard of a new golfer beginning to learn the game with a chipping lesson? Me neither. Most golfers begin at a driving range and try to hit the ball hard and far with a driver. Since the golf swing is not very intuitive, they usually whiff a number of times, laugh a lot, and suffer a little embarrassment or humiliation. Then what do they do?

Human instinct tells them they've got to stop missing the ball. To be sure of making contact, they let the hands and wrists dominate the swing since it is initially easier to control a club this way. By the time they get around to hitting their first chip shot, they know how to swing a club only with their hand and wrist muscles.

Golfers who start with a lesson from a qualified teaching pro usually do better because he (or she) won't let them make too many whiffs with a driver before putting a 7-iron in their hands. He teaches them a good grip and the fundamentals of the swing. However, few pros teach chipping in the first five lessons, by which time most golfers have already played a few rounds of golf, chipping to every green, and chipped enough to know how easy it is to chip with their hands.

If you're teaching a friend, a child, or even learning golf yourself for the first time, I recommend you start with putting and chipping, using the fundamentals of the finesse swing as detailed in this book. You'll be amazed at how easy it is to learn to chip, and how nicely the chipping motion leads into finesse (and other) swings in subsequent sessions.

pecially crucial when chipping. Hitting the big ball first produces a fat shot, which adds a stroke to your score, creates embarrassment, and takes the fun out of the game. Fat shots also lead golfers to change their technique, which usually produces thin and skulled shots. We see all these symptoms and bad chipping in nearly every session of my Scoring Game Schools.

The chip is a simple shot made with a simple swing. It's easy to learn, easy to hit, and crucial to your success. It also can wreak havoc on your score if not done well. Read the following instruction carefully, practice, and you shouldn't have too many problems.

8.2 Dead Hands ... Quiet Wrists

The chip swing is a finesse swing, rhythmic and smooth, employing a body turn away and a return-turn through (part of the same turns described in Chapter 4 and shown in Fig. 4.12.1.) There is no coil, so no power is generated by the lower body. The low-power turning motion helps maintain the synchronized swing rhythm of your arms, shoulders, and club. This motion also allows you to adjust the power transferred to your shots in small, controlled increments by changing the length of the swing. You do *not* use your hands or wrists for power.

I can explain a good chipping swing very easily: Imagine that your arms form two sides of a triangle, with the line across your shoulders the third side. When chipping, keep the shape of the triangle constant and swing it in synch with your body (Fig. 8.2.1). That's all: no hand power, no lower-body power, no adrenaline problems. Don't let your wrists hinge or break down (and, of course, there's no wrist cock since you don't want the power). Avoid the temptation to "hit" a chip with the muscles of your hands.

Figure 8.2.1: The chipping-swing motion: Turn back (left), turn through (right)

Standing in front of a mirror, and without a club in your hands, make the motion a few times to internalize in your mind how it looks. Then hold a club and, without a ball, make a few more chipping swings (Fig. 8.2.2). Remember: no body power, no hand power, no wrist power. It's just a smooth swinging motion. And keep your triangle intact.

Hold on just firmly enough to keep the grip of the club in the same position in the triangle throughout the swing. Don't strangle the club trying to keep your hands quiet. In fact, the tighter you grip the club, the more likely you are to have active hands, which will "fire" through impact. (Fig. 8.2.3 shows severe wrist

Figure 8.2.2: Watch your own chipping motion

breakdown.) It will take only a modest amount of "mirror" practice, as you concentrate on rhythm, to get you making a hand-and-wrist-free swing.

If you are still too handsy and can't get rid of the "hit impulse," chip with a "ChipStick" (Fig. 8.2.4; see section 13.8 for more details) or chip "left-hand-low." Reverse the position of your hands on the grip (right-handers place the left hand below the right, as in Fig. 8.2.5). Practice this way while focusing on the rhythm of the swing; you may find it an effective way to chip on the course.

Figure 8.2.3: Poor chipping motion with wrist breakdown

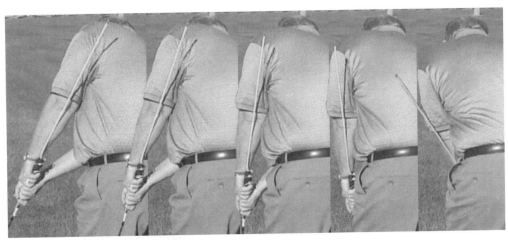

Figure 8.2.4: View from behind: ChipStick should never touch body

Figure 8.2.5: Left-hand-low chipping: makes no-wrist-breakdown chipping easy

Figure 8.2.6: Elbows out, large-wrist-angle chipping

Another way to quiet the wrists and hands is with the method taught by the great player and teacher Paul Runyan. He advocates swinging the club with a pure pendulum motion while setting and maintaining substantial angles among the elbows, forearms, and wrists (as set up in Fig. 8.2.6). As long as you don't "hit," and control the power of your chips with your muscle energy, it's OK by me.

8.3 Clean Contact

Crisp, clean contact is the number one requirement for good chipping. From normal fringe (fairly short grass) just off the green, you need to make a slightly descending blow to hit the ball cleanly. You don't want any grass getting between your clubface and the ball.

In keeping with the concept of requiring less and less power as you move from the distance wedge to pitch shots to chip shots, your chipping stance should be very narrow, only four to six inches between the insides of your shoes. Stand with 60% to 65% of your weight on your front foot, which will help you make a slightly more descending swing motion down and through impact for even cleaner contact.

Play the ball back about two to three inches behind your stance center. With such a narrow stance, that means the ball should be no farther forward than your back ankle (the right ankle for right-handed players), as pictured in Figure 8.3.1. Yes, that's what I said—the *back ankle*. To position the ball perfectly, address it with your feet pointed squarely at your target line (Fig. 8.3.2) and the ball across from your back foot. Then open both toes slightly, maybe 20 degrees toward your target, without moving your heels. You should be very close to the ball and standing tall. Raise your hands and bow both of your wrists a bit to keep them firm through the swing (Fig. 8.3.3).

Standing tall and raising your hands should have another result—the heel of your club will rise off the ground while the toe stays down. This is a good clue to look for as you set up (golfers who hit chips fat should be especially mindful of getting the heel up and toe down). Don't worry about stubbing the toe into the ground, because with the ball back in your stance, you will contact it well before the bottom of your swing arc, and the ball will be gone before the club scuffs the grass.

Be careful to align your clubface accurately in your setup, because with the ball two inches back in your stance, the tendency is to have your clubface open at address as shown in Figure 8.3.4. Left uncorrected, this would lead to shots starting out to the right, so be sure to check that your clubface is squared properly to your aim club and target line (Fig. 8.3.5). This may look slightly closed to you at

Arch Your Left Wrist

While you are reading this, run a quick test. Extend your left arm straight out in front of your body, keeping your palm vertical and your fingers horizontal to the ground. Move your hand from side to side in a fanning motion, with your eyes closed. Feel how easy it is to make that back-and-forth wrist motion.

Next, let your hand relax and, keeping your palm vertical, let your fingers point somewhat downward. Again, close your eyes and feel the energy required to move your hand from side to side. It will be a little harder than before to make this motion with your wrist.

Now, press your thumb downward and bow your wrist down as much as you can, positioning your hand at a strong angle to your forearm. Keeping the pressure on your wrist to stay bowed, try to move your hand back and forth. It will feel much more restricted this way. That's why you want to bow your wrists when chipping, to restrict wrist motion and avoid the possibility of any wrist collapse.

Figure 8.3.1: Ball position for chipping: on the back ankle

Figure 8.3.2: Start chipping setup with feet square to target line

Figure 8.3.3: Point toes toward target and bow wrists for chipping

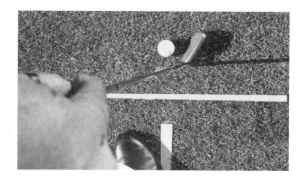

Figure 8.3.4: Golfer's view looking down. Chipping from back ankle allows clubface to open at address, which is wrong

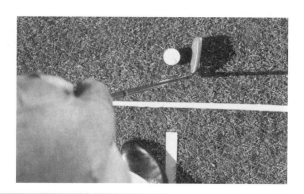

Figure 8.3.5: Always chip with clubface square to swing line and aim line

first, but don't worry, because when your chip shots are struck crisply, roll solidly toward the cup, and stop close to the hole, you'll learn to think this setup looks great!

8.4 Make a Stable Swing

The concept of stability, discussed at length in Chapter 4, is as important in chipping as in any other part of the game. To remain stable, use an accelerating swing but without trying to make it accelerate. By making a follow-through about 20% longer than your swing back (shown in Fig. 8.4.1), and using a rhythmic, smooth finesse swing (no "hit," no hands, no wrists, no fingers), you guarantee the clubhead will remain stable through impact.

Figure 8.4.1: Chipping swing: follow-through 20% longer than backswing

But don't overdo the follow-through, either. Forcing a normal backswing to go all the way through to waist level, as pictured in Figure 8.4.2, will force the use of some arm- and hand-muscle power that you don't want or need. Get into your rhythm as you execute your preshot ritual, make a rhythmic backswing, and let your natural finesse swing motion carry you to a longer finish.

Also avoid starting your backswing take-away with your hands. We often see this happen in our schools after instructing students to get rhythm into their chipping motion. Starting a chipping swing with the hands leads to cocking the wrists on the backswing (Fig. 8.4.3) and slapping at the ball through impact.

At address, position your hands in front of your left thigh (ahead of the ball) as

Figure 8.4.2: Active hand- and wrist-power promotes unwanted chipping follow-through

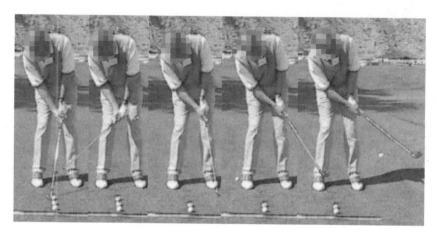

Figure 8.4.3: Chipping with hand-power leads to poor performance under pressure

you set your weight 60% to 65% over your lead foot. This puts your left side in the "pulling position," which, as you keep everything together through the swing, keeps your forward (left) arm ahead of and pulling the club into and through impact.

8.5 Chipping Recap

Always make a few preview swings through the same grass conditions that surround your ball. Once you see the perfect swing, step up to the ball, execute your preshot ritual, and go. Don't think or delay: Trust that when you repeat that swing, your result will be fine.

You should be standing close to the ball, your stance narrow, and the ball about three inches behind your stance center, on-line with your back ankle. As you lean slightly forward—about 65% of your weight on your front foot—keep your hands well ahead of the ball, aligned with the inside of your left thigh, your wrists slightly bowed. Stand close enough (crowd the ball) to raise the heel of your club slightly off the ground so the toe is down, and using parallel-left alignment, keep the clubface aimed squarely down the target line.

Make your finesse swing with your upper and lower body synchronized as you turn away and follow through. Keep your wrists firm but not tight; there must be no cocking or breaking down at any time. Use a light grip and dead hands. Your follow-through should be 20% longer than your backswing; as you hold the finish, watch your shot roll to the pin. Just learn to do this like Lee Janzen (Fig. 8.5.1) and you'll be excited about holing your shots often when you chip.

Figure 8.5.1: Lee Janzen chipping from 30 feet

Shot Behavior

8.6 What Happens on the Greens

Now that you know how to make a good chipping motion, the next questions are (1) How big a swing should you make? (2) What club do you use? and (3) Where should you land the ball? I'll discuss them in reverse order.

Every golfer has heard the advice to "get the ball on the green as quickly as possible," so it rolls toward the hole like a putt. That makes a lot of sense, but trying to cut it too close to the edge of the green is a surefire way of finding trouble.

Golfers are human, so there's a great likelihood of not always striking the perfect shot. This means you'll often be landing the ball a little longer or shorter than intended. For that reason, I recommend building in a margin for error by trying to drop the ball on the green about three feet from its edge: If you're a little short, the ball will still land on the green and roll nearly as expected; land it a little long and the ball will run just past the hole (which isn't bad, because you can watch it roll by, which helps with the read of the green when you're putting back). Just be sure to get the ball safely over the fringe, because reading how a ball will react through the fringe is less reliable than reading how it will react on the smooth, evenly watered, well-maintained green. And you'd always rather be putting than chipping your next shot. Always.

Which club should you use? Some golfers chip with only one, usually the 7- or 8-iron. But do yourself a favor and practice so you're comfortable with a number of different clubs, from the 4-iron to the pitching wedge. Then you can make your club decision based on the shot you need and the conditions: The worse your lie and the closer you are to the green, the lower the trajectory you're likely to produce. Experiment to find out how far shots roll with each club after landing (see data on page 213) and how far they carry.

Remember that when you position the ball back in your stance, while keeping your hands forward (over the inside of your left thigh), the effective loft of a club drops. So your 8-iron will now play like your 6-iron. If you want a little more height in any situation, go to a 9-iron or wedge and make a slightly longer swing.

Another part of the equation is that golf balls bounce and roll different distances when coming in and landing with different trajectories and differing amounts of backspin (e.g., a low, running 7-iron shot vs. a higher flying chip hit with a delofted wedge). That's another reason to vary club selection, especially near the green, where a lower-lofted club usually means less backspin.

How long a swing should you make? That's actually the easiest question to answer for yourself, because if you've committed to a dead-hands finesse swing, making approximately a turn #1 backswing and following through to about a turn #2 position (see Chapter 5 to review turn positions), the length of your swing will be directly related to the length of the shot within the tolerances around this average "reference" swing. Shorter swings for shorter shots, longer swings for longer shots. With just a few practice sessions, your touch will tell you "a little more" or "a little less" as you tune in to your practice swings.

8.7 Lower Is Straighter

To amass some data on how chip shots behave on the greens, several years ago I enlisted the aid of Perfy, the mechanical robot (Fig. 8.7.1). I also use Perfy for putting tests. This time, I mounted chipping clubs in his "hands" and tested to determine the best chip shots under varying conditions. Starting with the ball 30 inches off the edge of the green, I had Perfy chipping to the flagstick with every club, from 4-iron through pitching wedge.

I programmed Perfy to repeat a "normal" chipping stroke: slightly descending blow, clubface square, follow-through moving straight down the line through impact. As the clubs (and lofts) changed, the trajectories, carry distances, and roll distances changed systematically. By this I mean the more lofted the club, the higher the ball flight; less loft, lower flight. Very much as you would expect.

Two results are worth noting. First, and fairly obvious, the greater the loft, the bigger the swing necessary to get the ball to the hole. And, of course, the lower the loft, the shorter the swing to cover the same distance.

Second, and more important, the results consistently showed that the lower the ball flight, the straighter the bounce when the ball landed on the surface (see data in Fig. 8.7.2). This means that whether you face a normal green surface or one with side slopes or minor inconsistencies in your landing area (but no unusual up- or downhill slopes that would make shot reactions difficult to judge), the lower-lofted

Figure 8.7.1: Perfy chipping from the fringe

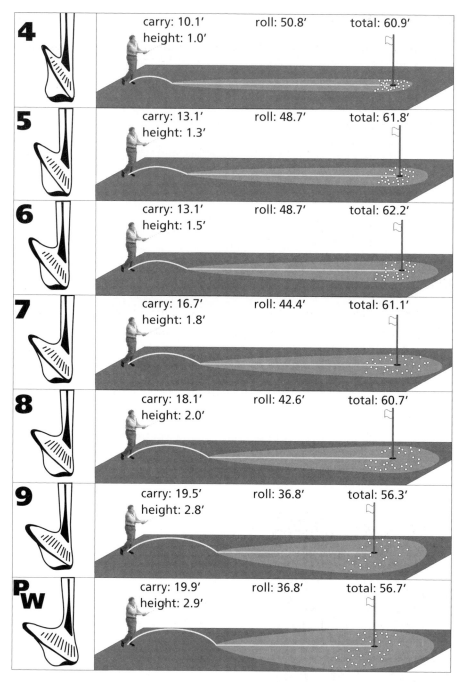

	carry: 10.1'	roll: 50.8'	total: 60.9'
4	height: 1.0'		
5	carry: 13.1'	roll: 48.7'	total: 61.8'
	height: 1.3'		
6	carry: 13.1'	roll: 48.7'	total: 62.2'
	height: 1.5'		
7	carry: 16.7'	roll: 44.4'	total: 61.1'
	height: 1.8'		
8	carry: 18.1'	roll: 42.6'	total: 60.7'
	height: 2.0'		
9	carry: 19.5'	roll: 36.8'	total: 56.3'
	height: 2.8'		
PW	carry: 19.9'	roll: 36.8'	total: 56.7'
	height: 2.9'		

Figure 8.7.2: In chipping: lower flights for straighter bounces and smaller scatter patterns

club will make the ball bounce and initially roll straighter on your expected line than a higher-lofted club.

Remember to give yourself a good margin for error. Even though you want the straightest bounce, it's more important to take enough loft to fly the ball at least three feet onto the green so it doesn't land in the fringe by mistake.

8.8 No Backspin

In another Perfy test, I gave him a pitching wedge and set him up to loft the ball safely onto the green. Then I had him hit shots with the ball positioned in three different places in his stance—the center of his stance, one ball-diameter (slightly more than 1.5 inches) behind center, and two ball-diameters back. As shown in Figure 8.8.1, the farther back in the stance the ball was positioned, the lower it flew and the more backspin it had upon landing.

Initially, these results surprised me because I had assumed backspin was the main factor controlling a ball on the green and was good. However, watching Perfy, I learned a lesson: The greater the backspin Perfy put on his chip shots, the greater the dispersion pattern of balls on the green.

This disparity in direction and distance seemed to have two sources. First, the greater the spin on the ball, the more inconsistent the "action." So from the center-stance position, Perfy produced very little backspin and the balls rolled almost the same distance every time. But from the two-balls-back position, there was significantly more backspin, which produced a much wider range of distances.

A similar, but perhaps more important, finding was that the greater the backspin, the farther off-line the ball bounced. Put another way, more backspin means more difference in direction. This surprised me at first, but again it makes sense: The more backspin on your shot, the more its reaction depends on the condition of the landing area. Put less spin on the ball and it will have a more consistent reaction and be less dependent on what's happening in the landing area.

Both of the above reactions mean that good chipping calls for less backspin. However, one result seems to fly in the face of the no-backspin recommendation. Clubhead-to-ball contact was most consistent from the farthest back-ball position, because that was when the least amount of grass got between clubface and ball. So not only did that setup produce the most backspin but those shots carried the most consistent distance.

What's my conclusion? From good lies, chip the ball low with minimum backspin: Take a lower-lofted club (as long as you can make solid contact) and carry the ball onto the green without rolling it too far past the hole. However, as the lie

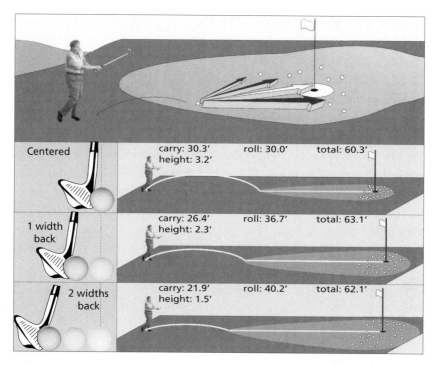

Figure 8.8.1: In chipping, less backspin produces more consistent roll

gets worse, move the ball farther back in your stance and use a more lofted club to assure clean, solid contact. Because without good contact, your shots won't land near your projected landing area and you won't produce good shot patterns.

Of course, this data depends on your ability to execute the shot. Just because Perfy proves one ball position is statistically better doesn't mean that's the shot you must use. If you feel more comfortable with a different shot, it's probably the one you should hit. So give the different combinations of club and ball position a try to see which are best for you and your game.

8.9 Keep the Face Square

Another Perfy test produced one more interesting result: Reactions on the green are more consistent from chip shots when the ball starts with no sidespin. In other words, people who cut across or try to hook their chip shots are doing themselves a disservice.

In this test, I set Perfy to roll three distinct sets of chip shots: one, a square clubface traveling squarely along the line through impact; two, a swing line aimed to the left and clubface opened 20 degrees to the right; three, a swing line aimed to the right but clubface closed 20 degrees to the left.

The results (Fig. 8.9.1) were very consistent. The more sidespin Perfy put on shots, the less consistent was their pattern of bounce and roll. Compare this to previous tests that proved a lower flight produced a straighter bounce. With sidespin, this effect was negated. Even the lowest shots, produced with the clubface shut down (closed), produced slightly more scatter than those with less sidespin.

The cut shots were obviously less consistent, because they had not only more loft but increased sidespin, both of which make the ball behave erratically on the green. It was clear from this test that, all other things being equal, if you can roll the ball with a square clubface, avoiding all sidespin, your results will be more consistent.

So whenever possible, aim your clubface square to your aim line (the line you

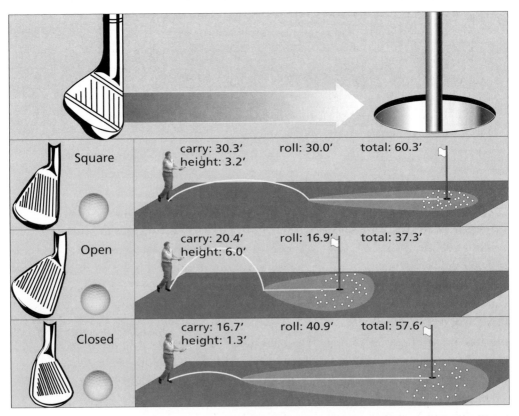

| | carry: 30.3′ | roll: 30.0′ | total: 60.3′ |
| Square | height: 3.2′ | | |

| | carry: 20.4′ | roll: 16.9′ | total: 37.3′ |
| Open | height: 6.0′ | | |

| | carry: 16.7′ | roll: 40.9′ | total: 57.6′ |
| Closed | height: 1.3′ | | |

Figure 8.9.1: In chipping, sidespin increases scatter

wish to start the ball on) when chipping. Depending on the openness of your stance, "square" actually might look slightly left of the line you want, but this compensates for the ball-back position at address. And I assure you, square will look just fine after a few good practice sessions.

Avoid the Humps, Aim for the Dips

Most pros try to land their short shots on a level surface, because it's much easier to predict the ensuing roll. When you can't hit to a flat spot, try to follow this rule: Avoid humps; aim for dips. If this sounds familiar, that's because I said it in the last chapter when referring to pitch shots. What was true then is true now, and for the same reasons.

Landing the ball on top of a hump or rise in the green magnifies any error in your swing or green-reading judgment. Underswing, so the shot is short, and you'll hit into the upslope of the hump: The ball will bounce up at double the angle of the slope, slowing it considerably and leaving you well short of your target. Hit the ball long and it will land on the far side of the hump, kick forward at twice the angle of the downslope, and run well past the hole.

However, if you can land the ball in the middle of a dip or depression in the green, go for it. If you land short, the downslope will kick the ball forward, making up for your lack of carry. Hit it a little long and you'll catch the upslope on the far side of the dip, slowing the ball's progress. Total distance of all three shots—off the middle, downslope, or upslope of the dip—will be about the same, offering the largest possible tolerance for error in your shot execution.

8.10 To Putt or to Chip?

How to play from the fringe of the green may be the most difficult decision in golf, the reason being that there are so many options in clubs and shots. You can successfully use any of the 14 clubs in your bag. From driver to putter, I've hit every club from the fringe and have seen the Tour pros do the same.

You also can make many different swings. Because not much power is required, you can hit hands-only shots, left-hand-low shots, even split-grip shots. You can play the ball forward, center, or back in your stance, use sweeping or descending impacts, and the results will be reasonable at least some of the time. So the important question when you're standing in the fringe isn't "What shot can I get away with" but "What shot can I reliably get closest to the pin, or even possibly hole?"

I have several general rules for playing from the fringe (or within three steps of the green's edge), rules I recommend to my students both in our schools and on the pro Tours:

1. All other things being equal, simpler is better.
2. Commit before you hit.
3. See it (imagine the shot), feel it (practice the swing until you sense the perfect preview swing), then do it (within eight seconds of the preview swing).

I have several more specific rules, which give some order to the decision-making process:

1. From inside 50 feet to the hole, if there's no reason not to putt, then putt using your putting stroke.
2. From outside 50 feet, if there is no reason not to use a putter, use it with your chipping motion (see the "chiputt" in section 8.11).
3. If you're not going to putt, and the landing area is predictable, use the lowest-lofted club that will land the ball three feet onto the putting surface.
4. If the landing area is unpredictable (and likely unforgiving), fly the ball as close to the hole as you can.

If you are now slightly confused, don't worry. All will become clear once you start to practice these shots around the green.

Here are some examples of the sort of options you'll face the next time you have a chip shot. Remember, you want to choose the simplest shot that will handle the situation. Since the putt is the simplest shot in golf, it should always be your first choice, unless:

- You are so far from the hole, your distance perspective is poor and you're not sure you can putt it all the way there. Then chip using your putter (see section 8.11).
- The lie is bad, down in a divot, so the putter won't roll the ball forward but pop it up. Then chip with a somewhat lofted club.
- The grass between the ball and the green is too long so the roll through it will be unpredictable. Then fly the ball over the grass, landing it three feet onto the putting surface.
- The grain of the fringe grass is against your swing and the grass is long enough to catch your putter. Then use the lowest-lofted club that will land the ball three feet on the green with the least amount of backspin.

Never make a swing if you're undecided on how to play the shot. You must commit to doing your best every time. Choose the shot, imagine it (seeing in your mind's eye that it will work), feel the motion that will produce it (a perfect preview swing), then make your real swing. You must hit the ball within eight seconds of making your preview swing so you don't lose the feel of the perfect motion.

The key is to hit enough chips to learn which of your shots work best and which are the easiest for you to execute well. All the shots described in this chapter so far are from good lies, so good contact is easily achieved if you make a good chipping swing.

The shots described toward the end of this chapter are from more difficult lies and situations. However, most chip shots, even the tough ones, aren't hard to execute. What's difficult is choosing the option that will work best. Most golfers never take lessons on the unusual shots, and they certainly don't practice them, so they don't know where to begin when faced with one. That means you're about to read instruction most golfers don't even know exists. Read about the different chips (several times, if necessary), then practice. Remember, whether you're on the practice green or the golf course, you must see it, feel it, and do it within eight seconds of making your perfect preview swing. And simpler *is* better, all other things being equal.

Chipping Variations

8.11 The Chiputt

Earlier, I said when you're more than 50 feet from the flagstick and on a good lie you should hit what I call a "chiputt." This is nothing more than holding your putter with your chipping grip, taking your normal chipping stance, positioning the ball a little forward of the center of your stance (not back in your stance as for normal chip shots), and making your normal chipping motion (turn #1 away, followed by a turn #2 through), with dead hands.

I've already said, and proven, that the most reliable way to play short shots from good lies is putting. But from more than 50 feet, most golfers leave putts short because their instincts don't let them make a big enough stroke to get the ball to the hole. The chiputt provides a more powerful swing and starts with an upright posture that provides a better perspective for distance, yet still rolls the ball like a putt.

The main difference from normal chipping is that you don't play the chiputt back in your stance. There's no grass to get between clubface and ball, and no need to be concerned about hitting the shot fat. In fact, your putter never hits the ground. Other than that, and your choice of club, Figure 8.11.1 shows that the chiputt is in every way a chipping swing. The longer the shot, the more it runs uphill, or the more against the grain, the longer you make your chiputt swing.

Figure 8.11.1: The chiputt: chipping with a putter

Don't get confused and try executing the chiputt from your normal putting stance, as the more bent-over putting posture limits the length of your swing and leads to leaving the shots short.

Besides handling extra-long putts, the chiputt works from well off the green, and on well-manicured courses with difficult slopes surrounding the greens. For example, at Augusta National or Pinehurst #2, where the fringes roll fast and true, it is often the most reliable shot. (Putting from off the green is sometimes referred to as a Texas Wedge. What's different here is you're not really putting, since that will probably leave the ball well short. You're chipping with a putter—chiputting. A crucial distinction.)

8.12 Get It Down and Rolling

As you move farther from the green and/or find worse lies, you need more loft to reach the green on the fly, a more descending blow to make good contact, and a bigger swing to supply more power. None of these are as much of a problem for a good golfer as the uncertainties presented by unpredictable landing areas.

When it's not the lie but the landing area that causes you difficulty in reading what your shots will do, minimize your interaction with problem areas such as level changes, saddlebacks, and double breaks. Most pros try to pick their short shots based on landing on a level surface, because it's so much easier to predict the resulting roll. However, you can't always hit to a flat spot, so when you can't, follow this simple rule: At all costs, avoid landing on top of humps, but when you can, aim for dips.

Of course, you don't need to worry about eliminating or dealing with the effects of ridges, humps, and valleys if your ball is down and rolling on the green before it encounters them. When a ball rolls over or through valleys and humps, there is no net gain or loss of distance. What energy the ball loses going up, it gains coming back down.

On the other hand, all chip shots will be affected by changes of level on the green. While there is no way to completely avoid this, planning to fly a chip onto a level-change area is one of the worst-planned shots you could come up with. Because every shot will bounce differently off each different area of the slope, this will maximize your uncertainty in the result in the same way as the hump explained above. The key to minimizing the level-change effect is to get your shot down and rolling purely on the surface before it encounters any slope of the level change. As long as your shot is not bouncing as it changes level, the effect will be simply the rolling energy lost or gained by the level difference, which is very consistent and can be learned with a little practice.

8.13 Down Lies, No Problem

Let's deal with some bad lies. When you find your ball sitting down in short fringe grass, either in a bare spot between clumps of grass or in a divot made by a previous incoming shot, don't try to putt. Your flat-faced putter probably will pop it in the air and leave it far short of the pin. The worse the lie and the farther down the ball is sitting, the more loft you need at impact to get the ball up, through the impediments in front of it, and rolling on the green.

Look at the three lies in Figure 8.13.1. The three sequences in Figures 8.13.2 to 8.13.4 compare the initial behavior of three shots from the worst lie, as they leave the fringe grass. Obviously, if three swings of the same power were applied to all

Figure 8.13.1: All lies—good, bad, and awful—are part of golf

Figure 8.13.2: Putting stroke
pops ball up from a down lie

Figure 8.13.3: Seven-iron chip moves ball forward but still up from a down lie

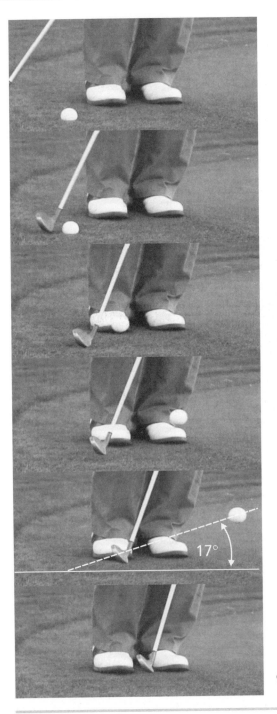

Figure 8.13.4: Delofted wedge gets ball out and moving forward best from a down lie

three shots, the putted ball (Fig. 8.13.2) would travel the shortest since it started almost vertically and lost much of its forward energy doing so. The 7-iron shot (Fig. 8.13.3), although better, still began significantly upward because of the ground in front of it. The best performance was produced by the somewhat de-lofted sand wedge (Fig. 8.13.4), which came down on a descending angle, got the ball up more quickly (thanks to the club's remaining loft), and propelled it more forward initially.

From down lies, the more lofted club sometimes produces the lowest trajectory and the best roll. To simulate such lies, drop a few balls in the long grass around a practice green and step on them (Fig. 8.13.5), creating a crater for each one. Practice with many different clubs to learn which produce the best results for you.

Figure 8.13.5: Chipping practice from bad lies prepares you for bad breaks on-course

Expect similar results when the ball sits in Bermuda grass with its grain growing into, rather than with, the path of your swing. Once again, practice with different clubs including your putter, short irons, high-lofted fairway woods, and wedges, and note the different results. Don't get careless and start using your hand and wrist muscles if your first few shots finish short of the hole. Be patient, learn which club best handles the grass, and then practice rolling shots the proper distance with your finesse chipping motion (20% longer follow-through swing, stability through impact, and, as usual, dead hands).

8.14 Against the Rough—Or in It

When your ball is up against the rough (Fig. 8.14.1), a special shot is required. Don't use your normal 8-iron chip shot, with the ball off your back ankle, because too much grass will get trapped between the clubface and the ball, destroying the consistency of energy transfer—and control—to the ball (Fig. 8.14.2). You want

Figure 8.14.1: Ball tucked against rough line requires special chip

impact that is clean (minimal grass between club and ball), solid, and transfers a consistent percentage of the swing's energy to the ball.

The traditional shot from this lie is the bellied wedge: using a putting stroke action to swing a wedge so its leading edge contacts the equator of your ball (Fig. 8.14.3). A wedge is used because it has more weight, and is more solid along its bottom leading edge, than most other clubs. By lifting the wedge off the ground and aligning its leading edge with the ball's equator, the club doesn't have to travel through much grass. Look for a wedge with a straight leading edge: The straighter

Figure 8.14.2: Standard chipping swing traps grass between clubface and ball

Figure 8.14.3: Bellied wedge contacts ball at equator as wedge skims across top of grass

the leading edge, the easier it is to keep this shot on-line. If the leading edge is rounded (Fig. 8.14.4), you'll have to worry about the ball squirting left or right.

Focus your attention on keeping your swing level and making solid contact at the center of your ball. When you execute the bellied wedge properly—take your normal putting posture and place the ball two inches forward of the center of your stance (the exact bottom of your swing arc)—the shot will have very little loft or bouncing (Fig. 8.14.5), and the ball will roll on the green like a well-struck putt.

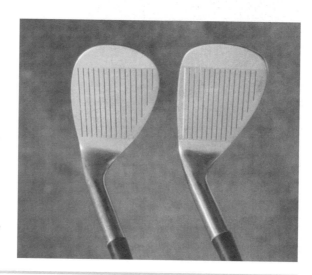

Figure 8.14.4: Straighter (less curved) leading edge, on right, makes bellied wedge shot easier

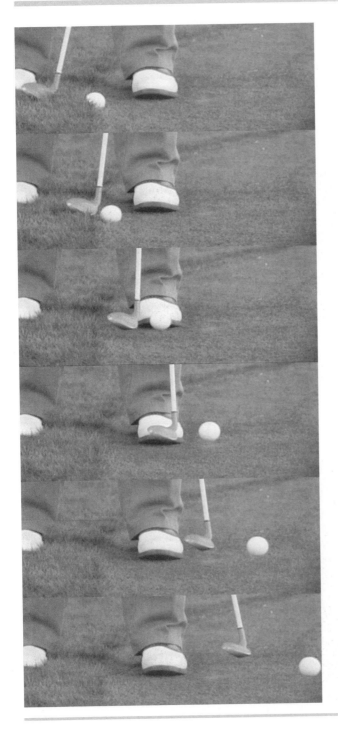

Figure 8.14.5: Bellied wedge shot rolls almost like a putt

When your ball is in heavy rough, it's time for another nontraditional shot—the wood chip. By "wood" I mean the 5- or 7-wood (okay, they are made of metal) from long grass, and the 3- or 4-wood from lighter rough. As you can see in Figure 8.14.6, a small wood head separates and slides through the grass, unlike an iron, which has to cut through it. Stand very close to the ball and set the wood on its toe (Fig. 8.14.7) to minimize the amount of clubface exposed to the grass. The club's loft will start the shots slightly up and out, above the surrounding grass (which is

Figure 8.14.6: Five-wood slides through grass, rolls ball well from rough

Figure 8.14.7: Set 5-wood on toe, bow wrists, and then chip normally

why you want more loft, like that of a 5- or 7-wood, from the longer grass). These shots will come out without backspin, so they'll roll like mad.

In lighter, shorter rough, you have a choice of chipping with your 3-wood, a 9-iron, or one of your wedges. If you choose one of your wedges, use your standard finesse chipping swing. With the ball positioned on or just behind your back ankle, assume a narrow stance with your weight forward and your hands in front of your left thigh (Fig. 8.14.8). This motion (Fig. 8.14.9) will deliver a descending blow and make clean, solid contact. If your practice swing shows that your downswing is not descending sharply enough, choke farther down the shaft to assure clean contact.

Figure 8.14.8: Position ball on back ankle for wedge chip from rough

Figure 8.14.9: Even with ball behind back ankle, wedge chip lofts ball softly onto green

8.15 The Cock-and-Pop

One of the most difficult chip shots around the greens is the nesty lie (shown in Fig. 8.15.1). What makes it so difficult is that it looks a lot easier than it really is. Most of the ball is visible, and the surrounding grass is not too deep. It looks as if the normal back-in-the-stance chipping swing would produce clean contact. But when you try it, the club catches grass first and impact is so cushioned it feels like you hit the ball with a headcover on. Your shot doesn't get even halfway to the hole. The technical reason for the difficulty is that too much grass is lying sideways around the ball, causing it to provide more cushion and energy loss than expected.

Figure 8.15.1: The nesty lie

When you face this lie, forget any kind of chipping swing. Instead, I normally recommend the blast shot, as described in section 6.15. However, if there's no room under the ball or you don't have room to make a blast swing, the "cock-and-pop" may be the best way out.

The cock-and-pop is a weird little shot that violates almost all the rules of my finesse-swing theory. Rather than no hands, you must be totally handsy. Rather than a finesse turn-away-and-through, there's no body motion at all. There's not much arm swing, either. Since it is so weird, I don't suggest practicing it too often or using it much on the course. But it can come in handy, so try it a few times before putting it into your on-course repertoire.

Set up by gripping well down the shaft, opening the clubface, and positioning the ball just behind the middle of your stance (Fig. 8.15.2). Your posture should be somewhat crouched so you get down to the ball, and your stance should be about half your shoulder-width. Without moving your body or arms, hit the shot by both cocking and collapsing your wrists, popping and slapping through impact (sequence in Fig. 8.15.3). The shot works especially well from nesty lies, because the small radius of the swing arc does the best job of any technique in getting the club in and out of the grass quickly and accurately.

Figure 8.15.2: Setting up for the cock-and-pop

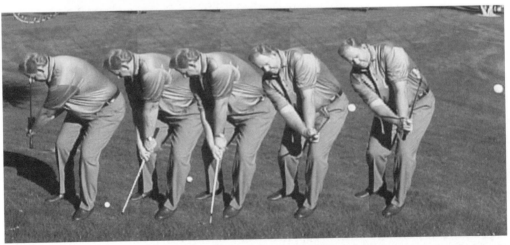

Figure 8.15.3: The cock-and-pop is all hands and wrists, no body

The cock-and-pop is not a high-powered shot. If you need to swing your arms for more power, you can't count on making an accurate entry into the nest at the back of the ball. Once you're that dependent on timing, the shot becomes too dangerous to use.

8.16 Flagstick in or Out?

A few years ago, I was asked by GOLF Magazine to answer an age-old question: When chipping, should you leave the flagstick in the hole or pull it out? I conducted a test and was surprised by the results.

It was impractical to hit shots from the fringe, fairway, or rough, because no human (not even Perfy, my putting/chipping robot) could hit the flagstick often enough or accurately enough to run the test in a reasonable amount of time. However, by precisely rolling balls on a green from a short distance to the hole, I could measure how the flagstick affected the results.

To guarantee measurable, reliable results, I used a putting machine called the "TruRoller," which I invented to roll balls precisely controlled directions at carefully controlled speeds. For each test, I set the TruRoller about two feet from the cup (Fig. 8.16.1) and measured (1) how far the ball rolled past the hole when the hole was covered, (2) how many putts stayed in the hole when the hole was not covered and the flagstick was out, and (3) how many putts stayed in the hole when the flagstick was left in.

Each test was run at three different speeds: On a perfectly flat green, the speeds were fast enough to send balls three feet past the hole, six feet past, and nine feet past. Each test also included putts that approached the target at different parts of

Figure 8.16.1: TruRoller measures approach speed with hole covered, then rolls balls to cup with pin both out and in

the hole: dead center; left and right center of the pin; left and right edge of the pin. Finally, the tests were run first on level greens, then on ones that sloped sharply uphill and downhill. (The speeds remained consistent, but because the slope changed, the balls, if they missed the hole, would finish considerably farther away on downhill putts and closer on uphillers. But it is the speed, not the final distance from the hole, that matters.)

All told, TruRoller launched thousands of "shots" at the hole, an equal number with the flagstick in and out, on a number of different greens, at five different parts of the hole. Once that was done, PGA Tour veteran Tom Jenkins did his best to duplicate those tests with his own putting stroke. While Tom couldn't control his putts as precisely as the TruRoller could, I felt it was important to compare machine and human results. Tom's putting results supported the TruRoller's results in every testing category (with just a little more scatter).

Of course, there were variables in conditions, including imperfect green surfaces, the edges of some cups being ragged or worn, the hole being higher in back than in front and acting as a "backstop," and so on. But after thousands of putts, with pins both in and out, these variables were averaged out.

What did I learn? All the evidence points to one very simple rule: Leave the flagstick in whenever the Rules allow, unless it is leaning so far toward you that the ball can't fit. Here are a few special cases:

- Perhaps most surprising, when the flagstick leans either slightly toward the golfer or away, the odds of it helping to keep the ball in the hole increase: With the flagstick leaning away from the golfer, the hole becomes effectively larger; when the flagstick leans toward the golfer, the ball rebounds downward, again helping shots to stay in the hole.
- Only in the most obvious case—when the flagstick is leaning so far toward the golfer that there isn't enough room for the ball—is leaving the flagstick in a bad idea. Check the flagstick before you chip to be sure it is sitting properly in the cup. (The Rules of Golf prohibit you from positioning a flagstick to your advantage. But you may leave a tilting flagstick as is or else center it in the hole.)
- Even if you don't hit the flagstick dead center, it still will aid you. This was true in every test I ran, and even on the off-center hits, the flagstick proved especially advantageous when chipping downhill and at faster speeds.

I even believe the flagstick should be left in when you're putting from an inch or two off the green in the fringe. The flagstick is going to help you make more putts unless it is leaning severely toward you or it's so windy the flagstick is moving around and might knock your ball away.

8.17 Chip Yips

The "yips" are not purely a putting disease. They can attack your short game and make a hash of your chipping. You can tell if you're a victim by answering the following: When you chip, do you regularly hit the ground behind the ball and occasionally bounce your club over it, missing completely? Do you use a putter even from ridiculously thick lies in the rough? Are you so awful from the fringe that you're afraid to take the club back? A "yes" to any or all of these means you have the chip yips.

Like the other yips, these are caused by fear, an understandable reaction after witnessing a long spell of bad results. But take heart: They can be cured.

Chip yips usually can be traced to one of three swing faults, all of which result from poor setup and swing technique. Here are explanations of these faults, along with quick solutions and a practice drill that will help rid you of them.

Fault #1: Poor Ball Position. If the ball is too far forward in your stance, even just in the middle of your stance, then the club can easily hit the ground first (Fig. 8.17.1). Fat shots and skulls result.

The solution is easy: Move the ball back in your stance as described earlier, so it is on-line with your back ankle (right ankle for right-handed golfers). Now the club will for sure contact the ball before reaching the bottom of your swing arc—and the ground (Fig. 8.17.2).

Figure 8.17.2: Proper ball position (back ankle): encourages clean contact

Figure 8.17.1: Ball too far forward: encourages chipping fat

Fault #2: Zero Body Motion. If you're not using a little body motion—a slight turn away, followed by a turn-through, shifting your weight from the right foot back to the left foot, the chip stroke becomes an all-hands-and-wrists action (Fig. 8.17.3). But as I've said over and over, a good finesse game comes from a free rhythmic swinging of the arms, shoulders, and hips synchronized together; your hands simply supply guidance and control.

Cure no-body motion chipping with the "left-arm-only" (LAO) drill (Fig. 8.17.4). Prepare to hit a chip, then put your right hand on your right thigh. Using only body motion, with your left elbow touching your upper stomach throughout

Figure 8.17.3: Chipping with no body motion: forces hands and wrists into action

Figure 8.17.4: The left-arm-only (LAO) drill

the swing, swing your left shoulder back and through. Feel the club swinging along with your chest, shoulders, left arm, and hips, and feel nothing from your left hand. You should be able to chip relatively well with the LAO.

Fault #3: Left Wrist Breakdown. After repeatedly hitting behind the ball (fault #1), many golfers develop a swing in which the left arm stops almost immediately after impact, with the club continuing to move as the left wrist breaks down and the right hand supplies power. This action results in thin and skulled shots, but at least you avoid the "fats."

The easiest way to correct this fault is by finishing the through-swing, keeping the left wrist firm. This, however, is easier said than done for golfers who have in-grained a wristy stroke. They need the following practice aid:

The "ChipStick." Practice chipping with a "ChipStick" (Fig. 8.17.5) attached to your club to extend its length and help remedy all three faults cited above.

Fault #1: At address, with your left hand in front of your left thigh, the angle of the shaft extension tells you if the ball is back far enough in your stance. The ChipStick should angle forward, clearing the front of your body when you position your ball properly on your back ankle (figure on far right, Fig. 8.17.5).

Fault #2: Practice the LAO drill using the ChipStick. If you can keep the long extension parallel to your left arm, your hands will stay out of the swing and let your body learn the swing motion it needs.

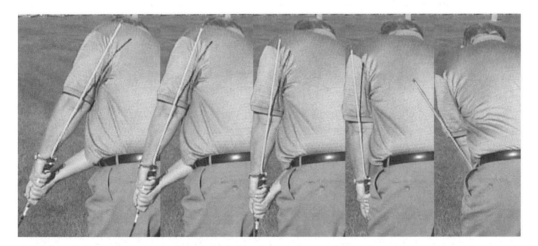

Figure 8.17.5: View from behind: Chip swing from address (far right) to follow-through (far left) with "ChipStick"

Fault #3: Practice chipping with the ChipStick, making certain to swing through 20% farther than your backswing. If you feel the ChipStick extension hitting your left side, your wrists are breaking down. Practice until it no longer hits you and your wrists remain firm through to your finish (far left of Fig. 8.17.5).

A Drill to Cure the Chip Yips

Here's a four-step program to cure your chip yips. Understand that it will take some time. It took many bad shots to convince your brain to fear your chipping results, so it will take time to restore your confidence in these shots.

1. To remove the swing faults that originally caused the yips, get a ChipStick, and practice your finesse chipping swing in front of a mirror. Chip for five minutes a day for three weeks, with an imaginary ball positioned across from your right ankle (see Fig. 8.17.6 ball position).

Figure 8.17.6: ChipStick should never touch your back on follow-through

2. In your living room, create a chipping routine in which you make a practice swing, then step into the address position you grooved in step #1 above, take one look down the line, and chip a plastic (Wiffle) ball (Fig. 8.17.7). Don't aim at anything; results don't matter. Just repeat your practice swing, take your address position, and chip the Wiffle ball for 10 minutes a day for two weeks.

3. In the third week, add a real ball to your living-room routine. Continue to chip 10 minutes a day, first the practice swing, then the Wiffle ball chip,

The "Golden Eight" Feet

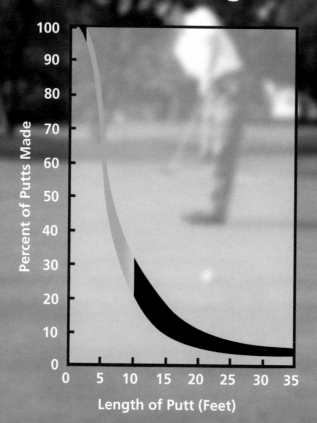

Putt Conversion Curve

"Where you putt from . . .
is more important than how well you putt."

The Wrist Cock
(CHAPTER 4)

The Finesse Grip
(CHAPTER 4)

Perfect Practice (CHAPTER 12)

The 12-Yard Pitch (CHAPTER 7)

The Lob Over Sand (CHAPTER 7)

The Chiputt (CHAPTER 8)

Max Velocity (CHAPTER 4)

The Knock-Down Wedge (CHAPTER 6)

The Swing Plane (CHAPTER 4)

Uneven Lies (CHAPTERS 6, 7)

The Cock-and-Pop (CHAPTER 9)

The Scoot-and-Spin Blast (CHAPTER 9)

Chipstick
(CHAPTER 8)

Aim Left—With Open Clubface (CHAPTER 9)

The Perfect Pitch (CHAPTER 7)

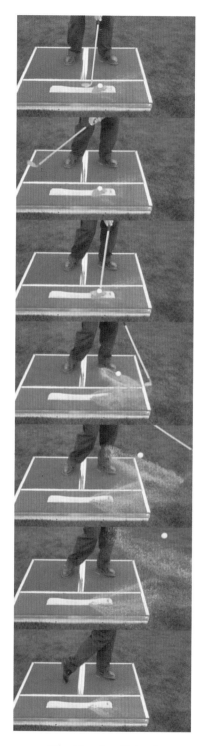

The BunkerBoard
(CHAPTER 12)

Maximum Backspin (CHAPTER 9)

Pitching to the "Golden Eight" (CHAPTER 1)

7:30 Finesse Swing (CHAPTER 5)

Chipping with a Wedge (CHAPTER 7)

7:30 Finesse Swing (CHAPTER 5)

9:00 O'clock Finesse Swing (CHAPTER 5)

10:30 Finesse Swing (CHAPTER 5)

The Chip (CHAPTER 8)

Super Cut Lob (CHAPTER 6)

Horizontal to Vertical (CHAPTER 7)

Down and Chasing (CHAPTER 8)

The Blast from Rough (CHAPTER 6)

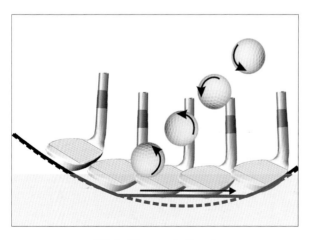

Club Through Sand
(CHAPTER 9)

Club Passes Ball
(CHAPTER 9)

Short Courses for Short Games (CHAPTER 8)

The Hard-Pan Shot
(CHAPTER 6)

The Shanker's Delight
(CHAPTER 12)

The Chop from Rough (CHAPTER 6)

Gripping Down (CHAPTER 7)

The High, Soft Blast (CHAPTER 9)

Ball Above Feet
(CHAPTER 9)

Backyard Practice (CHAPTER 12)

Ball Below Feet
(CHAPTER 9)

Uphill
(CHAPTER 9)

Downhill
(CHAPTER 9)

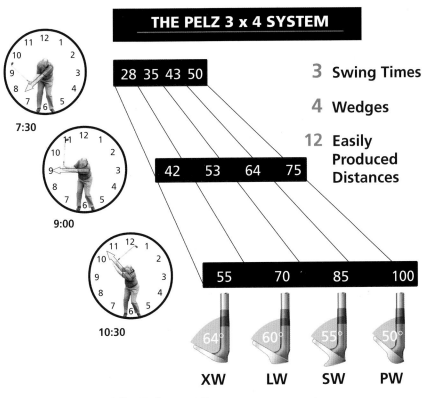

THE PELZ 3 x 4 SYSTEM

7:30

9:00

10:30

28 35 43 50

42   53   64   75

55   70   85   100

64°   60°   55°   50°

XW   LW   SW   PW

3 Swing Times

4 Wedges

12 Easily Produced Distances

The Pelz 3 x 4 System (CHAPTER 5)

The Bump-and-Run (CHAPTER 8)

The Golden Rule

"He who rules the short game wins the gold (or silver)."

Tom Kite, 1992 U.S. Open Champion

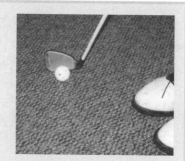

Figure 8.17.7: Chipping with a Wiffle ball

then the real ball. Develop a rhythm for moving from your practice swing to your Wiffle ball address—one look and swing. Then move from the Wiffle chip to the real ball address, take one look down the line, and swing.

4. After four weeks you are ready to go to the practice green and begin chipping to holes. Don't allow yourself to change any of the routines and rhythms you've been grooving. Good chipping rhythm must become a habit. Keep chipping in your living room until you can carry the same practice routine onto the course: practice swing, step into the ball, take one look, and chip. Stay with it until it works, because different people take different lengths of time to form a habit. Once you form a good chipping habit, it will save you strokes.

The Bump-and-Run

8.18 Bump-and-Run Mechanics

The bump-and-run is a shot all golfers should know how to play. It has been a vital part of golf since the game began. Although many Americans have lost the ability to play this shot, it doesn't have to be gone forever. If you are enough of a golf enthusiast to be reading this book, then I think you deserve to learn and successfully use the bump-and-run. It is an asset to anyone's short game.

First, a definition. The bump-and-run is a low, running shot that lands short of the green with minimal backspin, bounces, and runs along the fairway or rough up to the green and flagstick. The bump-and-run is largely unaffected by wind, and is sometimes the only shot capable of handling a hard, fast green. Unlike chip shots, which land on the green (or at least very close to it), the bump-and-run lands at least two or three bounces—and sometimes many more—short before running on. Bump-and-runs are much longer than chips, sometimes covering 50, 60, or even up to 100 yards, but still land only about halfway to the green before rolling the rest of the way. Yet, as you should have noticed, there is no place on the scorecard for indicating where the shot landed. What matters is whether or not the shot finishes close enough to the hole to let you make a good score.

In truth, the bump-and-run is not a chip shot, but it's in the chipping chapter because its action is more similar to chipping than any other finesse swing. And it has two characteristics also common to the chip:

1. The lower, the better (as long as it can bounce along the grass without getting caught up in it and stopping short of the green).
2. The less spin, the more predictable the results.

The mechanics of the bump-and-run swing are similar to the finesse chipping swing, except: the synchronized turn is longer both back and through; a partial wrist cock is employed (to produce more power as required); and the ball is positioned at the stance center as shown in Figure 8.18.1.

The swing requires a low, sweeping motion through impact, not a descending blow. The shaft should be gripped at full length (never gripped-down), to encourage the flattest angle of attack and minimum backspin. The 5- and 6-irons are most commonly used for the bump-and-run, although any loft from 3-iron up can be used.

Figure 8.18.1: Ball positioned at stance center for bump-and-run

Many people say the bump-and-run should be hit with overspin so it will run a long way and not bite. However, any ball hit below center with a lofted iron will have some backspin. What the bump-and-run requires is minimal backspin and solid impact from a low-lofted club, swung with a normal release through impact (see Fig. 8.18.2). Thanks to the low trajectory, that little bit of backspin is gone after the first few bounces.

Figure 8.18.2: Bump-and-run swing employs natural forearm release through impact

8.19 Why Play the Bump-and-Run?

If you sometimes play on windy days, you need the bump-and-run. If you play on courses with hard, fast greens, you need it. If you want to be good at match play, you absolutely need it. And if you ever play in England, Scotland, Ireland, or Wales, you really, really, *really* need the bump-and-run.

I remember when Corey Pavin beat Nick Faldo in the 1993 World Match Play Championship after hitting only 17 greens in a 36-hole match (vs. 27 greens hit by Faldo). The shot that set the tone for Pavin's win was a bump-and-run. On one hole, Faldo was on the green in two with a 12-foot putt for birdie. Pavin, also lying two, was under a bush 30 yards short of the green.

Pavin walked up to the green, surveyed the contours, and slowly walked back to his ball. He carefully studied his situation and took a number of practice swings. Then he hit the most beautiful bump-and-run shot you have ever seen. It stopped one inch from the hole. Nick almost fainted, and knew right then that no matter what happened, Pavin would be in every hole. He saw how good Pavin was from trouble spots, which made him *very* difficult to beat.

By practicing the bump-and-run, you learn a feel for distance, as well as how your ball will react on fairways, approaches to the greens, and the greens themselves. All of which helps you better read your short-game shots before you hit them.

Then there is the bad-shot advantage of the bump-and-run. At a clinic a few years ago, I ran a test comparing the average amateur's ability to hit to a green from 70 yards with two clubs—a sand wedge and a 5-iron. From that distance, nearly every golfer had to make an almost-full swing with the sand wedge, but only a half-swing with the 5-iron (Fig. 8.19.1 top and bottom sequences, respectively). The data showed that the sand-wedge shots had about 40% greater "scatter" (dispersion) than the 5-iron shots. While the closest shots were about evenly

Figure 8.19.1:
The scatter test: full sand wedge swing (top) versus half 5-iron swing (bottom)

split between the two clubs, the worst shots definitely came off the wedges. Since then, I've repeated this test several times, always with the same results. From this I've concluded that amateurs find it is easier to make a half-swing than a full swing. The data also shows that (1) in windy conditions, (2) when water guards a green right or left, or (3) from uphill or sidehill lies, the half-swing bump-and-run is often the highest-percentage shot, especially if you practice it just a little.

You should practice and use the bump-and-run so it's there in your game when you really need it—and you *will* need it!

8.20 Land on the Flat Spots

I've spent many days watching Tour professionals play in Scotland, home of both golf and the bump-and-run. After many discussions about strategy on those old courses, the pros taught me that the key determinant of bump-and-run success is choosing the best landing area and being able to hit it.

Landing the ball on a flat, firm area of short grass guarantees that the first bounce is strong and straight forward. This produces a low, running shot that will chase up a hill, around a slope, or through the desired opening between two sand traps and onto the green.

So if you can't make a half-swing and land your bump-and-run on a flat area, then you probably should hit a different shot. Making a half-swing is key, because a faster clubhead speed through impact will produce more backspin, which you don't want. It's also important that the landing area be relatively smooth and flat: If not, predicting and controlling the bounce and roll become risky business.

Several of my players prepare to compete overseas by playing practice rounds hitting bump-and-run shots to every green. Although heavily watered fairways and trouble in front of many greens make this difficult on numerous American courses, it's still good practice to visualize where you'd land a bump-and-run and try to hit it there. As you walk up to each green, pull a spare ball out of your pocket, drop it somewhere 30 to 50 yards short of the surface, and bump it up to the flagstick with your 5- or 6-iron. A few practice rounds like this will help you acquire the touch for the power and swing you need. You'll also develop the confidence that's necessary to use this shot in your game.

8.21 The Texas Turn-Down

The bump-and-run can be a real asset to your short game. But it won't always work, especially if you are trying to bump the ball through Bermuda grass or really long ryegrass. Then you may have to take your shot creation to a new level by executing the "Texas Turn-Down." This shot was taught to me by Tom Jenkins, who learned to hit it on the Bermuda grass courses in Houston, Texas, where he grew up.

The Texas Turn-Down should be used only in emergency situations when no other shot is available, when you can't hit a high shot because of overhanging trees, and when a normal bump-and-run won't get through the rough between you and the green (as shown in Fig. 8.21.1). You'll be trying to remove all backspin from the shot, giving it a chance to kick forward on its first bounce. But be warned: Because you exaggerate hand action through impact, it is very easy to hit this shot badly, smothering it at impact and possibly leaving yourself in an even worse situation.

Begin by positioning the ball in the center of your stance and lined up off the toe of your club. On the backswing (Fig. 8.21.2), roll your forearms open and to the inside of your normal swing plane. On the downswing, make a quick, almost violent rotation of your forearms back toward the target so the club is nearly back to square just before impact and "turned down" on your follow-through (Fig. 8.21.3). Herein lies the problem: If you roll the clubhead over too early, the shot will be smothered and the ball driven even deeper into the grass.

As seen in Figure 8.21.4, the ball should be struck far out toward the toe of the club, as far out as you have confidence to hit it. This toe impact will minimize

Figure 8.21.1: The Texas Turn-Down: your best chance to run balls through high grass

Figure 8.21.2: Texas Turn-Down: backswing

Figure 8.21.3: Texas Turn-Down: follow-through

Figure 8.21.4:
Texas Turn-Down: ball
position at address

backspin and also significantly reduce the power transmitted to the ball. Therefore, you have to make a longer-than-normal swing for the distance.

If you have fast hands, like T.J. or Chi Chi Rodriguez (the fastest I've ever seen), you can reliably hit this shot and get away with some amazing recoveries. However, the Texas Turn-Down is not an easy shot to hit, and I don't recommend trying it unless you are in dire circumstances and have practiced it a few times first.

8.22 The World Game

One of the most enjoyable learning experiences I've had came during one of my stays in St. Andrews, Scotland, home of the Royal and Ancient Golf Club and the University of St. Andrews, which hosts the World Scientific Congress of Golf every four years. I was presenting a research paper to the Congress in 1990, a week before the Open was to be played on the Old Course. Every morning at daybreak I walked the Old Course for my morning exercise. During these walks, I closely studied the contours and hazards of the game's original great layout.

Early the next week, I worked with several of my players. Then I stayed on, hoping to watch one of them win the Open. What an experience! I spent most of my time near the par-4 17th hole, the famous Road Hole, because it is one of the game's greatest tests. It was at that tournament, that week, that I became a true believer in the value of the bump-and-run.

I watched every pro I worked with self-destruct on the Road Hole that year. One of them would have won the tournament had he simply parred the hole every day, but his scores ranged from five to seven. Several others played billiards against the stone wall behind the green, flying beautiful 4- to 7-iron shots onto the green—and watching them bounce over. A few others landed in the Road Bunker short of the green and couldn't make better than bogey or double bogey.

Then I watched the British and Scottish pros play through, hitting half-swing 3-iron bump-and-runs that flew quail-high toward the right side, landed in the fairway 50 to 100 yards short of the green, and chased up and onto the putting surface. No problem, thank you very much. The worst result I witnessed for any of them was a short chip from in front of the green to save par. Most two-putted for par, while one or two actually made birdie.

Not one American even thought about bumping-and-running a shot into that green. Not one realized, as I had learned on my walks, that the contours of the fairway would funnel such a shot from the right side into the green. The hole was made for that shot, but the Americans never noticed because they never looked for it.

By the end of that week, I had decided how to design my Scoring Game Courses.

8.23 We Need More Short Courses

The Dave Pelz Short Course at the Club at Cordillera is not just a course that plays short. Let me explain.

The Short Course is in Edwards, Colorado, on a plateau 1,500 feet above beautiful Vail Valley. I designed it as an exercise in short-game shot execution and experience (Fig. 8.23.1), and it turned out wonderfully. The Vail Valley is perhaps the finest place to play summer golf in the United States. The weather is perfect, the views are spectacular, the air is clean, and the course is not only beautiful, it will improve your short game. (There are quite a few full-length courses in the area, some quite challenging. But only my Short Course is set up as a short-game learning experience.)

The Short Course invites and challenges you to use your short game (Fig. 8.23.2). It allows you to hit 80% of the shots of golf (everything but drives and fairway woods), on 25% of the land needed for a normal course, in less than 25% of the time of a normal round of golf. Hole distances range from about 100 to 215 yards, with a variety of tees on every hole. The traps are large, the rough is tough, and the greens are good-sized, undulating, and fast.

Every hole also has both level and uneven tees. Why? Because I want you to be able to practice realistic iron and short-game shots. Every hole has been designed to be played either through the air or on the ground with a bump-and-run game (Fig. 8.23.3).

If I had my choice on how you should practice to improve your short game, I would put you on a schedule of practice drills (described in Chapter 12) five

Figure 8.23.1: Cordillera Short Course: hole #2

Figure 8.23.2: Cordillera Short Course: hole #4

Figure 8.23.3: Cordillera Short Course: hole #9

days a week, and have you play nine holes on the Short Course on four of those days:

Day one: Take all your clubs and play through the air from the level tees.

Day two: Take all your clubs and play through the air from uneven tees.

Day three: Take your 5-iron and putter only. Play on the ground, using your bump-and-run game, from the level tees.

Day four: Take your 6-iron and putter. Play on the ground from the uneven tees.

If you could do what I suggest here, your entire game would improve. I don't want you to practice your full-swing game less. Rather, I want you to practice your short game more. And I can assure you, if you both practice and use your bump-and-run game on a regular basis, your scores will improve on every course you play.

The Sand Shot

Blast Shots from Sand

9.1 How Not to Do It: The Dig-and-Push

The fourth shot in the finesse game is the one most dreaded by the average golfer—the sand shot. Early in my teaching career I didn't understand why amateurs were so terrified of sand play; after all, it's the only golf shot where you don't actually have to hit the ball: You simply swing, move your club through the sand, and the ball comes out onto the green. If anything, I thought there would be less anxiety, since there's no direct ball-to-club contact. But what I didn't know then was that average golfers didn't understand how the club and the sand interact, or how the blast out of the sand really works. As a result, they were hitting poor shots, bad shots, horrible shots. And some of them were swinging with paralyzing fear, swinging with all their might, closing their eyes and "hoping" something good would happen!

This is the only chapter in this book where I'll spend more than a few words explaining how *not* to do something. Because what follows is an explanation of what most people think happens in the sand (Fig. 9.1.1). Remember as you read it—and nod your head in agreement—this is the *incorrect* technique.

With your clubface aimed square at the target, your wedge enters the sand about an eighth of an inch behind the ball. As the leading edge digs down two or more inches, it pushes both sand and the ball out ahead of it.

Is that what you try to do? Because if that's the way you think the sand shot should be done, your mind will do whatever it can to make it happen. And that's a big reason there are so many poor sand players: misconceptions about the shot that become self-fulfilling prophecies of disaster.

Figure 9.1.1: Common perception of a sand shot: club digs and pushes ball plus lots of sand out of bunker

I call the shot just described the "dig-and-push." It may, occasionally, get the ball successfully out of a bunker and perhaps, with some luck, get it to stop not too far from the pin. But the dig-and-push has almost no margin for error, no consistency, and leads to especially poor performance from sand under pressure.

Imagine how much energy it takes to get the ball out of the sand with this dig-and-push technique: The club hits the sand a little fat (half an inch behind the ball rather than an eighth), so the leading edge digs even deeper into the sand before reaching the ball. Since the clubhead is pushing so much sand, the ball can't have much backspin. If the ball gets out of the bunker—and it may not—it can't be controlled or stopped consistently near the pin.

After leaving a few dig-and-push shots in the sand, you're going to find a way, consciously or subconsciously, to avoid hitting future sand shots fat. That's when you begin hitting them thin, catching the ball cleanly without ever contacting the sand (Fig. 9.1.2). These home runs lead to very high scores—and even greater anxiety the next time you're in the sand.

So you can see the intolerance of the dig-and-push sand shot: It is very unforgiving. Of course, if you manage to hit the sand precisely an eighth of an inch behind the ball, you'll produce lots of backspin (assuming you also make a descending blow and drag the ball through sand), so the ball comes out and stops quickly on the green. However, contact the sand a little too early or a little too late and you

Figure 9.1.2: Skull—thin shot from sand: club hits ball first

can count on a disaster. Furthermore, when the clubhead digs deep into the sand, it loses so much of its velocity (like a wedge being pushed rather than pulled) that it loses stability. That leads to loss of control, improper direction, and often even a shot left in the bunker.

9.2 The Right Way: Scoot-and-Spin Mechanics

You don't have to get technical to master sand play. But if you don't know how you should be trying to swing, or where the ball should be in your stance, or how your club should react in the sand, you won't be successful.

Don't lose heart. Because sand play is *not* all that difficult. If you can master the distance-wedge techniques prescribed in Chapter 6, you will simplify and improve your sand game. The finesse swing I've been describing up until now works beautifully from a normal lie in the sand if you make three vitally important adjustments:

1. You must set up and aim your body and swing line a little to the left of the flagstick (Fig. 9.2.1). Not a lot—about 17 degrees (two or three steps) left of your target—but with every part of your body, stance, shoulders, and swing line. Everything.

2. Set the clubface extremely open, more open than most golfers realize is possible (Fig. 9.2.2). The face should aim 45 degrees to the right of your swing-line

Figure 9.2.1: Proper setup in sand: your body and swing line aim left

direction (the clubface lines will pass directly in front of your left toe), so it scoots through the sand without digging into it. Your club should penetrate only about half an inch below the surface.

3. Position the ball forward in your stance on a line at the inside of the heel of your left foot (Fig. 9.2.3). If you don't make any compensations, your natural

Figure 9.2.2: Proper setup in sand: clubface wide open

Figure 9.2.3: Proper ball position
in sand: on-line with inside edge
of heel of left foot

swing arc will have the clubhead contact the sand at about the center of your stance, about five inches behind the ball.

If you make these three changes at address, then all you need to do is make a normal finesse swing parallel to your foot/body line (don't steer the club back toward the flagstick during the swing); swing back to a 9:00 o'clock position (left arm straight out, parallel to the ground); and swing through to a full, high finish

Figure 9.2.4: Proper sand swing:
club scoots under and past ball, not much sand leaves bunker

A Distance-Wedge Refresher

Rather than sending you back to reread Chapter 6, here are the highlights of the distance-wedge swing, which, as of this moment, becomes your basic sand swing from here on out.

Your feet should be 14 to 18 inches apart, about shoulder-width. Stand tall, with knees slightly flexed, upper body bending forward slightly from the hips, and weight centered on the balls of your feet. Let your arms hang loosely, almost straight down from your shoulders, leaving four to six inches of space between your hands and legs.

Use your finesse (neutral to weak) grip and reasonably light grip pressure. Your upper hand should be about a quarter inch from the butt end of the club. You should be able to feel the clubhead as you waggle and swing.

Don't crouch, as this pushes your arms away from the body and flattens your swing plane, which is determined by your size and posture. With short clubs such as your wedges, your body is fairly close to the ball, so your swing plane should be quite steep.

When you're in the sand, remember to set up and aim slightly to the left of your target, open your clubface wide, and position your ball on a line with the inside of your left heel.

(don't ever leave your club in the sand). Finish with 99% of your weight on your left (front) foot, the back of the right foot turned up and right toe touching the ground for balance (Fig. 9.2.4).

We call this the "scoot-and-spin" blast shot. Your club will scoot under and past the ball, blasting it out high, soft, and with a fair amount of spin. The ball should bounce once or twice, check, roll slightly to the right (because of the open face), and stop near the hole. All you have to remember is to aim left, open the clubface, and play the ball forward on the inside edge of your left heel.

Now, will you be able to forget what you thought you knew about sand play and learn the proper method? Yes, if I explain why. If I can get you to understand exactly what happens with your club, your ball, and the sand on the "scoot-and-spin," you'll be better able to learn it, internalize it, and realize what was wrong with what you had been doing.

I want you to see a good sand shot, the "scoot-and-spin" shot, and what actually happens through impact. As the club moves toward the bottom of its arc, it enters the sand well behind (about four to five inches) the ball with its face wide open. The back and bottom of the clubhead—called the sole—are all that hit the sand. This causes the clubhead swing arc to flatten (bounce) and scoot horizontally through the sand, never digging into the sand deeply (Fig. 9.2.5). Most good wedges, when opened properly, are designed to bounce and scoot about a half an inch below the surface. Then two things happen: (1) The club passes under the ball, never actually touching it, and (2) the club continues out and up, leaving the sand well before the ball and throwing only a little bit of sand forward. The force that actually moves the ball is applied by the sand, not the club.

Watching the world's best sand players, I've noticed a key result of a well-struck scoot-and-spin blast from a good lie: For the first few feet after impact, the clubhead should be moving at least twice as fast forward (therefore, twice as far) as the ball. This is demonstrated by Jim Furyk, one of the best sand players on the PGA Tour, in Figure 9.2.6. Watch for this if you have a video camera, looking at your sand shots as they leave impact in slow-motion replay on your VCR.

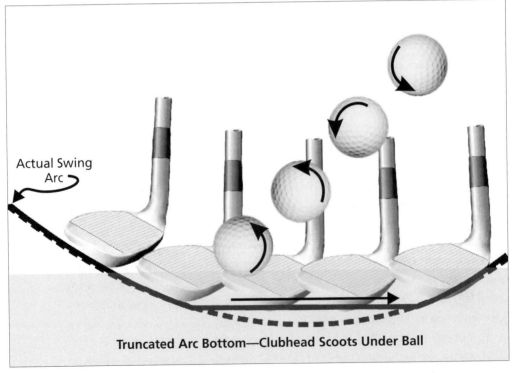

Actual Swing Arc

Truncated Arc Bottom—Clubhead Scoots Under Ball

Figure 9.2.5: The scoot-and-spin reactions of club, sand, and ball

Figure 9.2.6: Proper action through sand: clubhead scoots under and past ball, club leaves sand first, ball spins upward

9.3   Blast Calibration

To learn and groove the scoot-and-spin blast shot, follow the eight-step calibration test below. Not only will you learn how to execute the shot, but you'll also understand why you must make those three crucial changes in your setup and alignment mentioned earlier.

1. In a practice bunker, draw a line aimed at a flagstick (your target). This establishes your target line (Fig. 9.3.1).

2. Draw a line perpendicular to the target line, which will become the ball line. Smooth the spot where the two lines intersect (Fig. 9.3.2), which is where you will initially place a ball.

3. Take your normal distance-wedge address, except position the ball line just inside your left heel (raise your pants so you can see your feet and ankles) and keep your hips, shoulders, and feet set up square to and parallel left of the target line (left image in Fig. 9.3.3). Rotate your left toe 30 to 45 degrees toward the target (center Fig. 9.3.3), and loosen your grip and rotate the face of your club open so the grooves are at 45 degrees to your body line (right image in Fig. 9.3.3).

4. Keeping your body parallel to the target line, move back away from the ball, keeping your left foot heel touching the ball line. Now picture an imaginary ball positioned on the ball line, ready for you to blast out of the sand.

Figure 9.3.1: To calibrate your sand setup alignment, first draw a line directly at your target, the flagstick

Figure 9.3.2: Then draw a ball line perpendicular to that target line

Figure 9.3.3: Position left instep at ball line (left), rotate left toe 45 degrees toward flagstick (center) leaving heel on ball line, rotate clubface to wide open (right)

5. Make a perfectly synchronized 9:00 o'clock distance-wedge swing, contacting the sand four to five inches behind the imaginary ball. Your swing should take a divot out of the sand about eight to 10 inches long, starting in the center of your stance, five inches behind where the imaginary ball was sitting.

6. Repeat steps 4 and 5 three more times, backing six inches away from each previous divot before swinging. Stop and examine all four divots. If you have a perfectly grooved distance-wedge swing, the divots will look like those in Figure 9.3.4, each beginning at your stance center, scooting just under where the imaginary balls were sitting and continuing another five or so inches forward.

Looking at the divots should tell you something else important about your sand play. If your clubface is properly open through impact, the divots should only be about a half inch deep. If they are deeper, it means your club is digging in and, therefore, is not open enough.

7. With this new understanding, rake the sand and start over, but this time

Figure 9.3.4: Four perfect finesse-swing divots

after drawing the ball line, place six balls along it, each spaced six inches apart. Without worrying where the balls go, keeping your left heel on the ball line, make six more 9:00 o'clock distance-wedge swings. Every good swing should hit a good-looking blast shot out of the sand (Fig. 9.3.5).

That's the good news. The bad news is, these good-looking sand shots will fly consistently to the right of the flag because your clubface was open. Never mind. Rake the sand and hit another six good shots this way. Now look at the average angle error your 12 shots missed to the right of the flagstick. This is your "sand-aim-calibration" angle, the angle you must set up, aim, and swing to the left of any target to hit your sand shots close to that target. Now you are ready to blast perfect sand shots on the golf course to a flagstick, by aiming your setup to the left of that flagstick by that angle.

8. It's now simple to hit sand shots to any target. You know exactly how far left of the target to aim your swing line (your sand-aim-calibration angle), where to place the ball (at the heel of your left shoe), and exactly how far to open your clubface (45 degrees) to your swing line (Fig. 9.3.6). Plus, you understand that to execute a beautiful blast shot, you just have to make your good distance-wedge swing. Don't try to hit the sand a specific distance behind the ball; instead, try to make good finesse swings, trusting that you were smart enough to position the ball properly in the middle of where your sand divot will naturally occur (Fig. 9.3.7).

Figure 9.3.5: Perfect swings down target line produce perfect shots angling to right of flagstick

Figure 9.3.6: Perfect sand setup aims swing line left of target line

Figure 9.3.7: Perfect swings produce perfect shots from perfect setup positions

How *Not* to Grip an Open-Faced Sand Club

Many golfers, when told to open the clubface, do so by maintaining their grip on the club and rotating their hands and forearms clockwise. As a result, what they're really doing is temporarily addressing the ball with a stronger-than-normal grip and an open clubface (Fig. 9.3.8). As they swing through impact, their hands return to their natural position, so the clubface is square when it hits the sand (Fig. 9.3.9). The club digs in rather than scooting under, and the results are a dig-and-push sand shot . . . not good!

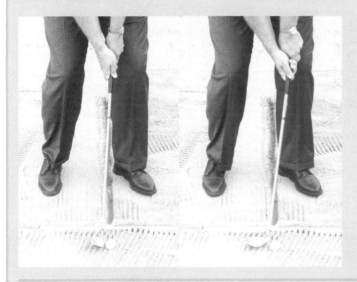

Figure 9.3.8: Improper method to open clubface: from normal finesse grip (left), rotate hands under and behind into strong position (right)

Figure 9.3.9: From improper strong grip, clubface returns to square through impact

How to Grip an Open-Faced Sand Club Properly

1. Start with your normal finesse grip (Fig. 9.3.10), the clubface square to your swing line.
2. Remove your right hand from the club and, without moving your left hand, loosen its grip on the club.
3. Still without moving your left hand, use your right thumb and forefinger (left side, Fig. 9.3.11) to rotate the shaft until the clubface is opened the desired amount (45 degrees). Retighten your left hand in its original position.
4. Replace your right hand exactly as it was in your original square-faced setup (right side, Fig. 9.3.11). This grip position will let you swing the clubhead through impact while maintaining the clubface open, to produce the proper "scoot-and-spin" blast shot.

Figure 9.3.10: Start with normal finesse grip (weak)

Figure 9.3.11: Proper method of opening clubface in sand: rotate shaft while maintaining weak grip

The eight-step calibration process is an excellent way to learn the scoot-and-spin blast shot. Repeat it until you have it down. Every time you practice sand shots, draw a swing line that aims the proper angle to the left of the pin, draw a ball line perpendicular to the swing line, and be sure your setup includes careful placement of your left heel on the ball line, keeping your shoulders, feet, and body alignment parallel left of the swing line (Fig. 9.3.12). Keep drawing lines and hitting shots until you get really good at it, until you can accurately escape from the sand without drawing the lines but knowing where they would have been.

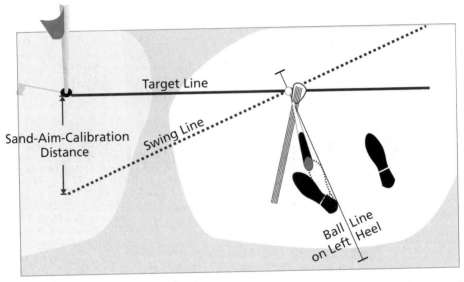

Figure 9.3.12: Proper setup for scoot-and-spin blast from sand
(as seen from golfer's view looking down)

Before I end this section I want you to see some photographs of a few sand setup positions we regularly see in our Scoring Game Schools. Houdini could not have escaped from the sand using some of these. Combine these positions with a generally poor knowledge of the sand swing, and you'll understand why so many people fear the sand (Fig. 9.3.13).

And a final point, when the ball is positioned perfectly on the inside of your left heel with respect to your swing line, it will be five inches in front of your stance center and will look to someone standing face-on to you (perpendicular to the target line) as if you are playing the ball off the toe of your front foot, as it appears in Figure 9.3.14. Don't worry; this is as it should be.

Figure 9.3.13: Bad ball position promotes bad golf swings in sand

Figure 9.3.14: Perfect ball position on left heel line relative to swing line in sand

9.4 Margin for Error

A few years ago, I tested some features of my own sand game by measuring my performance using both the scoot-and-spin and dig-and-push techniques. They should provide you with some insight into how valuable the scoot-and-spin can be. (I don't expect you to measure these parameters for your own performance, and the actual numbers are not important. What you get from my numbers is an understanding of how the proper technique makes your sand play easier because it is more forgiving and minimizes the consequences of making normal human errors.)

In the test, I hit 10 consecutive shots with one technique, with an assistant recording how far short or past the target flagstick each ball finished (Fig. 9.4.1). I also stopped, measured, and recorded the positions of my sand divots to see how far behind each ball my wedge entered the sand (Fig. 9.4.2). Then I hit 10 shots using the other technique, recording the same data. I alternated techniques and repeated each sequence five times, then correlated the results, which are summarized as follows:

1. Most of my best shots (those that landed softly, bounced once, checked, and dribbled closest to the pin) were scoot-and-spin shots. On the best 10 of those—all stopping within two feet of the hole—my wedge entered the sand almost exactly 4½ inches behind the ball.

Figure 9.4.1: I tested fifty shots with each of two techniques

Figure 9.4.2: Divot parameters and shot performance was recorded for every shot

2. A group of scoot-and-spin shots that flew a shorter distance but rolled farther than normal ended up at almost the same place as the best shots on the green. On these shots, my wedge had entered the sand about 5½ inches behind the balls.

3. A third set of shots flew farther than my best ones but had more backspin so they stopped quicker. They also traveled almost the same total distance and ended near the pin. On these, my wedge had entered the sand only three to 3½ inches behind the balls.

4. On those shots when my wedge entered the sand more than five inches or less than three inches behind the ball, all stayed on the green but were also more than five feet from the flagstick.

5. Then there was the erratic scatter pattern of my dig-and-push shots. Only three (out of 50) stopped within two feet of the hole; 14 missed the green completely. On my best dig-and-push shots, the wedge entered the sand less than a quarter inch behind the ball.

6. On those dig-and-push shots when my wedge entered the sand between half an inch to one inch behind the ball, the balls finished from three to 17 feet short of the pin. On those shots when I hit the ball cleanly before entering the sand, every one airmailed the green (traveling about 30 yards).

A very clear pattern emerged from the results. The scoot-and-spin has a margin for error of about two inches (plus or minus one inch from the perfect point of entry), for producing shots that finish where I want them to. On the dig-and-push, if I was not within a quarter inch of perfect entry into the sand, I was in trouble.

Whichever method you choose is your choice. If your timing and coordination are significantly better executing dig-and-push swings, then by all means use that shot (as long as you can maintain that performance under pressure). Or, as you'll see in the next section, you can learn to chip (pick all your sand shots clean) or putt from sand, but then you'd better not play courses with high bunker lips. For my money, I'll stay with the scoot-and-spin and its large margin for error.

The Chip-and-Putt from Sand

9.5 Chipping Mechanics in Sand

Have you ever been in a bunker and thought the shot looked so easy that you could pick the ball off the surface and roll it to the pin? Sometimes you can, and if the conditions are right, it's not a bad idea. I refer to this play as a chip, not a pick.

"Picking" the ball suggests that you might lift the ball with your hands, and your hands are the last things you want to use in this shot.

Before you get all excited about having an alternative to the standard sand blast shot, understand that the chip has almost no tolerance for error: You can't hit fat or thin and get away with it. But it is an easy shot to execute. There are three fundamentals to worry about. If you can handle them, and the physical circumstances of the bunker allow for the somewhat limited capabilities of the shot, the chip may be a shot for you to try.

1. Because there is no tolerance for hitting fat or thin, you must establish a fixed reference height for your swing during setup. I suggest making this reference your sternum and/or your head. You must commit to keeping them level, at a constant distance from the ground, throughout your swing.

2. From your fixed reference, establish a swing-arc radius—the length of your left arm extended—and keep it constant throughout your swing. And when I say constant, I mean *precisely* constant. Unlike most golf shots, where perfection is rare and you have a reasonable margin for error, on the chip from sand, the clubhead must contact the bottom quarter of the ball without digging into the sand.

3. You must execute a dead-hands swing on a ball positioned half an inch behind your stance center. Don't mindlessly put the ball "somewhere" back in your stance and chip it: You're likely to thin the shot because your swing radius is holding the club a quarter inch off the sand to begin with. Likewise, you have no chance if your ball is even slightly too far forward: Your club will dig in if it hits the sand first. *Any* error in clubhead height through impact is serious.

Even with these qualifications and warnings, the chip is still a good shot under certain conditions because it is not too hard to learn. Its best application comes when you can chip with a 6- to 8-iron over a low bunker lip to a pin a long way from you. If you hit the shot cleanly, it will behave about like a normal chip from grass from that distance, except it will have a little more backspin and stop about 10% to 15% shorter than the normal shot.

You also can get good results from your pitching and sand wedges with this technique if you learn to judge how high your shots will come out, and, again, if you're not looking at high bunker lips. But you'll never hit this shot high enough on the face to produce really high shots, no matter which club you use. Always play for the ball to come out a little lower than you would normally expect for the club you are playing.

From the standard chipping address posture (see Chapter 8 for details), position the ball precisely half an inch behind your stance center (Fig. 9.5.1). Keeping your club always a quarter inch above the sand, make your normal finesse chipping motion, except swing as though you intended to roll the shot about 15% farther than the distance to the flagstick (Fig. 9.5.2).

Figure 9.5.1: Address position for chip from sand

Figure 9.5.2: Maintain head level and swing radius constant to chip from sand

9.6 The Putt from Sand

If you haven't already, please read about the chiputt in section 8.11. Because if you are going to putt a ball out of the sand, the chiputt—nothing more than swinging your putter with a chipping motion—is the shot to use.

The chiputt works well from the sand because of the increased power generated by the chipping swing. But it will work only if the sand is firm enough to let a ball roll through it; I've seen sand so soft that rolling balls stop short and seem to sink. Most sand, however, especially if it has not been freshly raked, can be negotiated by a fast-rolling ball, as long as there is no lip at the edge of the bunker to stop it.

Start from a narrow stance and make a smooth finesse chipping motion. If you position the ball two inches ahead of your stance center (Fig. 9.6.1), at exactly the bottom of your swing arc, the ball will start above the sand by the amount of loft on your putterface. Give it too much loft, by playing the ball too far forward, and the ball will pop up and land, stopping in the sand. And if you play it back and hit it down, the ball will go nowhere. So the initial launch condition is critical. You must keep the ball moving almost horizontally immediately after impact to have a chance of getting it out of the bunker (Fig. 9.6.2).

Because you will almost always hit the chiputt solidly, it has none of the precision requirements of the chip from sand explained in section 9.5. However, it does

Figure 9.6.1: The chiputt works well from sand (if no bunker lip is there to stop it)

Figure 9.6.2: Keep ball moving horizontally after impact

have one major drawback: You can't predict exactly how the ball will transition from rolling in sand to rolling through the grass between the bunker and the green. Even with no bunker lip, the ball may bounce and take off in the grass, or get caught in the grass and die. That's why I recommend putting from sand only when the sand is firm and flat, there is no bunker lip, and the pin is 50 feet or more away (the greater the distance the better, to minimize the uncertain efficiency of the ball's roll through the sand and grass).

9.7 Accuracy Benefits

Many golfers will try chipping and putting from sand because they're uncomfortable hitting a blast shot. Specifically, they don't know which club to use, or how hard to swing, to blast long bunker shots close to the pin.

In fact, the scoot-and-spin blast is a higher-percentage shot than the chip or putt, because it has a much greater margin for error. But if the golfer has any anxiety about blasting normal sand shots, the long ones will make him terrified. Many accomplished players don't have a feel for the long blast shots. Even the Tour pros who hit close behind the ball on their bunker shots fear the long ones under pressure: They have to swing so hard to carry their shots the longer distances that if they miss just a little and hit the ball first, it will fly way too far.

But if (and I stress *if*) the bunker lip is low enough, the golfer can be pretty certain that a chip from sand will roll about the same distance (within 15%) as a chip from grass. And a putt probably will roll about the same distance as if putted through the fringe. That creates a level of comfort that, if the golfer hits the shot properly, he knows approximately how it will turn out.

9.8 Disaster Is Close

The real moment of truth in sand play comes when you're evaluating what shots are possible, and then which of those leaves the highest probability of converting the next putt. A final factor could be "Which shot makes you feel most comfortable?" Of course, all of this has to be evaluated with your situation: Do you need to sink the shot, or is out and two putts good enough? Is there a hazard behind the pin and anything less than out and three putts is okay?

When you look at the options this way, the scoot-and-spin blast shot again wins in most situations. It has the largest margin for error, and it produces the most shots close to the pin, from all distances (see section 9.12). But this applies only if you know how to hit the shot. Many golfers don't.

Rule out the scoot-and-spin, and the chip and putt become viable options if the bunker lip is low enough. Neither shot requires much touch for distance, but the golfer must make a level swing and precise contact for the chip, or have no lip to clear with the putt. On the chip, the club is moving so slowly that if it does hit the sand it stops almost immediately, and the ball doesn't get out. Or if you skull it, the ball likely hits the lip and remains in the sand. Both of these shots, when executed poorly, turn out far worse than a scoot-and-spin shot that is struck poorly by plus or minus an inch or two.

The last choice is the worst of all, the dig-and-push. It offers almost no margin for error, and its bad results are worse than bad—they're terrible.

My advice is simple. Get into a practice bunker and learn the scoot-and-spin blast shot. While there, try chipping a few, and if you have a bunker with no lip, putt a few balls out, too. These three options will allow you to handle any situation.

Sand-Shot Behavior

9.9 Spin Controls Behavior on the Green

Unlike distance wedges, most well-hit sand shots land softly on the greens and don't make deep divots. The club that blasted them onto the green never actually touched the ball. It's the sand brushing past, carried by the passing club, that imparts the spin and soft trajectory.

Because there is no deep divot to halt the forward momentum of a sand shot, it needs lots of spin to stop it. Otherwise, it can roll a long way. And you very well may not want that to happen.

Imagine a two-tiered green. The hole is cut close on top of the second tier. In Chapter 7, I explained how dangerous it is to fly a shot into a slope (it magnifies whatever error you make): It is much smarter to land your sand shot well short of the slope (where the levels change) and let it roll up the hill, rather than trying to fly it just past the slope. However, most players don't know how to hit a sand shot that runs after landing.

Or how about a sand shot into a green that slopes sharply toward you? If you put your normal full amount of backspin on this shot, it might come right back at you, spinning off the green and back into the bunker. But you don't want to push a ball up past the pin with no spin, because that likely will leave you a treacherous downhill putt. So put just a moderate amount of spin on your sand shot. Do you know how?

9.10 Spin Mechanics

The sand is one of the few places in golf where I see great players allow their left wrist to break down in the follow-through. This happens because when playing difficult courses with difficult pin positions, they use lots of backspin to help hold fast greens. Adding slap or zip through impact creates extra clubhead speed, and spin, as the clubhead scoots under the ball.

To maximize spin on a 60-yard bunker shot, the best method is to strike the ball first with a descending blow with your sand wedge, dragging the ball along the top of heavy, damp sand (pinching, or trapping, it against the sand). Under those ideal conditions, you'll probably produce more spin than you want.

Much more useful is the maximum-spin shot from a greenside bunker, which you have to do without hitting the ball too hard, since you usually want to carry it only about eight to 10 yards. Scoot the blade of your wedge through the sand very quickly and very close to the ball, so the sand that touches and spins the ball is being dragged by the clubface. The faster and closer the club passes the ball without actually touching it, the greater the spin.

There are two ways to hit this shot. First, you can take a longer backswing and "zip" your hands and wrists through impact as fast as you can, then stop them immediately. Paul Azinger is the best I've seen at this technique. The other way is to hit a normal scoot-and-spin swing but, again, zipping the hands through impact. Steve Elkington and Phil Mickelson are both great at this shot. The clubface must be wide open through impact for both shots to maximize spin while not transmitting too much forward power to the ball.

When less knowledgeable golfers try to hit the maximum-spin shot, they often hit a "blocked-hands" shot instead. The leading wrist stays above the trailing wrist after impact, so the club never releases. The club slows down so much through the sand that stability and control are completely destroyed.

On the opposite side of the spin world, to minimize spin and produce a shot that runs on the green, you must push the ball out of the sand. Your clubhead cannot scoot past it. From your normal setup position, create the push shot by positioning the ball two inches inside the heel of your left foot so it is just short of the middle of your soon-to-be sand divot. Keep your clubface square to your target line (which, in this case, is also your swing line) and turn your grip under (to a slightly strong position, as on the left in Fig. 9.10.1). Make an essentially normal sand swing, but consciously roll your hands back to square through impact. This lets your clubhead (usually a pitching wedge or 9-iron) enter and dig a bit into the

Figure 9.10.1: The minimum spin bunker shot

Figure 9.10.2: The minimum spin shot will roll all the way across a green

sand, but then quickly roll over so it doesn't get stuck there (right side, Fig. 9.10.1). Be sure to follow through so you push the ball out with low spin. This is a more dangerous shot than the face-open blast, because it requires that the bottom of the swing be very level so the club doesn't dig too deeply into the sand. But you sometimes need your ball to roll, so practice enough to have the shot ready (Fig. 9.10.2).

While you should know how to hit the above two shots, the most predictable way to get out of the sand and stop where you want on the green is to fly the ball most of the way there, stopping it after one bounce, a check, and a dribble. Again, that's the normal "scoot-and-spin" blast. It has enough spin to stop the ball within about six to eight feet of where it touches down, plus consistency in distance control, and a large margin of error (plus or minus one inch on your entry point in the sand). If your practice time in sand is limited, work until you *own* the "scoot-and-spin." It will serve you well.

9.11 Generic Expectations

Not all bunker and green configurations are the same. You're sure to face high and low bunker lips, different types of sand, and elevated greens, as well as lousy lies. Even though my data over the years show that almost 80% of all sand shots actually begin with good lies (so you want to become good from good lies before you worry about the bad), many golfers' results from bad or unusual lies are so bad that these shots also must be learned and practiced to save scores.

Here are a few tips and truths that may help you to play from different sand situations. Try some of these suggestions in a practice bunker before trying them on the course. As you'll see, some require you to make rather significant changes to my previously stated "standard" sand procedures.

Sand-shot height is controlled by:

1. The effective loft of your clubface as it passes through the sand. The greater the loft, the higher and shorter the shot.
2. Clubhead speed as it passes the ball. The faster the speed, the higher and longer the shot.
3. How close the clubhead passes to the ball. The closer it gets to the ball, the higher the shot will fly, and the greater the spin.
4. How far left you have aimed and swung. The farther left you aim, the higher and shorter your shots will fly.
5. The height of your hands on the follow-through. Just as with distance wedges, the higher your hands finish, the higher the ball comes out; the lower the finish, the lower the ball comes out. On most shots, finish with a

high, full follow-through to be sure of getting the ball out high and soft, and controlling the overall distance.

If you stab at the ball with a punch-shot swing, there's nothing lifting the ball except the loft of the club. That's why a swing without a follow-through hits low shots. Also remember that to produce spin, the club must pass the ball coming out of the sand, and that can happen only when the face is very open.

When the sand becomes harder, coarser, or wetter than normal, the ball will come out quicker, because the club bounces and scoots through the sand in a more shallow divot. Ultimately, the only way to handle these situations is with experience, which tells you how much hotter the ball will fly from different sand. From "hot" sand, don't change your technique except to use a shorter, more lofted club with less bounce on its sole. And whatever you do, if the sand is so hard your club won't penetrate (e.g., hardpan dirt), don't try the blast shot. That's when the chip or putt will do better (as long as there is a low, or no, lip on the bunker).

For fine, sugarlike sand, in which the ball sits down because of its own weight, use a wedge with a bigger flange and more bounce (see section 9.13). Use the same scoot-and-spin technique discussed earlier, but expect your club to dig deeper into the sand than the normal half inch before it bounces and scoots under the ball. These shots will fly shorter distances but roll farther with less spin than shots from firm-sand bunkers.

Sand-Swing Variations

9.12 Distance Control for Blasting

I've already said that you want to restrict your backswing in the sand to about the 9:00 o'clock length. So how do you control the distance of your shots? Here's how *not* to do it:

1. *Don't* change the rhythm of your swing.
2. *Don't* change how close you hit behind the ball.
3. *Don't* change how hard you swing through the sand.

The easiest way to vary the distance of your sand shots is to use clubs of different lengths and lofts, all the time continuing to use the same swing.

There's a great misunderstanding in amateur golf that the only clubs allowed for use in a bunker are those labeled "sand." But the name of a club doesn't have anything to do with its performance in the sand or anywhere else.

I recommend that most players carry four wedges, two of which have more loft than the traditional sand wedge. All four wedges can be put to excellent use getting out of the sand, as can all the irons down to the 6-iron. Don't be surprised: All eight of these clubs (6-iron to fourth wedge) will handle the sand if you position the ball forward in your stance, open the face so the bottom and back of the club bounce and scoot through the sand, and keep the leading edge from digging in.

Say your "normal" 55-degree loft sand-wedge (the one with "SW" stamped on the sole) carries the ball on average a distance of 12 yards in the air when you make your 9:00 o'clock backswing. That means if you take your pitching wedge and make the same swing, the results will be a 16-yard carry. Your 9-iron will produce a 20-yard carry from the same swing.

This steady increase in distance has two causes. First, even with the face of your 9-iron open so it will bounce and scoot through the sand, it still has eight degrees less loft than the sand wedge, so it will propel the ball more forward. Second, each shaft is longer than that of the preceding club, so the same-rhythm swing, with the same hand speed, produces more clubhead speed, which again translates into longer carry. This progression continues as you go on up through the irons.

I've seen Seve Ballesteros hit beautiful, high, soft sand shots with his 2-iron. But I don't think most golfers, including most Tour players, should hit anything less lofted than a 6-iron (long irons just take more practice time).

The Tour pros are not afraid to choose the right club for the situation. Table 9.12.1 shows the average distances sand shots should carry for the different clubs (plus or minus a few yards for individual golfers' swing differences).

Combining your rhythmic finesse swing with your four wedges provides you

CLUB	LOFT (degrees)	SHAFT LENGTH (inches)	CARRY DISTANCE (yards)
X-Wedge	64	34	8
L-Wedge	60	34.5	12
S-Wedge	55	35	16
P-Wedge	50	35.5	22
9-Iron	46	36	27
8-Iron	42	36.5	33

Table 9.12.1: Average carry distances for various clubs from sand (9:00 o'clock swings)

with a good range of carry distances, adequate for most greenside situations. And although most bunkers are located near greens, not all are. Go to your practice range and calibrate your 9-, 8-, 7-, and 6-iron distances from sand, too. This will increase your yardage coverage and come in handy on many long par-5 holes, where the bunkers are not close to the greens.

What if you need a shorter shot—say, one to a pin cut very close to the bunker? Take your most lofted wedge and grip down on it. Just as longer shafts produce more carry distance through increased clubhead speed, so do shorter shafts decrease head speed and carry distance (see Fig. 9.12.1). It's an easy way to hit soft short shots without trying to decelerate. Stand closer to the ball, but other than that, the swing fundamentals and ball position remain the same.

Don't be afraid to try this technique in practice: I've taught many fine players, including Tour pros, to wrap their lower hand completely around the metal of the shaft, below the grip, and hit shots that carry only three to four yards out of the sand. It's easy and requires only a normal, smooth, rhythmic, 7:30 or 8:00 o'clock bunker swing.

Figure 9.12.1: A short club produces short, soft shots from sand

9.13 Bounce vs. Conditions

Because I advocate using multiple wedges, I think the differences in loft, length, flex of their shafts, and weight of the clubheads are very important to your game. All can affect your wedge-shot performance and your ability to score. But there is something else about these clubs that can have an even bigger effect on your ability to hit shots. That something is the shape of the bottom, the sole.

You don't need to understand much about a wedge's design to hit good shots with it. At least that's true if your wedges have reasonably well-designed bottoms. But if your wedges have bad sole configurations, then you're in trouble. That's when knowing a little about design will help you determine if your clubs are help-ing or hurting your game.

Wedge loft, lie, shaft length, and flex are detailed in Chapter 10, so I won't go into them here. But sole design is independent of those parameters, and affects your wedge play in an entirely different way. While lies, lofts, and lengths deter-mine how far and in what direction your wedge shots go, the sole determines how the head of your wedge reacts with the ground, or sand, through impact. For example, sole design can determine if your club bounces into—and skulls—your ball, or contacts the ball first, then tears through the turf, creating a perfect shot trajectory.

Whenever I work with a player on wedge-game performance, I check the soles of his or her wedges to make sure the equipment will allow that golfer to play the game properly. They often don't. I look for three qualities:

1. How much bounce is on each wedge, and is that the right amount for the intended general use of that club?
2. How deep is the bounce? Is it a depth that will let the golfer play the special shots he intends to play with that club?
3. Does the player's set of wedges have the proper variation of sole designs to handle a wide variety of lies?

Let's define our terms. The amount of bounce on a wedge (or any club) is the distance that the bottom of the sole extends below the leading edge of the clubface (when the club is soled squarely in the impact position). Figure 9.13.1 shows the bounce for five different wedges, all of the same loft. In the golf industry today, bounce is completely independent of a wedge's loft, length, weight, or shaft flex. This means there is no assigned bounce to a particular type or loft of a wedge; the amount of bounce is the preference of the designer. It might be nice to have a standard set of rules for bounce, but golfers swing so differently, and teachers teach so differently, that no consensus has ever been reached.

Have no doubt, though, that there is an optimal bounce for each of your wedges, one that will provide the best results for your swing and game. So it behooves you to understand how to select your wedges.

Don't run out and try all the bounces shown in Figure 9.13.1. First understand that the *depth* of bounce also matters to wedge performance: The depth of bounce, as shown in Figure 9.13.2, determines whether or not the "effective" bounce—the amount of bounce at the moment of impact—changes when the clubface is opened through impact.

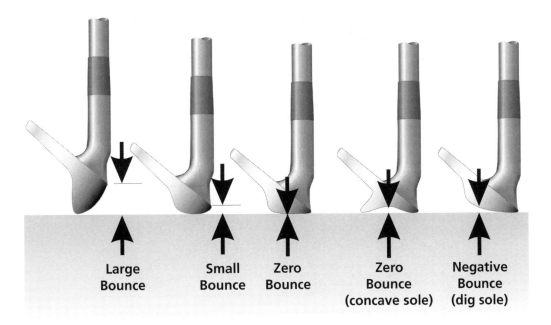

Figure 9.13.1: Different bounces produce different play characteristics

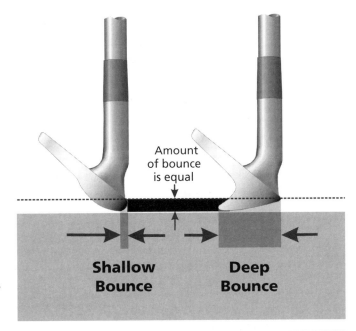

Figure 9.13.2: Wedge bounce can be shallow, deep, or anywhere in between

Effective bounce depends not only on how much bounce is designed into the sole, but also how deep it is in the sole and how much the face is open. As shown in Figure 9.13.3, shallow-bounce wedges don't change effective bounce much, if at all, as the face rotates open. However, deep-bounce wedges change effective bounce dramatically.

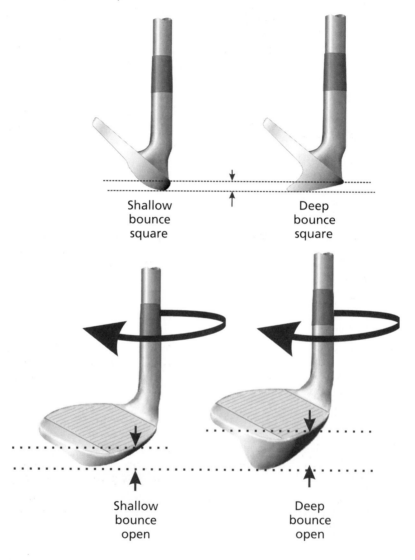

Shallow
bounce
square

Deep
bounce
square

Shallow
bounce
open

Deep
bounce
open

Figure 9.13.3: Opening the clubface usually changes the effective bounce of wedges

Depth of Bounce

Bounce vs. Application (in inches)	SHALLOW .10–.40	MEDIUM .40–.70	DEEP .70–1.0
MINIMUM .20–.35	Hardpan Tight Fairways Fringes Hard Sand	Fairways Light Rough Firm Sand	Plush Fairways Light Rough Moist Sand
MEDIUM .35–.50	Fairways Firm Sand Moist Sand	Light Rough Plush Fairways Medium Sand	Medium Rough Soft Sand
LARGE .50–.65	Medium Rough Soft Sand	Heavy Rough Very Soft Sand	Very Heavy Rough Fine, Soft Sand
MAXIMUM .65–.80	Heavy Rough Very Soft Sand	Very Heavy Rough Fine-Soft Sand	Super-Deep Rough Sugar-Fine Sand Pine Needles

Amount of Bounce

Table 9.13.1: Amount and depth of bounce affects how wedges perform from different lies

If you never play open-faced shots, you need bounce specifications different from those of the golfer who opens the clubface on many shots. For example, the golfer who carries only one low-lofted wedge, and therefore must open it to hit high shots, can't afford to have it be a deep-bounced club, because its bounce changes so drastically when the face is opened, and becomes so large, that the club could never be used from tight lies.

I don't want to make the discussion of bounce too confusing, but I must say a few general statements about the way the amount and depth of bounce will affect your wedge game. After you read them, examine Table 9.13.1 to determine what will best serve your wedge game on your home course. Also note that if you play other courses, with different short-game situations (e.g., tighter fairways or finer/coarser sand in the bunkers), you may want to take different clubs to handle the conditions.

General rules about bounce:

1. The greater the bounce, the earlier in the downswing and the more violently a wedge will bounce (reflect from the surface) upon hitting firm ground. Always carry at least one wedge with a small and shallow-bounce sole, allowing you to make contact on the third or fourth face line up from the leading edge, even when open. You'll need this wedge for hardpan and other hard-ground lies.

2. Don't carry wedges with either the same amount or depth of bounce. You never know what lie awaits on your next shot. We all face hardpan sooner or later, and you'll need a small, shallow-bounce club to handle it. But on the next hole you may find your ball sitting up in deep rough or on top of sugar-fine sand, and that's when you'll need a large, deep bounce.

3. Don't give up and select the maximum and minimum extremes of bounce if your courses don't call for them. Tailor your wedge set to fit what you face most frequently. And own a substitute wedge or two that you can call to duty on trips to other courses with other conditions.

9.14 Ball Position vs. Lie

I said earlier that 80% of all sand shots are hit from good lies. So why do those other 20% seem to occur so often? (And why, you might ask, just to you?) You know you're going to face a bad lie some of the time, so do you know how the ball will behave from them? Do you know what swings handle those lies best?

Three bad lies are the most common: the fried-egg, the completely buried, and the one-third-buried lie. An example of a fried-egg and a one-third-buried ball, along with how they compare to a perfect lie, is pictured in Figure 9.14.1. To help

Figure 9.14.1: The fried-egg, one-third-buried, and perfect lies in sand

you prepare for them, Table 9.14.1 lists my "all-other-things-being-equal" rules of sand play. Table 9.14.2 is a matrix of setup parameters to handle these lies.

As you can see in the tables, you can't open the clubface very much when the ball sits down in the sand. That means (because the club won't scoot under and spin the ball) you should allow for a lot more roll from bad lies once the ball gets on the green. Bad lies also require a wedge with less bounce, which allows the club to dig deeper and get down to the ball. Obviously, you don't want to scoot the clubface a half inch beneath the sand's surface when the ball is half buried; you'll strike the ball in its belly and fly it across the green and into more trouble.

A buried lie also demands gripping down on your club to produce a more descending blow from a shorter swing arc. The "shorter" the club shaft, the steeper the angle both into and out of the sand.

When a third of the ball is below the surface of the sand, open your wedge only half as much as for a good lie, set your swing line only half as far left of the target, play the ball a little less forward (two inches behind your left heel line), and use a club with not too much bounce. Then swing and try for a full follow-through. The ball will come out as shown in Figure 9.14.2, and run at least as far as it flies, usually farther.

The more the ball sits down, the farther back toward your stance center you play it, and the more you square the club (so it digs in). If you play the ball forward, as on good-lie sand shots, the square face will dig so deep that by the time the club gets there, it won't have enough energy left to get the ball out.

For the buried lie, when the ball is visible but mostly under the sand, move it back to the center of your stance, close the club so it's square, maybe even toed-in a little, and grip down on the shaft. Make sure to supply enough power to get

THE BETTER YOUR LIE (the higher the ball sits on top of the sand), the farther forward the ball should be positioned in your stance.

THE WORSE YOUR LIE (the deeper your ball is buried), the farther back in your stance the ball should be positioned.

THE FARTHER FORWARD the ball is positioned in your stance, the more you should open the clubface.

THE FARTHER BACK the ball is positioned in your stance, the more you should close the clubface.

THE MORE YOU OPEN THE CLUBFACE:

- the more left you must aim
- the shallower the club moves through the sand
- the higher the trajectory of the shot
- the more backspin the shot will have
- the softer the shot will land

THE MORE YOU CLOSE THE CLUBFACE:

- the more square or right you must aim
- the deeper your club will dig into the sand
- the lower the trajectory of the shot
- the farther the ball will roll after landing

THE MORE COMPLETELY YOU FINISH YOUR FOLLOW-THROUGH:

- the less likely you are to leave your ball in the sand
- the more consistent your carry distance will be
- the more "muscle-free" your club will travel through impact

THE SHORTER YOU STOP YOUR FOLLOW-THROUGH:

- the less forward momentum your shot will have
- the softer the shot will land
- the more likely you are to leave your ball in the sand

Table 9.14.1: Rules of sand play (all other things being equal)

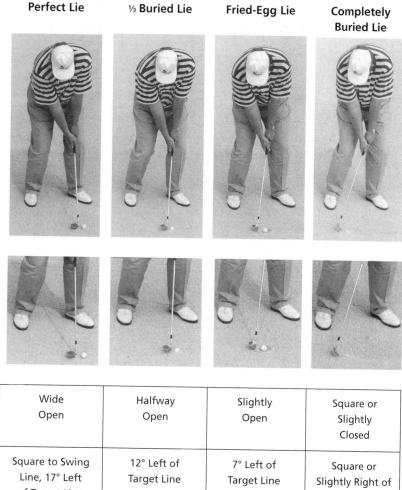

	Perfect Lie	**⅓ Buried Lie**	**Fried-Egg Lie**	**Completely Buried Lie**
Face Angle	Wide Open	Halfway Open	Slightly Open	Square or Slightly Closed
Stance and Shoulder Position	Square to Swing Line, 17° Left of Target Line	12° Left of Target Line	7° Left of Target Line	Square or Slightly Right of Target Line
Ball Position	Inside Left Heel	2" Behind Left Heel	Slightly Forward of Center	Stance Center
Club Through Sand	Bounce at ½"-Deep Scoot under Ball	Some Bounce, Some Dig 1" Deep	Slight Bounce, Medium Dig 1½" Deep	Zero Bounce, Complete Dig 2" Deep Push Ball Out

Table 9.14.2: Setup and ball position vs. lie in sand

Figure 9.14.2: From a one-third-buried lie, a full finish will produce a running shot

through the sand. A good rule of thumb says the more you are worried about getting the ball out, the more you should try to make a full finish. Striving for a finish guarantees that the ball will get out of the bunker, albeit with very little backspin. From the completely buried lie (Fig. 9.14.3), the ball always comes out low and will roll two to three times as far as it flies.

The fried egg is the ball sitting in a little crater somewhat below the surface (Fig. 9.14.4). Play it as if the ball were about one-third buried: Position the ball about two inches ahead of your stance center and open the club half as much as for the normal sand shot (about 20 degrees). The ball will roll a pretty long way on the green. You'll likely face quite a few fried eggs, especially when new sand has recently been added

Figure 9.14.3: From a buried lie, the full finish produces a low-running shot

Figure 9.14.4: From a fried-egg lie, a full finish will produce a soft shot but not much backspin

to a bunker, so practice it. To create a realistic lie, swirl a ball around in a small circle, pushing the sand away from the center, as shown in Figure 9.14.5.

Always remember that the desired action of your club through the sand, and the resulting behavior of the ball, are important choices you need to make *before* choosing which club to use. But if you use the right club, and make a few subtle changes in your setup alignment and ball position, you can execute all these shots with relative ease, because they all come from the same swing motion. I validate this statement by asking you to see how similar all of my swings from these bad lies are, compared to the sand swing from a perfect lie by Jim Furyk in the following sequence (Fig.

Figure 9.14.5: Making a fried-egg lie

9.14.6). You see, the swings are not so different. It is the setup, ball positions, and club selections that cause the differences in ball behavior (by the way, Jim is a great sand player, and while his swing plane doesn't follow all the rules, his clubhead action through the sand shows why he's among the world's best from bunkers).

Now, if you want to tackle some difficult sand shots, try hitting from sidehill lies. When the ball is above your feet, forget the scoot-and-spin blast shot; it won't work even if the ball is sitting up on top of the sand. You've got to be careful and make a good swing, because you have no margin for error. Try the dig-and-push blast, aiming slightly to the right of the target, the clubface almost square (Fig. 9.14.7). If the ball is one-third down in the sand, aim still farther right and square the blade completely. Play the ball three inches in back of your left heel line. The ball will pop out without too much power or spin, so expect it to roll a little farther than normal. Also, be firm through impact with a little greater grip pressure than normal, to be sure the toe of the club doesn't dig in and get stuck in the sand.

If the ball is completely below the surface of the sand, aim farther right and "toe-in" the blade to your target. Play the ball from the middle of your stance and grip down on your shaft as far as you can. Be sure to swing in balance, and expect more roll than normal. The toe of the club will definitely dig in on this shot, so be sure the club enters the sand with enough energy to get the ball out. Don't worry about getting up and down: Just be sure you get the ball somewhere on the green, take your hazard medicine, and move on. One last thing: Practice this shot before trying it on the course.

When the ball is below your feet, another tough lie, it is still important to maintain your balance, so try to make the smoothest swing possible. Don't open

Figure 9.14.6: Jim Furyk: the scoot-and-spin blast

Figure 9.14.7: For ball-above-feet shots, the dig-and-push blast is your only option

the face all the way, play the ball just ahead of stance center, and be conscious of staying down through impact (don't come up out of the shot or sway toward the ball as you swing). If you change your height during the swing—because you lean forward—it will lead to skulls and shanks. Stand close to the ball, aim farther left than normal (Fig. 9.14.8), and try to make a good finish despite the fact that your knees are more bent than usual and it is difficult to complete the swing.

Figure 9.14.8: The ball-below-feet shot is most difficult for me

9.15 The Cock-and-Pop from Sand

A still more difficult situation arises with the above three lies (one-third buried, fried egg, and completely buried) when there isn't much green between the ball and the hole. In this case, try the cock-and-pop with all three lies.

Just as you do when playing from a nesty lie in the grass, the cock-and-pop calls for violating most of the rules of a good finesse swing. You are most concerned with supplying enough power to get the ball out, some of it must come from a hand-and-wrist muscle pop, and you are going to have no follow-through.

Play the ball from the normal positions for all three lies. The difference is that you want to cock your wrists as much as you can early in the backswing, which shortens the radius of your swing. This gives you the ability to make a very descending blow into the sand, popping the ball up and out without too much forward power, because of your abbreviated follow-through. Look at Figure 9.15.1 for the cock-and-pop from a one-third-buried lie, then compare it to the swing finish for the same lie but a full swing (Fig. 9.14.2).

The same technique works on the completely buried lie, but you have to supply even more pop, so a lot more sand comes out (Fig. 9.15.2). The more you follow through with this shot, the more sure you are of getting the ball out and onto the green, but the farther it will roll. Don't get too cute, or exacting, with this shot unless you have practiced it many, many times. I can't tell you how many cock-and-

Figure 9.15.1: The cock-and-pop from a one-third-buried lie

Figure 9.15.2: The cock-and-pop from a completely buried lie

pop shots I've seen *almost* get out of the bunker. (If you want to see the best at this shot, watch Paul Azinger practicing it before a tournament. I don't know why, but he loves the cock-and-pop from a buried lie and is unbelievably good at it, which proves that it can be done.)

9.16 Downhill Lies

Most golfers—yours truly included—consider the downhill sand shot one of the most difficult plays in the game. But some downhill shots are easier than others. For example:

• If the bunker has no lip, a simple chiputt might do the trick.

• If the slope isn't too steep, place the ball at the left heel position, tilt your shoulders so they're parallel to the sand, and make a normal finesse blast to scoot-and-spin the ball out. This technique succeeds only when the slopes are fairly minor (less than about 10 degrees from horizontal) and you can keep your balance throughout the swing (see Fig. 9.16.1). And it helps if you've practiced the shot beforehand.

• Gentle slopes also can be handled with a chip, but the tendency is to hit these chips fat, and if you don't hit them fat, they come out incredibly low and roll a long way.

It's the steep downhillers that are real tough. By steep I mean when it's impossible to tilt your shoulders parallel to the surface and still keep your balance during the swing. In this case, consider putting if the bunker has no lip (but such

Figure 9.16.1: Be sure to stay with (swing through) the downhill bunker shot

bunkers are increasingly difficult to find). So, assuming there is a lip to clear, here are a number of adjustments that may help you achieve a reasonable result:

1. Plant your left (front) foot solidly, deep in the sand, so it can support nearly all of your weight during the swing. You'll have to flex your knees excessively, and doing so will limit body rotation during the swing.

2. Tilt your body so your shoulders are as nearly parallel to the slope of the sand as you can get them, while not losing your balance. (I sometimes use my wedge to help get my shoulders as close to parallel as I can and still get steady, as seen in Fig. 9.16.2.)

3. Grip down on the wedge at least three or four inches. Lower the right shoulder so you can address the ball, which is positioned perfectly centered in your stance.

4. Without any delay, hit the shot with an upper-body-and-arms swing. The swing momentum probably will carry you down the hill after the shot. It may look a little odd, but walking through this shot actually helps, since it keeps the club-head going downhill longer (see Fig. 9.16.3).

On the steepest downhillers, move the ball a little farther back in your stance, aim significantly more to the left than normal, and open your clubface to the absolute maximum. You will hit closer to the ball than normal, take less sand and keep the shot from coming out too low, and rolling too far (Fig. 9.16.4).

Fortunately, we don't face many downhill bunker shots. Therefore, they aren't

Figure 9.16.2: On downhill sand shots, set your shoulders parallel to the slope

Figure 9.16.3: Walking through the shot helps you stay down through impact

Figure 9.16.4: Plan for a lower trajectory and more roll on downhill bunker shots

worth too much practice time. But when you do face one, keep your expectations realistic. I tell my Tour players to forget performing a miracle from truly tough bunker lies; you just want to be sure of getting the ball onto the green. The worst result from a downhill lie is skulling the ball or leaving it in the bunker, both of which lead to double and triple bogeys. So minimize your penalty, keep it to one stroke, and try to get that shot back later on in the round. One stroke can be handled. Two or three are a *lot* more difficult to recover.

9.17 Uphill Struggles

The uphill bunker lie can work in your favor. The key is to create forward swing momentum, which will help you maintain your balance as long as you keep moving forward during the through-swing, and don't fall back or reverse pivot.

From gentle upslopes, aim slightly left of the target and tilt your shoulders as near to parallel to the sand as you can. Use a normal, left-heel ball position, and open the clubface relative to your swing line. Make a normal scoot-and-spin swing. I suggest using one club stronger (less loft) than normal for every five degrees of upslope. This makes up for the higher trajectory and quicker stopping on the green that result from the uphill lie. This concept works well on slopes less than 15 degrees and distances less than 30 feet to the pin (Fig. 9.17.1). From a good lie, you should be able to get close to the pin if you take enough club.

Figure 9.17.1: Uphill sand shots are much easier

When the uphill shots get longer, the scoot-and-spin technique provides even higher trajectories, which begin to make deeper divots on the green, so the ball spins back quicker and farther than normal. Take less-lofted clubs (try a 6-iron) for long, uphill blast shots. Don't take the normal-lofted sand club and try to make a harder swing, as "rip" swings seldom work from the sand. Again, these shots take practice, particularly to learn how much club you need to reach the hole.

9.18 Deep Problems

What do you think happens when the ball sits down in the sand on uphill bunker shots? Surprisingly, the shot gets a little easier, because the ball comes out lower, with less spin, and will run farther once it lands on the green. That helps, since the biggest problem with an uphill shot is getting the ball to the hole. As long as the uphill slope is not too great (no greater than about 20 degrees, as shown in Fig. 9.18.1), allowing you to make a balanced swing, this shot can be accomplished safely and your up-and-down percentage can be high.

But the scoot-and-spin will no longer work, which means you have to use the dig-and-push, moving the ball back to only two inches ahead of stance center and

Figure 9.18.1: Use the dig-and-push
on plugged uphill lies

using a square clubface to dig through impact. If you can get your shoulder line parallel to the sand, this shot isn't too difficult.

Even when your ball completely buries in an uphill bank (Fig. 9.18.2), don't throw in the towel. This shot isn't nearly as difficult as a bad downhiller. Although the commentators on television like to say how the player got a tough break, don't believe it. Just change your technique.

When you can't get your shoulders parallel with the surface of the sand and keep your balance, go vertical. Stand almost straight up and down and forget about a follow-through. While this may sound bizarre, the shot works very well because your instinct is to hit the shot hard, and, for once, that instinct is correct. The ball will come out with very little spin, so it will roll a long distance on the green, again helping you get it close.

Set up to this shot by positioning the ball two inches forward of your stance center and squaring the clubface, with your swing line aimed directly at the target. Using your sand or pitching wedge at full-shaft length, take a long, powerful shoulder turn going back. Then give it all the acceleration you've got coming down (use your power swing, not your finesse swing), letting the square clubface

Figure 9.18.2: Swing hard when the ball is plugged in the bank

stick into the sand and stop. Don't worry about a follow-through, because you can't move a mountain. You'll like the results when your club (because of proper ball position) enters the sand very close to the back edge of the ball.

Don't worry about hitting this shot thin or skulling it: I don't think you could skull it if you tried. But be sure not to hit it fat or the ball might not move an inch.

9.19 Imagination Helps

A chapter on sand play is a good place to remind you that you can never prepare too much or too well for what is going to happen in golf. That doesn't mean you must have practiced every shot 10,000 times. What it does mean—and I base this on my experience working with some of the world's greatest players—is that the most successful sand play comes from those who understand the principles of sand play and know how the shots will react if they do this or that.

Players like Steve Elkington, Tom Kite, Phil Mickelson, and Seve Ballesteros understand their sand games very well. Of course, they have practiced them a lot both to develop and refine that knowledge. But here's a story, told to me by PGA

Tour professional Tom Sieckmann, which indicates that success sometimes comes from something in addition to experience and practice.

Playing a European PGA Tour event some years ago, Sieck was paired with Seve Ballesteros, who hit a long iron over and left of a green into a deep, bowl-shaped bunker. Seve's ball plugged under the top edge of the back of the bunker. The ball was plugged deep under the lip, and at the back of the bunker, no less. What did Seve do next? He couldn't take an unplayable-lie penalty and a drop, because the ball would have been closer to the hole. He couldn't hit it out backward, because there was a hazard there. He didn't want to go back to his original position and hit another long iron, and there was no way to hit it toward the hole.

Sieck told me he thought the only shot was to stand at the bottom of the bunker, take a big swing sideways, dig the ball out with the toe of a club, and hope it would come down to the bottom without hitting Seve (which would have been a penalty). From there, he would then have a chance of getting up and down.

Seve looked at the lie for about 30 seconds, went to his bag, and pulled out his putter. He stood on the bank above and behind the ball, and to Sieck's absolute amazement turned the toe of his putter down, drove it through the grass of the bunker lip, and hit the ball. Seve didn't hesitate, or seem surprised, as the ball ran through the bottom of the bunker, back up the other side, hopped onto the green, and rolled toward the pin. The ball didn't go in, but Seve holed his putt for par, as Sieck almost had an "amazement" heart attack.

Now, for the interesting part of the story. When Sieck could speak again, he asked Seve how in the world he had learned that shot. Where did he learn it? How did he know how hard to hit it? Did he have any other shots he hit with the end of his putter? Seve looked at him and said, "No, I've never tried it before. I just *imagined* it might work."

So, my friends, I suggest that you keep your brain in gear when you practice. What you learn while practicing just might help your imagination. That was how Seve built his imagination, and it has definitely helped him.

CHAPTER 10

Short-Game Equipment

Generic Equipment

10.1 Generic-Set Design

In my opinion, there is a problem with most generic sets of golf clubs sold today: I don't agree with the way they have been designed for the job they are supposed to do.

When I say a "generic set," I mean the off-the-rack clubs sold in pro shops, off-course golf shops, sporting-goods stores, discount stores, and mail-order catalogues. It's the same, basic set of clubs everybody is familiar with, beginning with a driver and going down through the long, medium, and short irons, plus a pitching wedge, a sand wedge, and a putter.

This is the standard in golf, the set almost everybody buys. Yet, despite their widespread acceptance, I cannot for the life of me understand why these sets are designed the way they are. Not my education in physics, my 15 years of space research at NASA, my 24 years in the golf-research business (including 12 years designing and developing clubs), or all my years playing and studying the way the game is played, help me understand the design principles behind this generic set.

I believe a set of clubs should be designed to let you hit your shots and play the best you can. They should help you score your best and enjoy the game to the max, from your longest drive to your shortest putt. The distance range of those shots is from roughly 300 (Tiger-drive) yards to near zero (tap-in putts). Within that range, the generic set provides 12 clubs, including a driver, a fairway wood or two, and irons (usually 3-iron through pitching wedge) for distances between 300 and 100 yards: That's 12 clubs for a range of 200 yards. From 100 yards to about 15 yards, most sets provide you with one club, usually a sand wedge. For the last 15 or so yards, when you're on the green—where nearly half the game is played—you get one club, the putter.

Look at that lineup on a distance scale (Fig. 10.1.1). Twelve clubs for 200 yards, one club for 85 yards, and one club for 15 yards. Does that seem well balanced? Okay, put it another way: Twelve clubs for the power game, one club for the short game, and one club for the putting game. Not a lot better, is it? There's something very peculiar about this, particularly since you now know that it's the shots inside 100 yards that control your ability to score.

Maybe we're looking at this all wrong. Let's look at generic-set design not by distance but by the frequency of shots hit (Chart 10.1.1). Does that make better

STANDARD GOLF-SHOP SET (AS DESIGNED)

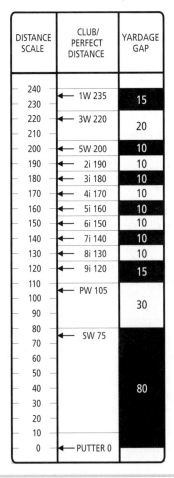

Figure 10.1.1: Yardage gaps between clubs (men)

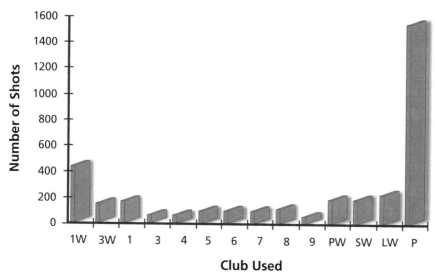

Chart 10.1.1: Club-use frequency

sense? The wood clubs hit 20%–25% of the shots; nine or 10 power-swing irons hit 15%–20% of the shots; one wedge hits about 15% of the shots; and one club, the putter, hits 43% of the shots.

Looking at these figures, it's clear to me that the generic set was created by someone who loved hitting the ball a long way. Why else would it include 12 clubs for the one-third of the game that involves power, and only two clubs for the two-thirds of the game that determines your ability to score? And does this change for women or Tour pros? No, absolutely not! We are all given two clubs—a sand wedge and a putter—to handle 55%–65% of all our shots in golf. And if you're concerned with scoring, the percentages are even worse, since these two clubs account for almost 80% of all your shots lost to par.

I think this set design is bizarre. Actually, *biased* might be a better description. I was taught that the challenge of golf is to shoot the lowest score while playing within the rules. I deeply believe that the joy of golf competition stems from the incredible challenges it presents to posting a good score. Take away scoring and the game that remained wouldn't be nearly as much fun or exciting. So when I see today's clubs being designed almost exclusively to hit the ball farther, to the detriment of your ability to score, it bothers me.

Stay with me in this chapter and I'll show you why using generic-set-design clubs hurts your game, and what you can do about it.

10.2 The Standard Way

When you pull your 7-iron out of your bag, you have a pretty good idea how far you are going to hit it. Say, 140 yards: That's the distance you expect if you are the "average" American male, make a good swing, and hit the ball solidly. For the most part, golfers associate a distance with each club, and they base their club and shot selections on these expectations.

If you hit your 7-iron 140 yards, your 6-iron likely goes about 150 yards. So what does that mean for the yardages in between? Making a full swing, you have control of the 140- and 150-yard shots. But what do you do when your ball is 145 yards from the flag, halfway between your 6- and 7-iron full-swing distances? You learn to "finesse" each club, to cover the distance gaps between them. You cover these differences by "laying off" a little on the longer club or "leaning on" (swinging harder) the shorter one.

If the gap between two clubs is 10 yards, then the distance that must be finessed is five yards extra for the shorter club and five yards less than the normal full-swing distance for the longer club. With the distances I've just used, that means you normally hit your 7-iron 140 yards but can finesse it from about 135 to 145. And while you normally hit the 6-iron 150 yards, you can finesse it from 145 to 155.

So if you have a 147-yard shot, you ease up a little on your 6-iron. And if you're halfway between the two, at 145, you choose whichever shot is more comfortable, either leaning on the shorter club or laying off on the longer club. (You should have practiced, or at least noticed over the years, which option suits you better.) And if there is a slight breeze, you probably play the club that produces the lower-trajectory shot.

Such is the way golf is played, and it solves the distance problems, right? Well, yes, it *is* the way golf is played. But does it solve the distance problems? It sounds reasonable, and most golfers, even Tour pros, believe it. But I don't.

10.3 Sets in the Field

Look at Figure 10.3.1 and check the distances and yardage gaps I measured for real sets of clubs played by real golfers at the famous Medinah Country Club in Chicago. The gaps between most pairs of clubs are even less than 10 yards, and everything looks under control—until you look inside 100 yards, where the gap is enormous!

To have to hit all your shots inside of 100 yards with one club is, to my way of thinking, absurd. But, in fact, the real world *is* the way it *is*.

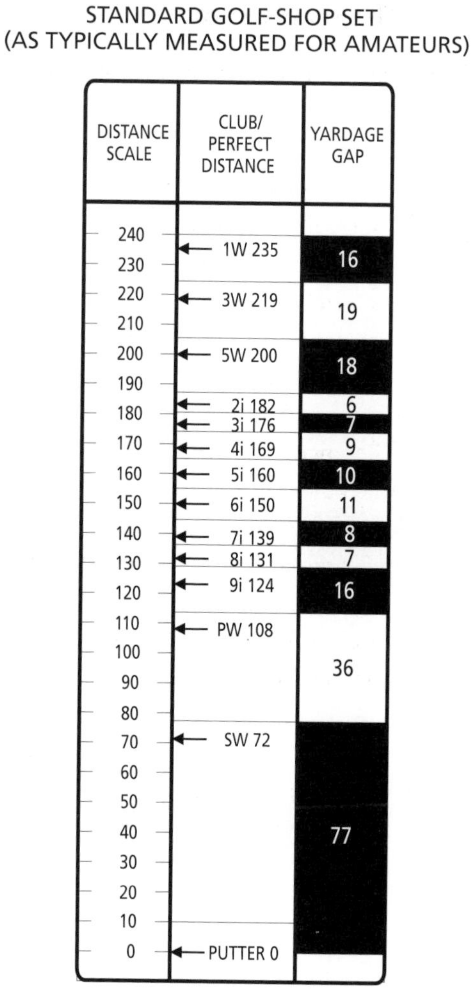

STANDARD GOLF-SHOP SET
(AS TYPICALLY MEASURED FOR AMATEURS)

DISTANCE SCALE	CLUB/ PERFECT DISTANCE	YARDAGE GAP
240		
	1W 235	16
230		
220	3W 219	19
210		
200	5W 200	18
190		
180	2i 182	6
	3i 176	7
170	4i 169	9
160	5i 160	10
150	6i 150	11
140	7i 139	8
130	8i 131	7
120	9i 124	16
110	PW 108	
100		36
90		
80		
70	SW 72	
60		
50		
40		77
30		
20		
10		
0	PUTTER 0	

Figure 10.3.1: Yardage gaps between clubs (amateurs)

If you do a marketing study of golfers, you learn that they want to hit the ball better and farther, and to shoot lower scores like the pros. It's difficult to make clubs that hit the ball better, but it isn't hard to make some clubs that hit the ball longer. So companies redesign their sets to let golfers hit the 7-, 8-, and 9-irons and the wedges farther, while giving them some marketing "sizzle" to convince them that all the clubs in the set are longer. And you know what? Golfers buy the stories and these sets.

Please don't think I've got it in for marketing people. They're just doing their jobs. But I don't think they should control golf-club design, which, in some companies, they do.

How else do you explain that since I started playing golf, the average loft on a pitching wedge in the marketplace has decreased from 51 degrees to 46 degrees, while the standard shaft length has increased one inch? Both of these changes mean golfers are hitting their pitching wedges farther. And it isn't only wedges: 8-irons have become 7-irons. Today's club may have the loft, lie, weight, and length of an old 7-iron, but there's an "8" stamped on the bottom. The public is told that if they're hitting the ball farther, then the clubs must be better.

These new sets have stronger wedges that we hit farther, but the same old long irons that we can't hit farther. (If the loft of long irons is decreased, the ball won't stay in the air as long and actually will fly shorter distances.) Then we buy these new sets, shoot the same old scores, and blame ourselves for not playing well.

Here's a fact. When you hit your short irons farther, your scores get worse, not better. Hitting wedges farther hurts your ability to hit them precise distances, which is the crux of the scoring game. Hitting wedges farther also increases the size of the yardage gaps in your short game, which leads to higher scores. The numbers are real, measured for golfers who'd bought new clubs that promised longer shots (which they got from their short irons) and lower scores (which they didn't get). I guess some would say that's progress!

10.4 A Better Set Design

Forget marketing, forget distance, forget stronger lofts and longer shafts made of some never-heard-of-before material. What you really need from a set of golf clubs is help in scoring. No matter where you are on the golf course, you'd like to hit the ball as close to the pin as possible. You'd like your clubs to help you do that in the fewest possible strokes and as consistently as possible. So how do you do that?

Figure 10.4.1 shows what I believe is a better design for a set of golf clubs for women, men, and pros. Two clubs (for men the 2- and 6-irons) have been removed, and the gaps between the remaining irons have been adjusted so they are consistent 15-yard intervals. By eliminating two longer irons, there is room for more wedges while still fitting under the 14-club rule. Why do you need more wedges when you already have two? Because more wedges let you shrink the gaps in the scoring game, inside 100 yards, where your current set now gives you only one option, the sand wedge.

In this new set, the gaps between the long clubs are greater than those in the generic set, and you have two fewer long irons. But that won't hurt your game. It may make you uncomfortable at first to take the 2-iron from your bag, but it won't hurt your ability to score. I know, because I've measured in so many rounds, that golfers (including PGA and LPGA Tour professionals) seldom hit their long irons straight

PELZ-RECOMMENDED SET DESIGN

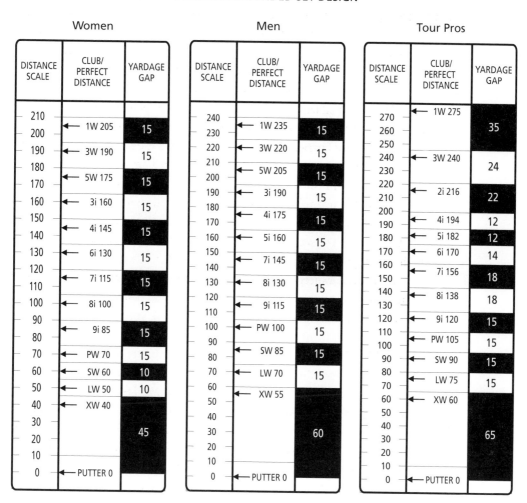

Figure 10.4.1: Yardage gaps between clubs (women, men, and Tour professionals)

enough to make their next putts. No matter how many long irons are in the bag, no golfer averages getting up and down from outside 100 yards more than 10% of the time. Most amateurs don't convert (make the next putt) from outside 100 yards even 5% of the time. So the fact that you remove a long iron and degrade distance accuracy by a small amount is insignificant. It won't affect your scores.

Put another way, no human can get up and down consistently from 150 yards. No one can hit 5-, 6-, and 7-irons that straight. So losing a little yardage accuracy in the long irons (if in fact you do; it hasn't been proven) won't bother your game a bit.

> **Prove It to Yourself**
>
> If you don't believe my gap theory on irons, prove it to yourself. You know the last 10 scores you turned in for handicap purposes. For your next 10 rounds, remove the 2-, 4-, 6-, and 8-irons from your bag. Carry only 10 clubs in your bag and make all your power swings with your 3-, 5-, 7-, or 9-irons. If you need a perfect 6-iron shot, lean on a 7-iron or take a little off a 5-iron. Make no other changes in your game, and keep track of your next 10 scores. I bet you won't see any difference from those made with all 14 clubs. They won't change because you wouldn't have hit the perfect 6-iron sufficiently closer than the soft 5 or strong 7 to make the next putt.
>
> I've done this and have had many of my students perform the same test, always with the same result: no measurable change in the ability to score with four fewer clubs. You don't miss those long irons because you never could hit them straight enough to make the next putt anyway.

However, it is absolutely critical that you maximize distance accuracy inside 100 yards, where you can *consistently* hit the ball straight enough to have a chance to make the first putt. By adding wedges, you optimize your chances of saving a stroke after every shot from inside 100 yards. The cost to you is the slight sacrifice in distance control from longer yardages that doesn't matter to your scoring.

You Need Four Wedges

10.5 Why Four?

Very simple: You will score better.

Why? Because having four wedges (each with different specifications) will let you hit more shots of consistent, repeatable distances in the most important area of golf—the short game. If you learn to make the three finesse swings described in Chapter 5, the four wedges will produce 12 surefire yardages (three swings times four wedges), which are sure to improve your up-and-down percentage. And that will improve your scores.

This is usually when I hear, "Come on, Pelz. You can't *really* mean you want me to carry four wedges all the time!" My answer is always the same: "Only if you care about scoring!"

Go back to the chart of the improved set design (Fig. 10.4.1) and look at the last four clubs. I've called them the pitching, sand, lofted, and extra-lofted wedges, but the names aren't important. What is important is that they're all just golf clubs, designed to hit short shots. With full swings, they still create 15-yard gaps like the rest of your set, so you're producing four times as many known short-game distances as you used to when you had only one wedge in your bag. By adding two wedges, you've become a better player.

And remember this: If you hit your sand wedge 85 yards with your full-finesse swing (a 10:30 backswing), that means you can also make that wedge throw the ball 64 yards from a 9:00 o'clock swing (75% of the 10:30 swing), and 43 yards (50%) with your 7:30 swing. It's a great system. The whole range is shown in Figure 10.5.1:

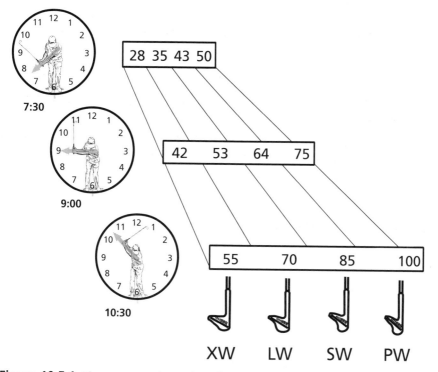

Figure 10.5.1: Time your wedge swings for distance control
(longer backswings produce longer shot distances)

These distances might not be the exact yardages you hit each club, but I think you can see what I'm driving at. Every golfer will have his or her own set of distances, and the more different wedges in the bag, multiplied by the three finesse swings, the more distances accurately covered inside the scoring game.

10.6 The Male Ego

Even with all the advantages, all the scientific and statistical reasons I have for enhancing your finesse game with more wedges, I am the first to admit that there is a very serious drawback in doing so. I run into it in every school, seminar, and clinic I teach. I run into it with pros and amateurs. I can't escape it: the male ego.

It's the "real men don't carry four wedges" syndrome. The male ego wants to be hitting long, high, penetrating shots with a plutonium driver. If the male ego designed sets of clubs (and sometimes I think it does), then everyone's bag would feature a driver, 2-wood, maybe a 3-wood, then a driving iron, followed by the 1-, 2-, and 3-irons. The male ego thinks it can emulate the swings of the best golfers in the world, the Tour pros, who can rip perfect 225-yard long iron shots into the teeth of a ferocious wind. Consequently, sets of clubs continue to be designed to stroke that ego, because that's what sells more sets.

Before giving you more equipment details, let me tell you about two tests my players ran at a time when they were intellectually convinced adding wedges made sense, but still emotionally tied to their full set of long irons.

When Jim Simons, a very intelligent player who since has won three times on the PGA Tour with this system, first heard me recommend dropping the 2-iron from his bag, he was stunned. He said, "But what will I do when I have a 2-iron shot?" He just couldn't bring himself to add a wedge and lay down his beloved 2-iron. After about six months of his procrastination, I convinced him that since I might be right, in which case his game would improve, he should run a test. He finally agreed to the test.

I convinced him to substitute his 6-iron for his 2-iron, which would show how unproductive the 2-iron really is. He said, "How can I do that? I can't get a 6-iron to the green from 210 yards. I only carry my 6-iron 165 yards." I agreed, then explained, "That's exactly the point. I want you to miss the green every time, then see if you can get up and down. We'll see how it affects your scoring."

With some trepidation, Jim agreed to play every pro-am event for six weeks without his 2-iron. During those rounds, every time he was faced with a 2-iron shot, he would hit his 6-iron. After six weeks and six pro-am rounds, he gave me all the scores he had made on his "6-iron-for-2-iron" substitution holes. His average score was 4.25 strokes, or 0.25 strokes per hole over par (he hit a 6-iron short of the green four times, and got up and down three out of those four).

Then, from all the data I'd collected, I showed him his average score on the Tour for the previous two years on holes where he hit a 2-iron to the green. His

High-Handicappers Need the Short Game, Too

It's a fact: High-handicap golfers need the short game more than low handi-cappers do.

A popular misconception is that the worse you play golf, or the higher your handicap, then the less you need a short game. Actually, the exact opposite is true. Which is why I say, "The poorer your game, the more wedges you need."

The players on the PGA Tour hit, on average, 12.5 to 13 greens a round. This means they miss five, maybe six greens each round, and a missed green usually means they're hitting a short shot of some kind—pitch, chip, or sand. They also normally play four par 5s a round, which account for a few more short-game shots. So seven to 10 times a round, the Tour players make "finesse swings" onto the green.

If you're not a Tour-quality ball-striker, then your number of short-game shots per round is higher (Chart 10.6.1). The average 10-handicapper hits four or five greens in regulation, so he's hitting short-game shots to 10 greens plus the par 5s. That's 13, 14, sometimes 15 wedges, chips, pitches, and bunker shots every round. So if you miss more greens, your short game is more im-portant to your scores. Ahhh . . . yes, the *scoring game!*

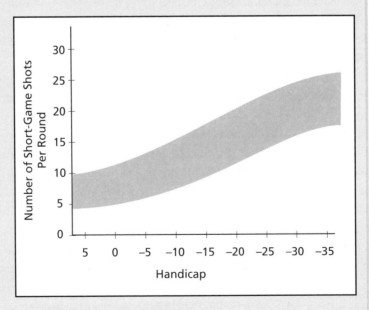

Chart 10.6.1: The higher the handicap, the more short-game shots per round

Tour scoring average was 0.46 over par after he hit with a 2-iron. He had averaged a better score with his 6-iron from 210 yards than with his 2-iron.

Some of his 2-iron shots plugged in greenside bunkers, or flew over the green into trouble, or went left into water. He seldom, if ever, hit 2-iron shots close enough to the pin to hole the next putt. But during the time he was conducting the 6-vs.-2 test, he converted 16 up-and-downs with his replacement for the 2-iron, his third wedge.

That's what it took to convince Jim Simons that a lofted wedge is more valuable than a 2-iron to scoring. With the proof in front of him, he removed the 2-iron from his bag and played every round thereafter with a third wedge.

Tom Jenkins couldn't break the emotional ties to his long irons at first, either. "How can I possibly give up my 3-iron?" T.J. asked. "I use it so often and it means so much to me. It's one of my better clubs."

My response to T.J. was: (1) You don't hit the 3-iron as often as you think, and (2) a 3-iron is incapable of being one of your better clubs in terms of scoring. It can be one of the better clubs for your ego, but they don't pay for ego on Tour.

T.J. agreed to keep his statistics on the clubs and shots he used in tournament play for the next eight rounds. It turned out he hit his 3-iron only seven times in eight rounds, while hitting 55 wedge shots. T.J. didn't hesitate: He recognized the value of his wedge game to scoring and hasn't played with a 3-iron since. He's now playing the Senior Tour with great success, still without a 3-iron.

Jenkins's approach was different from Simons's. T.J. simply dropped the 3-iron and didn't change anything else about the rest of his set. He determined from his test that he used the 3-iron the least of any club in his bag, so he just removed it. He kept the 2-iron (which he often used on par 5s) and 4-iron, creating a big distance gap between them. But since he used the 3-iron so rarely, he reasoned that it would be an easy gap to cover. From 200 yards, his normal 3-iron distance, he learned that he could either rip a 4-iron or feather a 2. And since he knew he probably wasn't going to make birdie anyway, putting the ball anywhere on the green was fine.

These examples should convince you that it isn't the end of the world to drop a long iron or two from your bag. In fact, if you're already carrying more than one fairway wood, you've probably got the long-iron distances covered, especially if you learn to grip down on the shaft of your 5- or 6-wood by three inches (cutting the carry distance 10 to 15 yards). Still, you should conduct your own test. Take the 2- and/or 3-iron out of your bag and see if you're suddenly at a loss. Keep track of the shots and clubs you hit over your next 10 rounds, and see which you use least. If you play most of your golf at the same course, you probably don't even need to chart your shots to know the club, or clubs, that never get dirty.

Remember, more wedges means better distance control around the greens, which means shorter putts, which means lower scores. If you can learn to turn three shots into two from off the green, you can transform your game, your handicap, your winning record, and sometimes even your outlook on life.

10.7 How Should They Perform?

You no doubt noticed few unusual changes in the makeup of my revised set. I'll start at the top and work down, ending with what I consider the most important change: adding wedges.

To fill the holes left by the extraction of your 2- and 6-irons, and to make your gaps consistent, you need to alter the yardages you hit with some of the rest of your clubs. The 3-iron, for example, needs to hit the ball 190 yards rather than 176; and the 9-iron needs to drop to 115 from 124 yards. How do you accomplish that? You have your golf pro or a custom clubmaker strengthen or weaken the lofts, add or reduce headweight, lengthen or shorten the shafts, and so on. These changes aren't difficult to make, and are readily available around any club or through your golf professional.

Many golfers find these changes intellectually hard to handle. All they think is that two clubs, the 2- and 6-iron, are missing from their game. "Now, wait just a minute," you cry. "I hit those clubs all the time. I can't give them up." That may be true with the set you now have, and the way you now play. But when you standardize the gaps between clubs, the 2- and 6-irons won't be doing the same jobs they used to, so you can, indeed, give them up. Remember, the typical and revised sets used here are simply illustrations of the concept. It may make more sense for you to give up your 3- and 7-irons, or your 2-wood, depending on the courses you play and your game. I say drop any club you like (except the putter), as long as you make room under the 14-club limit for more wedges.

Most of the PGA Tour players I worked with didn't think they could give up even one club—until they proved to themselves that it made sense. After I had a few notebooks and computer disks full of data, I held a meeting with six of my favorite players. I presented my data to them: I showed them the correlation among the finesse game, lower scores, and money earned; I showed them the beginning of the 3 x 4 wedge system; and I told them to drop a few long clubs and pick up more wedges.

They were impressed. Every one of them said, "Pelz, you're right, that's incredible. I never realized how my short game and the distance inaccuracy in my wedge game were tied to my scoring ability."

So five of the six left the room . . . and changed absolutely nothing. Only one player reacted the way I recommended. Tom Kite, who already was the best wedge player of the six, left the room and immediately added a third, more lofted wedge to his bag. To make room for it, he dropped his 2-iron. To get over that loss, he changed his 3-iron, strengthening its loft, removing a little weight from the head, and lengthening its shaft. He turned the club that said "3" on the bottom into his 2-iron distance club. He also strengthened his 4-iron by two degrees, his 5-iron by one degree, and his 6-iron by half a degree; he didn't touch his 7-, 8-, or 9-iron. He covered his complete long-distance range with one fewer club by adjusting the remaining clubs to provide slightly larger gaps, then went out and became the greatest wedge player in the history of the game.

Think about the implications of this new set design for your game. How often do you hit a 2-iron on the green and make the putt for birdie? Almost never. How often do you hit your 2-iron on the green and two-putt for par? Maybe sometimes. Now remember (perhaps painfully) the 2-iron ground balls you hit, the ones that went left into bunkers, those hit right into trees. And do you remember the one you flushed, that landed in front of the green but bounced over, down the hill, and into the creek? I've even known golfers, although I'm sure not you, who have hit 2-irons out-of-bounds.

What about you pros? You should do the same "game-searching" evaluation. My data proves that for club pros, and even Tour professionals, a good result for the 2-iron (roughly a 225-yard shot) is anywhere on the green and not in trouble. Why? Because you probably wouldn't have made the next putt even if you had hit your 2-iron shot 10 feet from the hole. So aim your 2-irons at the largest safe area around the pin (even including some fringe areas around the green), take your par, and move on to the next hole. Don't flirt with disaster.

Now here's the real shocker: Giving up the 2-iron is a blessing in disguise. Your scoring average will probably go down, not up, even if you *don't* replace it with a wedge! But when you learn to use your L-wedge and add it to your bag, your game—and scores—will improve. Then, someday, the X-wedge will come!

10.8 Are There Any Negatives to This?

Adding two wedges forces you to do two things: (1) drop two other clubs from your bag; (2) learn to hit higher-lofted wedges.

While eliminating long irons is emotionally difficult for established players who are used to their ways and resist change, it is the right thing to do for their scoring game. Even though many great players—more than 50 PGA Tour and 40 LPGA Tour players have paid to come to my schools—have been using this system, and more wedges, for years, I still get questions from golfers sniffing around the edges of this concept. Golfers who haven't read this book or haven't come to one of my Scoring Game Schools have heard something about leaving out clubs, adding others, and higher-lofted wedges, but they don't know the specifics. They don't understand why, how, or what they should do to improve their ability to score.

Some ask me, "If so many good players are doing this, why haven't I heard of your 3 x 4 System?" Or "Why don't manufacturers promote sets of clubs the way you describe them?" And "What's the downside of your system?"

Let me answer all three. First, why should Tom Kite or any Tour player say something about this to you, anyone in the press, or anyone else on the Tour? All that will do is make it harder to win the money out there. In fact, while I have worked with Kite on his short game for more than 20 years, you probably haven't heard him say a word about me. Not after he won any of his 19 tournaments, not after he became the leading money winner in the world, not after he won the Vardon Trophy for the lowest scoring average on the Tour. And why should he? He paid me for my time and I never hit a shot for him. He deserves the accolades. As a competitor, he asks no favors of, and gives none to, the competition. He does his job, I do mine; he is my friend, and that's good enough for me.

Second, do you really expect the manufacturers to deemphasize the long ball so they can sell fewer clubs? I can't expect them to promote the short game at the expense of their income. I am thankful that they aren't lying about the virtues of the short game. They largely ignore it, and I don't expect them to change their minds anytime soon. (However, many are now making a variety of wedges you can add to your bag. These wedges are almost never included in a full set of clubs, since the manufacturers would rather sell you a set and then have you buy a few additional clubs, making them a little better profit.)

Third, is there a downside to the system? All I can answer is, "only if your 1-iron mentality can't see the benefits of shooting lower scores." In all honesty, I can't think of a downside to the 3 x 4 wedge system or the "finesse-swing-for-the-scoring-game" theories. But if you find one, let me know.

One example might dissuade some doubters. In 1990–91, Tom Sieckmann played the PGA Tour with four wedges and without a 3- or 5-iron. He won more money than at any other time in his career, and finished third on Tour in birdies on par-3 holes. Understand that the Tour doesn't set up many par 3s to be hit with wedges. Sieck made more birdies while finessing with his 2-, 4-, and 6-irons than other pros made with twice as many clubs (1- through 6-irons).

Sieck did say one thing to me then that's too funny to be considered a downside. He said he kept getting odd looks from his fellow pros as they peeked into his bag to see what he was hitting on par 3s. (They aren't allowed to ask or touch his clubs, but the Rules allow looking.) How surprised do you think they were when he was holding his 4-iron and all they saw in the bag was a 2- and 6-iron, with nothing in between?

10.9 Is This Set Practical?

The primary consideration for deciding what shot and what club to hit is distance. It isn't until you know how far to hit a shot that you can think about trajectory, spin, carry, or anything else. So maybe clubs should be designed for a particular distance and identified that way.

Your caddie would say, "The yardage is 148 yards. Here's your 155 club. There's no wind, so take a little off of the shot." There wouldn't be much chance of a misunderstanding. Or how about "You're 68 yards from the pin, the wind will hold it up a couple, and the ball will stop dead on this green, it's so soft. Here's your 70-yard club. It should be perfect." Hearing that you were holding the perfect club would clear your mind to make a smooth 70-yard swing.

Building each club to produce the distance needed for perfect coverage and gap balance, based on your swing speeds, would create the ultimate set. But since all golfers have unique mechanics and swing speeds, this is impractical. No one set would fit all golfers. However, it is surprising how many golfers hit the ball similar distances, which makes it relatively easy to modify an existing set to suit your game and cover your specific gap distances.

Let's consider how to modify your existing set so you can score better.

The first and most important change: Learn how to make consistent 9:00 o'clock and 7:30 finesse swings with your existing wedges. Once you can, and know the approximate distances produced by your pitching and sand wedges, it's time to optimize the rest of your clubs. There are a few ways to go:

1. Drop one long iron and add one wedge, without changing the specs of any clubs. (This is what Tom Jenkins did.) If you add a wedge with the proper loft and length specifications, you have a 3 x 3 system—three swings (10:30, 9:00 o'clock, and 7:30) and three wedges, for nine distinct, consistent distances. This is the simplest option, and leaves just one large gap in your long-iron game.

2. Drop two long irons, add two wedges, and play a 3 x 4 System. Many students drop their longest two irons (usually the 2- and 3-) and learn to grip down on their 5-wood. Again, it leaves a gap, but it's a gap that can be covered without losing strokes.

3. Drop two clubs and alter the specs of the others to produce consistent distance gaps. This is what some pros do (see the Tom Kite example on page 314). They tend to go with 15-yard gaps between clubs.

4. Create a 16-club set by adding two wedges, dropping nothing, and picking the 14 you'll use each day according to the course you're playing.

Don't get overly concerned about trying to decide which club(s) to drop. You can always bring one back and drop another. But I'm convinced that most amateurs can drop all their even-numbered irons and shoot the same scores anyway. (By lightening their bags, it might encourage more golfers to walk, too.)

You also shouldn't worry about hitting the "in-between" shots now that some clubs are missing. The truth is:

- You don't have to make a perfect swing. You probably wouldn't have made the next putt even if you had all the clubs in your old set. Just make a good swing and put the ball safely on the green.

- You've already been making finesse decisions, covering the 10-yard gaps (and five-yard finesse distances) between clubs in your old set. Now that the gaps are 15 yards, do the same thing. Now your club can hit the ball within 7.5 yards of perfect (rather than the five yards you used to have).

- You usually would rather be long than short (to avoid bunkers). So if you're not sure, play the shot that, if it isn't perfect, will still get there. Of course, long can also spell disaster, so check out all the options, and all the trouble around the green, and make the smart choice.

It's not important which, how, or how many long irons you drop. What's most important is adding the wedges. You could put 115 clubs in your bag, one for every yardage between 100 and 215 yards, and you still wouldn't shave one stroke off your score. But add a wedge and learn how to use it, and you can lower your scores by three, five, even 10 shots a round. Add two wedges, plus your 9:00 o'clock and 7:30 swings, and you have created the almost perfect way to play the game.

Look at your old distance gaps inside 100 yards (Fig. 10.3.1). It's the size of those gaps that helped prevent you from becoming a good wedge player. Now look at those same wedge distances in Figure 10.9.1, showing the shots that can now be in your bag, shots all produced with just three swings. With this set, you can hit

PELZ-DESIGNED SET WITH 7:30 AND 9:00 O'CLOCK
SWING TIME ENHANCEMENT

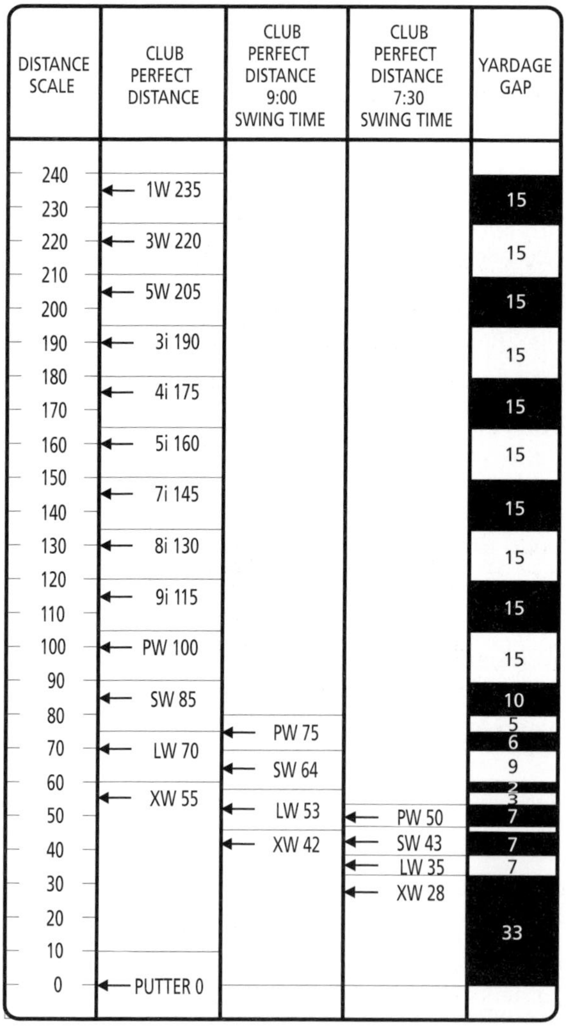

DISTANCE SCALE	CLUB PERFECT DISTANCE	CLUB PERFECT DISTANCE 9:00 SWING TIME	CLUB PERFECT DISTANCE 7:30 SWING TIME	YARDAGE GAP
240	← 1W 235			
230				15
220	← 3W 220			
210				15
200	← 5W 205			15
190	← 3i 190			
180				15
170	← 4i 175			15
160	← 5i 160			
150				15
140	← 7i 145			15
130	← 8i 130			
120				15
110	← 9i 115			15
100	← PW 100			
90				15
80	← SW 85			10
70	← LW 70	← PW 75		5 / 6
60	← XW 55	← SW 64		9
50		← LW 53	← PW 50	2 / 3 / 7
40		← XW 42	← SW 43	7
30			← LW 35	7
20			← XW 28	
10				33
0	← PUTTER 0			

Figure 10.9.1: The 3 x 4 System produces the ultimate small yardage gaps (men)

your wedge shots within a yard or two of the perfect distance by making reasonably good swings. Then there is a good probability of converting the next putt, saving par or making birdie.

Once you've practiced enough times to learn your 7:30 and 9:00 o'clock distances, and marked them on your shafts, you'll find a comfort and confidence you never dreamed possible. Because when you know your short game is good, you know you can score.

Set Designs for the Future

10.10 Club Specifications

Here are the four wedges mentioned earlier (Fig. 10.10.1), with the approximate loft ranges I recommend for each:

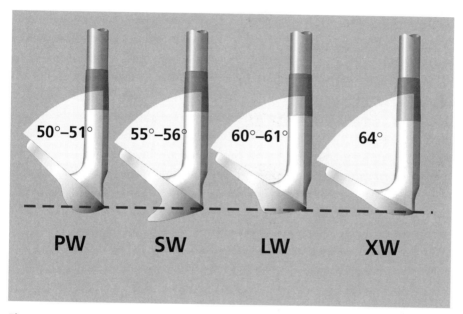

Figure 10.10.1: Four wedges that will help most golfers

Your pitching wedge (PW) loft should not be less than 50–51 degrees. This is weaker than some of the new PWs offered by manufacturers trying to get you to hit the ball prodigious distances. Resist the distance temptation. Also, be aware that some manufacturers, having decreased their PW lofts, offer a "gap" wedge to fill in between the pitching (which they made into a 9-iron with "PW" stamped on it) and the sand wedges. Is that great marketing, or what?

Your sand wedge (SW) should be 55–56 degrees. Don't confuse this with the new "strong" sand wedges in the 52–54-degree range, which aren't as useful.

Your lofted wedge (LW) should be either 60 or 61 degrees, no more, no less. This third or L-wedge has become popular thanks to the success of Tom Kite, the harder, faster greens in vogue the last few years, and maybe, just maybe, a few of my articles stressing short-game shots in GOLF Magazine (because I often get letters and e-mail messages reporting improved scoring and lower handicaps as a result).

Your extra-loft wedge (XW) needs about 64 degrees of loft. This club makes life around the greens very easy, because it hits high, soft shots without having to open the face.

Besides different lofts, other specifications of your wedges should change, too. As the loft of each wedge increases, make the following adjustments:

- Shorten the shaft by at least a half to three-fourths of an inch (whatever the length difference is between the other irons in your set as each club's loft increases). With shorter shafts, the resulting smaller swing arcs also help to hit shorter shots.
- Make the lie of each more-lofted wedge marginally (approximately half a degree) more upright. This allows the club to be soled properly as it gets closer to you (as the shorter shaft length demands). If you buy one of the multiwedge systems some manufacturers sell, be aware that the lengths and lies of the wedges may be the same; have your pro or a clubmaker make the necessary adjustments (usually cut down the successive shaft lengths and add headweight).
- The greater the loft, the heavier the clubhead. Adding weight to the clubhead of a wedge usually reduces the shot distance, which, again, is what you want.
- Weaken the shaft flex as loft increases, because gentler, smoother finesse swings require being able to "feel" the clubhead for better timing and rhythm.
- Every wedge should have a different amount and depth of bounce, to provide options for playing different shots from different lies (see Chapter 9).

For the X-wedge, with the most loft, I recommend a fairly small bounce flange that is only medium-deep. This lets you use the club from tight lies around the green as well as normal lies when you need a high-lofted shot that lands softly and stops quickly. Add a little more bounce to the L-wedge (but be careful not to add too much), and more still for the sand wedge, because you occasionally need a lot of bounce for fine, sugar-soft sand and high rough.

Don't put too much bounce on your pitching wedge, so it can be used from tight fairway lies and for longer, full-swing shots, when a big flange inhibits contact.

There are thousands of clubs to choose from that will satisfy your wedge needs. But as I've pointed out, you may want to take them to your pro or custom club shop for tweaking. The object is to build a set to help you create the most consistent, repeatable distances, and that might require customization in loft, lie, headweight, shaft flex, length, bounce, and so on.

A final note about crafting your set as closely as possible to your game. When you buy a wedge, it's likely that you'll pick it first and foremost for its loft. Be sure to check that the bounce is acceptable and fits into your set without duplication. If possible, before buying you should take it to the range and measure how far you hit it. You have no use for a wedge that hits shots the same distance as one you already have. If you're unsure about loft, bounce, and the other specifications, have the clubs checked by your golf professional or a knowledgeable clubfitter.

If the bounce and loft specs are right but the distances are still off, don't buy it! Keep shopping. I know from experience that if you buy a 60-degree L-wedge "off the rack," the true loft could be anywhere from 58 to 62 degrees. And who knows what the length will be? Don't go blindly into a store expecting the specifications given with any club to be correct.

Table 10.10.1 gives you the average specifications of the wedges I've hand-built or modified for PGA Tour players over the years. Again, don't make your set conform to these numbers or values if you don't hit them the right distances. In the short game, distances come first, so test them yourself. Once you know the actual yardages for all your wedges, write them down in one place and compare them to be sure that they provide you with balanced coverage and gaps inside 100 yards.

If some distances overlap, don't worry. That can be good, as you will see in the next section.

Wedge Type	Loft Angle (degrees)	Lie Angle (degrees)	Shaft Length (inches)	Bounce Amount (inches)	Bounce Depth (inches)	Shaft Flex Code letters (frequency)
PW	50–51	61–63	35–36	.20–.40	.30–.50	R (6.0)
SW	55–56	61½–63½	34½–35½	.45–.75	.45–.90	R (5.5)
LW	60–61	62–64	34–35	.20–.55	.20–.40	R (5.0)
XW	62½–64	62½–65	33½–34½	.20–.40	.35–.60	L (4.5)

Table 10.10.1: Wedge specifications (average)

10.11 Optimizing Your Set

When it comes to optimizing the equipment in your set, a properly fit putter is a top priority. Putting is the most frequent shot in golf (43%, according to my data), and a putter's specifications can have dramatic effects on green success.

Since your short game does more to determine scoring ability, fitting your wedges also counts as a top priority. But wedges are rarely as "out of fit" as putters, and short-game results are more affected by a lack of knowledge and finesse-swing skill than by club fitting.

The third priority, by the way, is the driver—because if you can wedge it, putt it, and drive it, you can play this game.

All that said, making the most of your wedges is still of the utmost importance. As explained earlier, you can—and should—tape to the shaft the distances that each wedge flies shots from your 10:30, 9:00 o'clock, and 7:30 swings. Be sure to do this when you're beginning to adopt the methods in this book. You don't want to read all this advice and then be so distracted trying to remember your distances that you forget to make good, rhythmic swings.

Write all three yardages on a self-adhesive dot, tape it to the underside of the shaft (Fig. 10.11.1), and don't be embarrassed to check it before every wedge shot. It's easier to make a good swing if you're confident that the wedge in your hand and the swing length in your mind are right. Even after learning the yardages, look at the dot every now and again to be sure.

Don't assume that once you know your yardages they'll stay the same forever. Recheck your distances at least once a season to be sure they haven't changed as a result of a change in your swing (conscious or unconscious) or equipment (such as a different brand or type of ball). Periodically hit at least two dozen or so solid shots with each wedge and pace them off.

Some students get confused when they see the yardages produced by different wedge-swing combinations overlap. But it makes sense that if you take a high-lofted wedge and make a fuller swing, it might go the same distance as a less-lofted wedge with a shorter backswing. (For example, in Fig. 5.13.1, the 10:30 swing with the

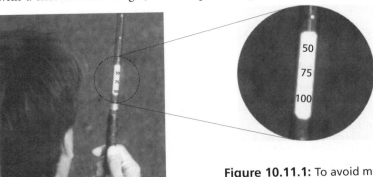

Figure 10.11.1: To avoid mistakes, keep yardages on your shafts

X-wedge flies 55 yards, while the 9:00 o'clock swing with the L-wedge flies 53.) This overlapping is good, because every player develops preferences in both wedges and backswing lengths. Most of my students find the 9:00 o'clock swing the easiest to visualize and repeat, the 7:30 the most difficult, and the 10:30 somewhere in between. When you have to select between overlapping distances, choose the shot you're most confident with.

Also, while the distances may be the same, the trajectories will not be. Shorter backswings produce a lower ball flight than do longer swings. A 9:00 o'clock pitching wedge may fly the same distance, but lower than, the 10:30 lofted wedge. This can matter depending on weather and green conditions. In windy conditions, you might want to use shorter backswings and less-lofted wedges to minimize the wind's effects. However, remember it will also make shots bounce and roll farther after impact.

As you learn and ingrain your wedge performance and distances, consider using an electronic rangefinder (we use the Bushnell Yardage Pro in our schools). During practice and casual rounds, it will supply accurate feedback to measure or verify your yardages. Say you think the yardage is 77 yards. You take out your 74-yard club—a 9:00 o'clock pitching wedge—make the swing, it feels great, and you know it's going to fly 74 yards, bounce once, and stop by the pin. But when you look up, the shot has landed short of the green and stopped well short of the pin. With a rangefinder, you can measure the distance to within one yard and learn what went wrong. ("Shooting" your distance with a rangefinder also is faster and more accurate than walking it off.)

That's when you learn that your distance estimate was off; you really needed to carry it 84 yards. Or you might learn that your distance was accurate but your shot didn't carry. Checking distances and performance will help you learn while keeping your judgment system based in reality. As you mature in this system, good feedback will help both your knowledge and your confidence, and let you become the best you can be in the scoring game.

10.12 Scoring Considerations

Sets of clubs that help you score should be designed by yardages, not by the numbers on the clubhead sole or someone's ego. What you call a wedge is not important, nor is how many wedges you "think" are in your bag.

If your ego won't let you carry more than two wedges, then rename your 51-degree wedge your 8-iron, and your 56-degree club your 9-iron. Then your 60- and your 64-degree wedges become your two wedges. The problem with this solution is you'll be hitting the 8- and 9-irons fairly short distances. But then you could always use the excuse of having a sore wrist, and ask your competitors not to squeeze too hard when they shake hands and pay you at the end of the round.

Another approach is to rename your 60-degree wedge "Tom." Then you could still say you carried only two wedges, plus a Tom. It might help some golfers if they could say, "Come on, Tom. We need a great 56-yard shot here. I'll make a perfect 9:00 o'clock finesse swing and you put the ball close to the pin." Maybe the association with Tom Kite or Tom Watson, two of the greatest wedge players ever, would help. Giving your wedge a friendly, talented name might remind your subconscious what a great short-game player you are becoming.

Also, think about the long irons in your new set by the distances they cover. As soon as you know how far you hit your newly bent 4-iron, begin thinking of it as your 170-yard club, knowing that with a little finesse you can fly it between 162 and 177 yards, depending on the situation. If you always think of your clubs by their distances, and remember that direction is a real problem with long irons (play away from hazards left and right), your approach to achieving proper results will be optimized for your skill level.

I'd also like you to consider assembling a 15-, 16-, or 17-club set. No, I'm not suggesting that the USGA and Royal and Ancient expand the current 14-club limit. But if you have other clubs you can hit with confidence, which also provide extra shots and extra distance coverage, you can put together the perfect set for the course you're playing that day. There are many courses where a 5-, 6-, or 7-wood is more useful than a 1-, 2-, or 3-iron. Or if the winds are up, you might keep the 1-iron. Depending on the rough, the thickness and type of grass, the width of the fairways, the green speed and hardness, the sand . . . and on and on, you can tailor the clubs you choose to optimize your performance. Expand this idea to include choosing different clubs to play the same course at different times of the year.

One thing you should not change is your approach to decision making on the course. Everything I suggest in this book is meant to improve your odds of shooting a lower score. So if you're not likely to get up and down after your next shot, avoid taking chances. Trying to get close to the pin from 200 yards doesn't make sense, because "close" from that distance is 24 feet (4% error), and you're not going to convert many 24-footers. Don't risk trouble or a penalty when there is no reward for success. Make the choice that keeps you out of trouble.

Play the percentages, evaluate the consequences of your different options, choose the right club, and play smart. Always remember: We're into scoring here!

CHAPTER 11

Everyone Has a Short-Game Handicap

What Is Your Short-Game Handicap?

11.1 The Overall Handicap

If you really want to understand how a golfer plays the game—and therefore begin to understand how to improve his or her ability to score—don't simply look at his USGA handicap index. That number is an "overall handicap," a measure of a player's entire game, and gives no indication where their strengths and weaknesses lie.

In my evaluation system there isn't one handicap but five, one for each of the five games I mentioned at the beginning of this book: the power game, short game, putting game, management game, and mental game. By carefully studying these, I have found that a golfer's scoring ability is primarily determined not by his strengths but by his weaknesses in these areas.

As mentioned back in Chapter 3, Jack Nicklaus in his prime was not the best at the power, short, or putting games, but he was good in all of them. He was the absolute best in the management game, which let him avoid his only real weakness, sand play, and become the best overall player, by far, of his time. During the same period, Lee Trevino was the best ball-striker, and excellent in the management game as well. Ben Crenshaw made up for a less-than-great handicap in his power game with a fine short game and a great, close to the best ever, putting game. You've already read my opinion of Tom Kite, Mr. Short Game.

I spend much of my time and energy studying and teaching the short game because my research has proven that it is the area that most closely correlates to lower scores (and in the case of the pros, fatter wallets). My studies also show that the short game can be drastically improved by golfers at all skill levels, because anyone can learn to control distances, mental understanding, practice time, and using the proper clubs. It is not just a game that requires massive doses of talent, strength, or athletic ability.

If you are going to improve your short game (and I hope that's why you're reading this), you need a method for measuring your progress. That would be your short-game handicap. It will let you know how good a short-game player you are now, and help you see improvement as you work on the skills discussed in this book. So whether you've already begun work on improving your finesse-swing mechanics or not, begin right now regularly measuring your short-game handicap.

11.2 Your Short-Game Handicap

Every golfer has a short-game handicap. If you learn and master both the finesse swing and 3 x 4 System as described in this book, your short-game handicap will get lower, and, in turn, your overall handicap will drop. How much? From measuring my students' abilities around the green, I've learned that almost 80% of the average golfer's handicap is determined by the scoring game. While this includes both your short game and putting, we can isolate the effects of those shots between 100 yards and the edge of the green.

What does that 80% mean? If the average 10- to 12-handicap golfer developed a "scratch" scoring game, his overall handicap would drop to between 2 and 4. Put another way, if Tom Kite hit all the scoring-game shots for a 10-handicapper, their combined score probably would be near par. Tom would save almost every up-and-down, as well as make a couple of birdies on the par 5s. Give the 20-handicapper a scratch scoring game and he'd drop to between 4 and 6. Give golfers scratch short games without changing their putting and they would still reduce their overall handicaps by a little more than half the difference.

"Scratch" generally means consistently shooting par golf. If you can develop a scratch short game, playing your up-and-down game "up to par" on every hole, 40% to 50% of your scoring ability would be at scratch. Then you'd have to look at the power, putting, management, and mental games for the rest of the strokes you lose to par.

What about putting? While I would like all golfers to improve their putting, and it is definitely important, the short game has a larger effect on your scores. There's nothing that affects the average number of putts per round more than a golfer's ability to chip, pitch, and blast close to the hole—specifically, to get the ball close enough that it is consistently inside the critical "Golden Eight" feet on the putting conversion chart.

By the way, I'm certainly not the first person to make this observation. John Henry Taylor, who won the British Open five times and was runner-up another six times between 1894 and 1914, is quoted as having said, "The man who can pitch doesn't need to putt." While I think this might be a slight overstatement, there is no question that besides being a tremendous golfer, Mr. Taylor had the right idea.

Another way to look at the importance of the short game to your handicap is that you can't do much to recover after hitting a bad pitch or chip shot, while you often can recover from poor longer shots. Just like a poor putt, a poor pitch, chip, or sand shot is usually another whole shot lost to par.

You will begin to understand all this as you take the short-game tests presented on page 328. And when I say take them, I don't mean just once; you should return to them time and again to chart your progress, isolate your weak areas, and provide yourself with invaluable practice time. I recommend executing the complete set of tests once a month to move your game to its optimum level. It's also fun to record your scores to stay aware of how you are improving.

If after all my exhortation and explanation you still don't put yourself through these tests on a regular basis, at least keep track of your up-and-down percentage when you play. If you work on your short-game and distance-wedge skills, there is no question that you'll get up and down more often.

11.3 How to Measure It

You need to find a good practice area or a deserted, quiet spot on the course to take these eight tests. If it's difficult to find a practice area with a green and realistic short-game conditions, then you begin to understand one of the inherent problems of the short game. Check out golf facilities around the world and I'll bet 90% of them don't offer a good place to practice your short-game shots. Most putting greens have little signs around them saying "No Chipping" or "No Pitch Shots." And it's rare to find a practice range with target greens closer than 100 yards for conveniently practicing, or testing, your distance wedges. This is just one more reason people spend most of their practice time on the power game. However, to really improve, you must get around this problem and find suitable practice areas. We can help you with some learning aids to make "at-home" practice beneficial, but it will still be worthwhile for you to find a good short-game area at a nearby course or range.

The directions for each test (Fig. 11.3.1) are straightforward and simple. Hit 10 shots for each test and score yourself as instructed. I strongly suggest you record your scores over time so you can see your skills improve. You also can translate

Instructions: Hit 10 shots in each test. Use scoring system to determine points. Use chart at bottom of each diagram to calculate handicap.

Scoring:
Shots outside 6 feet = 0, between 3 and 6 feet = 1, inside 3 feet = 2, in hole = 4

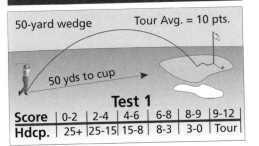

50-yard wedge   Tour Avg. = 10 pts.

50 yds to cup

Test 1

Score	0-2	2-4	4-6	6-8	8-9	9-12
Hdcp.	25+	25-15	15-8	8-3	3-0	Tour

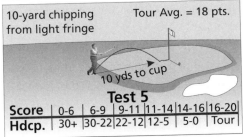

10-yard chipping from light fringe   Tour Avg. = 18 pts.

10 yds to cup

Test 5

Score	0-6	6-9	9-11	11-14	14-16	16-20
Hdcp.	30+	30-22	22-12	12-5	5-0	Tour

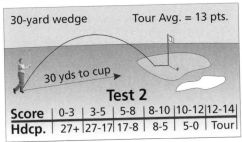

30-yard wedge   Tour Avg. = 13 pts.

30 yds to cup

Test 2

Score	0-3	3-5	5-8	8-10	10-12	12-14
Hdcp.	27+	27-17	17-8	8-5	5-0	Tour

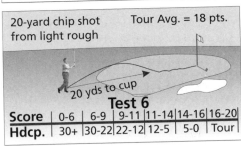

20-yard chip shot from light rough   Tour Avg. = 18 pts.

20 yds to cup

Test 6

Score	0-6	6-9	9-11	11-14	14-16	16-20
Hdcp.	30+	30-22	22-12	12-5	5-0	Tour

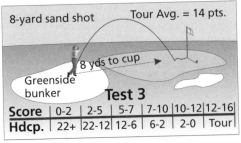

8-yard sand shot   Tour Avg. = 14 pts.

8 yds to cup

Greenside bunker

Test 3

Score	0-2	2-5	5-7	7-10	10-12	12-16
Hdcp.	22+	22-12	12-6	6-2	2-0	Tour

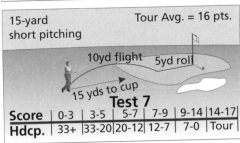

15-yard short pitching   Tour Avg. = 16 pts.

10yd flight   5yd roll

15 yds to cup

Test 7

Score	0-3	3-5	5-7	7-9	9-14	14-17
Hdcp.	33+	33-20	20-12	12-7	7-0	Tour

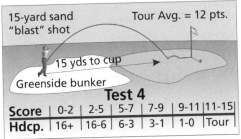

15-yard sand "blast" shot   Tour Avg. = 12 pts.

15 yds to cup

Greenside bunker

Test 4

Score	0-2	2-5	5-7	7-9	9-11	11-15
Hdcp.	16+	16-6	6-3	3-1	1-0	Tour

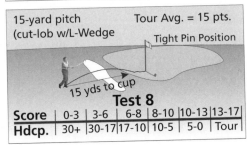

15-yard pitch (cut-lob w/L-Wedge   Tour Avg. = 15 pts.

Tight Pin Position

15 yds to cup

Test 8

Score	0-3	3-6	6-8	8-10	10-13	13-17
Hdcp.	30+	30-17	17-10	10-5	5-0	Tour

Figure 11.3.1: Short-game handicap tests

your score into your handicap for each shot category. Accurately learning and being aware of your short-game strengths and weaknesses will help you manage your game better on the course, too.

Figure your short-game handicap by totaling the points from all eight tests and finding the corresponding handicap on the short-game handicap chart below. No matter what it is, as you improve it, you will improve your ability to shoot lower scores.

Periodically take these tests (once a month during the golf season—it should take you less than 45 minutes), measuring your short-game handicap and recording your scores. If you haven't started working on your finesse swing as outlined in the earlier chapters of this book, take the test before making any changes. Be very careful not to let your ego take control as you take the test. It's easy to cheat on

---

Figure your overall short-game handicap by totaling the points from all eight tests and finding the corresponding handicap on this chart.

Score	Hdcp.		Score	Hdcp.	Score	Hdcp.
150	+8		83	8	42	24
145	+7		80	9	40	25
140	+6	PGA	77	10	38	26
135	+5	Tour	73	11	36	27
130	+4	Level	70	12	34	28
125	+3		67	13	32	29
120	+2	LPGA	63	14	30	30
115	+1	Tour	60	15	28	31
110	0	Level	58	16	26	32
107	1		56	17	24	33
103	2		54	18	22	34
100	3		52	19	20	35
97	4		50	20	18	36
93	5		48	21	16	37
90	6		46	22	14	38
87	7		44	23	12	39

Chart 11.3.1: Short-game handicap chart

yourself. However, it will help you much more if you can be realistic and honest recording your scores. You don't have to discuss the test or your handicap with anyone else, although you might try a little harder if someone is watching or competing with you.

I know from experience that if you practice the way I recommend in this book, your short game will improve and your scores will drop. You'll see steady improvement, not only in your short-game test scores and handicap, but on the course. It will motivate you and help you keep going over the long haul more than almost anything else you can do for your golf game.

11.4 How You Compare

If you want to know how your overall short-game skills stack up against other golfers'—LPGA or PGA Tour pros, any given golfer, or to the golf world in general—the easy way is to look at your relative short-game handicaps. By taking the eight tests of short-game skills and documenting your scores, you can see both where your skills stand now and how much improvement you can expect in the future (assuming you are going to go after that improvement with a consistent, dedicated program).

In particular, I think it is both interesting and instructive to compare your short-game ability relative to the Tour pros' because they set the standard. Simply measure your short-game handicap (as described on page 329) several times, maybe over three weekends in a row, and compare your average scores to the Tour players' scores in Chart 11.3.1. Don't get too excited or upset about your scores in the short term. This short-game-handicap comparison is meant to provide you with a yardstick, a way to measure and evaluate your progress and improvement, evaluating your relative weaknesses vs. strengths over time. It's like having a scale in your bathroom that keeps you up-to-date on how your diet is going. I mention this because many golfers have the wrong goal when practicing. Most players practice to improve their ability to hit great shots more often; I think they should learn to hit better bad shots first.

My point here is, if you see your short-game handicap falling, you know your practice is being effective, and you should keep at it. If your short-game-skills test scores are *not* going down, you're not practicing enough, or well enough, to improve, and you need to "get after it." Remember, improvement on the course is what is important, but it won't be measurable until you become good enough to make your first putts. If your short-game handicap is going down, you are getting there, you are becoming a better player, and you can see, feel, and measure that it really *is* happening.

11.5 Missemall

As discussed earlier, an important ingredient of any playing strategy is knowing the strengths and weaknesses of your game. Measuring your short-game handicap on a regular basis will keep you updated on what shots you can pull off and those you'd better not try. There's another way, a game I want you to play to help identify how good your short game is relative to the golf course.

When the pros I work with are out on Tour, I suggest they occasionally play a game we call "Missemall." That's short for "miss every green in the regulation number of strokes," or "miss them all." Play it as you're working on your short game because it will show you very clearly where you need the most practice. My pros play Missemall on the Monday or Tuesday before a tournament. There are two simple rules:

1. You are not allowed to hit your ball onto any green with your first shot on par 3s or your second shot on par 4s or par 5s. If these first or second shots inadvertently finish on such greens in regulation, you must putt them off into the sand, rough, or fairway before proceeding. This means you will have 18 chances to get the ball up and down from near the green (assuming you can get near enough on par 5s in two to have a short-game shot left).

2. You must miss the greens in a specific distribution of locations, such that you play six short-game shots from the sand, six from the rough, and six from fairway lies. (It's your choice on which hole you play which type of short-game shot—sand, rough, or fairway.)

This game will show how good your finesse game is at preserving your score. Say coming to the par-4 last hole that you've already hit the required number of rough areas and fairways but you haven't played from your sixth sand bunker. Under the rules, you must hit to the green from the sand. So if your second shot finds the rough, you must use a shot to chip into a bunker, then play from the bunker to the green. This rule proves quite difficult, because, believe it or not, bunkers are hard to hit when you're aiming for them: They are, on average, much smaller than greens.

PGA Tour pros playing Missemall have scored as low as 69. Several players regularly shoot between 71 and 73, and all the pros can shoot 75 or better just about whenever they play. On the extremely difficult courses, with nasty rough around the greens, they on occasion have a hard time shooting much below 75.

As for amateurs, most of you won't be able to break 80. If you think your short game is pretty good, Missemall will show you just *how* good. If you regularly bogey after missing a green in regulation, then you are definitely not yet a Tour-quality player. But if you can consistently save par and occasionally do better after missing a green, that's a short game to be proud of.

How Your Short Game Relates to Scoring

11.6 The Bad vs. the Good

Earlier in this book I made the observation that golfers like to practice most what they do the best. That is true of both the power game and the short game, and it is something to avoid. The weaknesses in your short game are far more important to your scoring than the strengths in your power game. And like the proverbial chain, your golf game is only as strong as its weakest link. It isn't the good shots that determine what you shoot, it's the bad shots. So pay special attention to the weak parts of your short game, as determined by your test scores, and practice them more than the stronger parts.

Some examples will help you understand.

Years ago I analyzed the game of Tom Weiskopf (unbeknownst to him), who was always known as a great ball-striker. I found that he did, indeed, hit many more "great shots" than most other players (a "great shot" defined as one with less than 2% error). When I compared him to Tom Kite, I found Weiskopf hit more great shots in one month (four tournaments) than Kite did in a whole year (27 tournaments). But I also learned that Weiskopf hit more "bad shots" (greater than 14% error) than Kite over the same time periods, they putted about the same, and, on average, Kite scored better. Why? Because hitting bad shots hurt Weiskopf more consistently than hitting great shots helped him. Because he too often hit his bad shots with wedges, meaning he didn't convert his next putt for birdie or to save par often enough. And when he hit great shots with his long irons or fairway woods, he usually didn't convert or hole the next shot either (which, while perhaps unfair, is understandable, as his great shots from 225 yards still left him with 12- to 15-foot putts).

What about Kite's game? My analysis showed the opposite. His great shots helped him more than his bad shots hurt him. Which you now know means his great shots were usually from inside 100 yards, allowing him to make his following shot, a short putt. Even when he hit a bad long iron, it cost him only about .15 of a shot, because he got up and down 85% of the time to save par. Compare this to Weiskopf, who converted less than 10% of his putts after great long-iron shots, and lost more than half a shot every time he hit a bad wedge, which he did all too often.

How does this apply to you? Just like Weiskopf, your score is less dependent on great shots in the power game than on great shots in the short game (while the exact opposite probably is true for your ego). Furthermore, you'll suffer greater punishment from bad shots in the short game than from bad power-game shots. (The farther from the hole you make a mistake, the greater your chance of recovery. Remember that.) So all other things being equal, it's better to be great in the short game and just good in the power game, than the other way around.

If you still don't believe it, look at money. Kite has won $10.4 million, Weiskopf $3.9 million. Weiskopf hit the ball longer, straighter, and more accurately, but Kite had the better (some would say best) short game.

(Don't shed too many tears for Tom Weiskopf. If he had had a better short game, we might never have discovered how good Jack Nicklaus was, or what a fine golf-course architect Tom is. If you haven't yet played any of his courses, you are in for a treat, as he is one of the best.)

Something else about Kite. His "bad" drives usually find the edge of the fairway, or at least stop in the first cut of rough. Over all these years, I've never seen him hit a ball out-of-bounds. He could almost always still play his bad shots.

Statistically speaking, no golfer's play from tee to green is as important as the quality of their short game, *unless* his ball-striking consistently gets him into trouble. That doesn't mean you have to hit the center of every fairway, but you do have to keep the ball in play. The rough is not out of play, the first cut is O.K. (in some ways better than the fairway, since the ball often is sitting up), and, of course, any part of the fairway usually is just fine. It's the trees, bunkers, water, and O.B. that lead to the big numbers.

But note once again, with everywhere from the center of the fairway to the rough qualifying as "good," that the power game is the most forgiving aspect of golf. The least forgiving? Putting and the short game.

Hit a bad chip and you have a much smaller chance of making the putt. You've penalized yourself by a large part of a stroke. From 30 yards away, if you pitch to 14 feet, you're likely to hole the putt only about 10% of the time; pitch it to six feet, and you'll make it half the time, gaining .4 of a stroke. Don't think about this as just numbers. I'm talking about your scores. If you hit 10 chips to 14 feet from the flagstick instead of 6 feet, your scores will be almost exactly four strokes higher. Try it: You'll see.

And all this is, as I can't stop repeating, more reason to learn, practice, and master your short game. You can aid that process by keeping track of your strengths and weaknesses with the handicap tests in this chapter.

11.7 Strategy

Mention strategy to most golfers and they think "Should I go for this par 5 in two?" or "How close can I cut this dogleg?" It's true that gambling on par-5 holes is part of golf strategy. But it's actually only a small part. Besides managing the course, you have to manage yourself and your game. And a lot of this management involves your short game.

Is there strategy to the short game? Absolutely. As in every other part of golf, the smart way to play isn't always aiming straight at the flag or flying your ball all the way to the hole. You've got to play the course, the conditions, and, more important, your personal percentages. That applies whether you're lining up a shot of 200 yards or one of 20 yards.

In fact, I think strategy is more important on the shorter shot. The shots inside of 100 yards, the scoring game, account for 60 to 65% of all the shots in golf, and as you've heard over and over, especially in the early chapters of this book, it is what you use to score. So the smarter you are in managing this part of the game, the better your chances of writing low numbers on the card.

The first ingredient of short-game strategy is much the same as that for the long game: knowing your strengths and weaknesses. But knowing them is not enough; you also must know how to play to the strong parts and away from the weak. That comes primarily with experience and thinking.

After I became friends with many Tour players and they were comfortable having me around during their competitive rounds, I spent a lot of time studying how they managed their games around the greens. I'm not exaggerating when I say I was amazed by what I saw. There are significant differences in how each player tries to play and work shots, to his or her advantage, around the greens. In my experience of 24 years watching and working with the pros, I have found several of them who, in my opinion, managed themselves rather poorly.

11.8 The Architect's Way

What I noticed was that many of these very good golfers play by somebody else's rules, usually those of either a great player or a course architect. For example, if Jack Nicklaus proclaims "the hole should be played like so—I designed it that way, it is meant to be played that way," many of the players believe him. These pros, experienced and talented though they may be, sometimes don't consider their own skills in that decision. They play the course in a way that fits another player's strategy, then complain that Jack, or whoever the architect is (particularly if that architect is, or was, a Tour player), designs courses to fit one of his own game strengths, such as Jack's high fade.

You must realize that from the strategic point of view, golf is played in quantum steps. That is, you make either a 3, 4, 5, or 6; there are no one-half or partial-digit scores. You either get it close enough to make the next putt, or you don't. You either make the putt, or you don't. There is no in-between in scoring. You save the stroke, or you don't. Therefore, you should choose the shot strategy that produces your lowest score the highest percentage of the time. And your highest score the lowest percentage of the time. If you can choose a shot strategy that satisfies these criteria, considering *your* game skills (not, say, Greg Norman's), you've got the right shot. I don't care what the architect says.

If you play safe and depend on your short game, but then don't perform well near the hole, your scores will go up. Remember, you get no credit or recognition for "almost" or "close" to making a score of one stroke less. If you have the ability to "turn three strokes into two," getting up and down a high percentage of the time, then you have the opportunity to use all kinds of strategy in the other (non-short-game) parts of the game. You can play the smarter shot, lay up to avoid trouble, play away from hazards, even take some high-risk chances when the rewards are there, knowing your short game will cover you if you don't pull it off.

Your short-game skills can have an enormous effect on the rest of your game strategy.

For example, facing a 150-yard shot from the fairway, your options are fairly limited. Unless it's windy or there's some kind of trouble in the way, you're going to make a normal full swing with your 150-yard club, maybe a 6-iron. If 150 yards is between clubs, then you have to use a little smarts and decide whether you want to lean on your 7-iron or swing easy with the 6. This isn't game strategy, it's shot strategy, and it's important.

However, there is a lot more shot strategy when you get close to the green, such as when you have a 30-yard shot to the pin. You can pitch or chip it, throw it high and make it stop, throw it halfway to the pin and let it roll, or you can bump-and-run it up. Plus, you probably have the option of using four or five different clubs.

You've also got to consider your skill and ability to execute the different swings, and whether or not you can control the flight and roll of the ball. You also have to know the types and grain of grasses you're hitting from and how they react, as well as the grasses you're hitting to. The firmness, moisture content, and detailed terrain of the landing area are also critical to your result. You need to understand how these factors affect the height of your shot, the spin your ball will have, how fast it will stop, and how likely it is to take breaks on the first bounce versus bouncing straight and rolling like a putt.

11.9　Play the Probabilities

Most golfers think there is "the right way" to play all short-game shots. In reality, there is no one right way to play a 35-yard approach, any more than there is a right way to play a 550-yard par 5 with water 15 yards short of the green. In both cases there is a "best-strategy" way to play, and it may be different for each golfer, every time he plays the hole. The best way for Greg Norman to play the par 5 after his 310-yard drive onto a perfect lie in the fairway is to hit his "normal" 240-yard 1-iron directly over water at the pin. For Tom Kite to consider a 270-yard 3-wood shot at the pin after his 280-yard drive into a slightly down lie would be silly. But this is an obvious decision, because Kite can't hit a 3-wood 270 yards from a bad lie (over 250 yards in the air), as this play would require. So this strategic decision is easy, because it is based on what the players can, and probably would, do.

Short-game strategy is different and generally much more complex to assess because it almost never depends on what a player can do. All golfers "can" hit a short shot around the green. Short shots don't require strength or tremendous physical ability. All golfers know they physically "can" hit the shot, so in many—far too many—cases, they try it.

What I want you to understand is why short-game strategy comes into play far more frequently, and in a significantly more complex way, than does long-game strategy. Because short-game strategy is in play in every round for every golfer in all weather conditions on every green missed in regulation.

Very simply, short-game strategy should depend on the *probability* of a golfer executing a shot successfully, not the *possibility* of doing so.

Obviously I can't tell you which shots you'll most probably execute well. As your finesse game improves, you will develop favorite shots in which you have supreme confidence because you have seen and proven that you are good at them. However, most students in my short-game schools don't even consider their probability of hitting a shot well before they try it. Instead, they attempt the shot that "should" be hit in that situation ("should" being determined by watching the pros on television), and experience anxiety during their swing because it is a shot they probably won't hit well.

The probability of success and the consequences of failure are factors you must weigh when planning your short-game strategy. I hope you are beginning to appreciate that there are many more options, possibilities, decisions, and judgments to make in the short game than in any other part of golf. Many golfers have poor short-game skills, not because they have such bad technique, but because there are so many shot options to develop, which they have never taken time to learn. Then they practice poor short-game strategy because they consider only what they "possibly can" do instead of what they "probably will" do.

It would be terrific if you had the ultimate skill, and could choose to always hit the smartest combination of shot and club for any given situation. But we both know that's not realistic. Even great players favor certain clubs and shots, which means they have performed successfully with these given sets of trajectories, spin tendencies, and so on in the past, and they have confidence in knowing what they probably will do with them.

I can't tell you which shots to hit. But I can tell you how various conditions will affect your shots, and this will ultimately help your shot strategies. There is a lot of detail to follow, and if you study it and think about it, the information will help you.

First, a few words of caution: Good short games take years to develop, so don't expect too much of yourself too soon. It's easy to overthink the grain of the grass, the closeness of the lie, the effect of backspin, and other variables, none of which matter if you can't execute shots from good lies that land where they are supposed to and have the trajectory, spin, and speed appropriate to finish close to the hole.

Also, please don't spend so much time and energy thinking about strategy that it screws up the rest of your game. Do, however, spend the time to develop a good short game from good lies over the next few years. Once you master both the mechanics and strategy from good lies, the tougher lies won't present such a problem. You'll enjoy the game more than ever. You'll be amazed how easy it makes the game, and you can empathize with your friends and playing companions who are still struggling with scoring worse than they think they played (since they still think playing is all about striking the ball, when ball-striking has very little to do with it). But you know, if you scored well, you played well; if you scored poorly, you played poorly.

Learn to Read the Shot

11.10 Reading Your Lie

The way your ball lies in the grass, or nongrass, is more important in the short game than in any other game of golf. This is partly because, in the short game, you don't swing hard enough to minimize the effects of grass on your trajectory and spin rate, as you often do in the power game. And, of course, your lie is always good in the putting game (I'm assuming you're on the green, not in the fringe).

The other reason lie is more important on short shots is that what happens *after* your shot lands is a large part of the total result. Full shots usually fly most of the way, then stop fairly quickly. Short-game shots often bounce and roll for more than half their total distance. Experience in knowing how the grass is going to affect your short-game shot, before you hit it, is a vital part of being able to make the ball finish near the hole.

The grass effects you need to predict are twofold. First, you need to know how it will influence the clubhead passing through the impact zone: Will it slow the club, grab the hosel and turn the face left, create an energy-absorbing pad between the clubface and ball, or spread apart and have no effect? Second, after estimating, or guessing, how the clubhead will react through impact, you have to imagine how such behavior will influence the trajectory and spin characteristics of your shot, and the ball's likely performance on the green.

For these reasons, it is absolutely essential that you take several, and maybe more, practice swings before hitting every short-game shot. Find an area of grass similar to that around your ball, and make practice swings that you believe are appropriate for the shot you intend to hit. Simulate the lie—uphill, downhill, side-hill—you will be standing on for the shot. Then, as you make practice swings, watch carefully how the club travels through the grass. It is this vision that will help turn practice swings into the perfect preview swing that will make your shot fly precisely the way you want, to finish in or very close to the hole.

If the grain of the grass you're hitting from is lying against the direction of your swing, and the grass is strong, take much larger practice swings, because you need more power than normal. Watch and feel the club go through the grass. The more resistance you encounter—the more the club gets hung up—then the quicker and/or more powerfully you have to get in and out of the grass to be successful.

As a general rule, as grass gets thicker, stronger, and deeper, you should:

1. Grip farther down the shaft. A short swing-arc creates a steeper, more vertical entry into and out of the grass. This gets the club into and out of the grass more quickly, and through the shot with minimal resistance.

2. Make a bigger, more powerful swing. The more powerful the swing (while keeping clubhead speed down by gripping down the shaft), the less the club's behavior is dependent on the thickness or strength of the grass.

3. Move the ball farther back in your stance, and use a more lofted club to produce the loft you want.

Of course, when you face a delicate shot, it's difficult to make a long, powerful swing and not have the ball go too far. This is when gripping down helps the most.

There will be times when the grass is so nasty and the grain so against you that the only way to get the ball out, and not hit it too far, is to open the blade and play the equivalent of a sand-explosion shot. Having the blade open, and the hosel leading into the grass, helps in this "against-the-grain" shot (as demonstrated by Vijay Singh in Fig. 11.10.1).

Let me end this section with a final, overview thought. Put it in the back of your mind, and someday when you can't decide how to swing on a shot, maybe it will help. From the low-running bump-and-run to the high-loft cut-lob shot, there is a sliding scale of forward energy transferred to the ball: On low-running shots, almost all of the swing energy transferred to the ball makes it run forward; on high lob shots, most of the swing energy lofts the ball high, and very little makes it move forward.

The result of this is that the bump-and-run shot roll is most sensitive to the length of your swing, while the cut-lob shot is the least sensitive. So whenever the lie allows it, consider the low-running shot. But if the lie is so bad that you can't figure out what it will do, open the blade and hit a big, high cut-lob shot. If contact is better than you expect, the ball will go a lot higher but not much farther. If club-ball contact isn't that good (because of too much grass), the ball won't fly so high while forward distance won't change very much (as illustrated in Fig. 11.10.2). Most important, the ball will be out of the mess and somewhere on the green.

Figure 11.10.1: Vijay Singh blasts from rough

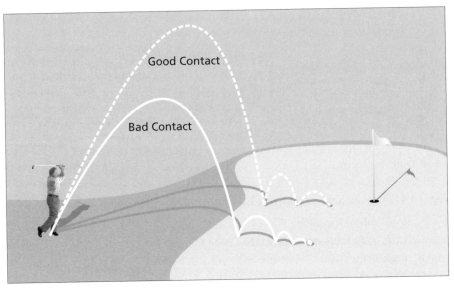

Figure 11.10.2: Cut-lob shots vary in height more than in carry distance

11.11 Reading the Green

If you are going to play a short shot into a Bermuda grass green, landing with a lot of backspin and a shallow pitch mark, and it lands against the grain, it will stop far more quickly than if it's flying in the same direction as the grain (Fig. 11.11.1). That means you should know how the grain runs even when you're not on the green. While this is usually a relatively small effect on bent grass greens, it can be a major consideration on strong-grass greens, like Bermuda and Kikuyu. The stronger the blades, the greater the effect. In fact, I've seen many instances where grain has a greater effect on finesse shots than it has on putting.

I recommend to all my Tour players that they note in their yardage books the grain on every section of every Bermuda green—not just where the holes will be cut. I encourage them to scrape the green surfaces with their putters (not during competition—that's illegal), so that when they miss the green and need to pitch to it in competition, there is no doubt in their minds as to whether they'll be pitching to the green with or against the grain.

In addition, hitting against the grain with a pitch or chip shot is like driving into the wind: Any error in direction will be exaggerated, and you need to play more break for the roll because the grain pushes the ball away from the line of travel. When an incoming shot is coming into heavy grain, I often recommend flying the ball all the way to the hole rather than trying the bump-and-run; it's just

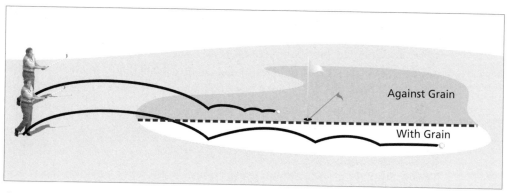

Figure 11.11.1: Grain can affect chipping results dramatically

too difficult to judge distance and direction against the grain. Another reason to hit the high-lofted shot is that the ball will stop more quickly when hit into the grain: You can throw it at the pin and know it will stop there.

Approaching with the grain, the opposite is true. Just as driving with the wind results in straighter tee shots, so pitching and chipping downgrain usually result in straighter roll. Play less break and your errors will be minimized. But it's also more difficult to stop a high-lofted shot downgrain, so I often bump-and-run these, figuring the expected extra roll into my mental calculations.

As described in Chapter 7, I like players to be aware of humps and valleys on the greens and how they affect both pitch and chip shots. The upshot is that you should always avoid having to land a shot on a hump and, when you can, select shots where you are trying to land in the bottom of a depression.

Another green-reading consideration is the location of the flagstick on the green (this keeps showing up in the data). As you develop your short game, you probably will notice varying degrees of success when the pin is toward the front, middle, and back of the green. While every golfer has personal swing tendencies and weaknesses (even great players; they just have smaller, more subtle weaknesses), and because the short game is less athletic ability and more acquired skill, your finesse tendencies occur more consistently day after day. Be sure to take note of them. For example, if you have more success with the hole cut up front (using high-lofted shots that stop quickly) and less when the cup is in back (where you tend to use bump-and-run shots), use this knowledge two ways: When the pin is forward, you should be brimming with confidence; and practice harder on the shots you tend to hit to pins in the back, the ones that give you trouble.

Finally, while my research suggests *always* leaving the flagstick in the hole when chipping or putting from off the green (see Chapter 8), you also should commit to playing a little more break than you "read" on these shots. Only one in 10 approach shots finish above the hole, while nine end up below. Although you might say you'd rather face an uphill putt, I don't think you'd rather face an uphill 12-footer than a one-foot downhill putt. Most holes are not cut on sidehill slopes, so don't worry too much about up- vs. downhill putts: It's more important to leave yourself a putt that is short. The percentages say that shorter, easier putts follow from playing more break.

11.12 Choosing Your Equipment

The quality of the grooves on your wedges is important, because grooves affect backspin, a critical element of short-game shot control. You should know what kind of grooves you have so when you get new clubs, you can specify the same type and quality groove. Keep grooves clean of dirt and grass and be sure they don't get too worn.

Although numerous parties (including the United States Golf Association) have claimed that square versus V-groove shape is not important and that players don't have enough control of backspin to have much influence on their performance, I think they are wrong. These naysayers have contradicted themselves anyway.

On one hand, they say that even if box (square) grooves do produce more backspin, it doesn't matter because players are not capable of taking advantage of them; on the other hand, they acknowledge that if the conditions of the greens are soft and the pros can "throw darts" on the course, they will score better (which is true). If you check scores over a period of years, you will know that lower-scoring rounds are played when the greens are soft, and the pros can throw the ball at the flag knowing it will stop. This is the same as giving the pros more backspin from their wedges, so they know their shots will stop quickly on greens, just as if they were wet and soft. When the pros can accurately predict the behavior of the ball, because their execution is already so good, they can perform at their best.

Along this same line, it should come as no surprise that one way the USGA makes a course play tough for its championships is by firming up the greens. This makes it more difficult for players to throw darts and predict what will happen afterward. If you can't have precise control over how much the ball rolls after it lands, it is much more difficult to score. This is the same result you see when hitting wedges with worn-down grooves.

I conducted the extensive "Box vs. V-groove" test for the PGA Tour a number of years ago. From that data I learned that:

1. Square (or box) grooves put more spin on wedge shots than do V-grooves (a little bit more on fairway shots, significantly more on rough shots, and a *lot* more on shots from wet rough).

2. Shots hit by square-groove wedges stopped faster on greens (Fig. 11.12.1).
3. The worst performers of all, in both stopping-distance control and shot-scatter patterns, were worn-down grooves (Fig. 11.12.2).

So if you want to get your shots to stop more quickly, get box grooves on your short irons and wedges. But beware, more spin on most modern balls makes shots

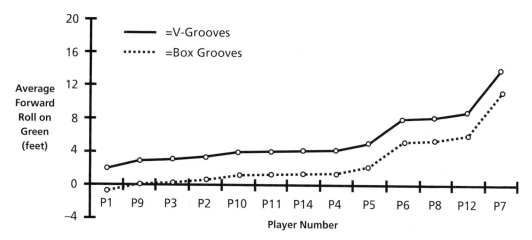

Figure 11.12.1: Ninety-yard wedge shot from 2-inch wet rough by 13 PGA Tour players

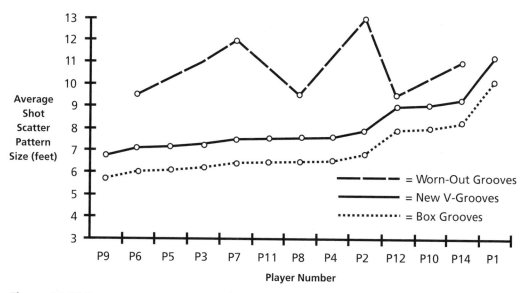

Figure 11.12.2: Average scatter-pattern size for 90-yard wedges from dry fairway lies

fly shorter (Fig. 11.12.3). This can be a real problem if you have box grooves on all your irons, especially the 6- and 5-irons you need to hit from rough when you want to hit "flier-shots," which run up to the greens. Groove shape gets less important as club loft decreases, so this effect can cause strange gaps between clubs set strictly by loft specifications (which most manufacturers do).

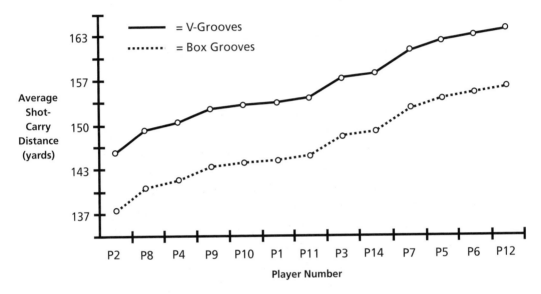

Figure 11.12.3: Shot-carry distance for box vs. V-grooves (7-iron shots from 2-inch rough)

11.13 Using the Right Ball

The type of ball you play is another factor. There used to be no question that balata-covered, three-piece balls (also called "wound" balls because of the rubber windings within) stopped more quickly with more backspin than did two-piece (solid center), Surlyn-covered balls. But this is no longer true. Some of the new two- and three-piece blended-cover balls have very high spin rates. Lower-spin balls are unquestionably longer off the driver and long irons, and there's no reason not to play them if distance is your problem, you're good around the greens, you play slow greens, and you don't have trouble stopping the ball near the hole.

But if you play on lightning-fast, Oakmont-, Pinehurst #2-, or Augusta-type greens, and have trouble controlling shots on those surfaces, then consider the slightly shorter but faster-stopping high-spin balls.

Don't be misled about how different balls feel. Two-piece balls were originally reported to feel harder and resist being worked, curved, and controlled. I don't believe feel has anything to do with any of this. I ran a test a few years ago that showed the main differences among balls that golfers could detect were the sounds made at impact, the distance they travel, and their spin rate. There is no question that low-spin balls both fly and roll farther, and that high-spin balls fly shorter and stop faster on the greens. But feel has absolutely nothing to do with it, so don't worry about it.

Weather is a definite factor. Hitting out of wet grass reduces spin, while wet greens will be softer and help the ball stop more quickly. Cold balls fly shorter, hot balls fly farther.

Despite the emphasis on spin in this chapter, I want you to remember what I said earlier about golfers who are the most successful around greens, often controlling their shots with trajectory. Wound balls will fly lower off the clubface on pitch shots, while two- and three-piece balls with large, rubber-compound centers tend to fly higher. Remember, a ball that is coming in low and hot, even if it has a lot of backspin, may or may not stop on the green, depending on the hardness and/or wetness of the surface. But a ball coming in high and soft is going to stop fairly quickly every time, no matter what the surface is like—wet or dry, soft or hard. If the ball is coming straight down—the ultimate, high-lofted shot—it will bounce straight up and down no matter how hard the surface, and stay just about where it landed.

Now a warning. You can't possibly think about all these things I've just mentioned while preparing to hit a shot. It would be too much, it would take too long, and it would paralyze your brain. You can't be worrying about trying to remember all the information presented in this book. I simply want you to read and understand the game, so that when you play it, it makes more sense. Over a period of time, your brain will work out how to incorporate many of the things you read. Till then, make your practice swings, feel free to experiment when you're practicing, and let the skills come to you. Play the game the best you can, every time you play it, and practice a little in between. The more you understand, the better you will practice, and in the long run, the better you will score.

Playing Your Own Game

11.14 Bad Mistakes Are Bad

What makes a golfer good? The good ones don't hit only good shots, they don't manufacture magical recovery shots, and they certainly don't all have more physical talent than others. What they do, what separates them, is they avoid mistakes they can't cover with their short games.

Good players tend to mishit thin, not fat: You usually can play thin shots, saving the par or even occasionally getting away with birdie. But fat shots rarely get lucky, and more often cost a full stroke. Good players don't mishit into spots from which they can't recover, and they don't hit the wrong shot at the wrong time. While all golfers make mistakes, it is the kind of mistake made and how you recover from it that determines your score. Good players know enough about their full-swing and short-game skills and tendencies that they avoid the really costly errors and play the safe shot. When they do err, they can still recover and save par.

In my years of teaching the short game, I've witnessed all kinds of mistakes. Here are some of the most common ones, and the ways to deal with them, so they don't keep you from becoming a "good" golfer:

1. Backswing too long. This is the most common mistake in the short game. When the backswing is too long, the only compensating move is to slow the downswing motion, and decelerate into the ball. This is a disaster, leading to all kinds of bad results, caused by unstable club motion through impact. If your backswing is too short, you may have to "get after" your follow-through; that's not good, but at least the club is stable through impact. If you find yourself hitting at the ball, flinching as you hit it or getting "yippy" (jumpy) during your finesse swing, make sure the ball is back in your stance, then imagine a second ball on a tee about a foot closer to the target than your real ball (Fig. 11.14.1). Make a backswing you know is shorter than your follow-through will be, and in your mind's eye imagine that the center of your swing arc (the point of maximum clubhead velocity) will occur at about where the second ball is sitting.

2. Ball too far forward. When hitting from grass, the ball must be positioned prior to (or behind) the point where your club reaches the bottom of your natural dead-hands swing arc, to ensure solid contact. Playing the ball a little too far forward produces fat shots; playing it too far back produces very playable shots, but on a slightly lower trajectory. If you are unsure about your ball position, move it a little back, not forward. It's always better to err on the safe side, and that's back.

3. Not holding the finish. When you don't hold your follow-through and finish position on a chip, pitch, sand, or distance-wedge shot, you lose the feedback of what your effort produced, so you don't learn anything from the results. I evaluate

Figure 11.14.1: Maximum clubhead velocity should occur past impact

practice sessions based on what I think the student learned. Players who learn from their practice sessions improve; players who beat balls and don't learn are wasting their time. So hold your finish as if you are posing for a photograph after hitting a great shot. This will give your brain both the look and feel of the swing, fresh in your memory, as you watch the result. The correlation of swing feel with outcome is what learning is all about.

4. Poor transfer of weight. You've got to transfer your weight from the right foot (for right-handers) to the left side through impact in the finesse swing. Many golfers never move any weight and their lower bodies remain stock-still. Others reverse pivot, transferring their weight forward during the backswing and backward coming through, the exact opposite of what's correct. This is a disastrous mistake.

Concentrate on the synchronization of your upper and lower body, with a rotating turn, which is vital if you want to make a rhythmic swing. (Please note, I don't refer to this as a weight *shift*, because the transfer of weight should come from a turning of your body, a rotation around your spine, rather than a sliding or shifting motion.)

5. Not enough lower-body turn-away. The average golfer in our schools turns his hips only about 30 degrees from the top of the backswing—where they are almost in the same position as at address—to the end of the follow-through. The proper hip rotation on anything longer than a 15- to 20-yard shot is more like 100 degrees, and for a 50-yard shot as much as 140 degrees. Remember, you're not trying to produce power, but simply trying to keep your rhythm consistent. I don't see one golfer in 100 who turns too much, so make sure you rotate your lower body away from address, keeping your lower body synchronized and moving with your upper body.

6. Grip too strong. Taking too strong a grip with the left (or upper) hand is a mistake. A strong grip leads to swinging back inside and low, below the desired plane, and sticking the club too far back behind the body. Without vicious rerouting on the downswing, the shot won't have the proper trajectory. A strong grip also gives control to the hands and small muscles, which flip the club at impact in an attempt to lift the ball up. Even if contact is made with such a swing (a big if), the results are inconsistent. When in doubt, again, make the safe mistake: A finesse grip that's a little too weak won't hurt your short game (but it can mean trouble if you take it to your power game).

7. Shanking. Believe it or not, if you start shanking as you begin working on your new finesse swing, you're on the right track. It often happens because the lower body is working with the upper for the first time; this creates more centrifugal force with less effort coming down through impact, which swings the club a little farther out and away from the body. To correct this, stand slightly farther from the ball and keep making your improved "finesse-lower-body turn." If you are a shanker for reasons other than a better finesse turn, however, order a "Shanker's Delight" learning aid (Fig. 11.14.2) and you'll have no further problems. Hit enough shots with the Shanker's Delight and it will prevent you from making either of the body or hand manipulations that lead to shanking.

8. The "styler" finish. While a low-hands-coiled-around-the-body "styler" finish (Fig. 11.14.3) occasionally gains popularity with younger players, and may look cool and different, it's a surefire way to ruin your short game. A low follow-through requires muscle and hand control, which means it will prove inconsistent, especially under pressure. It also creates a lower trajectory than does a high finish, again meaning less consistency in how shots react upon landing. My advice is to stay with the dead-hands swing, and let the club finish high and long (Fig. 11.14.4) when the shot-carry distance allows you to do so.

Figure 11.14.2: The Shanker's Delight

Figure 11.14.3: The styler finish indicates unwanted hand control

Figure 11.14.4: The higher your hands finish, the higher your shot will fly

9. *Block through impact.* Some players insist on holding the clubface "blocked" through and after impact. That means they never rotate or release the club or their forearms, so shots are blocked, sometimes out to the right but often with extra loft (Fig. 11.14.5). Trying to inhibit the release is an unnatural action that involves the muscles of the hands, wrists, and fingers, which makes it a difficult shot to hit under pressure. Stay with the natural, dead-hands finesse swing, which gives the club a complete release as it comes down through impact and swings up into a full, high finish.

Figure 11.14.5: Blocking through impact requires hand control

10. *No distance.* As players work on their finesse games, they are sometimes surprised that their shots don't go very far. But they do go high, so high they don't reach the target. There are several possible reasons:

a. A decelerating swing. Instead of accelerating through impact, the hands slow down, letting the club actually pass them. This can add 5, 10, even 15 degrees of loft to the club, causing the club to slide under the ball at impact.

b. Deceleration also causes instability at impact and excessive loss of energy, and, again, causes the shot to fall short.

c. Blocking past impact. As described above, the golfer doesn't release his arms, so the clubface is open through impact, sending the ball high and short.

d. Ball position too far forward in the stance. This position adds unwanted loft to the clubface, even if you don't hit the shot fat.

For all these problems the solution is a short backswing followed by smooth acceleration through impact, releasing the club, all after making sure the ball is properly positioned in your stance. The hands, arms, shoulders, and lower body should turn together (synchronized) throughout the swing, pulling the club through impact, and finishing with a "longer-than-the-backswing" follow-through motion. The club must be in the process of releasing as it meets the ball, and must be accelerating as a result of the centrifugal force generated by the body's synchronized turn movement.

11.15 Commit to Your Shot

You can't, and shouldn't, try to learn every shot in the short game. Tom Kite, David Duval, Tom Watson, and Seve Ballesteros have been working on their short games for so many years that you'll never catch them. While there's a lot of fun and creativity to be had in the short game, you can overdo it. As I said before, you don't want to think yourself out of a shot. I recommend practicing only two "specialty" shots for any given situation, if your normal finesse swing won't work: one with minimum backspin, the other with the maximum backspin you can routinely put on it (routinely means not the ultimate, all-time, most spectacular move to produce spin). On the course, you then decide which shot to use based on the lie, green conditions, pin placement, and so on. Then commit to that shot, practice the swing until you produce a good preview of it, step up, and hit it.

To avoid confusion, I use two slightly different preshot rituals for my two maximum- and minimum-spin swing motions; the difference lets my subconscious know which shot I'm going to hit, well before I do it. I use my normal preshot ritual, with my normal waggle, for my normal medium-high backspin shot. I change the waggle, but keep the same rhythm, when I'm hitting either of the other two spin-option shots. This way, if I haven't fully committed in my mind which shot I'm going to use, I can't waggle. This commitment check is good, because if you're not ready to waggle, you're surely not ready to swing.

11.16 Conservative Strategy, Aggressive Execution

I can sum up my thoughts on generic golf strategy in eight words: Conservative Strategy, Aggressive Execution, Know When to Go.

If you plan conservatively, you will never hit shots into the killer areas of the course and you will minimize the impact (or penalty) of your bad shots on your score. If you execute aggressively (by which I mean positively and optimistically, not forcefully), you will optimize your mechanical-swing skills by giving yourself the chance to make the best move you can. And knowing when to go means gambling at the right times.

Most amateurs think the man who makes the most birdies will be the winner. In reality, it's usually more likely that the man who makes the fewest bogeys wins. If a PGA Tour player could eliminate bogeys, I can't imagine how much money he'd make. All the players, even those not near the top of the money list, make lots of birdies. But they throw them away, cancel them out, with bogeys. The way to protect against bogeys is with conservative planning, so that not only do your average shots turn out okay, but your poor shots don't hurt so badly that you can't still make par.

You can't protect yourself from the really awful shots in golf—the shank or wild slice or hook that occasionally puts you out of play or in deep trouble. But you can protect against your "not-great" shots that aren't hit perfectly. When evaluating shot options, give yourself a safety margin—say, 10 to 15 yards on either side of your intended target. Be sure that if the shot doesn't come off within 10 to 15 yards of perfect, you'll still be okay. If you can't make that guarantee, hit a different, safer shot.

Having chosen a conservative strategy, make the most rhythmic, beautiful move you can through the ball. Be very positive in your mind's eye: Visualize the perfect shot; visualize and internalize the feeling and the vision of the move (or swing) that causes the shot; and while you have these images fresh in your mind, execute the shot and watch your ball fly to its target. Not having a clear image and feel of the swing you want to make, before you make it, is another mistake good players avoid.

As important as visualization and preparation are, I also believe you need to understand the mechanics of the swing you're trying to make. You need to know, as I've explained in detail over the last few chapters, what it is about the swing that makes the ball fly higher or lower, with more or less spin, longer or shorter. If you know the swing requirements for the shot you are trying to produce, you can practice, improve, and turn your short game into a subconsciously controlled, automatically performed "feel" game. But you can't get to that point without basing it on something sound and reliable, without understanding intellectually what it is you have to do to make a shot happen. Then you need to know when to gamble.

Because I know my game, I can tell you that I never gamble and try to hit a 3-iron to a flagstick near water. But I *always* go for that same flagstick when I have a wedge in my hand. The reward is much more likely, the penalty much less so. I like the odds.

11.17 The 90% Rule

That's the physical side of strategy. What about the mental side? I can deal with that with one comment: Never hit a shot if you have any anxiety about its outcome. If you haven't practiced the swing sufficiently, if you don't have the confidence to pull it off at least 90% of the time, then it's the wrong shot and you shouldn't try it.

That's right—90% of the time. I'm going to put 10 balls down and you're going to bet me your paycheck that nine out of 10 will land near (or somewhat near, and safe) the target. If you can't make that bet, don't try that shot. Ten safe shots to the fat of the green or 10 safe shots short of the bunker in the throat of the opening to the green are much better than 10 shots aimed at a dangerous pin placement, six of which end up on the green (you won't make some of the next putts anyway) and the other four of which finish in serious trouble buried in the bunker or worse. These shots lead to double and triple bogeys.

Here's what happens when someone attempts a shot with less than 90% confidence. I call it golf's version of the anxiety attack:

The player is worried as he thinks about the shot; worried a little more as he addresses the ball; takes extra time to think and make sure he's not going to do whatever it is he's worried about doing. But then the subconscious anxiety attack occurs at the top of the backswing. The player thinks, "Ohmygod, don't let this happen," which is the worst possible thought any golfer can have as he moves down toward impact.

Here's a saying I use with my players: "Trust is a must, because to bail is to fail." If your subconscious doesn't trust you, it will "bail out" in the middle of your downswing, guaranteeing a poor shot. You can't change your motion in the middle of the downswing; there isn't enough time and you don't have enough hand strength to override the centrifugal forces that have built up. If your subconscious bails out on you in the middle of a swing, *you will fail!*

11.18 Don't Be Too Conservative

If you have developed a solid short game, one that you trust, then play to it. Use it for all it's worth, because it will help you score better. When you have a good short game, you can gamble more profitably with your long game. You can try to get close in two on more par 5s (as long as you stay out of sand around the greens). You'll know you can always save par, and the closer you get, the easier the birdie putt your finesse shot will leave.

On a short, tight par 4, if you are a reasonably good driver you can go for it with full confidence. Even if you blow an occasional drive into the trees, you know you can chip it out into the fairway in front of the green, pitch it on, and save par. And you can make many more birdies from near the green with your wedge than you can if you lay up off the tee and have to hit an 8-iron into the green.

Playing to the strength of your short game can have a tremendous impact in a tournament. In fact, I think not gambling in your area of strength is as much an error as gambling (hitting poor percentage shots) in your area of weakness. For example, on that short, tight par 4, you might make two birdies and two pars teeing off with a driver during a four-round event. That gives you a huge advantage over the rest of the field, which is hitting 2- or 3-irons off the tee and 7- or 8-irons into the green, making three pars and a bogey.

While I encourage you to play aggressively when you play to the strength of your short game, there is need for some caution. When you hit into trouble, play safe coming out. Make sure you never hit two bad shots in a row—again, that's when double and triple bogeys come into play.

When you're in trouble, the smart policy is to give yourself a good chance for par (maybe a 60% likelihood of getting up and down), but a 100% chance for bogey. Never let a double bogey onto your scorecard. Don't try hitting a miracle shot out of the woods, low under the trees, then rising and turning left up and over a bunker, onto the green, then biting. That shot is just asking for a big number. Play smart, punch the ball out toward the front of the green, trusting that you can get it up and down to save par. That way, the very worst you'll ever make is bogey.

Another smart bit of self-management is to never gamble when there's a penalty such as water or out-of-bounds nearby. Penalties can't be erased from the scorecard, so avoid them at all costs.

Identify the "disaster areas" on your course (they don't have to be out-of-bounds; a particularly bad patch of rough will do). Treat them like penalties—and manage your game to avoid them.

If you've really worked at your short game, then by all means go for the par 5s in two. But forget trying for eagles. Trying for extra distance or hitting extra-difficult shots in order to chase eagles will cost you more strokes than you'll gain. If you never make another eagle, fine. What you want are birdies on par 5s, and lots of them.

Play to get as close as you can in two shots to all par 5s without finding the sand, problem rough, or hazard. This will allow you a third shot from close enough to the green to stop it in the "Golden Eight" range. You can make a lot more birdies from short range than if you lay back and hit full shots into the greens. There is no great full-swing player who, from 110 yards, can beat a good short-game practitioner from 40 yards at getting the ball close to the pin. Forgetting eagles and maximizing birdies is smarter, safer, and you'll be pleasantly surprised if a few eagles come your way.

Finally, whenever you have a wedge in your hands, fire at the pin. Don't play conservatively unless there's a potential penalty—water or something similarly severe—guarding the pin so tightly that your wedge skill can't match up to the 90% rule.

And while you're firing at the pins, enjoy it. Make a lot of birdies while thinking that this is your aggressive move. "Conservative strategy, aggressive execution, know when to go" will pay dividends over the long run.

Use conservative strategy to eliminate penalties and minimize bogeys. Forget eagles on par 5s and forget trying to make birdies on long par 4s. Use an aggressive attitude to execute every swing as perfectly as you can. And take no prisoners with your short game on easy or short holes and on par 5s. Go after every chance to make birdies with wedges. See how the game will come to you. This is the way the game is meant to be played. It also optimizes your scoring potential.

CHAPTER 12

Secrets of the Short Game

I haven't yet met a golfer who isn't looking for the secret that will unleash success in his golf, that elusive something that's going to make him or her a better, or even great, player. We all know it's out there, and we have been searching for it as long as the game has been played. No matter what we do or say, the search goes on. No matter how well he plays, in the back of his mind every golfer still wants to know the extra little "secret" that will unlock his ability to play even better. "But what's the *real* secret for me?"

I've noticed that no one asks, "*Is* there a secret?" Golfers are convinced there is one.

Well, they're right, there is a secret; that's the good news. The bad news is, there is more than one. In fact, there are many. And the worse news (if you choose to see it that way) is that these many secrets apply to all golfers.

And one more piece of news: The secrets aren't really secret. Many people know them, so perhaps they really shouldn't be called secrets. In any case, they are important "truths of the game." And I promise that if you believe in them and act upon them in the right way, you definitely will improve your ability to score!

12.1 Secret No. 1: The Secret of Feedback

As a teacher, a scientist, a physicist, and a player, I believe the "Secret of Feedback" is at the top of the list. Because if you don't receive, internalize, and benefit from the feedback provided by your shots—if you don't both consciously and subconsciously correlate your shot results with your actions and learn from your experiences—then you will never improve.

But you can't just practice. You must do "intelligent practice." My five rules for intelligent short-game practice with feedback are:

1. Never "rake and beat" balls.
2. Never hit a practice shot with bad alignment.
3. Know your precise yardage.
4. Watch the trajectory of each shot.
5. Hold your finish while you learn.

Rule No. 1: Never "Rake and Beat" Balls

Practicing with feedback means that you must be careful, you must be patient, you must work at a somewhat slower rate than what you otherwise might do. You can't beat balls, simply rushing from shot to shot, club to club. You must never rake over a second ball and hit that shot until the first one has landed—and you've watched it land. You must take the time to back away after each shot, then approach the new one and get into your setup the same way every time, just as you intend to do on real shots that count on the course. Getting into your address position is as important as, and can be more important than, the swing itself. Because if you're set up incorrectly or differently on each shot, there is no way to make or learn to groove a good, repeatable swing. So practice carefully, taking enough time to make proper setup a habit.

Rule No. 2: Never Hit a Practice Shot with Bad Alignment

Nothing is more ridiculous than standing at address in a poor position, with your shoulders, feet, or hips aligned in the wrong direction, trying to hit a good shot. Because with poor aim even a good swing will make the ball go to the wrong place. Your subconscious will always fight against that and will prohibit you from learning a good swing.

Your natural instincts, guided by your desire to hit the ball to your target, will force you to make a compensating swing, to try to make the ball go where it is supposed to. It is these subconscious compensations that make the swing so difficult for so many golfers. On the other hand, from a perfectly aligned position, a good swing results in a good shot.

It is very easy to practice with good alignment.

First, before hitting even one shot, take the club you are going to be hitting and place it on the ground, aiming exactly at your target. The butt end of the club should just touch the first ball (Fig. 12.1.1). From behind, make sure it is aimed *exactly* at the target.

Then put your 2-iron (which isn't good for much else) in the "aim-club" position of parallel-left alignment.

And finally, pick up your hitting club, set your feet and body parallel left, and without lifting your left (front) heel, turn the toe toward the target 30 to 45 degrees. Now you are ready to practice (Fig. 12.1.2). Be sure to hit all your practice shots this way. If you change your target, reset your hitting and aim clubs on the ground.

While setting up with an aim club is simple and takes no time, it is still ignored by almost all amateurs. PGA and LPGA Tour pros, however, are much better about this and work with aim clubs all the time. They know what an advantage it is to make perfect aim a habit. The more practice shots you hit with perfect alignment, the better perfect setup and alignment will feel to you on the course.

Figure 12.1.1:
Aim your hitting
club precisely

Figure 12.1.2:
Always practice
with an aim club

Rule No. 3: Know Your Precise Yardage

What matters with your distance wedges is the flight distance of your shots (hence their name). Yet when most golfers hit wedges on the practice tee they note only the shots' direction. And they usually hit to targets off in the distance, farther away than the club they are hitting can handle. So most golfers have no idea how far each wedge shot travels, which means they aren't learning or gaining in their ability to control yardages.

If you're hitting a wedge toward a distant target and you don't know how far it's flying, then all you are doing is warming up your muscles. You're not practicing your wedge game or finesse swing at all.

For valuable distance-wedge practice, you need a known-yardage target (or targets) that you have either accurately walked off or measured with a laser rangefinder (Fig. 12.1.3). You also need good enough visibility of the landing area to accurately evaluate—at the moment the ball hits the ground—whether you've hit it long, short, or the perfect distance. I try to have my students hit to nets that are sloped toward them so it is easy to see within inches of where the ball hits: on the net, short, or over it. To clearly see a shot's landing spot, it helps to be hitting to a slight uphill slope. If you don't have nets, lay down a towel as a target on a slight slope, shoot the distance, and you are prepared to practice distance wedges with accurate, reliable feedback for the distance each shot carries.

Whenever you practice distance wedges, don't be distracted by worrying about their flight direction; you'll note that instinctively. Focus on how far the shots fly. In practice, distance should be your sole criterion of a good wedge shot. The more you think that way in practice, the better your shots will fly on the course.

Figure 12.1.3: Shoot your practice distances to one-yard accuracy

Rule No. 4: Watch the Trajectory of Each Shot

Watch most golfers hitting wedge shots on the practice range and what you see are people beating balls. They think they're working on their wedge games, but all they're really doing is making a wedge swing, striking the ball, taking a quick glance to see whether or not it's airborne, then looking back at the pile of balls and raking another into place for the next swing. They don't watch how far the ball flies, they don't notice how high it goes, and they sometimes don't even have a target in mind. They have no idea what they—or their shots—are doing.

Whenever I see a "raker-and-beater" in one of my schools, I wait until he's hit a ball and begun looking for the next one to hit, then I say, "Joe, look at me, please." Once I have his attention, I ask, "Without looking back, what did that shot just do? Where did that ball go?" Most of the time they can't tell me. They have learned absolutely nothing, so they have wasted the time it took to get ball and body into position and make the swing. This isn't practice, because they aren't learning anything. It's just exercise.

Not that I'm against exercise. I just prefer exercise with good feedback, which is just as much fun, just as healthy, and has the added benefit that it helps you become a better golfer. So I want you to learn to notice and care about the height and character of each shot's trajectory, and make it a habit to watch your shots in flight (Fig. 12.1.4). If you are making a true finesse swing, with no hand-muscle control and no hitting action, you will create consistent trajectories and a consistent, repeatable amount of backspin on the shots as they land. (To evaluate backspin, you occasionally must hit to a well-maintained green surface for feedback on your shots' bounce and roll behavior, particularly on shots inside 30 yards.)

Figure 12.1.4: Watch your shots, internalize their feel

These are the questions you should be answering after every shot you hit: Did it land the distance you wanted? Or was it too long or too short? (Instinctively you already know if it was right or left of the target.) Did it have the trajectory you wanted? Did it have the same trajectory as the previous shots you'd been hitting, and if not, why not? Finally, would it have behaved as desired on the golf course, to a real green with a real pin?

Rule No. 5: Hold Your Finish While You Learn

If you want your short game to be the best it can be, you must be able to see and feel the swing you need (to produce the shot you want) before you need it. This "mind's-eye visualization" must happen before you swing so it can help you make the perfect motion.

The only way to achieve this ability is with experience, seeing and feeling how different swings cause different golf-ball behaviors. You can't learn this by watching someone else hit, from videotapes, or from books. Those can teach you why and what to do and how it is done. But you must make the swings yourself so you can add feel to the swings you've observed, giving your mind's eye the complete correlation between actions and results. Once the feelings and images are internalized and accurate in your mind's eye, make enough practice swings until you see and feel the one that will produce the result you want.

What do I mean by "holding your finish"? Remain in the completed follow-through position of the swing, without moving, so you have the feel (kinesthetic awareness) of that swing as the ball lands (Fig. 12.1.5). This simultaneous experience of shot result and swing feel is what enables a golfer to learn and internalize the swing mechanics/ball-flight correlations for future use in the short game. If you hold your finishes (maintaining swing feel) until your shots land, you learn these correlations. With continued practice you will develop great touch. If you don't hold your finish, as soon as you stand up, step back, look away, or turn your back, you lose the feel of the swing and with it the chance to learn another swing/result correlation. Unfortunately, this is exactly what most golfers do and why their practice doesn't help them when they get to the course.

The secret of feedback can be summed up this way: If you are raking and beating balls; if you're not set up with good aim; if you're not getting good distance feedback from your shots; if you're not aware of the trajectories of your shots; and if you're not forming a habit of holding your finishes, then you would be better off lying on your back, looking at the sky, and daydreaming about a good short game.

The other way to think of it is this: Bad practice is worse than no practice.

Figure 12.1.5: Make holding your finish a habit

12.2 Secret No. 2: The Secret of Productive Time

The most valuable, most irreplaceable asset we have in this world is time. We all start with the same amount of time each day, and at day's end we've spent it all, never to have it again. What you have to ask yourself is "How productive is the time you spend trying to improve your game?" The time you practiced yesterday either made you a little better, made you worse, or left you the same. No other choices. It is not the person who practices the most or the longest who wins: It is the person who improves the most who wins.

In golf, as in life, if you gain knowledge, understanding, and insight from the use of your time, you will be successful. However, if you expend time, effort, and energy in practice and don't consistently learn, internalize, and improve from it, your game is in serious trouble.

My concept of productive time is not simply about how many hours or minutes you allot to practice. Nor is it about how long it takes you to learn. Productive time is making the time you have productive in improving your ability to score.

The pros I work with fall into two basic categories. The first are the "grinders," like Tom Kite, Lee Janzen, Tom Sieckmann, and Payne Stewart. It does absolutely no good to work with these guys for 10 minutes on anything, because after 15 minutes they're still warming up, getting involved, and just starting to turn their full attention to whatever we're working on. Their first few attempts at changing things, if they are not yet focused, are not always impressive, and they get little benefit from practice sessions if they are short.

The grinders benefit most from long, intensive, repetitive sessions in which they drill over and over and over what they need to do and how it feels to do it. They have to see the results many times, and they seem to internalize these results very carefully. It seems to take them a long time to learn or improve. However, the upside to this is that once grinders learn something, once they have it, they don't lose it. Apparently because they have repeated the actions so often, and have ingrained the lessons so deeply into their systems, they form habits that stay there and are there when they need them later.

The other category is what I call the "quick hitter." I don't mean they strike the balls quickly, but pros like Peter Jacobsen, Steve Elkington, Paul Azinger, D. A. Weibring, and Howard Twitty use shorter, more variable practice sessions to avoid boredom and loss of concentration. Jake may be the quickest of all.

Whenever I ask Jacobsen to do anything, he does it very well very quickly. But he then gets bored with it and says, "I've got it, I've got it. There's no reason to waste any more time on it. Let's go do something new." And he does have it, which he shows me by hitting several more perfect shots to prove it. The quick hitters usually are very talented physically, and learn very quickly. They can produce excellent results in a short time no matter what I ask them to do. However, the next time I see them they've often learned something new and have forgotten the old. It's gone, out the window. It never became a habit. They're off learning something different and exciting every time they practice. They have difficulty sticking with the same system or technique long enough to really get *great* at it.

My strategy when working with quick hitters is to arrange short practice sessions often enough to stress the old principles, the same old fundamentals (which never actually change), and keep them distracted by getting them to think about scoring or ability tests. They need to keep their minds off the fact that they're doing something boring and repetitive, something they already know how to do and did yesterday and the day before.

Obviously you need to determine if you are a grinder, a quick hitter, or somewhere in between. If you are creating a practice routine for yourself, take this personality trait into consideration. If you like to grind and learn slowly, leave yourself enough time to work on each improvement over and over and over again in a single session. If you get bored quickly and easily, don't build in failure by staking out more than 15 minutes for each practice session on any one aspect of your short game. Rather, you should keep things short and sweet while competing or keeping score, and move on to other shots to keep things interesting.

That's *how* to allocate your practice sessions. Now, to *what* should you allot that time?

Start by eliminating the old habit of spending 80% of your time practicing 19% of the game: the power game composed of woods and long, medium, and short irons. Just as bad, don't practice at the same percentages of time that the shots occur in the game—43% putting, 25% woods, 13% finesse wedges, etc. The amount of time you need to practice the various aspects of your game should be determined by combining three factors: They are (1) "importance to the game"; (2) how weak/strong your game is in each category; and (3) how fast/slow you learn and improve from practice.

The most important game to scoring is (you've heard this before) the short game. Therefore, it should be allocated the first available block of every golfer's practice time every time they practice. So under "importance to the game," the short game is top priority. I rate the other four games in this order: (2) putting, (3) power, (4) management, and (5) mental. Understand this is the order you should practice them in, not the time spent on each one.

Practice Time Priority Per Week

First: 30%—the short game (inside 100 yards to the edge of the green)

Second: 30%—the putting game (on the green)

Third: 30%—the power game, divided equally between woods (emphasis on driving) and irons (outside 100 yards)

Fourth: 5%—the management game (how to manage your game strengths and weaknesses around the course)

Fifth: 5%—the mental game (fear, confidence, aggression, determination, organization, frustration)

In each practice session, practice your short game first. Then your putting. Next go hit balls on the range and work on your power swing. If you run out of time after your short-game and putting practice, so be it. In your next practice session, give yourself more time so you can also hit balls.

If I were creating a practice schedule for the generic golfer, I'd recommend time be allocated as shown in Figure 12.2.1 on the next page.

Within the total of your short-game practice time (which is 30% of your total practice time), the first priority should be the 15-yard pitch shot around the greens, followed closely by distance wedges (30 to 75 yards), then chipping from close to the greens, then bunker play, and lastly indoor mirror practice.

If 30% of your total practice time is one hour per week, this gives you 60 minutes to devote to improving your short game. Break it into the following areas:

1. Assuming you have no particularly weak areas that require immediate and special attention (remember, your weak areas determine your scoring ability), start with a 15-minute session hitting pitch shots, 15 minutes hitting distance wedges, 15 minutes chipping from around the green fringes, followed by a 10-minute session in the sand. You can expect to hit 20 to 50 shots in each of these sessions if you carefully address and hit each shot to a target and watch it until it stops. If you hit fewer shots, that's fine. You want careful, meaningful practice with feedback on results. Anything else is a waste of time, so don't even bother to practice if you're not going to do it right.

2. Assuming you do have a weakness in one area, say the sand, take five or so minutes from each of the other areas and emphasize sand practice. Once again, your weakest area of performance is where the game of golf will always get you.

3. Finally, in this 60 minutes of short-game practice, spend five minutes in front of a mirror at home. Wear shorts and a light-colored top so you can see and feel what your body is doing. Practice your synchronized finesse swing to the 7:30, 9:00 o'clock, and 10:30 backswing positions, and swing through to a full, balanced, complete finish. The more you watch, see, and feel these swings—in your perfect body rhythm of "saaawish-swish"—the sooner your subconscious will repeat these motions on the course.

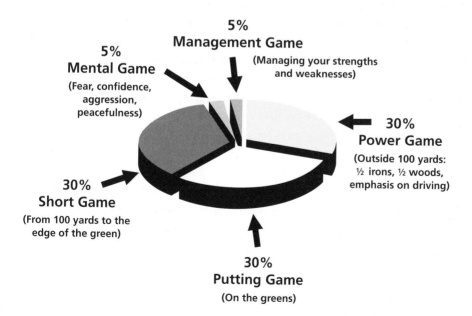

Figure 12.2.1: My recommendation for practice-time allocation

Of course, I'm not saying to practice your short game for only one hour a week. But doing more means increasing your total practice to more than 3½ hours a week. If you can handle this, great. The more you practice properly, the faster you will improve your short game and your ability to score.

As to the rest of your practice time, the second priority for improvement is your putting game. Spend 30% of your practice time putting, divided evenly between indoor stroke-mechanics practice and outdoor putting touch, feel, and green-reading. With good feedback on the results of your practice, you will see the greatest benefits.

Don't forget to spend 30% of your total practice time on your power swing. You always need to work on this part of the game. Even though I believe it should come after you've practiced your short game and putting, you still must do it. You can't consistently shoot pars if you can't get your first shot into play and your second shot somewhere near the green (on par 4s), no matter how good your short game and putting.

My last piece of advice on time allocation is don't neglect your mental and management preparation. Look into working with one of the sports psychologist/mental-side teachers like Bob Rotella, Richard Coop, David Cook, Deborah Graham, and Chuck Hogan. They can teach you to develop and improve the control of your mental and management games, and I guarantee it will be worth your practice time. You must consistently work on all parts of your game if you want to develop the talent necessary to consistently post your best scores.

That's how to allocate your practice time. Don't confuse practice with "warming up" before a round. Warming up is not practice but a sequence of exercises that loosen, lubricate, and tone your muscles to prepare them to play. But warming up can also be used for more than just stretching.

Optimize your warm-up time by carefully preparing yourself to execute the shots you are most likely to face and will have the greatest impact on your scoring. Always start with your finesse swings. If you are warming up before a round and have only a few minutes, hit some chip and pitch shots around the greens, because you're probably going to have more of those in a round than any other shot except putts. Make sure you feel and groove the synchronized-turn motion of the finesse swing—that you aren't handsy, hitting these shots with your hand/wrist muscles.

Move on to a few distance wedges and again warm up the finesse-swinging motion of your entire body; if these can be hit at a 30- to 50-yard target, to which you can check your distance, all the better. (If you're not hitting or coming close to these targets, spend a few extra minutes sharpening your focus on distance, hitting these shots the right length.)

If you have time, next practice your full swing, especially up to and including a few drives. But if you don't have time, you're still okay if you stretch enough to loosen your back and legs. As you think about the first drive, don't worry about how long it is going to be: Just get it into the fairway. If you can't get warm and loose, take a 3- or 4-wood off the first tee, make a three-quarters swing, and just put the ball in play. You don't want to start your round hitting a second shot out of trouble.

Of course, you *must* do a little warm-up practice putting. Do this in place of full-swing warm-up if time is limited. You need to stroke a few lag putts to learn the general speed of the greens; a few 20-footers to focus on the exact green speed; then be sure to make a few short putts before walking to the first tee, because you may well face a three- to six-footer on the first hole to save par. My data show that golfers hit more bad chips, pitches, and putts on the first three holes than on the last three, even though there often is more pressure at the end of the round. I think this is because golfers rush to the first tee, play away, then encounter short-game and putting-game shots they haven't faced in a week (or at least a few days), and they are not physically or mentally ready to execute these simple little shots.

12.3 Secret No. 3: The Secret of Hand Muscles

Hand muscles are about as good for the finesse game as they are for putting: no good at all! They do nothing but screw up both games.

Humans are used to pounding hammers, playing games, cutting meat, manipulating implements, and performing other tasks that involve using the small muscles of the fingers, hands, wrists, and forearms. Therefore, they believe instinctively that golf clubs are meant to be manipulated and controlled in the same way. This is true of most golfers in general, and of male golfers in particular.

Everything I've learned from observing and teaching thousands of golfers to improve their scoring games tells me that the more you let your small hand muscles get into determining where your shots go in your short game, the less consistency and more trouble you're going to have scoring.

That's why I say the dead-handed short game is the way to go. By learning and using dead-handed swing motions, you eliminate the effects of an increased heartbeat and adrenaline, which occur when you are excited and nervous. And excited and nervous are what you always become when facing an important golf shot.

It's easy to practice and groove a muscle-controlled swing on the range, where you get 10 or 15 tries at every shot, and you can do it over and over again until it feels just right. You can have the timing down and have complete control over the hit impulse, and everything can be just fine—on the practice tee.

The problem is reproducing that exact muscle function and performance energy when the heat is on, when pressure is applied, when your heart rate goes up and the adrenaline begins to flow. You can't do it, because you can never practice under these kinds of pressure-filled conditions. You can't turn up your heartbeat to 150 or 200 beats per minute for a full practice session. You can't make the adrenaline flow into your muscles, making them stronger and quicker under pressure during practice. Long hours of practice will not teach you how to overcome these influences.

The only way to beat these conditions is to eliminate the muscle-strength variable from your performance. If you use the rhythm of your finesse swing—which you can watch, evaluate, and refine during practice swings on-course before the pressure shot in question—then you can produce the exact results you want. You can see, watch, and feel yourself, not by watching the club or your hands or arms, but by letting your mind (your subconscious) be aware of and feel what the swing is doing. You'll be able to see and feel if your swing is a pure, rhythmic, finesse swing, moving the length and speed required to produce the shot you want.

An increased heartbeat does not affect the rate at which your mind's eye sees and judges the rhythm of your swing. Adrenaline will not change how the swing looks and feels in your mind's eye, even when your muscles feel stronger. So if you can make your swings look and feel right for the shot, they will be right under all conditions, and you'll produce the results you want when you need them under pressure.

A great example of controlling heartbeat and adrenaline under pressure is Tom Kite on the last hole of the 1992 U.S. Open at Pebble Beach. On that ocean-lined par 5, he intentionally laid up with his second shot—even though he could have hit the green with a 3-iron because he had hit an incredibly good drive. However, Kite laid up with a little half-swing 6-iron second shot, leaving a 75-yard finesse wedge to the hole. He did this because the 75-yard wedge is his favorite shot in golf, which he knows he can hit better than any other shot in his bag. He took a few dead-handed practice swings, exact duplicates of the finesse swing he wanted to make for real, saw and felt that he was doing what he wanted, made the real shot, and flew it inside the "Golden Eight" to take home the trophy (Fig. 12.3.1)!

I cannot stress enough that the other system—using the muscles of the hands and arms—will work on the practice tee when there is no pressure. It will feel good, it might even seem easy. But don't be deceived. Don't be misled into thinking that because you can make something work on the practice tee you can make it work under pressure on the course.

There are millions of golfers who say, "I'm a great player on the practice tee, I just can't take it to the course." They blame themselves, lose confidence, think they haven't got what it takes in their heart to win under pressure, and sometimes lose

Figure 12.3.1: 1992 U.S. Open
Champion . . . Tom Kite

self-esteem after blowing a lead or a shot under the gun. All this because they learned the wrong short-game control system. They never learned that if you use a hand-muscles-controlled swing, you will not perform well under pressure. You *must* understand this and not fall into that trap.

The secret of hand muscles is to keep them out of the short game, and rely instead on a pure, rhythmic, consistent, muscle-free finesse swing as detailed in Chapter 3.

12.4 Secret No. 4: The Secret of Repetition and Drills

One of the most important aspects of improving your game is learning how to practice. You can significantly improve your short-game skills by repeatedly performing drills with proper feedback over an extended period of time. The feedback-heavy drills detailed on the following pages will help you develop, groove, and habitualize these skills. Some drills can be done at your home or office, away from the golf course. Others must be done outdoors at a course with good practice facilities. Together, they can immensely improve your ability to score. Remember: Just as perfect practice produces improvement, it is only perfect repetition that leads to the formation of those quality habits that produce good results under pressure.

12.5 At-Home Drills

1. The Synchro-Turn Drill. This will help you synchronize the turning of your upper and lower body. Take a correct finesse stance face-on in front of a full-length mirror: Bend slightly in the knees and hips and assume a perfect address position as if you are holding a club. Move your hands onto your hips, thumbs forward, and pinch your elbows toward each other behind your back. This will lock your shoulders and hips together, forcing you to turn one when you turn the other. Turn your lower and upper body together, away from the target, to about a 40-degree angle away from your address position. Stop and hold this position for a few seconds, as it approximates the proper body position for a 7:30 backswing (Fig. 12.5.1).

Your hips should be turned far enough that your lead knee (the left knee, for right-handed golfers) has been pulled slightly toward the back knee. It's important that the lead knee hasn't moved out toward the target line but back toward the trailing knee.

Start the downswing by moving everything together. Imagine you have pointers sticking out of your chest and belt buckle; they should be pointing in the same direction at the top of the backswing, as you move through impact, and as you

Figure 12.5.1: The synchronized finesse turn

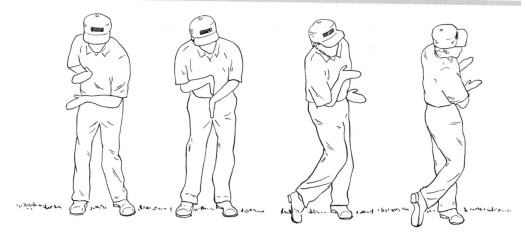

Figure 12.5.2: If your turn is synchronized, both pointers (hands) always point in the same direction

move into the finish (Fig. 12.5.2). At the end of your follow-through, the pointers should have turned past and be aiming to the left of the target for right-handed golfers (to the right of the target for left-handers). At the finish, you should have turned more than 90 degrees (closer to 100–105 degrees) from your original address position. All your weight should finish on your left (forward) foot; your back toe is to be used only for balance, having almost no weight on it; and your right (back) knee should be covering the left (front) knee. By repeating this complete turn motion 25 times, while keeping your spine and head positions fixed, you will begin to see and feel the perfectly synchronized turning motion of the perfect finesse swing (the full finesse turn is shown in Fig. 12.5.3).

Figure 12.5.3: The complete finesse turn

2. The Power Drill. In our Scoring Game Schools, we use a 40-pound medicine ball (filled with sand) to teach the feel of "synchronized body power," as opposed to "hands-and-arms" power, in the finesse swing. (To make your own, take an old basketball, punch a small hole in it, pour in sand, and seal with a bicycle-tire repair kit.) A 40-pound ball is very heavy, so anyone with back problems is cautioned not to use this drill without first consulting a physician.

Hold the ball from underneath with your hands and arms while your body is in your normal address position, knees bent slightly. Tuck the elbows together so they're no more than four to six inches apart and almost touching your stomach; your elbows must stay "attached" to your stomach throughout this drill. Be sure you are bent at the waist until you approximate your swing position. (Bend slowly and carefully to avoid straining your back; if you feel even the slightest twinge or strain, stop immediately.)

Move in a good rhythm and make a normal 30-yard finesse swing (as described in the Synchro-Turn Drill, page 370), except turn back only about 30 degrees. As you reach the top of the backswing, be sure your hands, arms, and the ball remain exactly in front of your chest and stomach as they were at address. On the through-swing, turn only with your lower-body muscles, letting your upper body go along for the ride as you toss the medicine ball forward to a partner. (Make *sure* he also has no back problems.) Repeat this drill 25 times, every other time with your eyes closed, to begin internalizing the look and feel of your synchronized upper and lower body turn utilized in the finesse swing (Fig. 12.5.4).

This drill differs from the Synchro-Turn Drill by letting you feel your synchronized finesse turn with your arms, hands, and ball (or golf club) out in front of

Figure 12.5.4: The medicine ball toss teaches a synchronized finesse turn (only if you have a well-conditioned, strong back)

you, while letting your body turn provide the power of the swing. It is imperative that you not use your arm or hand power to toss the ball in this drill. Simply turn your upper and lower body in a synchronized motion to toss the ball forward along your target line. Then fold your arms and elbows up, over your left shoulder, to feel the proper finesse-swing finish.

3. *The Stance Drill.* Many golfers have trouble getting comfortable with the correct ball position on the golf course, yet it is such an easy problem to solve. If you have ball-position problems, use a teaching aid called the "PositionMat." It indicates exactly where the ball should be positioned in your stance under good-lie positions for pitch, sand, and chip shots.

To use the "PositionMat," place it on the floor in front of a mirror, and with a club in hand (but no ball), take your address position on the shoe positions as indicated. Start with your feet on the dotted outlines, then switch to the solid shoe positions for your final setup (as shown in Figure 12.5.5). Go through your preshot ritual and actually make the appropriate finesse swing (pitch, sand, or chip). Repeat this sequence five to 10 times for each position, actually simulating hitting the "PositionMat" ball each time. The more you repeat this drill at home (a few swings on many different days is better than many swings on a few days), the more comfortable you'll become with the feel of good ball position on the course. Occa-

Figure 12.5.5: Getting "into position" to swing is as important as "making" the swing

sionally during this drill make sure to watch your body turn in the mirror to keep it smooth, proper, and completely synchronized.

4. *The Release Drill.* This drill helps you see and feel the proper rotation and release of your forearms and club through the impact zone of a 15-yard pitch shot.

Stand perpendicular to a mirror, take your address position with both hands on the club, and start the turn as in the above drills. Stop your backswing when the shaft is horizontal. At this point, your upper and lower body should be turned about 20 degrees away from address and both the toe and leading edge of the club should point straight up to the sky. If the leading edge is past vertical, pointing behind you, you've rotated your forearms too much; if it hasn't reached vertical, you haven't rotated the arms enough (Fig. 12.5.6).

On the through-swing, stop when the shaft is horizontal on the other side. Again, the toe should point straight up, indicating a complete release. Your forearms should have turned 180 degrees from the same point on the backswing. Finish this swing by taking the shaft to vertical as you turn another 5 degrees to the completed 15-yard pitch swing position shown in Figure 12.5.7.

Do not hit balls with this drill. Instead, perform it in slow motion to imprint on your mind's eye the look and feel of your proper release motion as viewed from both behind and in front of your swing.

Figure 12.5.6: The shaft horizontal, leading-edge vertical position

Figure 12.5.7: The 15-yard pitch finish

5. The Backswing Drill. Once you understand the synchronized turn, the dead-hands finesse swing, and the 3 x 4 System for controlling distance with the length of your backswing, it is vital that you internalize the feel of your own perfect 9:00 o'clock backswing position. As mentioned earlier, 9:00 o'clock is most golfers' favorite, and most reliable, swing because it is the easiest to visualize and the horizontal left arm position is somewhat visible through your peripheral vision.

First, practice this position in front of a mirror, swinging with a club but no ball. Use the mirror to get the feedback of exactly where 9:00 o'clock is; get the feel and view of that backswing length (Fig. 12.5.8). After some practice, I'm sure you'll find 9:00 o'clock your easiest and most reliable backswing length.

However easy 9:00 o'clock is for you, 7:30 will be much more difficult. Initially practice this length the same way: Use the mirror to see when your arm reaches the 7:30 position, noting how it feels and looks. Close your eyes, go through your preshot ritual, swing to the top of your 7:30 backswing, then open your eyes and check (Fig. 12.5.9).

Remember, it's always easier to learn the feel and sight of these backswings without a ball on the ground, when you are not making a shot, and not worrying about results. For every backswing you make, go ahead and swing through to a full, synchronized finish. You may as well commit your perfect finesse move to subconscious control that much sooner.

Figure 12.5.8: The 9:00 o'clock backswing **Figure 12.5.9:** The 7:30 backswing

Once you feel reasonably good about being able to execute both your 9:00 o'clock and 7:30 finesse swings, take them to your backyard and the "ShotMaker" platform. Attach the "SwingStop" (Fig. 12.5.10) and hit 10 or 20 shots to a target each session. Keep your total focus on the length of your backswing, making a

Figure 12.5.10:
The SwingStop calibrates
backswing length

quality finesse swing with good ball contact and a perfect full finish. Don't worry about where or how far your shots are going until you have mastered the ability to make the desired-length backswing.

6. *The Plane Drill.* The plane of the finesse swing extends from the ball, up through your shoulders, and above and behind you. It is the "pane of glass" that Ben Hogan made famous years ago, as detailed in Chapter 4. This is the plane you want the head of your club to travel on throughout your finesse swing. You can accomplish this swing plane simply by executing a synchronized body turn and swinging your arms upward during the backswing, then letting the centrifugal force created by your turn down and through the impact zone control the motion of the club.

While there are many swing-plane training devices for the full power swing, we like to use the "SwingSlot" attachment to the ShotMaker platform to train proper finesse swing planes (Fig. 12.5.11). The SwingSlot, when properly adjusted for your height and address posture, defines your proper swing plane through the impact zone by means of a plate positioned just below your actual swing plane. (You can also use the "Shanker's Delight" attachment to define your swing plane further.) By repeatedly swinging through the slot, without hitting either guide plate, you can groove your finesse-swing feel and reach the subconscious control level for the mechanics of your wedge swing. While we use the SwingSlot to hit shots in our schools, I recommend you first swing slowly in one in your backyard

Figure 12.5.11:
The SwingSlot defines
your finesse swing plane

without hitting a ball. Once your clubhead is repeatedly passing through the slot without touching the plate, then start hitting balls into a net (with no concern as to where the shot actually would fly). Finally, hitting 25 shots with the SwingSlot to target baskets every few days (Fig. 12.5.12) will advance your wedge game to a new level.

Figure 12.5.12: The SwingSlot grooves a proper finesse-swing plane

7. The Sweet-Spot Drill. After, and only after, you have internalized the concepts of (1) a synchronized finesse turn; (2) smooth, hands-free body-rhythm power; (3) perfect ball position and parallel-left alignment; (4) proper release of your forearms; (5) timing your backswings; and (6) the proper finesse swing plane, it is time to practice hitting your wedge shots on the sweet-spot of the clubface. I emphasize this order of practice because to try to learn to make sweet-spot contact from bad setup or swing positions will do more harm than good to your short game.

Once you can produce good-looking wedge swings with a dead-hands finesse turn, however, it becomes important to make consistently solid contact before you try to learn to control how far shots go. Exactly where contact is made on the clubface determines the percentage of swing energy transferred to the ball on every shot. So, if you can't make consistent contact, it destroys your ability to correlate your swing time with shot distance.

That's why I recommend practicing solid contact with the "SweetSpotter," as shown in Figure 12.5.13. The SweetSpotter is a pad of energy-absorbing material that adheres to the face of your wedge during practice, which exaggerates the energy loss on shots struck significantly away from the sweet spot. When you hit the energy-absorbing SweetSpotter, you feel it and see the yards lost. Then you can

Figure 12.5.13: The SweetSpotter exaggerates the effects of mishits

properly blame the impact quality of your swing (rather than your swing speed, as most golfers do) for not hitting the shot the proper distance.

8. *The Basket Drill.* Assuming you have grooved reasonably good swing mechanics in the seven drills just discussed, you should now be ready to polish your wedge game. When a golfer misses a green, he or she usually faces either a pitch shot or a distance wedge to the pin. You can groove these shots in your backyard by hitting balls into laundry baskets.

Place several baskets in different positions from 10 to 75 yards' carry distance away (walk them off, or shoot them with a laser for accurate distances), always in line with either your aim club or the swing line of the ShotMaker. Hit shots to the baskets in random order. Hitting 25 shots from time to time (Fig. 12.5.14) will teach you to control where your shots land on the green. Once you can hit (or come close to hitting) the baskets with consistent trajectory and spin, you'll be very effective at saving par (and making birdies on par 5s) when you play.

Be sure to hit some wedge shots from longer grass (like the rough at your course), rather than always hitting from artificial grass, which simulates shots from fairway lies on the course. (Don't get too used to hitting only from fluffy lies in a plush lawn, either.)

Figure 12.5.14: You can't get too good with your distance wedges

9. The Uneven-Lie Drill. I recommend the previous drills for all golfers, beginners to Tour players, to improve their short-game skills. But for those of you who want to go the extra mile, or are having problems in a particular area, some additional drills will help develop your short games.

Sooner or later, all golfers face pitch shots around the greens from uneven lies. I don't know any better way of learning this skill than on the ShotMaker, hitting shots to baskets in your backyard when the ball is above or below your feet, or from uphill and downhill lies (Fig. 12.5.15). If you can pitch into a basket from these lies in your backyard, you can land your shots where you need to on the course.

Don't rush into practicing on these difficult lies, however, until you've developed your swing skills from level lies. While it might be more fun to hit from sidehill lies, and to play games and keep score on the ShotMaker, about 80% of your pitch shots on the course will be from relatively level lies. When you do practice these shots, review the techniques in Chapter 6 before wasting your time and forming bad habits.

10. The BunkerBoard Drill. All golfers eventually must play out of sand. For those who fear this shot, the BunkerBoard drill can have a very calming effect. The

Figure 12.5.15: Use the ShotMaker to develop techniques for uneven lies

BunkerBoard eliminates the possibility of your wedge digging into the sand too deeply and leaving the shot "flubbed" in the sand.

Once you are convinced that you won't flub the shot and leave the ball in the sand, you will find it easier to use your normal finesse-wedge swing in a real bunker. The plastic surface of the BunkerBoard forces the open-faced wedge to scoot properly under the ball (Fig. 12.5.16 shows how little sand is blasted out of a bunker by a good scoot-and-spin shot). Because you can't dig in the Bunker-Board, with a little practice you also will stop digging in real sand. Start this practice hitting into a net set slightly to the right of your swing line direction. Remember, as detailed in Chapter 9, when you open your clubface in the sand, your shots will fly somewhat to the right of your swing line.

When you can confidently stand over a BunkerBoard shot, make a good, smooth, aggressive, 9:00 o'clock finesse swing, end with an all-world finish, and produce a high, soft, spinning shot, you can begin to become a good sand player (Fig. 12.5.17). I say "begin" because hitting good sand shots from real bunkers is more difficult than hitting them from a BunkerBoard, and you need to move your practice to the next level to master the on-course sand shot.

11. The BunkerTray Drill. Hitting from the BunkerTray attachment to the Shot-Maker (Fig. 12.5.18) is good practice precisely because it is no easier than hitting

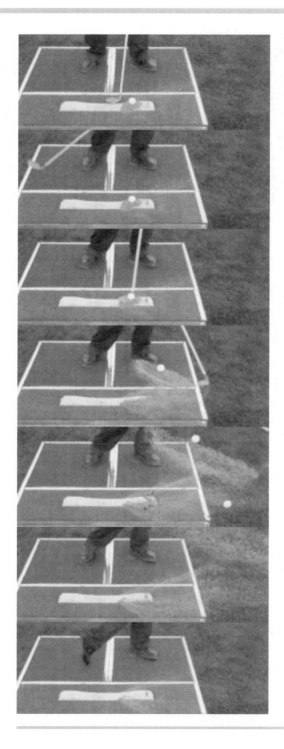

Figure 12.5.16: Learn proper feel for the scoot-and-spin blast on the BunkerBoard

Figure 12.5.17: Swing line to towel, clubface open, ball flies to BunkerBoard target basket

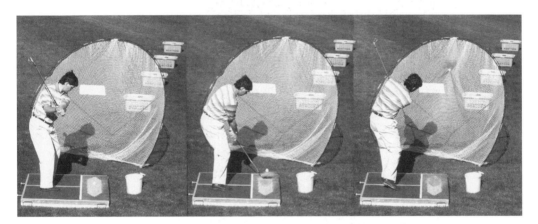

Figure 12.5.18: Scoot-and-spin practice from real sand in the BunkerTray

from real sand. The sand in the BunkerTray is about two inches deep, enough to let your club dig in and flub the shot. (If the clubface isn't open enough, you'll hit weak dig-and-push shots and spend most of your time replacing the sand.)

Once you're good enough, and have enough confidence to hit to baskets, re-move the net from interfering with the ball flights (Fig. 12.5.19) and practice all lengths of shots from the sand. Purchase a few bags of the same sort of sand found in the bunkers at your course (your golf course superintendent may sell or give you some), so your sand touch is calibrated to the sand you see the most often (but you'll have to adjust to supersoft or fine sand, or extra-coarse sand, when en-countered at other courses).

Figure 12.5.19: Groove your bunker game at home to save strokes on the course

You also can practice the difficult uneven lies in the sand by adjusting the Shot-Maker to the extremes with the BunkerTray (Fig. 12.5.20). I don't suggest spending too much time on such shots, since they don't occur too often. But they can be fun and educational to try on occasion. Always be sure to try them initially into the net.

12. The Knee-Slide Drill. If your knee slides forward during your through-swing, join the crowd (Fig. 12.5.21). Tall golfers, including yours truly, have a difficult time stopping this habit. We understand intellectually that we should turn (rotate) onto our leading foot instead of sliding forward into the outside of that foot. Doing it, however, is more difficult.

The best device for combating this problem is the KneeSlider attachment for the ShotMaker (Fig. 12.5.22). It simply won't let you slide! When I first tried this device I almost broke my left knee. Then I learned to swing without hitting balls and thought it was great. I learned the feel of the proper turning on the through-swing and thought I had it. However, when I then tried hitting balls, my long-ingrained knee slide was back. So once you've eliminated your slide and learned the feel of a proper turning motion, hit as many balls as you can with the Knee-Slider in place. When you finally learn to hit shots without touching it, you will have ingrained a much improved finesse turn and swing.

13. A Drill for Shankers. There are several reasons for shanking, and most are just minor deviations from a really good swing. That's right: A shank swing is usually pretty close to being a good swing. But no matter which reason for yours, there is an easy solution: the Shanker's Delight.

Figure 12.5.20: Be sure to use a net when first practicing from uneven lies on the ShotMaker with BunkerTray attachment

Figure 12.5.21: The greater the forward slide, the less consistent the contact at impact

Figure 12.5.22: Hitting shots with a KneeSlider stops the forward slide

This is another attachment for the ShotMaker, primarily for use in the backyard. As shown in Figure 12.5.23, the Shanker's Delight places a wall a few inches from your ball, which will keep your clubhead from traveling outside the proper swing plane through impact. Set out a few baskets as targets, and hit a lot of shots with the Shanker's Delight. You won't shank them (Fig. 12.5.24). Then alternate between hitting from next to the Shanker's Delight wall and hitting from the open mat by stepping back six inches (keep your net in place for a while, just in case) on every other shot. You'll quickly learn the differences in feel between the shank and nonshank swings.

Having learned the difference, hit shots from the mat concentrating on that nonshank feel. Every time you shank one, hit a few shots from next to the Shanker's Delight wall; just addressing balls next to the wall will give you the feel of the nonshank swing again. Then move back and hit a few more open shots. Learning to make good, in-plane swings normally takes only a few sessions a week for a few weeks.

(By the way, I'm sorry if explaining my drills sounds like commercials for the ShotMaker or any other feedback device. I don't mean to sound like a salesman. However, I have to tell you what I believe to be the best ways to learn, and these are the best I know. All of these learning aids are used in my Scoring Game Schools, so I know that if used properly, they will help you.)

Figure 12.5.23: Practicing with the Shanker's Delight cures the shanks

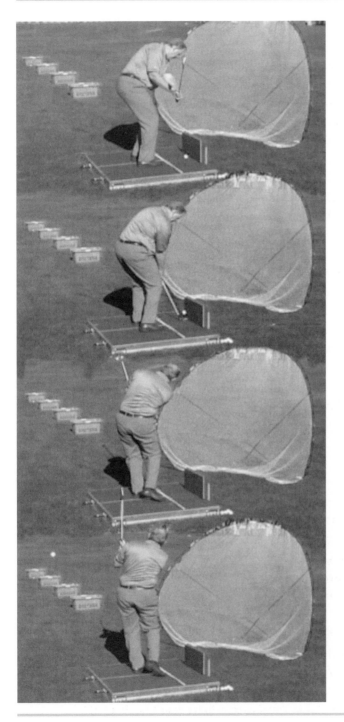

Figure 12.5.24: Alternate shots from 6 inches away to alongside of the Shanker's Delight wall. You won't need the net for long.

12.6 At-the-Course Drills

Of course, you also must go to the course to practice your short game. If you don't have a short-game facility at your local course, find one in your area that will allow you to chip, pitch, and hit bunker and distance-wedge shots to a pin on a realistic green surface. Many facilities have opened up in the last few years with short-game practice areas, but it can still be difficult to find one.

The importance of at-the-course practice should not be underestimated, even if you have already perfected your finesse-swing mechanics and positions with at-home practice drill sessions. Because every short-game shot challenges your ability to execute in two areas, you must learn both if you are to become a good player. The first component is swing mechanics, which start the moment you start the backswing, through impact, to the finish. It determines the shot's trajectory and spin until the ball lands on the green. Swing-mechanics execution is the physical motion of your swing, which creates clubhead speed, face angle at impact, flight pattern, carry distance, trajectory, and the backspin of your shot.

The second component of your shot execution involves how well you estimate the behavior of the ball on the green as it moves toward its final resting point. This component depends not only on how you hit the shot, but also how hard the green surface is, the slope of the landing area, grain of the grass, wind, and several other factors that result in your choice of which shot to hit. Your "reading" of the shot comes from your past experience, a learned skill from hours and hours of practice at the course. To get good at this component, you first must be able to produce a consistent, repeatable trajectory, then do it many times so you learn how greens and balls react. If you don't know how to read greens and judge the second component of each of your finesse shots, it's like making perfect putting strokes just as you intended to make them, but reading the greens incorrectly: Your results will be spectacularly unsuccessful.

So I recommend first practicing at home to get your finesse-swing mechanics grooved and proper, then incorporating some at-the-course practice to learn the second half of all the shots. The course drills I suggest follow.

14. The Lead Arm Only (LAO) Drill. As you prepare to hit balls at the range, first assume your finesse-swing address position, and put both hands on the club in your normal grip position. Take your trailing hand (right for right-handed golfers) off the grip and put it into your pants pocket. Stick it as far into the pocket as you can and press your right arm against your right side. You are ready to hit your first shot LAO.

Begin this drill the same way you began your turn in the Synchro-Turn and Power at-home drills, but making a 9:00 o'clock swing away with the upper and lower body synchronized. Keep the lead (left) arm and club in front of your body as you cock your left wrist on the backswing, turn down through the ball, and turn up into a high finish on your left (lead) side. Finish with 100% of your weight on the lead foot, using your back foot only as a balance point, turning it up on the tip of the big toe (Fig. 12.6.1).

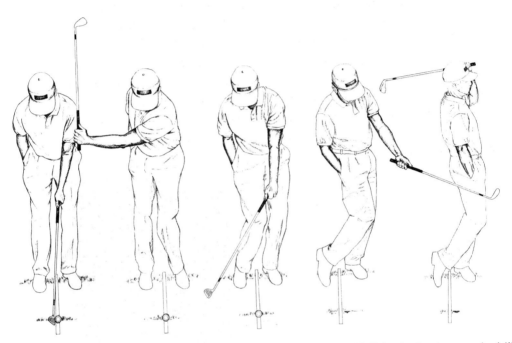

Figure 12.6.1: The lead arm only drill

Perform this drill first without a ball, then hit at least 10 to 15 balls LAO. After a few sessions, you should be able to make a good enough swing to hit a reasonably good 30-yard shot with your LAO swing. If you can't swing LAO with reasonable accuracy, keep doing the drill for the first 15 shots every time you warm up to hit practice balls. You need to strengthen your left side and improve the lead arm's participation in your normal finesse swing, and LAO is the best way to teach your left arm, shoulder, and body to achieve this move.

15. The Chipping Drill. The low-running chip shot from just off the edge of the green should be practiced with a 7- or 8-iron, with the ball placed directly across from your right (back) ankle. This ball position assures crisp, clean contact between clubface and ball, and leaves your distance control to the length or size of the swing selected to execute the shot.

By taking only three balls, and repeatedly hitting three shots from 30 feet, then three shots from 45 feet, followed by three shots from 60 feet (distances to the pin), you will become familiar with and reasonably accomplished at these three distances. They are the most frequently required chip shots on the course, and most other chips will require only minor modifications from one of these three.

After practicing these three shots repeatedly during your allotted practice time, leave enough time to test yourself at the end of each session. For my last attempt at each of the different shots, I always try to get three in a row inside three feet, even if it takes several repeat attempts (Fig. 12.6.2). By picking three new shots to work on for each new practice session, you can experience and be prepared for all the uphill, sidehill, and downhill shots you will encounter on the course. And each time you face a chip that counts, you'll know the last time you practiced that same shot you hit three in a row close to the pin.

Figure 12.6.2: Close out practice sessions with three in a row

16. The 15-Yard Pitch Drill. This is the shot you have most often when you just miss a green with a pretty good shot. It calls for carrying the ball about 10 to 12 yards in the air and having it then roll another few yards to the pin. If you master it, this shot will save you many strokes over the long run.

Practice with only three balls, changing positions after every three shots. Each time you pick up the three balls and select a different shot, lay down a handkerchief as a marker, giving yourself a well-defined landing-area target. By moving around the practice green, you will experience all kinds of grass lengths, all kinds of lies, slopes, and slightly differing carry distance requirements. Pay particular attention to exactly where your ball lands relative to where you tried to land it (evaluate your shot execution) on every shot. Then watch how far it moves on the green after it lands and bounces on the surface (evaluate your shot "read"). Learning how balls react on greens is difficult, because even if you watch carefully, the green can fool you with some of its unknowable conditions (variable surface softness, moisture content, etc.). However, if you don't watch carefully, learning to predict these reactions is impossible. So pay attention. Practice with intensity. Always be aware of how closely you pitched to your target spot on the green (swing-mechanics execution) and then how the ball reacted compared to how you expected it to react on the green (your read execution). That's the only way to learn to pitch it close.

To close out this drill, pick one shot and hit it repeatedly until you stick three in a row within the length of your wedge shaft (Fig. 12.6.3). It's a great confidence builder.

Figure 12.6.3: Don't cheat yourself: Facing reality will help you later

17. The Lob Drill. The high, soft lob shot is more difficult to execute, but easier to read, than the normal pitch shot. Because you use a more lofted club, solid contact at the proper place on the clubface is more important to the carry distance of the shot. But because the shot flies higher, it will land more softly and stop more quickly (in general), so there is less uncertainty in how far it will roll.

As a result of these differences between lobbing and pitching, you should select different and tighter landing areas for your lob-shot practice and drop your target handkerchief closer to the pin. Because most of the success in lobbing is achieved by being able to drop the ball on the proper spot, pay particular attention to your trajectories and carry distances. Getting comfortable with lobbing shots over sand traps to tight pin positions (Fig. 12.6.4) will help your nerves when you face such shots on the course. And, again, three in a row to close your practice session will help your confidence.

Figure 12.6.4: Three in a row and you are ready to go

18. The "Cut-Lob-Right" Drill. I always recommend following each lob-drill session with about a dozen cut-lob shots. You don't need this shot too often, but by practicing and developing the skill necessary to hit it, you gain the confidence that makes your standard lobs look easy.

By hitting a lob shot with an open-faced lob wedge, you produce the highest, softest landing shot in the short game, the cut lob. As detailed in Chapter 6, this shot is nearly the same as the ordinary lob except for the setup alignment to the left and the open clubface. Learning and grooving this shot should be accomplished with two drills, similar to my earlier explanation of the shot. Most golfers try to control all their wedge shots with the hands, and by doing so lose their ability to hit the shots under pressure. Periodically practice a few cut-lob-right shots to remind your brain to keep your hand muscles from taking control.

To hit six cut-lob-right shots, pick a target pin, aim directly at it by setting up normally (feet, body, and shoulders aligned parallel left to the target line, stance open slightly by flaring the lead toe toward the target), then open the face of the lob wedge to the right. Execute your preshot ritual and make your normal lob wedge swing to the original setup target. With the clubface open through impact (as set by address), your shot will miss the target short and to the right. If you make six really good swings without hand-muscle manipulation, all six shots will finish in a tight short-right pattern.

Notice how far right and short your open-faced shots missed your original target pin. Transfer that same distance differential to the other side of your target flagstick, i.e., to the left and past the pin. This identifies a new setup target to the left and past your real target pin. Setup parallel left of your long-left setup target, open the lob wedge face, execute your ritual, and hit six more shots as if you were trying to hit a square-face wedge shot to your long-left target. If you choose that target well, and swing without hand control, your cut lobs will go straight to your real target and form a nice pattern there.

A few sessions of cut-lob-right shots, followed by cut lobs at a real target with a well-chosen, long-left setup target, will teach you to hit your ultrahigh and soft cut shots close when you need them on the course. But don't try to hit three consecutive shots inside three feet to close this drill: It might take longer than the time you allotted to practice.

19. *The Distance-Wedge Drill.* You need to spend a significant amount of time honing your ability to hit wedges consistent, repeatable distances. If the range at your course doesn't have target nets like those we use at our schools, place some kind of target—a flag, handkerchief, or basket—on an uphill slope so you can clearly see how close to it each ball lands. Even better, pick a practice green with a pin and hole, pace off three different distances, and drop three piles of balls. Then fire away (Fig. 12.6.5).

If you can't see precisely where the balls land, you aren't getting accurate feed-

Figure 12.6.5: Real greens provide the ultimate feedback

back on your distance control and are wasting your time. Remember: Bad practice is worse than no practice. You must know within one yard how far every ball is flying. So besides being able to see where shots land, you must know the precise distance to that spot. Either walk your distances off or use a laser rangefinder to know your target distances in every practice session. Once you've done this drill a few times, your shot control will improve where you need it most—on the course—and you'll face shorter putts as a result.

Why are drills so important? Because learning doesn't happen only in your mind. Yes, you must understand the concepts, you must have images and visions in your mind's eye of what you're trying to do. But you also must feel and connect these with the body's kinesthetic awareness of what those motions feel like. Golf is played with a combination of images and feelings. You need to experience, correlate, and internalize your thoughts and images with the feelings of motions that produce them, often enough that they become habitual, controlled completely by your subconscious, during your swings. And *that*—subconscious control—is what you learn from drills.

I said at the very beginning of this book that one of my major goals is to help you become your own best teacher. To help you learn efficiently, you need to understand the concepts and how to put them into practice, because no one can be with you at the moment of truth when you must hit an important shot. When your shots count the most, you must always rely on the training you've provided yourself. If you have practiced enough properly, using consistent preshot rituals and always with feedback on shot results, you should be able to create the practice swings that become the preview motions you need, which you then simply repeat to produce the results you desire.

I understand that these practice drills are not easy. There often will be perfectly good reasons why you can't practice. But good excuses are just that—excuses. Neither the game, the ball, nor the greens on the course care why you can't practice. Very simply, if you don't practice, and practice intelligently, then you won't improve.

To provide convenient places to practice optimally, you must find a range, a practice bunker, and a good target green at a course, as well as a yard or field near your home. And you must do these drills.

It also will help if you have a video camera with a high shutter speed so you can occasionally film yourself and review your swing action. It is always helpful to look at the positions of your golf swing and compare what you see to what you feel and what is in your mind's eye. Compare your motion to that of a great player of similar size and personality whom you see on television or in this book. Although I don't want you to copy other golfers, it can be instructive to see what they do, then analyze yourself on video, trying to see if you are actually achieving the things you are working for.

12.7 Secret No. 5: The Secret of the Preshot Routine and Ritual

Once again, I want to explain the difference between a preshot routine and a preshot ritual. The routine a player uses before hitting any shot starts when he or she arrives at the ball and begins to prepare to hit it. A good routine includes the following:

1. Assessment of shot conditions
   a. lie of ball
   b. distance to target
   c. conditions in target landing area
   d. wind
   e. danger/penalty possibilities
   f. risk/reward percentages
2. Imagine the desired shot, visualize the entire shot
   a. impact reaction/launch action
   b. flight pattern and trajectory

    c. landing, bounce, and roll characteristics

    d. final resting point (probable spread)

3. Imagine the swing that will produce the desired shot

    a. visualize yourself swinging

    b. feel the swing in your mind's eye

4. Practice the desired swing as you imagine it, through grass similar to what you will encounter in the real shot's impact zone

5. Feel if the imaginary shot hit by your practice swing seems as if it will go the desired distance as you hold and focus on feel at the finish of your practice swing

6. If your practice swing didn't feel perfect, make another one that is longer or shorter, until you feel the perfect swing to hit the perfect shot

You are now prepared to hit your shot, and you have prepared yourself by going through the routine that you always use to lead into your preshot ritual.

Your preshot ritual is separate from, and has to follow immediately after, your preshot preparation routine for any shot.

As many times as I tell students about the importance of a preshot ritual (and how it differs from preshot preparation), many of them still ask, "Why do you emphasize the ritual so much?"

It's true that the preshot ritual doesn't have anything to do with the shot itself. You don't hit the ball with the ritual, and it slows down practice. It's also true that you could hit more shots in a shorter period of time if it were eliminated. And you'd certainly hit more shots in practice if you "rake and beat" and never notice where the shot goes. But I hope by now you've realized that practice is not just about hitting balls. It is about getting feedback so you learn from every shot. Without feedback, practice has no benefit.

Golfers who "rake and beat" don't learn from their practice. And golfers who don't use a preshot ritual don't form the habits required to carry what they've learned *from* the practice tee *onto* the golf course.

The preshot ritual is not about hitting the ball. It is about training your subconscious to perform at the proper rhythm when you're scared, when you're nervous, when your heart is beating at two or three times its normal rate and the adrenaline is flowing. A consistent, repeatable, never-changing preshot ritual before every shot allows you to produce that shot, and its desired result, no matter what else is happening around and to you.

The ritual is a series of timed motions, and both the order of these motions and the timing between them must be repeatable, and it must be used in all of your practice and with all of your shots on course. It's the "one, two, three, go" or "ready, set, go" that tells your subconscious that it's time to go to work, to execute the same motions you grooved thousands of times on your practice shots on the range and in your backyard. Your ritual allows your subconscious to completely control your swing motion. You can't think your way through a golf swing. You have to have practiced enough that after your ritual you don't have to think, you just swing. Out of habit.

12.8 Secret No. 6: The Secret of the Secrets

Remember: Practice doesn't make perfect; practice makes permanent. If you practice poorly, you will become consistently poor—and I say you deserve it! Just as important, perfect practice makes for good progress and improvement. Finally, be assured that only with continued, consistent, perfect practice will you ever approach perfection in your short game.

You should practice until you improve your average shots and eliminate your really poor ones altogether. Your golf scores are determined not by your good shots, but by the severity of your bad shots. The more you practice and improve on your weaknesses, the better a player you will become.

If you read and look carefully at the secret of the ritual, and the other secrets in this chapter, they will allow you to find the best secret of the game, the one golfers have been searching for. And what is it? Very simple: Play like you've practiced and practice like you'll play!

Think about it. If you have practiced with feedback, your subconscious will know how hard to swing when you play. If you have practiced with a dead-handed swing, your subconscious can do the same when you play. If you've practiced in a rhythmic manner, your subconscious will be properly prepared to recognize good rhythm when it is time to play. If you have practiced your drills properly, your subconscious will have developed the necessary skills for when it is time to play. And if you have always practiced all this using your preshot ritual, your subconscious will know when it is time to take over.

You must have practiced being great to be great. And you must have practiced in a way that you can take to the course and play. Then you must remember to play exactly how you practiced so your subconscious can be great when you're playing. The same tempo, the same rhythm, the same swing habits. No thinking. Just creating previews, then repeating.

To make this all work, you must be smart enough to practice the way you want to play. Decide how you're going to play in the most important moments, on the most important holes, when making the most important swings of your career. Then begin practicing just that way.

If you have the discipline and patience to practice like you want to play, then you can, in fact, play to your full potential under all the pressure that the game has to offer.

CHAPTER 13

The Future

The Composite Player

13.1 A Scoring Machine

I have created three composite players, combining my choices of the world's best in six shot categories. I've taken enough data on most of these guys, so I know something about their games.

Here they are by shot categories (or games):

1. Driving and fairway woods (power game): Greg Norman, Tiger Woods, Colin Montgomerie
2. Shots of longer than 100 yards to the green (power game): Steve Elkington, Ben Hogan, Moe Norman
3. Wedge shots inside 100 yards (short game): Tom Kite, Tom Watson, David Duval
4. Trouble shots (from sand, bad lies, trees, high rough): Seve Ballesteros, Phil Mickelson, Jose Maria Olazabal
5. Chipping (short game): Paul Azinger, Raymond Floyd, Payne Stewart
6. Putting (putting game): Ben Crenshaw, Lee Janzen, George Archer

Don't make too much of these choices. They don't mean that Loren Roberts, Dave Stockton, Justin Leonard, and Brad Faxon can't putt, or that Davis Love III is not a great driver, or that Peter Jacobsen and Ernie Els can't get out of a bunker. Of course they can (in fact, they are right at the top in those categories). But I chose the players I did because I have more data or personal knowledge of some part of their games.

Why are composite players important to you and the game of golf? Because they provide a realistic view of how well each part of the game can be played, what can be accomplished in each area, and a glimpse of what future players might be able to achieve.

For example, imagine if you could assemble the six first choices in each category into a composite player, enter "him" in a tournament, and watch him play the course. Norman drives magnificently off all the par-4 and par-5 holes, and hits incredible fairway woods to the long par 5s. Elkington stripes the full-swing irons to the greens, including the par-3 holes, leaving most of them close to the hole, while Kite nestles all the wedge shots dead to the pins. Azinger almost chips in on the hole where Elk left his 4-iron shot in the fringe, while Ballesteros lips out his bunker shot for eagle on the longest par 5 and leaves a 2-inch putt for birdie. To top it off, Crenshaw rolls every putt so beautifully that you think they're all going in! What a group. What a player. What a scoring machine!

Three Composite Players . . . Three Scoring Machines

Shot Category	Game	#1	#2	#3
Driving, Fairway Woods	POWER GAME	Greg Norman	Tiger Woods	Colin Montgomerie
Shots to Green from Outside 100 Yards	POWER GAME	Steve Elkington	Ben Hogan	Moe Norman
Wedge Shots from Inside 100 Yards	SHORT GAME	Tom Kite	Tom Watson	David Duval
Trouble Shots	SHORT GAME	Seve Ballesteros	Phil Mickelson	Jose Maria Olazabal
Chipping	SHORT GAME	Paul Azinger	Ray Floyd	Payne Stewart
Putting	PUTTING GAME	Ben Crenshaw	Lee Janzen	George Archer

Table 13.1.1: My three composite players

That's what my composite player is all about: scoring. By my calculations, which are nonemotional evaluations of individual players' skills in the various games of golf (based on shots they've hit in competition), any one of these three composite players would win every tournament on the current PGA Tour.

Does that sound bizarre? How could any one player, even a composite player, win every tournament? The computer calculations say it's true, and if you think about it, it actually makes sense. Imagine on every hole in one of your club events that you had the best driver in the field teeing off, the best iron player hitting all your iron shots, the best wedge player hitting your wedges, followed by the best putter rolling it for you. How could you *not* win? If no one else in the tournament could consistently hit shots as well as your designated player in each category over 18 holes, the composite would have to win. This is what my three composite players could achieve, and it gives us all a glimpse, in our imaginations, of what may be possible in the future.

13.2 The Awesome Talents

Notice, I didn't have to select a different individual for every iron or wood shot. My data shows that when players excel, they excel through entire shot categories, throughout the games of golf. That means when they are good at something, they are *really* good at it; even on the days when they're not at their best, they're still pretty good.

I find it interesting that not every golfer making up my composite players are of the "awesome," "world-beater," or "Incredible Hulk" variety. Although the power-game selections tend to be very good athletes (the full swing requires athletic talent), the rest of the players have few attributes that would single them out as especially gifted. This validates my belief that short-game expertise is a learned, rather than a "God-given" talent. If hand–eye coordination and talent were the main ingredient, Seve Ballesteros would be more than a short-game magician: He would also be a great driver of the ball, a great iron player, and a great putter. Although he has his moments, he is far from the best in the power or putting game.

Mac O'Grady is another talent who can hit the ball incredibly well. But his short game and putting often let him down, and keep him from competing with the composite players in scoring ability. Then there's Moe Norman, probably the most consistent, most repeatable ball-striker who ever lived. But he doesn't chip and putt anywhere near that same exalted level.

Why can't one golfer do it all? Why can't Tiger Woods—who seems to be many people's choice to be the next truly great player—wedge and putt as well as he strikes the ball? He has all the physical talent anyone would ever need, and he can hit every conceivable shot in the book. But his putting is generally weak, even though he works at it very hard, and his wedge game is not even close to that of Duval, Watson, or Kite.

I think he *can* learn it all, if . . . if he knew what he needed to learn, and how to learn it.

But I believe neither Tiger nor anyone else has learned to be great in all of golf's games, probably because they don't realize that there *are* different games to be learned.

13.3 Future Greatness

When you take young golfers who are reasonably athletically talented, put them into an environment where they can totally focus, and simultaneously teach them the fundamentals of all five games of golf, you will begin to develop composite-like skills in individual players. I emphasize all five games so you understand that I'm not only a short-game proponent, I'm a *reality* proponent. You can't leave out the short game, the putting game, or the management game, all of which have been left out of golf instruction far too often, and expect to come up with the best. And you can't leave out the power or mental games, either. The greatest golfer will have to have them all.

Is this really possible? Why not?

Don't tell me Tiger can't learn to putt. Or that Crenshaw can't learn to drive the ball into the fairway. Or that Greg Norman can't manage his game. Of course they can. They already do it sometimes, and extremely well. I think they could do it *all*, given the proper training. Just the way Crenshaw putts, Greg drives, and Jack Nicklaus manages his game. They can learn to do it all well, all the time.

Maybe you can learn the skills required to become the composite player, the greatest, most dominant player to ever play the game. Despite what you might think, Jack Nicklaus never did it. He couldn't compete with any of my composite players or even a composite player of his time. But don't sell Jack short. He came the closest anybody ever has—so far. For a long time, he had the Tour believing he was the one to beat, and he had himself believing it, too. (He believed even back when I played against him in college.)

You'll never convince me that, perhaps someday soon, there won't be a true composite player. I've seen too much progress in this direction. I've seen too many golfers, thought to be weak in certain parts of the game, turn those parts around and become experts at them. I know composite skills are possible in one person, and expect to see someone in my lifetime exhibit them all. I know in my heart that when a player learns all five games, optimizing each unto and of itself, and puts them all together, he or she will eclipse the feats of all who have played before.

A Review of Fundamentals

13.4 Finesse-Swing Mechanics

Whether or not you can become a composite player is not really important. What you're interested in is improving your current skill level, soon, in the time you have available to work on it. And that is exactly what you should work on. So remember this: If you can improve the swing mechanics of your short game, then many other improvements become not only possible but relatively easy to achieve. However, if you have bad short-game mechanics, and don't improve them, improvement will come slowly and painfully, if at all.

Finesse-swing mechanics provide a base for your short game, upon which you can build the ability to execute the scoring shots. Develop good mechanics, then practice them often enough to internalize them and commit them to subconscious control. The ideal is to be able to forget about the swing mechanics, yet still have good mechanics when you swing. Good players make good swings out of habit.

Before working on your scoring ability, review the short-game system presented in this book, which is summarized below. Be sure you understand it all, both the fundamentals of finesse-swing mechanics and the short-game principles. The more clearly your mind's eye sees and understands what you are trying to learn, the more efficiently you can internalize it. Read through the review carefully, and if anything doesn't make sense, go back to the earlier chapters and read the details until it does.

Alignment: If you can't aim your club and body properly, you can't learn a good finesse swing. If you can't set up to a ball with your shoulders and body aligned parallel left of your target, you have little chance of hitting to it consistently. The finesse swing requires swinging the club along a natural arc, without hand control, so your clubhead moves parallel to your shoulder line, and at the target, through impact. If you set up perfectly, your body instinctively wants to make a good finesse swing. But set up too far right or left, and your instincts will never let you groove a good swing. Your subconscious will always know that poor aim sends the ball to the wrong place and will try to compensate.

Ball Position: Where your ball is positioned in your stance is critical. If the ball is too far forward, you can't make solid contact without maneuvering the club from its natural swing arc. To maneuver the club, you have to use your muscles, which will cause you trouble (the adrenaline effect) under pressure. If you are nervous, or unsure of your ball position, move it back in your stance a little, because there is more margin for error being too far back than forward.

Ball Position: One More Time

Even though I've said this before, it bears repeating. Ball position is crucial to a successful finesse game.

Perfect finesse swings produce perfect shots only if the ball is in the proper place. This means to allow yourself to learn good swings, you must carefully position your ball properly during your finesse-swing practice sessions.

Please never forget that appearances can be deceiving when it comes to ball position. When golfers look down, their shoes dominate their visual landscape. This generally results in ball placement that looks centered, but is actually well forward of their true stance center. Always, *always* be aware

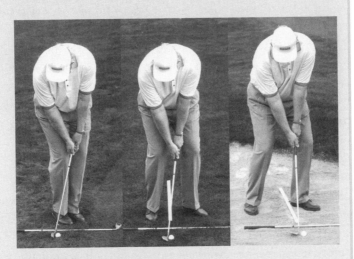

Figure 13.4.1: Perfect ball position (good lies) for the chip, pitch, and sand shots

that your stance center is midway between your ankles and is not related to your toes.

Another confusing aspect of proper ball position is what sometimes appears on television. Because the position of the camera lens can move the "apparent" position of the ball by several inches, you must never pay attention to where the ball "appears" to be in a player's stance on TV.

Remember, in any photograph or on any TV screen, where the ball appears to be depends on the camera's angle of view. If you don't know exactly where the camera is, you can't tell where the player's ball is positioned.

The following rules of ball position apply for normal, good lies:

SAND	GRASS	FRINGE
Scoot-and-Spin	Distance Wedge and Pitch Shot	Low-Running Chip
Ball on line with *inside edge* (instep) of lead-foot heel	Ball on line *centered* between ankles	Ball on line with *back ankle*

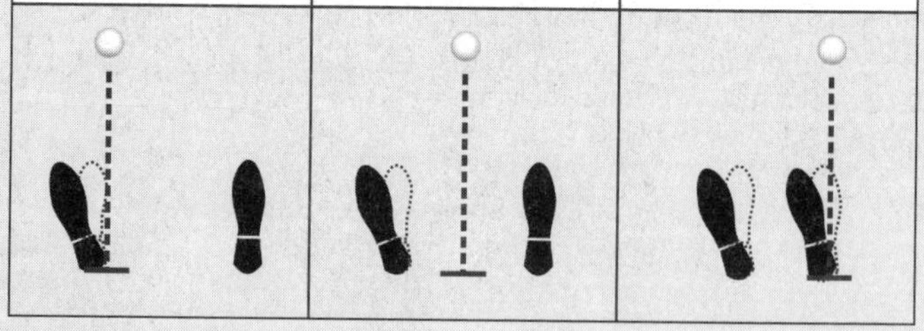

Figure 13.4.2: Correct ball position is fundamental to a good short game

Shorter Backswing: The backswing should be shorter than the follow-through to create stability (sequence in Fig. 13.4.3). Notice I didn't say the backswing must be short, just shorter than the through-swing.

Left-Arm Radius: Keep your left arm extended throughout the finesse swing, until your arms fold at the finish. A constant swing radius (sequence in Fig. 13.4.4) produces solid, repeatable contact. Phil Mickelson is the best model to watch for this (maybe that is part of why he is so good with his wedges). Changing the radius during the swing leads to inconsistent clubhead position through impact.

Figure 13.4.3: Short-to-long swings are stable

Figure 13.4.4: Phil Mickelson demonstrates the 7:30 finesse swing

Synchronized Turn: Your arms, shoulders, chest, hips, and lower body should stay together, turning in a synchronized motion, throughout the finesse swing (Fig. 13.4.5). Nothing should ever lead, trail, or separate, as in the power-swing coil, which produces too much power. While there are many ways to be "off" in the timing of your power swing (days when all your shots go wrong), there is only one "together" in the synchronized finesse swing. With a little practice you can see and feel together, and you can easily judge when you are out of sync. Then just make a

Finesse-Swing Positions, Back and Through

FINESSE-SWING POSITIONS		
Swing Description	Backswing Turn	Through-Swing Turn
Chip	#1	#2
7:30	#2	#5
9:00	#3	#5
10:30	#4	#5

Table 13.4.1: The finesse-swing, back and through

Figure 13.4.5: The synchronized finesse turn

few practice swings, even out on the course, until you are together again. And your short game will be right back on track again.

Wrist Cock: The wrist cock is a cocking-up motion (Fig. 13.4.6), which should occur to some extent in every short-game shot (except chipping and the "super soft" shot). It is not a wrist hinge, collapse, load, flip, or breakdown. Properly

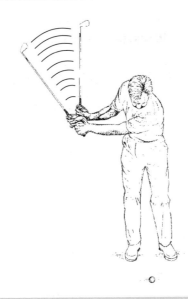

Figure 13.4.6: The proper wrist cock

cocked wrists uncock naturally on the down and through swing, and produce crisp, on-target finesse shots. (Exceptions where hinging is allowed are the "cock-and-pop" shot and the sand or cut-lob shots, to help produce extra spin or height.)

Finesse Grip: This is a fairly weak grip, with both "Vs" formed by the thumb and forefinger pointing approximately to your nose (Fig. 13.4.7). This grip positions the hands neutral (or parallel) to the clubface, and minimizes forearm and clubface rotation through impact. This grip also minimizes the power produced by the hands and forearms, while maximizing consistency and accuracy. You can't build a successful finesse game with an overly strong grip (the Vs pointing out past, to the right of, your right shoulder). A strong grip, with your hands more under or behind the club, produces too much power, harming finesse, touch, consistency, and control (one reason many great ball-strikers have poor finesse games).

Finesse-Swing Plane: Your perfect swing plane is like a sheet of glass that passes from the ball up through your shoulder sockets at address, and extends past the top of your backswing (Fig. 13.4.8). Because you stand close to the ball when holding the shorter, more upright wedges, this swing plane also is very upright. If the clubhead stays "on-plane" throughout the finesse swing, the result will be a high, full finish and high, soft shots. Your right hand should almost touch your left ear as you finish distance-wedge swings.

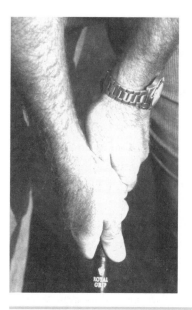

Figure 13.4.7: The finesse grip

Figure 13.4.8: The finesse-swing plane

13.5 Essential Short-Game Principles

If you now have an understanding of what the finesse swing should look like, you are ready to internalize it and make it your own. To do this properly, and develop your scoring ability, incorporate the basic principles listed below as you groove your swing mechanics. These principles are enormously important to your short game, but are not often taught, because you can't see, touch, or feel them. They are concepts that will help build your swing mechanics when you practice in your backyard or on the range, and keep them with you when you play on the course. They will help you avoid bad habits and eliminate future problems.

1. The short game is its own game within golf. The finesse swing is different from the power swing in that it has no coil of the upper body against the lower, and the lower body does not lead through impact. While the intent of the power game is to hit each club as far as possible within the bounds of reasonable accuracy, the intent of the short game is to execute finesse swings that fly shots as short as possible, for whatever size swing you have made. (For example, if you choose a horizontal-shaft backswing to vertical-shaft follow-through, as in Fig. 13.5.1, the shot you hit with that swing should fly only 15 yards, not 18, 20, 25, or 30 yards.)

2. Stability is to the wedge game as aim is to putting. Without stability, your short game will never be very good. If the head of your wedge is unstable at impact, your mistakes will be magnified.

Figure 13.5.1: Horizontal to vertical: the 15-yard pitch

3. Nonmuscular control of distance is essential to performance under pressure. To avoid the adverse effects of an increased heart rate and adrenaline, you must develop a dead-hands (no-muscle) swing, which is "timed" to control distance.

4. The rhythm of your finesse swing must be constant—shot to shot, hole to hole, day to day, year to year. With a constant rhythm, distance can be controlled by the length of your backswing. You can see and feel your rhythm, and evaluate it during your practice swings, no matter how excited or scared you are.

5. Time your wedge swings. By making 7:30, 9:00 o'clock, and 10:30 backswings, you can learn to control distance to within one yard. Standardizing three wedge swings (Fig. 13.5.2) at the same rhythm gives you three known, reliable distances from every wedge in your bag.

6. Add two wedges. After grooving three finesse-wedge swings, add two wedges and remove two longer irons from your bag. Your scoring game will gain more accuracy, your long game won't be measurably affected, and you can learn to be deadly on those shots around the greens with your 12 swings inside 100 yards (Fig. 13.5.3).

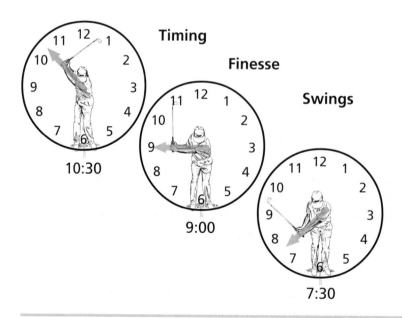

Timing

Finesse

Swings

10:30

9:00

7:30

Figure 13.5.2: Three backswing times produce three consistent distances with every wedge

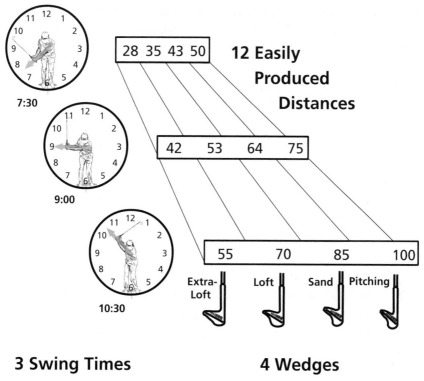

3 Swing Times   **4 Wedges**

Figure 13.5.3: The Pelz 3 x 4 System

7. Use a preshot ritual. Think about how you'd waggle before hitting the most important shot of your life, and establish that preshot ritual for all your future play on-course and in practice (even in your backyard). This ritual must be repeatable, less than eight seconds long, and contain enough motion to make you comfortable when scared. Practice it religiously so your subconscious takes over under pressure.

8. Hold your finish until your shot has stopped, so you learn the correlation between the move you made (and still feel) and the shot that resulted (Fig. 13.5.4). Learning this relationship is what practice is for, so make good use of it. Don't waste your practice time, because you'll never have that same time again. Remember, this is not a rehearsal.

9. Accurate feedback. When you practice, be sure to receive feedback accurate to within two yards, one if possible. If you don't know within two yards how far your

Figure 13.5.4: Hold your finish, watch, feel, internalize

wedge shots are flying, you're wasting your time. One-yard accuracy is better, and inches would be perfect. If you can't see and feel your result within eight seconds and two yards, go take a nap on the couch.

10. Remember the "Golden Rule": He who rules the short game wins the gold. And focus your short-game shots on the "Golden Eight" feet, between two and 10 feet around the flagstick. Remind yourself on the course and in practice that the scoring question in golf is whether you make or miss your next putt (Chart 13.5.1).

11. Play like you practice. This is the best secret of the game. And the only way to do that is to be smart enough to practice like you are going to play. It's slower, it takes more effort, and you have to be more careful, but it works.

When you get frustrated and discouraged (and you will), ask yourself this question: "Do I have the patience to practice smart enough to improve?" An honest answer is your key to whether you should practice or not and to your success.

13.6 Don't Forget Your Secrets

If your motivation to improve is strong and you understand the message of this book, then you know how much improvement is possible. However, I have to warn you to avoid the mistake I sometimes see after my Scoring Game Schools.

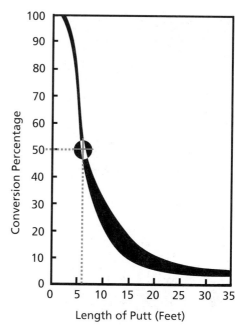

Chart 13.5.1: The conversion curve causes the "Golden Eight" to create the "Golden Rule"

Students, a mile high after seeing and feeling the tremendous improvement in their games, rush off to practice and improve some more.

They do fairly well at first, because what they are working on is fresh in their minds, and they are well focused on what they need to work on. But over time, two things change: (1) As they improve, they need to work on different things; and (2) they get more careless in their practice habits. Both changes lessen their improvement rate, and can dampen enthusiasm.

Don't let this to happen to you. Don't practice the wrong way or the wrong things. Remember, bad practice will make you worse!

My advice (and this is not a sales pitch) is to come to a three-day Dave Pelz Scoring Game School: I know that sounds self-serving, but it's true; nothing else is as good for improving your ability to score. If you can't make that commitment, the next-best thing is to attend a one-day Dave Pelz Scoring Game Clinic (which travels around the country to towns near you). All my schools and clinics are taught by our Scoring Game Teaching Professionals, who are thoroughly trained in the ways of this book. Their teaching is focused on the Scoring Game, and they are the best instructors you can find anywhere.

If a clinic is still more than you can manage, take some short-game lessons from your local golf professional. And if none of these is on your schedule, read this book carefully, taking notes on what and how you are going to practice. The worst thing you can do is go to the practice tee and simply start hitting wedges. There's too much to remember, and you'll probably make mistakes if you haven't plotted a course of practice from this book. Here are some of the key ideas for successful practice.

- If you don't form habits of "intelligent practice," you'll waste a lot of time. Intelligent practice demands feedback, so you must receive immediate, reliable knowledge of the results before you lose the feel of each swing that caused them.
- Use visible yardage markers, so you know how far each shot flew, and use an aim club: Never hit shots when improperly aimed or you are unaware of the precise distance to the target.
- Don't "rake and beat." If you look away from your shot before it stops, you are throwing away the feedback and swing correlations. If you're not going to take the time to watch your shots, you might as well practice in the dark.
- Don't simply watch a shot's direction. Note its trajectory, too. If you don't know how high shots are going to fly, you won't be able to predict how they will behave when they land.
- Tailor practice time to your personality and your game. If you're impatient, don't schedule long practice sessions. No matter how good a player you are, regularly evaluate the amount of time you spend on each part of the game. Devote about one-third of your time each to the short game, putting game, and power game—in that order. Always practice your short game first, so if you run out of time, it's the power-game practice that gets dropped.
- When practicing the short game, work on your worst shot first. It's your weaknesses that determine your score. (If you don't know your weaknesses, take the tests in Chapter 11.) Before every round, practice 12- to 15-yard pitch shots, chipping, and a few distance wedges (with feedback). At least once a month, schedule a session for the sand and other fun shots such as backhand, left-hand, hardpan lies, and whatever other bizarre situations you can devise.
- Keep your hand muscles out of your normal finesse swings; they'll fail you under pressure.
- I can't overemphasize the value of proper repetition: Just because you *can* hit a shot doesn't mean it's committed to memory and will be there when the pressure is up. Practice, practice, and practice some more until it will be there whenever you need it.

- Include your preshot ritual in every practice shot so your finesse swing becomes a subconscious response to the ritual.

- Forget trying to be perfect in practice. Of course, you want to hit perfect shots, but it is far more important to learn to make consistent finesse swings.

- Finally, remember that bad practice is worse than no practice. I would rather see you relaxed, stretched out on the couch, than see you practice poorly. At least on the couch you won't be hurting your game.

Learning Aids Help

13.7 Don't Try It Alone

Every day, from every bit of research I do, I'm reminded that it is impossible to learn anything without feedback. One of the best ways to get feedback when learning in golf is to use learning aids.

The best aids I know help you feel the proper motion you are trying to make as you make it. They don't force you to make it, nor do they make it for you. They identify your good swings as well as your bad, and provide feedback on the feel of the differences. Since the USGA wisely banned the use of such aids while actually playing, you must learn to play on your own, guided by your body. We play by feel, so you must learn the proper feel well enough that it stays with you on the course.

One of the best learning aids is an expert short-game instructor, standing by your side, watching, talking to you before and after swings, and helping you feel positions and reactions. Even better is a knowledgeable instructor using a learning aid that helps you be aware of those feelings on every swing over time. That is what we try to do in our Scoring Game Schools and Clinics. But the schools last only three days, the clinics only one, and then you're on your own. However, you can continue to get expert help after you leave, if you use learning aids.

13.8 At the Course or Range

Yes, learning aids make practice more cumbersome, slower, and require more mental focus, energy, and patience on your part. But if the point of practice is to improve, then why beat a bunch of balls and learn nothing that will stand up for you later? You have to want to practice properly and maximize your improvement.

Possibly the best learning aid of all is the aim club. It costs you nothing, takes

only a few seconds to set up, and helps ingrain the look and feel of proper alignment. It also helps you learn a good dead-hands swing, since bad alignment encourages compensating moves. Yet most golfers don't use an aim club in practice.
Well, here's a strong statement: If you are too lazy, careless, or have some other
reason not to use an aim club when you practice, then throw this book away and
forget you ever read it! You have no chance of learning what I'm trying to tell you
if you can't see the value of the aim club.

Another great learning aid is a practice green that will hold wedge shots at least
close to the way normal greens do. A green a learning aid? Absolutely. It helps you
learn by providing reliable feedback on the quality of both your swing execution
and shot read. If it's nothing more than cement painted green, don't bother—it
can't help you. But a real or artificial-grass green (yes, they do exist) in your backyard that will hold pitches and wedge shots is priceless.

Always be sure you know the exact distance to your landing target. I recommend a rangefinder like the Bushnell Yardage Pro (it doesn't require special reflectors). "Shoot" the distance to every target you hit to, or walk it off. Don't waste
time hitting wedges to targets at unknown distances. (I also suggest using the
rangefinder during your casual and practice rounds.)

Use an aim club when practicing chipping, too. Then attach the ChipStick to
the club you're chipping with and practice that way (Fig. 13.8.1). Hold your finish

Figure 13.8.1: When you can chip well with a ChipStick,
you can chip well without one

until each shot stops. Once aimed properly, check that the ball is back in your stance, and don't let your wrists break down on your follow-through (the Chip-Stick should never hit your body on the follow-through).

Once your short-game practice session at the range—10 to 15 minutes each with the distance wedges, pitches, and chipping—is over, you can head home and improve some more with a session in your backyard.

13.9 Away from the Course

A number of learning aids are perfect for use in your yard, garage, rec room, or office. Practice wherever you can. I find that home short-game practice is surprisingly effective because there's less focus on results (where the ball goes) than in on-course practice. You tend to pay more attention to your swing motions, which means more internalization of the feelings that go with them.

A good exercise to help wedge and bunker play, and one you can do anywhere, is the WristTwist (Fig. 13.9.1). Twisting for three minutes a day, five days a week, strengthens the last three fingers of each hand, both wrists, and your forearms, making them strong enough to resist breakdown during the swing. This is especially important to seniors and women who have lost some of the muscle tone needed for good wedge play. Your wrists and last three fingers need to be strong enough to hold on to and swing your wedges without hinging or breakdown, and

Figure 13.9.1: The WristTwist strengthens hands, wrists, and forearms

feeling as if you are stressing (at the limit of) the strength of your hands. Remember, you must always think "dead hands."

Two more learning aids that can be used at home are the PositionMat (Fig. 13.9.2) and the medicine ball (Fig. 13.9.3). The PositionMat positions the ball in your stance for chips, pitches, and sand shots from good lies. Hitting a few Wiffle ball shots in the den each night off a PositionMat can do wonders for making correct ball position feel comfortable.

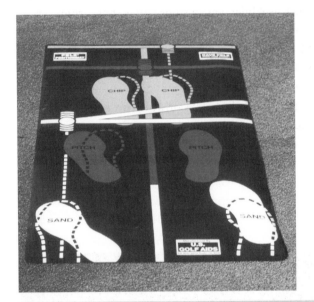

Figure 13.9.2:
The PositionMat

Figure 13.9.3: The medicine ball toss (watch your back)

For help keeping the upper and lower body synchronized, tossing a medicine ball around will give you the feeling of a synchronized finesse swing. (Don't use the medicine ball if you have a weak or bad back.)

The ShotMaker is an extremely effective learning aid for use indoors and out. Its artificial-grass hitting surface can be aimed and tilted into different positions, making it a great way to learn how to handle uphill, downhill, and sidehill lies (Fig. 13.9.4). Among the available attachments are the Shanker's Delight, for correcting that most upsetting of shots; the SwingSlot, to address any swing-plane problems you might have; the KneeSlider, which stops the left knee from moving past the outside of the left foot; and the SwingStop, to help you internalize the feel of timing your 7:30 and 9:00 o'clock backswings. There's even a collection of attachments that duplicate sand play—the BunkerBoard and BunkerTray.

No matter which learning aids you use (for information on sources for these learning aids, see page 427 at the end of the book), or what part of your game you work on, it's important to maintain good practice habits when working at home. Just as you do on the range and on the course, always use your preshot ritual, dead-hands finesse swing, synchronized turn, and hold your finish while you watch your results!

Figure 13.9.4: The ShotMaker set for uneven-lie practice

Set Realistic Goals

13.10 The Golfer's Achilles' Heel

I'm often asked to identify the worst problem golfers have in the short game and putting. A few years ago, I would answer with an explanation of the intricacies of forearm rotation in putting, of ball position in the pitch shot, or any one of many common mistakes we regularly see in our schools. However, as I gain more experience with what I call the overview of golf, I have come to believe the primary problem golfers face on their road to improvement is impatience.

What makes impatience the great killer of learning? Too many golfers want instant gratification (to see perfect shots immediately), and when they don't get it, they think they're not improving. If it doesn't work in the first three swings, they give up, try something else, look for a different secret. We are confronted with the "instant gratification syndrome" in our schools every single day.

Some golfers believe that once they learn how to do something, they should be able to repeat it correctly from that point on. Practice? Why practice? They already think they know how to do it. In fact, they just *proved* that: Didn't you see that last shot?

They have no understanding that it takes tens of thousands of good repetitions to ingrain a habit in long-term muscle memory. Even the most gifted athletes need thousands of practice shots to get good. Yet weekend golfers, intelligent and successful in their workday worlds, expect to own a good swing right away.

So they learn how to hit a shot, hit one good one, and assume they've got it. Three weeks later, when they hit a bad shot, they assume there must be something wrong with the technique or the theory behind it. They're willing to drop it, start over again, recycle all that hard-earned muscle memory, and forget what they learned.

Believe me, instant gratification does not work in golf. If you have a problem in your swing and I tell you how to fix it, expect your next few shots (and it could be dozens or more) to be worse, not better, than before. Your mind already developed subconscious compensations to correct every swing flaw, and those compensations don't leave after your first new swing. They took time to develop, and they will take time to go away.

If you want to become a better golfer, begin by saying to yourself, and to anyone who is going to work with you, "I am willing to get worse before I get better." Like it or not, that's how golf works. If you truly want to improve, you must be willing to suck it up and keep swinging the right way even though you're hitting bad-looking shots. Nobody ever said golf was easy.

13.11 Work Hard and Smart

Hard work alone is not enough to make you a good golfer. It doesn't matter how many practice shots you hit, how much your hands bleed, or how much frustration you can tolerate. If you are practicing the wrong thing the right way, or the right thing the wrong way, you're not going to "get it." The more you practice a shot poorly, the more consistently and permanently poor you become. This doesn't mean you can improve without hard work. Just understand that hard work is a "necessary-but-not-sufficient" component of improvement.

A golfer with the chip yips worked hard to develop them. If you asked if he meant to do that, of course he would say no. But he did. By practicing his chipping hard but poorly (say, grooving a bad move with the ball in a bad position), he convinced his subconscious that he was a bad chipper. And that's all it takes, knowing you are going to perform poorly. Poor practice ingrains poor habits. (That's why I say bad practice is worse than no practice.)

But when you practice smart and carefully, you will improve.

13.12 Keep the Trees *and* the Forest in View

I tend to get wrapped up in my players' short games and swing problems when I work with them in schools or one-on-one. Whether the student is a Tour pro or a beginner, I assume he or she wants to become the world's best player, so I want to help them achieve that goal. However, sometimes when I'm beating on them to do what it takes to be better, I realize I need to stand back, take a deep breath, and listen to the breeze in the Aspen trees. Or lean back in my chair in front of the video monitor and listen to some background music.

I try to remember that real improvement takes time. No one goes straight from crawling to running, and no one jumps from awful to great in golf. Chart 13.12.1 shows my estimate of the spectrum of golfers, as projected from the skill levels of those I have measured. Where your game falls on that spectrum determines where you go next in your personal improvement program. And you definitely can get better. We all can improve. I've worked with a number of the world's best players, and they *all* still have marked room for improvement.

Despite all the detail I've gone through in this book, the short game really is physically fairly simple to execute: The mechanics of the finesse swing don't re-

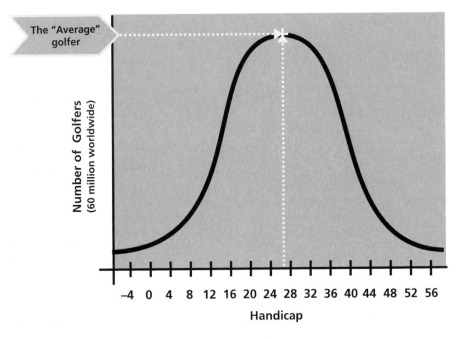

The "Average" golfer

Number of Golfers
(60 million worldwide)

–4 0 4 8 12 16 20 24 28 32 36 40 44 48 52 56

Handicap

Chart 13.12.1: The spectrum of golfer skills

quire inordinate physical prowess and you don't have to be a genius to understand them. The key ingredient—practice with good feedback—is accessible to us all. So you *can* move your skills up the chart; believe me, it's been done many times by golfers with less talent than you have. That's the good news.

The bad news is that as you improve, there are several levels you must pass through before you reach the top. And there are many things anxious to get in your way: bad advice from different sources, the instinctive human desire for instant gratification, the counterintuitive nature of the game, the lifestyle and lack of good practice facilities of most golfers, and the tendency for newly improved swings to hit worse shots before they hit better ones. Allowing any of these to lead you down a road of poor practice will groove poor performance habits and inhibit your progress.

You must keep some perspective. Give your program a chance to succeed by providing enough time, and feedback, to see results. Gradual improvement is as good as it gets in golf, so make that your goal. If you see that you're making progress, it's easy to keep a great attitude and stay with the program. However, if you expect perfection right away, you are doomed to disappointment.

The Challenge

13.13 Keep Your Priorities Straight

You *can* get yourself the information you need to improve your short game. You may have to read a few chapters of this book over a few times, or come to a school, or whatever. But you *can* do it. One of the great benefits of understanding the finesse swing is the simplicity it instills for what is actually involved. The realization of exactly what you have to learn makes learning it so much easier than before.

You must always keep the realities of the game somewhere in the back of your mind when you make your decisions in golf. The penalties for bad shots are a lot more certain than the rewards for good shots. When you knock your ball out-of-bounds, you add two strokes every time. In the water, at least one stroke. In a sand bunker, about half a stroke, at least. Leave a chip shot 25 feet from the pin, add almost one stroke.

Your good shots do have rewards, but not so clearly, or so often. Hit your shot to within two feet, you save one stroke, for sure. But after that, it's maybe, maybe not for saving strokes. At six feet, you save one-half stroke at best. At 10 feet, you're down to a small fraction of a shot. After that, maybe nothing.

During practice, remember it is your bad shots that determine your score. Practice your weaknesses, while spending only routine maintenance time on the strengths of your game. Try to hit 10, then 15, then 20 shots in a row, without a really bad one. Only after you eliminate your bad shots are you ready to focus on making your good shots better.

If you don't know enough about your game to identify your weaknesses, take the short-game handicap tests detailed in Chapter 11. Then adopt a system of periodic practice drills, laced with feedback, aimed at improving those weaknesses. Identify what they are, and attack them. And take no prisoners. Try to make your former weaknesses the strength of your game. Practice at the course or in your backyard, but always practice with feedback. Have a goal to your practice, of learning or improving something. Don't beat balls, and learn from your bad shots (what not to do again) as well as your good shots. Hold your finish and watch the beauty (there is something beautiful about a soft, high shot landing where you aimed it, bouncing once and checking, then releasing to the pin). And don't ever, ever, *ever* let me see you practicing without an aim club!

You must also remember that you can't afford to focus on only one game, you've got to look after all five of your games in golf. If you can't drive the ball into play, no matter how sharp your short game is, you can't score. If you can't hit your irons somewhere near the greens, you can't score, either. And if your mental game isn't strong enough, the game will sooner or later throw enough bad breaks at you to tear you down. In golf you've got to try to cover all the bases, just like in life. It's the best microcosm of life I know. That's why we all love this game so much.

13.14 Understanding Comes First

I hope my *Short Game Bible* has helped you understand more about your short game, and has given you the information, and encouragement, necessary to improve your ability to shoot better scores. I have spent many hours, days, and years compiling this data, trying to understand this great game better. I hope I have presented the information in a way that can help you. I'm not conceited enough to think this book contains everything you will ever need to know, or that I know it all. But I hope you can learn from this book, and find in it what you need to score better and enjoy the game a little more. I sincerely believe that the better you understand the game, the simpler it will be to improve your ability to play it.

Still, there is a lot of information here, so if it seems too much at first, take what you want and don't worry about the rest. If you improve just one shot in your short-game repertoire, the results will show up in your score. And if that's enough to make you happy, I'll be happy, too. Then if you want more, it will be here for you. In the meantime, I'll be out taking more measurements, compiling more data, and trying to learn how to teach golf so it will be even easier to play and enjoy in the years to come.

Reading this book won't make you a better short-game player. But understanding this book, then doing something about it (like practicing properly) will! Once you understand both what you are trying to learn and how you are going to learn it, the actual learning becomes fun.

Better scoring is out there for you if you want it. But you have to go get it. You have to earn it. And in the words of the greatest mind in golf, Yoda, "Try not. Do, or do not. There is no try."

Good scoring to you!

Resources

Postal Addresses, Telephone Numbers, Fax Numbers, Internet Web Site Addresses

Pelz Golf Institute
1310 RR 620 South
Suite B-1
Austin, TX 78734
Phone: (512) 263-7668
Fax: (512) 263-8217
Web site: www.pelzgolf.com

The Pelz Report (newsletter of the Pelz Golf Institute)
"An entertaining and scientific look at golf"
1310 RR 620 South
Suite A-17
Austin, TX 78734
Orders: (800) 833-7370; Offices: (512) 263-7668
Fax: (512) 263-8217
Web site: www.pelzgolf.com

Dave Pelz Scoring Game Schools (3-day schools) and
Dave Pelz Scoring Game Tour (1-day clinics)
1310 RR 620 South
Suite B-1
Austin, TX 78734
Enrollment: (800) 833-7370; Offices: (512) 263-7668
Fax: (512) 263-8216
Web site: www.pelzgolf.com

Learning Aids available from U.S. Golf Aids:

ShotMaker™	SwingStop™	Shanker's Delight™
SwingSlot™	BunkerBoard™	ChipStick™
KneeSlide™	PositionMat™	WristTwist™

BunkerTray™
Dave Pelz Videotapes
Dave Pelz Audiotapes
Dave Pelz CD-Roms

U.S. Golf Aids
1310 RR 620 South
Suite B-0
Austin, TX 78734
Orders: (800) 833-7370; Offices: (512) 263-7668
Fax: (512) 263-8216
Web site: www.pelzgolf.com

Everlast Medicine Ball
Rooster Andrews Sporting Goods
3901 Guadalupe Street
Austin, TX 78751
Phone: (512) 454-9631
Fax: (512) 454-9935

Backyard Putting Greens and Wedge Target Greens
SportCourt Home Golf Centers
939 South 700 West
Salt Lake City, UT 84104
Phone: (800) 972-0260

YardagePro Laser Rangefinder
Bushnell Sports Optics
9200 Cody
Overland Park, KS 66214-3259
Phone: (800) 423-3537
Fax: (913) 752-3550

The Dave Pelz World Putting Championship
1310 RR 620 South
Suite A-16
Austin, TX 78734
Phone: (888) 972-7888
Fax: (512) 263-7946
Web site: www.worldputtingchamp.com